Rethinking Peace and Conflict Studies

Series Editor
Oliver P. Richmond
University of Manchester
Manchester, UK

This agenda-setting series of research monographs, now more than a decade old, provides an interdisciplinary forum aimed at advancing innovative new agendas for approaches to, and understandings of, peace and conflict studies and International Relations. Many of the critical volumes the series has so far hosted have contributed to new avenues of analysis directly or indirectly related to the search for positive, emancipatory, and hybrid forms of peace. New perspectives on peacemaking in practice and in theory, their implications for the international peace architecture, and different conflict-affected regions around the world, remain crucial. This series' contributions offers both theoretical and empirical insights into many of the world's most intractable conflicts and any subsequent attempts to build a new and more sustainable peace, responsive to the needs and norms of those who are its subjects.

More information about this series at
http://www.palgrave.com/gp/series/14500

Birgit Poopuu

The European Union's Brand of Peacebuilding

Acting is Everything

palgrave
macmillan

Birgit Poopuu
Department of International Politics
Aberystwyth University
Aberystwyth, UK

Rethinking Peace and Conflict Studies
ISBN 978-3-030-19892-3   ISBN 978-3-030-19890-9   (eBook)
https://doi.org/10.1007/978-3-030-19890-9

Cover design by © MC Richmond

This Palgrave Macmillan imprint is published by the registered company Springer Nature Switzerland AG
The registered company address is: Gewerbestrasse 11, 6330 Cham, Switzerland

Chapter 4 'Artemis in the Democratic Republic of the Congo: A Necessary "Success Story"' appeared in: "Telling and acting identity. The discursive construction of the EU's common security and defence policy", as published on pp. 134–153 in the journal: "Journal of Language and Politics", volume 14:1 (2015). Published by John Benjamins Publishing Company. Amsterdam/Philadelphia.

To my people, because they are everything

ACKNOWLEDGEMENTS

The fact that this book has materialised owes a lot to the many people who have helped and been there for me along the way.

First of all, I would like to thank Maria Mälksoo who has been incredibly supportive throughout the whole research project and has devoted a lot of her time to engage with me and my work. I have truly appreciated her insights and enjoyed our many conversations—a dialogue that has made me into a much better researcher. I am also enormously grateful to all the people who have read and commented on parts of my work, especially Jevgenia Milne, Siobhan Kattago, Falk Ostermann, Elina Hartikainen, Caterina Carta, Ruth Wodak, Thomas Diez, Stefanie Kappler, Christian Bueger, Oliver Richmond, Karin Fierke, Xymena Kurowska, Emily Pia, Luis Simón and Patrick T. Jackson. Of course, any errors or omissions remain my own. I am very thankful for the support that the Johan Skytte Institute of Political Studies at the University of Tartu has provided, together with the Centre for EU-Russia Studies and the support and funding of the Doctoral School of Behavioural, Social and Health Sciences, the Archimedes Foundation, the University of Tartu Foundation and Kone Foundation together with the Helsinki Collegium for Advanced Studies.

I am greatly indebted to the many people who have helped me in the different stages of my project. In particular, I am very thankful to Melina Sadiković and Dani Ilazi, who provided me with advice, shared their insights and personal stories during my research in Sarajevo and

Pristina. Further, I wish to thank all those people who agreed to meet and converse with me during my time in Sarajevo and Pristina. I extend my great appreciation to the people I have had the pleasure to converse and share thoughts and ideas with in the course of my research, notably Elizabeth Tapscott, Falk Ostermann, Giovanna Bono, Sandra Fernandes and Jevgenia Milne.

Above all, my warmest thanks go to my mum and dad—*sorbus intermedia* for life—who have always believed in me and encouraged me throughout my project. Their support and sunny-side-up attitude have made my travels to where I am now feel so light. I am incredibly happy and thankful that throughout this stage in life I have been surrounded by good friends—waves to you all—who have always been there for me and inspired me in countless ways. An especial thanks to the strong and courageous women in my life—Maria, Kati, Liisa—who I know I can always lean on and who have significantly widened my horizons and who continue to animate my thoughts day in, day out. My heartfelt thanks—to Pluto and back—go to my life partner Silver who has been a constant source of support and laughter and every now and then reminded me that there is life beyond my project.

This research was supported by the programme DoRa, which was managed by Archimedes Foundation and funded by the European Social Fund and by the Kone Foundation.

Tallinn, Helsinki, Aberystwyth
March 2019

Contents

ABBREVIATIONS

AF BiH   Armed Forces of Bosnia and Herzegovina
Artemis   EU military operation to the DRC
BiH   Bosnia and Herzegovina
BRICS   Brazil, Russia, India, China and South Africa
CFSP   Common Foreign and Security Policy
COM EUFOR   Commander of EUFOR
Commission   European Commission
Council   Council of the European Union
CSDP   Common Security and Defence Policy (previously ESDP)
CSO   Civil Society Organisation
DA   Discourse Analysis
DHA   Discourse-Historical Approach
DRC   Democratic Republic of the Congo
EFP   European Foreign Policy
ESI   European Stability Initiative
ESS   European Security Strategy
EU   European Union
EUFOR Althea   European Union military operation in BiH
EUISS   EU Institute for Security Studies
EULEX   European Union rule of law mission in Kosovo
EUPF   EU Peacebuilding Framework
Europol   European Union's law enforcement agency
EUSR   EU Special Representative
GAERC   General Affairs and External Relations Council
GFAP   General Framework Agreement for Peace in Bosnia and
                Herzegovina (or Dayton Peace Agreement)

HoM	Head of Mission
HR	High Representative of the European Union for Foreign Affairs and Security Policy
HRRP	Human Rights Review Panel
HRW	Human Rights Watch
IC	International Community
ICG	International Crisis Group
ICO	International Civilian Office
IFOR	Implementation Force
IKS	Kosovar Stability Initiative
ILP	Intelligence-Led Policing
(I)NGO	(International) Non-Governmental Organisation
IO	International Organisation
IPOL	Balkan Policy Institute
JRCB	Joint Rule of Law Coordination Board
KCSS	Kosovar Center for Security Studies
KFOR	Kosovo Force
KIPRED	Kosovo Institute for Policy Research and Development
KJC	Kosovo Judicial Council
KLA	Kosovo Liberation Army
KP	Kosovo Police
KWN	Kosovo Women's Network
LOT	Liaison and Observation Team
MCSC	Municipal Community Safety Council
MIP	Mission Implementation Plan
MMA	Monitoring, Mentoring and Advising
MONUC	UN Mission in the Democratic Republic of the Congo
NATO	North Atlantic Treaty Organisation
OC	Organised Crime
OHR	Office of the High Representative
PIC	Peace Implementation Council
PISG	Provisional Institutions of Self-Government
Presidency	The presidency of the Council of the European Union
PSOs	Peace Support Operations
R2P	Responsibility to Protect
RoL	Rule of Law
SAP	Stabilisation and Association Process
SCT	Social Choice Theory
SFOR	Stabilisation Force
SRSG	Special Representative of the Secretary General
SSR	Security Sector Reform
TOC	Transnational Organised Crime

UN	United Nations
UNDP	United Nations Development Programme
UNMIK	United Nations Interim Administration Mission in Kosovo
UNODC	United Nations Office on Drugs and Crime
UNSCR	UN Security Council Resolution
US	United States
YIHR	Youth Initiative for Human Rights

CHAPTER 1

Introduction

Commemorating the tenth anniversary of the inception of the European Security and Defence Policy (ESDP), the Council commended the success of this policy which saw the deployment of some 70 000 personnel in 22 ESDP missions and operations, of which 12 are ongoing, in support of international peace and security. (Council 2009, November 17)

[CSDP] missions 'are deemed to be successful' from the moment the decision about the deployment has been taken. Hence, there is only one conceivable scenario in which the Council might publicly criticise its deployments, namely if it decided to re-engineer the ESDP, say, the way missions are planned and run. In such a case, the criticism of mission performance would function as a means to justify major institutional change. (Kurowska 2008, 37–38)

One of the reasons that prompted me to explore the European Union's (EU's) peace missions was the incredibly disproportional attention paid to the means versus the ends of these missions. Even in cases where the ends were emphasised, the stress fell on how a particular end would affect the EU's capability to act on the international stage. I felt that the discussions reified the EU's identity by totally disconnecting the debate from the target(s) of these missions. Furthermore, the frequent encounter with the commonsensical argument that the CSDP offered more of a short-term toolbox and was hence justified to have as blinkered a view of the particular "goods" its missions were supposed to offer as it pleased further pushed me to enquire for whom the CSDP operations were meant.

© The Author(s) 2020
B. Poopuu, *The European Union's Brand of Peacebuilding*,
Rethinking Peace and Conflict Studies,
https://doi.org/10.1007/978-3-030-19890-9_1

With this concern in mind, I investigate within this book the European Union's identity as a provider of peace missions, that is its Common Security and Defence Policy (CSDP) identity.[1] The prime purpose is to critically disturb the nature of the EU's peace missions by asking *what* they offer, *whom* they serve and *how* they go about it. The supplementary questions underline the significance of the following aspects: (i) who is able to script peace, (ii) how the EU affects/is affected by the liberal peace, (iii) to what extent does the EU appraise its missions and finally (iv) what are the real-life effects of conceptualising the EU peace missions in the way they are presently imagined. Liberal peacebuilding, representing the received approach to conflicts among the international community (IC), inescapably affects the way the EU's peace missions are imagined. Concurrently, the CSDP arm of the EU's external policy allows to shape—and/or reinforce—the preponderant way of doing peacebuilding. Moreover, as much as the EU's missions are about solving problems, they are in the first instance about defining the problems we are allegedly facing (see ESS 2003). The EU has identified itself as a peace project and articulated its aspiration to widen the zone of peace and security, to promote a ring of well-governed countries, to bring stability. It is vital to bear in mind that throughout the EU's CSDP career the substance of its missions has been pushed into the background. Hence, when Solana is asked about the future developments of the CSDP in 2005, his argument is "no concept, however beautiful or sophisticated, can be a substitute for practical improvements" (Council 2005, December). The rub is that the way CSDP missions are envisioned—cookie-cutter predilection aside—is not the only way to think about them, but rather *a very particular way of thinking and understanding* (cf. Viktorova Milne 2009; Autesserre 2010, 2014). Put differently, EU's peace missions are loaded with particular conceptual energy, pivoting on how they make sense of the ultimate goods the missions should offer. Therefore, with some thirty missions under the EU's belt it is indispensable to examine the "peace" the EU has offered. By investigating EU's CSDP identity from a critical standpoint, as opposed to the more common problem-solving one, this work offers new perspectives on the CSDP. The book not only explores the solutions offered through the EU's missions but also scrutinises how the problems are presented in the first place as requiring specific solutions. Furthermore, through questioning the CSDP identity, the overall coherence of the EU's identity is brought under scrutiny. Approaching the CSDP in this manner does not intend to offer the "whole story"—it rather zooms in on aspects that have previously remained peripheral, with the intention of questioning the received image of CSDP.

The Council's excerpt to this introduction demonstrates the manner in which the EU measures the success of the CSDP. The EU utilises quantified metrics that are more tilted towards the EU's internal factors, such as the number of troops, number of operations deployed,[2] rather than analysing the effect of the operations on the ground. Indeed, it can be noted that the majority of policy-oriented literature and academic writing on CSDP missions are guided by problem-solving frames that have focused their energy on the effectiveness and efficiency of CSDP missions rather than interrogating the substance and purpose of these missions. Conversely, this book focuses on the substance matter, not seen as something that is natural and commonsensical (cf. Kurki 2013), but rather something that is pregnant with certain assumptions and visions of how a better life can be brought about.

The goods, such as security, the rule of law, support of international peace and security (see the quote introducing this chapter), and others that the CSDP offers are very often utilised as taken-for-granted articles of peacebuilding, where debate on them is made redundant. Indeed, as many authors have pointed out, there is a specific template that international actors follow, i.e. the liberal peace model (e.g. Mac Ginty 2008, 2011). While the Commission's side of the EU's externality has been successfully brought into the discussions of the critical strand of peace and conflict studies literature, the same cannot be said about the CSDP. Pogodda et al. (2014, 2) argue that the EU as a whole does not have an "explicit peacebuilding strategy", yet a number of recurrent motifs emerge within the EU's speech acts communicating particular goods (e.g. the rule of law) and policies (e.g. the rule of law missions). In all, Pogodda et al. note that rhetorically the EU subscribes to conflict resolution and peacebuilding themes, yet in practice the EU seems to oscillate between liberal peacebuilding and neoliberal statebuilding models (ibid. 15, 17). Within this work, the emphasis is placed on one element—the CSDP missions—of the EU's peacebuilding framework (EUPF), a concept relating to the overall EU presence in peacebuilding (see Björkdahl et al. 2011).[3]

The next paragraphs will tap into a selection of state-of-the-art literature on the CSDP, in order to better locate my own approach—which will offer a significant contribution to a critically informed study of the CSDP, since critical approaches to the CSDP are rather sparse. In 2010, a group of researchers mapped the prevalent topics and approaches to the CSDP (see

Freire et al. 2010) and divided the literature on European peace missions into three thematic groups: (i) European Union cooperation with other international organisations in crisis management; (ii) decisions and planning; and (iii) the evaluation of missions (ibid. 2010, 3). The first two topics in this group are definitely more predominant when it comes to research on the CSDP. Also, the mapping exercise reveals—even if this is not explicitly stated—that positivist frameworks and logics have been applied more often (cf. Manners and Whitman 2016), whereas there is a dearth of critical frameworks in the study of the EU's peace operations. As Kurowska notes, research on CSDP "is said to be notoriously undertheorised" (2012, 1; see also Bickerton et al. 2011). In particular, as the mapping exercise manifests, the evaluation part of CSDP has been patchy and "highly subjected to individual interpretations" (Freire et al. 2010, 40). More often than not, the evaluation process is not conceptualised: it is executed implicitly, which does not provide a solid grounding for the evaluation itself. Furthermore, the study refers to the problem of terminology in accounting for the impact of the mission, in that different terms are used and not always coherently, not always differentiating, for example, between outputs and outcomes (ibid.). It is crucial to take note of the fact that the evaluation of CSDP has, similarly to the direction of the overall research on CSDP, been more focused on the EU's internal dynamics (e.g. logistics, decision-making, number and quality of staff, etc.). In contrast, the impact of CSDP on the conflict society is not very often evaluated, although rhetorically, the CSDP habitually takes the credit for promoting international peace and security. All in all, the object of evaluation has rarely anything to do with the local context in which the CSDP operation is deployed.

More specifically, in order to illustrate the themes in the literature dealing with the evaluation of the CSDP up until now, the existing research will be divided into two groups. In the first group, I will discuss the works that either do not apply a theoretical framework explicitly and/or adopt a problem-solving lens. In the second, I will inspect the more critically inclined works that as a rule explicitly subscribe to a theoretical frame/approach, linked to a wider literature pool in peace and conflict studies, particularly to its critical strand.

Merlingen and Ostrauskaite's edited volume (2008c) puts forward a pre-theoretical argument to examining CSDP, in their own words (2008a, 4):

We believe that there are good reasons at this stage in research on the implementation and impact of the ESDP to privilege them [inside stories]. There is simply too little known about this dimension of European foreign policy to theorise it. The latter demarche would run the risk of abstract academic work running ahead of actual developments. Theory-building and testing has to wait for further empirical research.

Although the authors take note of the theoretical drawback of this route, they nonetheless phrase it as a caveat and follow the logic precised above (ibid.). The vast empirical knowledge that the chapters in the edited volume display is commendable; however, at the same time their value is diminished by the pre-theoretical approach. This is so because the latter choice is essentially presented as the truest medium of presenting the empirical material, which seemingly places it above theory. In the conclusion to the edited volume, the authors attempt to bring in "select theoretical concepts to sketch out, in tentative fashion, patterns emerging in the implementation of the ESDP" (2008b, 197). This, however, remains a rather circumscribed exercise as the analysis of the empirical material is already from the start "biased" towards *a particular view*—notwithstanding the pre-theoretical lens—and thus getting quasi-theoretical in the conclusion of this edited work seems rather blinkered (ibid., Ch. 13; see Zehfuss 2002, Ch. 5).

There are a number of other works that fall into the same genre as the work of Merlingen and Ostrauskaite (2008c). Their chief characteristic is that they have largely "shelved" theory, and/or they put forward systematic evaluation criteria without sufficiently questioning their purpose or origins—that is, without conceptually clarifying their ground.[4] For example, Ginsberg and Penksa assert that "however important theory is, it does not measure the effects of CSDP activity" (2012, 16). Crucially, these frameworks do not seriously interrogate the conceptual apparatuses they employ, or any biases therein: while their vocabulary is rooted in conflict management literature, they ignore a large part of literature in the peace and conflict studies which takes issue with conflict management approach (see, e.g., Emerson and Gross 2006; Grevi et al. 2009; Asseburg and Kempin 2009; Peen Rodt 2011; Galantino and Freire 2015; Gross and Juncos 2011; Merlingen 2012b; Ginsberg and Penksa 2012; Whitman and Wolff 2012). Without paying attention to the substance of the missions it is assumed (even if implicitly) that, for the most part, peacebuilding has a particular recipe. It is not just the fact that a theoretical frame should be applied it is also the case that it be a critical theoretical frame since by and large EU scholarship has been dominated by mainstream approaches whereas dissident voices have been living on the fringes (see Manners and Whitman 2016).[5]

As for the more critically attuned works, their value lies in problematising the whole process of straightforward evaluation of CSDP, by exposing the power relations and by problematising the knowledge that is presented in common-sense, natural, technical or apolitical terms (see esp. Merlingen 2012a, 188).[6] The works that can be categorised under this label are also much more connected to the relational aspects of evaluation and therefore emphasise the relevance of the local context (see, e.g., Merlingen and Ostrauskaite 2006; Schlag 2012; Merlingen 2012a; Dias 2013; Kurowska and Breuer 2012). It is noteworthy that some of the authors also tap into the critical literature of peace and conflict studies (see Merlingen and Ostrauskaite 2006; Dias 2013), which in turn allows them to evaluate the EU's peace missions within the pool of literature that has perhaps most to say about conceptualising peace. Accordingly, my approach sets out to further advance the critical project in researching the CSDP. This work will explicitly benefit from openings and findings the critical camp of peace and conflict studies has provided. Specifically, my work goes beyond the current critical engagements by problematising the core concepts (such as rule of law, security or alternatively "peace") the CSDP discourse makes use of. Therefore, instead of accepting these concepts at face value this work critically reviews these in deeply relational and contextual terms.

According to Merlingen and Ostrauskaite, "the EU's presence is the result of both *what it is* and *what it does*" (2008b, 202; emphases mine). The latter assertion is rooted in the vast literature on the "EU as an X kind of actor" debate.[7] The latter discussion has been so wide-ranging that it would be difficult to rehearse it again. Instead, I reflect on two strands of criticism directed against parts of this debate, as they prove useful for introducing the theoretical frame of this work. First, Pogodda et al. (2014, 3) point out that the concept of "normative power" comes with a baggage of recipes that "imply a reconciliation of difference within a *common framework*". The authors add that the latter instance could be considered conflict transformation or resolution if the mentioned *common framework* would be the fruit of a dialogical process "in the absence of significant power, social, economic or cultural hierarchies". In reality, this equality has proven difficult to achieve and thus subjecting policy tools to concepts like the "normative power" may result in "contradictory effects on conflict dynamics" (ibid.; emphasis mine). Second, Cebeci (2012) takes issue with

European foreign policy (EFP) research by critically analysing the impact of constantly naming the EU a certain type of power. Doing so, she observes, the EFP research constructs an "ideal power Europe" meta-narrative. The gist of the matter is that this meta-narrative both empowers and legitimises the EU in its actions and simultaneously discourages and inhibits the ones that the EU is engaging with, and in consequence cements asymmetry. It also prepares the ground for assigning the universal/liberal/positive and "good" to the side of the EU, whereas the others are seen as lacking in these qualities (cf. Diez 2005; Bono 2006).

The book is divided into two larger parts. Chapters 2 to 3 lay a solid theoretical and methodological foundation for the following empirical analysis, which will be taken up in Chapters 4–6. Here the label "normative power Europe" is challenged, in the sense that *what the EU is* is contingent on how it expresses itself through telling and acting. This is a particularly context-sensitive frame of analysis as it does not fixate on a certain moment in time but challenges this knowledge by delving deeper into the contextual dynamics. To start with, this chapter outlines the framework employed to interrogate the EU's CSDP identity, the telling and acting model. The idea is to probe in detail the overarching good, that is, peace, which the CSDP offers. The telling and acting frame nuances the subject matter of the EU's missions as it sheds light on the Union's expressive realm, that is to say, how the EU speaks and acts peace. My work explores how, through examining the twin-processes of telling and acting identity, it is possible to deconstruct an actor's identity. The analysis aims to examine the traits the EU's role identity reveals and the implications of that, without trying to capture the essence of CSDP identity by putting a concrete label on it. Within this work, telling and acting refer to a particular *modus operandi* for how actors express themselves. The crux of the matter is that these two processes, on the one hand, are qualitatively different in social reality (that is, doing something is not the same as talking about it; cf. Van Leeuwen 2008, 6); on the other hand, these processes are redolent of one another. That is, these processes both involve speaking and doing, but in different ways and to different degrees. It is not the separating line between them that directs this work, but rather the *logics in plural* by which the two stages inform identity construction in a much more nuanced way.

While the analysis of telling and acting lays the groundwork for my work, the theoretical frame—a constellation of post-positivist perspectives—permits to flesh out the lens through which the CSDP missions are studied here. The fragmentary set of theories used in this work champion the interrogation of common-sense categories. In this sense, they provide a particularly fresh take in the situation where the research on the CSDP has been basically wedded to problem-solving accounts. The two chief concepts underlying my work are *dialogue*

and *just peace*. The concept of dialogue, also taken up in Chapter 2, draws attention to at least two very crucial moments in researching identity: (i) that it should be seen as a process (thus avoiding reification), and (ii) that identity is always constructed in dialogue/interaction with multiple selves and others. Chapter 3 presents the particular grammar I utilise in the analysis of the EU's missions. Just peace functions as a conceptual toolbox that guides the interrogation of CSDP missions by focusing on questions *what peace is, who it is for* and *who can script peace*. The debate on just peace does not just underline the significance of asking these questions, but it also provides a clear—although not closed—theoretical frame through which the case studies will be inspected. Of course, the particular grammar of just peace is enriched by the diverse vocabulary that the critical strand of peace and conflict literature has to offer.

The second part of Chapter 2 details the toolbox employed to address the EU's telling and acting of CSDP. I tackle the EU's CSDP identity with a pluralist approach to discourse analysis (DA), since it provides a solid basis from which to study the meanings/representations of peace(building) that the EU communicates, and the implications these meanings have. Chapters 4–6 feature, respectively, the analyses of the Artemis mission in the Democratic Republic of the Congo (DRC), EUFOR Althea in Bosnia and Herzegovina (BiH), and EULEX in Kosovo. The case selection purposefully features the EU's most lauded (and loved) peace missions that have all been declared successful with the launch of these missions (or sooner). Crucially, these peace missions provide a glimpse into the EU's telling and acting of CSDP for almost a decade. The empirical material mostly consists of EU speech acts, centring on the public and official texts of different EU bodies, and non-EU speech acts, inter alia NGO reports and analyses of the missions in order to destabilise the hegemonic script. Additionally, in case of the EU missions in the Balkans I also include the material gathered from interviews with both EU officials and various local presences (predominantly local NGOs).

In sum, this study critically investigates the EU's CSDP identity to enquire into the promise of the deployed missions to the country they are deployed in. To do this, the missions are located in the terrain of literature on just peace in order to challenge the usual frames through which the

CSDP is conceptualised. It is my hope that the telling and acting technique will both enable to detail the CSDP identity and to shake the foundations of the CSDP that have been regarded for far too long as unassailable. Throughout this book, I attempt to demonstrate how crucial a contextually detailed account—taking note of the telling and acting moments—is to apprehending the EU's CSDP identity.

NOTES

1. The label *CSDP* is used throughout the work, albeit this policy area was formerly, before the Treaty of Lisbon, known as the *ESDP*. For an accessible overview of what the EU's CSDP is, how it has historically developed, how far it has come, i.e. the stock-taking of the EU's operational record, consult the European External Action Service's (EEAS) web page together with the European Union Institute for Security Studies's (EUISS) web page.

2. Refer back to the second introductory quote to this chapter by Kurowska and observe the logic of evaluation of the CSDP.

3. Peacebuilding is not approached in a linear fashion or an a priori manner, it denotes the whole spectrum of activities from prevention to post-settlement reconstruction (see Viktorova Milne 2009; Fetherston 2000; Buckley-Zistel 2006).

4. One of the characteristics of this group of literature seems to be its often implicit subscription to neopositivism (see Jackson 2011, esp. Ch. 2, 3).

5. Consult the special issue "Another Theory is Possible: Dissident Voices in Theorising Europe" on this matter (see Manners and Whitman 2016).

6. Importantly, theoretical frames prove crucial as is demonstrated by the present literature overview that houses the same authors on both the problem-solving and critical side of the debate with very oppositional conclusions on the CSDP.

7. .1This literature is so vast that I do not even attempt to capture it in its entirety, just to point out some of the labels applied to the EU: civilian power (François Duchêne); normative power (Ian Manners); regional normative hegemon (Hiski Haukkala); empire-like power (Jan Zielonka); global power (James Rogers); ethical power (=as a force for good) (Lisbeth Aggestam); (non-)normative power (Elisabeth Johansson-Nogués); risk-averse actor (Zaki Laïdi); postcolonial power (Nora Fisher Onar & Kalypso Nicolaïdis); transformative power (Thomas Risse); soft power and the capability-expectations gap (Christopher Hill; Kristian Lau Nielsen); normative power as hegemony (Thomas Diez).

References

Asseburg, Muriel, and Ronja Kempin, eds. 2009. *The EU as a Strategic Actor in the Realm of Security and Defence? A Systematic Assessment of ESDP Missions and Operations*. Berlin: German Institute for International and Security Affairs (SWP).

Autesserre, Séverine. 2010. *The Trouble with the Congo: Local Violence and the Failure of International Peacebuilding*. New York, NY: CUP.

Autesserre, Séverine. 2014. *Peaceland: Conflict Resolution and the Everyday Politics of International Intervention*. New York, NY: CUP.

Bickerton, Chris J., Bastien Irondelle, and Anand Menon. 2011. "Security Co-operation Beyond the Nation-State: The EU's Common Security and Defence Policy." *Journal of Common Market Studies* 49 (1): 1–21.

Björkdahl, Annika, Stefanie Kappler, and Oliver Richmond. 2011. "The Emerging EU Peacebuilding Framework: Confirming or Transcending Liberal Peacebuilding?" *Cambridge Review of International Affairs* 24 (3): 449–469. https://doi.org/10.1080/09557571.2011.586331.

Bono, Giovanna. 2006. "The Perils of Conceiving of EU Foreign Policy as a 'Civilising Force.'" *Internationale Politik und Gesellschaft* 1: 150–163. http://library.fes.de/pdf-files/id/ipg/03647.pdf.

Buckley-Zistel, Susanne. 2006. "In-between War and Peace: Identities, Boundaries and Change after Violent Conflict." *Millennium—Journal of International Studies* 35 (1): 3–21. https://doi.org/10.1177/03058298060350010101.

Cebeci, Münevver. 2012. "European Foreign Policy Research Reconsidered: Constructing an 'Ideal Power Europe' Through Theory?" *Millennium—Journal of International Studies* 40 (3): 563–583. https://doi.org/10.1177/0305829812442235.

Council of the European Union. 2005. "ESDP Newsletter. European Security and Defence Policy." December, Issue 1. https://www.iss.europa.eu/content/esdp-newsletter-no-1.

Council of the European Union. 2009. "Council Conclusions on Democracy Support in the EU's External Relations (2974th External Relations Council Meeting)." *Brussels*, November 17. http://www.consilium.europa.eu/uedocs/cms_data/docs/pressdata/en/gena/111250.pdf.

Dias, Vanda Amaro. 2013. "The EU's Post-Liberal Approach to Peace: Framing EUBAM's Contribution to the Moldova-Transnistria Conflict Transformation." *European Security* 22 (3): 338–354. https://doi.org/10.1080/09662839.2012.712039.

Diez, Thomas. 2005. "Constructing the Self and Changing Others: Reconsidering 'Normative Power Europe.'" *Millennium—Journal of International Studies* 33 (3): 613–636. https://doi.org/10.1177/03058298050330031701.

Emerson, Michael, and Eva Gross, eds. 2006. *Evaluating the EU's Crisis Missions in the Balkans*. Brussels: Centre for European Policy Studies.

European Security Strategy (ESS). 2003. "A Secure Europe in a Better World—The European Security Strategy." *Brussels*, December 12. https://www.consilium.europa.eu/en/documents-publications/publications/european-security-strategy-secure-europe-better-world/.

Fetherston, A.B. 2000. "Peacekeeping, Conflict Resolution and Peacebuilding: A Reconsideration of Theoretical Frameworks." In *Peacekeeping and Conflict Resolution*, edited by Tom Woodhouse and Oliver Ramsbotham, 190–218. London: Frank Cass.

Freire, Maria R., et al. 2010. Mapping Research on European Peace Missions. The Hague: Netherlands Institute of International Relations 'Clingendael'.

Galantino, Maria G., and Maria R. Freire, eds. 2015. *Managing Crises, Making Peace: Towards a Strategic EU Vision for Security and Defense*. Basingstoke: Palgrave Macmillan.

Ginsberg, Roy H., and Susan E. Penksa. 2012. *The European Union in Global Security: The Politics of Impact*. Basingstoke: Palgrave Macmillan.

Grevi, Giovanni, Damien Helly, and Daniel Keohane, eds. 2009. *European Security and Defence Policy: The First 10 Years (1999–2009)*. Paris: EUISS. https://www.iss.europa.eu/content/esdp-first-10-years-1999-2009.

Gross, Eva, and Ana E. Juncos, eds. 2011. *EU Conflict Prevention and Crisis Management: Roles, Institutions, and Policies*. London: Routledge.

Jackson, Patrick T. 2011. *The Conduct of Inquiry in International Relations: Philosophy of Science and Its Implications for the Study of World Politics*. Abingdon: Routledge.

Kurki, Milja. 2013. *Democratic Futures: Revisioning Democracy Promotion*. Abingdon: Routledge. Kindle edition.

Kurowska, Xymena. 2008. "The Role of ESDP Operations." In *European Security and Defence Policy: An Implementation Perspective*, edited by Michael Merlingen and Rasa Ostrauskaite, 25–42. London: Routledge.

Kurowska, Xymena. 2012. "Introduction: The Role of Theory in Research on Common Security and Defence Policy." In *Explaining the EU's Common Security and Defence Policy: Theory in Action*, edited by Xymena Kurowska and Fabian Breuer, 1–15. New York: Palgrave Macmillan.

Kurowska, Xymena, and Fabian Breuer, eds. 2012. *Explaining the EU's Common Security and Defence Policy: Theory in Action*. Basingstoke: Palgrave Macmillan.

Mac Ginty, Roger. 2008. *No War, No Peace: The Rejuvenation of Stalled Peace Processes and Peace Accords*. Basingstoke: Palgrave Macmillan.

Mac Ginty, Roger. 2011. *International Peacebuilding and Local Resistance: Hybrid Forms of Peace*. London: Palgrave Macmillan.

Manners, Ian, and Richard Whitman. 2016. "Another Theory Is Possible: Dissident Voices in Theorising Europe." *Journal of Common Market Studies* 54 (1): 3–18. https://doi.org/10.1111/jcms.12332.

Merlingen, Michael. 2012a. "Applying Foucault's Toolkit to CSDP." In *Explaining the EU's Common Security and Defence Policy: Theory in Action*, edited by Xymena Kurowska and Fabian Breuer, 188–211. Basingstoke: Palgrave Macmillan.

Merlingen, Michael. 2012b. *EU Security Policy: What It Is, How It Works, Why It Matters*. Boulder: Lynne Rienner Publishers.

Merlingen, Michael, and Rasa Ostrauskaite. 2006. *European Union Peacebuilding and Policing: Governance and the European Security and Defence Policy*. Abingdon: Routledge.

Merlingen, Michael, and Rasa Ostrauskaite. 2008a. "Introduction: The European Union in International Security Affairs." In *European Security and Defence Policy: An Implementation Perspective*, ed. Michael Merlingen and Rasa Ostrauskaite, 1–8. London: Routledge.

Merlingen, Michael, and Rasa Ostrauskaite. 2008b. "The Implementation of the ESDP: Issues and Tentative Generalisations." In *European Security and Defence Policy: An Implementation Perspective*, edited by Michael Merlingen and Rasa Ostrauskaite, 189–205. London: Routledge.

Merlingen, Michael, and Rasa Ostrauskaite, eds. 2008c. *European Security and Defence Policy: An Implementation Perspective*. London: Routledge.

Peen Rodt, Annemarie. 2011. "The EU: A Successful Military Conflict Manager?" *Democracy and Security* 7 (2): 99–122. https://doi.org/10.1080/17419166.2011.572790.

Pogodda, Sandra, Oliver Richmond, Nathalie Tocci, Roger Mac Ginty, and Birte Vogel. 2014. "Assessing the Impact of EU Governmentality in Post-Conflict Countries: Pacification or Reconciliation?" *European Security*. https://doi.org/10.1080/09662839.2013.875533.

Schlag, Gabi. 2012. "Into the 'Heart of Darkness'—EU's Civilising Mission in the DR Congo." *Journal of International Relations and Development* 15 (3): 321–344. https://doi.org/10.1057/jird.2011.17.

Van Leeuwen, Theo. 2008. *Discourse and Practice: New Tools for Critical Discourse Analysis*. New York, NY: OUP.

Viktorova Milne, Jevgenia. 2009. *Returning Culture to Peacebuilding: Contesting the Liberal Peace in Sierra Leone*. PhD diss., University of St Andrews.

Whitman, Richard G., and Stefan Wolff, eds. 2012. *The European Union As a Global Conflict Manager*. Abingdon: Routledge.

Zehfuss, Maja. 2002. "The Politics of Reality: Derrida's Subversions, Constructivism and German Military Involvement Abroad." In *Constructivism in International Relations: The Politics of Reality*, edited by Maja Zehfuss, 196–249. Cambridge: CUP.

CHAPTER 2

Identity *in Motion* and *in Dialogue*

Whatever the concrete terms applied, speech and action—via versatile theoretical/positional lenses—have always been the categories used to decipher world politics. The debate about these containers of meaning and their intricate relationship is ongoing. Arendt aptly demonstrates the deeply relational character extant between these terms:

> Action and speech are so closely related because the primordial and specifically human act must at the same time contain the answer to the question asked of every newcomer: "Who are you?" This disclosure of who somebody is, is implicit in both his words and his deeds; yet obviously the affinity between speech and revelation is much closer than that between action and revelation, just as the affinity between action and beginning is closer than that between speech and beginning, although many, and even most acts, are performed in the manner of speech. Without the accompaniment of speech, at any rate, action would not only lose its revelatory character, but, and by the same token, it would lose its subject, as it were; not acting men but performing robots would achieve what, humanly speaking, would remain incomprehensible. Speechless action would no longer be action because there would no longer be an actor, and the actor, the doer of deeds, is possible only if he is at the same time the speaker of words. The action he begins is humanly disclosed by the word, and though his deed can be perceived in its brute physical appearance without verbal accompaniment, it becomes relevant only through the spoken word in which he identifies himself as the actor, announcing what he does, has done, and intends to do. (Arendt 1998, 178–179)

© The Author(s) 2020   13
B. Poopuu, *The European Union's Brand of Peacebuilding*,
Rethinking Peace and Conflict Studies,
https://doi.org/10.1007/978-3-030-19890-9_2

My approach below offers one possible reading of this debate. This work avows that the EU tells and acts its identity, and it is through problematising identity *in motion* (or in process) that a fuller grasp of it is achieved. In order to situate my take on telling and acting, the discourse and practice approaches serve as analytical guidelines. The merit of drawing from both discursive and practice approaches lies not in creating something detached from the mentioned perspectives—on the contrary, it is about exploring the inescapable cohabitation of the two views. Apart from resting on key post-positivist premises, the discussion on identity draws on Mikhail Bakhtin's concept of dialogue, which underlines the fact that identity cannot but include the word(s) of others. This chapter closes with the methodological discussion delimiting the ways of how one can study social phenomena *in motion* and *in dialogue*.

Identity as a concept allows for problematising the issues/components of international relations without starting from a ready-made script or a privileged referent. It enables to effortlessly move between the purportedly distinct levels of ir/IR.[1] It invites a myriad of questions, as Zalewski and Enloe point out:

> who are "we" in international relations? Who become identified as important in international political events? Which identities are perceived as relevant and which are not? Which groups are allowed to self-identify? What role does the politics of identity play in contemporary international relations theory and practice? (1995, 279)

As an illustration of the above enquiries, consider the concept of identity vis-à-vis an EU's Common Security and Defence Policy (CSDP) operation and an imaginary country X undergoing this operation. Being represented as lacking European/international standards legitimises certain actions towards that country, opening some routes and foreclosing others. These standards contain a number of value judgements on what a move for the "better" would look like, and when, as is the case with most of the Balkans, a country gets labelled as lacking these standards, it is liable to forfeit certain aspects of its agency to an entity that allegedly possesses these standards (cf. Cebeci 2012).[2] In this instance, the role of identity politics is profound. Consequently, the value of identity as a concept in researching international relations is immense. In this way, the *dramatis personae* of international relations ("ir" as well as "IR") is never seen as established, but always under critical inspection (see Zalewski and Enloe 1995, 279–305), always in dialogue (in a deeply Bakhtinian sense, as explained below).

Positivist approaches, from the start, already unnecessarily circumscribe the reach of identity to certain pre-given foci.[3] To a large extent, these approaches are limiting due to their ontological-epistemological commitments. Their belief, for instance, that theory and reality are two autonomous and separate categories (see Jackson 2011, Ch. 2; mind-world dualism vs. mind-world monism; see also Hamati-Ataya 2010, 2012), limits the versatility of ir/IR, and in effect, does harm, as its viewpoint tends to be monologic and universal. Especially when

> this understanding of the world allows the possibility of thinking that defining specific referents or identities as the central issues in international relations theory is not particularly political or epistemologically significant act; it is merely one of choice. … the choice of referent is seen as a neutral activity by positivists. (Zalewski and Enloe 1995, 299)

Another equally problematic issue is the fact that, as Hobson (2012) demonstrates, IR theory—mainly its mainstream strands—tends to privilege certain subjects, explicitly or implicitly, and thus narrow down possible research routes and spaces.

The study of identity harbours an array of approaches from a number of positivist and post-positivist approaches. This work relies on the post-positivist platform, especially since it allows space for reflexivity—in fact, more often than not considering it an ineluctable category of any research programme. This means that I take seriously the premise that knowledge and reality are mutually constitutive (Lynch 2014; Hamati-Ataya 2012, 2014; Khalili 2010; Butler 1992). At the core of this stands the argument that social reality is not an exogenously given realm, but a space where individual knowing subjects leave their imprint. Therefore, both the tools of construction—knowledge and meaning—and the construction itself—the social space—are simultaneously a creation and co-creation (Hamati-Ataya 2014, 47–48). The concept of dialogue will further explain this logic. A similar dynamic also applies to the research process itself. The researcher is not outside of the social construction process and whatever number of caveats one makes, a particular positional bias shines through her/his work (cf. Holquist 2002, 20). This moment, although at times frustrating, distances my work from positivist excursions that allegedly have an alibi that makes their theoretical viewpoint "neutral" (cf. ibid., 150).

I have decided to open the debate on identity by focusing on the work of Goff and Dunn (2004), since it represents post-positivist work on identity in a variety of hues and thus provides a solid point of departure. Their approach is multidimensional, referring to four primary features of identity—*alterity, fluidity, constructedness* and *multiplicity*. The key point that they make is that the more specific content of each of these categories is subject to empirical research and thus cannot be determined a priori. In this way, it is possible to avoid a narrow focus on just one mechanism of identity construction, e.g. "othering", or, the reification of actors (see Jackson 2004, Ch. 10). It is worthwhile to elaborate on these concepts as they form the point of departure of my approach to identity. First, *alterity*, as they suggest, denotes primarily that identity is relational, and thus does not strictly refer to "othering" strategies, i.e. when difference translates into inferiority. Rather than fixing neat parameters within which difference operates, they leave it open-ended (cf. Diez 2005): in other words, their belief is that identity is contextually laden. Contingent on the contextual specifics, Goff and Dunn stress, "an identity that emerges from efforts to specify an other need not necessarily exclude or include, but rather carries the potential to do either" (2004, 238). *Fluidity*, secondly, means that identity is spatio-temporally sensitive. As Frueh maintains (2004, 64), "identity labels, as a critical component of social power, are susceptible to the same pressures of continuity and change as other aspects of reality". Thirdly, *constructedness* hints at the social nature of identities, with the accent put on who has more leverage in this process and the implications of this. Finally, *multiplicity* highlights the importance of actors' multiple roles. Taking a step even further, this might raise questions of the stability and coherence of an actor's identity. Hansen (2006, 42; cf. Rowley and Weldes 2012, esp. 523) has pointed out that as a researcher of a specific identity, one might be inclined to iron out the cracks in a particular identity. Thus one can stretch the multiplicity even further by arguing that a coherent identity might be a mere chimera.

The mentioned aspects unpack the main features of identity. The cardinal logic of identity—*dialogue*—extends the idea behind alterity and functions as a key to understanding meanings. Therefore, my work rests on the concept of dialogue that has by now been successfully introduced to the field of IR and is experiencing a revival of interest in IR and beyond (e.g. Dépelteau 2018; Hobson and Sajed 2017). Both Mälksoo (2010) and Guillaume (2011) take their cue from Bakhtin's work and thus manage to draw attention to at least two very crucial moments in researching identity: (i) that it should be seen as a process (thus avoiding reification), and (ii) that identity is always constructed in dialogue/interaction with multiple selves and others. The idea of dialogue goes well beyond the notion of conversation or a normative/ethical expectation (see Guillaume 2011, 40). According to one of the foremost scholars of Bakhtin, Michael Holquist:

> dialogism argues that all meaning is relative in the sense that it comes about only as a result of the relation between two bodies occupying simultaneous but different space, where bodies may be thought of as ranging from the immediacy of our physical bodies, to political bodies and to bodies of ideas in general (ideologies). (2002, 19; cf. Shapiro 1984, 1)

It is crucial, as implied by Holquist (2002, 21, 36), not to reduce dialogism to just dualism (which may also be true), but to preserve the awareness of an unlimited multiplicity that receives a more concrete shape once a specific empirical instance is selected. The emphasis on a processual account (Guillaume 2011) points to the rich social fabric in which identities transact, thus shifting the emphasis from entities to the moment of exchange (cf. Jackson 2004). In this way, it is clear that an identity is responsive to and contingent on both the spatio-temporal specifics and other identities. The emphasis on process and dialogue allows one to escape treating identities as ready-made and bounded categories.[4] Rather, it invites seeing identities as an ongoing process/transaction, which never occurs in a vacuum—cf. the Bakhtinian idea that "nothing is anything in itself" (see Holquist 2002, 36), or in monologic/static terms (Bakhtinian idea of becoming, identity is always in process; Todorov 1998, xi–xii; Bakhtin 1986). Dialogue, inextricably interwined with the notion of process, allows better to understand the workings of identity. Crucially, in this perspective, both the ontological and epistemological commitments are grounded in the concept of dialogue/dialogism. As Holquist aptly points out, "dialogism may indeed be defined as an epistemology based on the assumption that knowing an entity (a person or a thing) is to put that entity into a relation of simultaneity with some-thing [*sic*] else, where simultaneity is understood as not being a relation of equality or identity" (2002, 154). In this way, taking a dialogical approach means that the object of study refers to a set of relations.

In more specific terms, this relational aspect translates into the following dynamics. Bakhtin places the premium on not treating identity/self as a ready-made entity; rather the logic of dialogue prevails. That is,

> Existence is *sobytie sobytiya*, the event of co-being; it is a vast web of interconnections each and all of which are linked as participants in an event whose totality is so immense that no single one of us can ever know it. That event manifests itself in the form of a constant, ceaseless creation and exchange of meaning. The mutuality of differences makes dialogue Bakhtin's master concept, for it is present in exchanges at all levels – between words in language, people in society, organisms in ecosystems, and even between processes in the natural world. (Holquist 2002, 40)

This approach escapes the ontological fixity of discrete identities and stresses the dialogical nature of identity. "Dialogic relations" are taken as "relations (semantic) among any utterances in speech communication" (Bakhtin 1986, 117). For Bakhtin, an identity presents itself via utterances, referring to the communicative aspect of interaction. It is easy to misread Bakhtin's concept of dialogue as a mere byword for a physical conversation, yet as Bakhtin himself and a number of scholars that have taken it upon themselves to dissect his work (e.g. Kristeva, Todorov, Neumann, Holquist, etc.) have underlined, the dialogic quality of utterances does not necessarily hinge on there being two concrete entities; rather it tries to communicate that, as Bakhtin himself contends, language "is populated – overpopulated – with the intentions of others" (1981, 294). Indeed, "any utterance is a link in a very complexly organised chain of other utterances" (Bakhtin 1986, 69). Therefore, Bakhtin, root and branch, enriches our understanding of identity, by not a priori limiting the number of participants, by not subscribing overwhelmingly to one single strategy of self-other relations, by stressing the weightiness of the moment of utterance that conveys—from (a) specific viewpoint(s)—meaning(s). It is crucial, at this juncture, to put an emphasis on the importance of both expressivity and addressivity (1986, 92–95): as Bakhtin argues, "the expression of an utterance always responds to a greater or lesser degree, that is, it expresses the speaker's attitude toward others' utterances and not just his attitude toward the object of his utterance" (ibid., 92; see Butler 2004). Furthermore, Todorov, in discussing Bakhtin's thought, suggests that "every utterance always has a receiver (of different nature; different degrees of proximity, specificity, consciousness, etc.) whose responsive understanding is sought and anticipated by the author of the verbal work" (1998, 110).

My own point of departure draws from the above literature, adopting the construction process of identity as it was succinctly posited above, especially through the invaluable loans from Bakhtin's thought. The aspect that my approach aims to discuss and elaborate upon further concerns the vehicles of meaning, that is, the telling and acting processes of a specific identity. Many IR scholars have referred to the discourse-practice conundrum in researching identity, but it has not really been taken up more substantially (see, e.g., Goff and Dunn's edited volume [2004], and more recently Lebow [2012]).

My work slices up identity spatio-temporally, hence referring to moments of telling and acting that make up the expressive realm of an entity's identity. It is also pertinent to draw attention to the inescapable fact that this act of slicing up identity spatio-temporally is at the same time an axiological move, i.e. driven by value judgements (cf. Holquist 2002, 150–153). Owing to the problematisation of discourse and practice— seeing that these concepts acquire different guises spatio-temporally—I attempt to provide a more contextual and nuanced picture of identity. Yet, by way of an empirical exploration of the dynamics of telling and acting, this work does not pretend to resolve this question (nor to urge others upon this quest), but rather to emphasise the value of open-endedness in accounting for the varied dynamics that identity construction entails. In this way, although the poststructuralist concept of discourse is a direct loan (see esp. Hansen 2006), my approach to action/practice is not directly taken from practice literature. Analogously to Fierke's (2013b) recent work on political self-sacrifice, I treat action as an "act of speech" where different authors—relying on their symbolic capital (Bourdieu 1989)—provide representations of what happened/what is done. Of course, Fierke's work remains an influence and allows for a nuanced not a verbatim translation of how to make sense of "action". Additionally, I adopt De Certeau's position to practise as it contests the artificial dichotomy between discourse and practice, and the attitude to practise as somehow providing a "true" insight into an actor's nature (as opposed to the deliberate "lies" of discourse). He maintained that practice, far from being an unbiased insight into an actor's position, is a construct just like discourse (1988, esp. 67; but also see 45–81).

Although the debate is very much at the zenith, the emergence of the practice turn in IR scholarship has raised some issues for both discursively and practice-inclined authors.[5] First, ontologically and epistemologically speaking, what are the ethico-political implications of naming something discourse and practice, or alternatively, rhetoric and action? The fact that these are concepts that the researcher applies calls for reflexivity (see Hamati-Ataya 2012). On many occasions, the practice theorists resort to a line of attack according to which discourse analysts are too linguistically inclined. With this move, language is reduced to text rather than meaning-making. In doing so, of course, practice theorists demonstrate a very superficial reading of discursively inclined authors (see, e.g., Hansen 2006; Epstein 2008, 2013; Fierke 2013a). Scholars working with discourse, for their part, have largely dismissed practice turn authors, since they take it that discourse already comprises practice, and/or that discourse and practice are so closely interlinked that there is no use in separating them (see Epstein 2013, 514–515; cf. Pin-Fat 2010, esp. 16). This proves that the larger debate revolves around the definitions of both discourse and practice. It is interesting to observe how much emphasis is placed on the speaking-doing divide, and how—if not always explicitly—the doing realm of an actor is seen in more glorious terms (value judgements *par excellence*).[6] Thus, deciding on the "right" concepts (either discourse or practice or both together) is ethico-politically laden and needs further reflection to account for the many implications. It is at this juncture that the knowledge-reality mutuality finds its expression: that is, the researcher as well as the research object render meaning to these realms of operation, as well as to the ways these realms—if kept separate—can be accessed. The entry-points to telling and acting—in case these categories are isolated, or to reality in more general terms—are *either* discourse or practice, according to linguistic and practice theorists. The questions that different entry-points would raise are numerous: can these access-points be seen so linked that there is no worth in separation; if separation is essential, what sort of separation; and, of course, a question about the legitimacy of picking either of these entry-points?

Methodologically, practice theorists occasionally claim that they have a more immediate access to the research object, as researching practices demands the use of "observation" (e.g. esp. Bueger 2014). This claim, of course, remains somewhat futile, as a focus on discourse does not only propagate analysis of documents from *afar*, but also includes interviews, ethnographic research and the like. "Observation" of action is often conducted through the medium of text (accounts, reports, documents, etc.)—so largely the same material. Only a focus on action in this case may blind the researcher to the salient discursive realities which may otherwise impact on the conclusions. Thus, the divide remains crude. Yet, what this problematique draws attention to is the need for a more fruitful discussion over both research methods and methodology. Furthermore, it is worthwhile to interrogate the claim that reducing the distance between the research object and researcher per se solves the age-old crisis of representation (see Vrasti 2008, esp. 295–296).

There is no straightforward way to solve these issues. However, what remains paramount is that the researcher acknowledges the above polemics and is conceptually as lucid and thorough as possible to allow for engagement with them. Below, a rudimentary example is presented to illustrate the simultaneous complementarity of and difficulty contained in the relationship between the two entry-points, i.e. discourse and practice. The EU's reference to European best practices is a recurrent motif in its relation to the multiple others for whom the CSDP missions are intended. From a discursively inclined perspective, it is possible to note how power relations are played out through the way in which the EU wields this term. From a practice turn perspective, it is possible to note that this is a repetitive "practice" that is characteristic of the EU's praxis in the case studies covered in this work.[7]

What does this example imply? This state of affairs places me as a researcher in a very difficult position, because what I am inclined to do is to refer to the baggage of knowledge (both theoretical and contextual) that can provide interpretations of this practice. The difficulty is twofold, for the interpretative moment is vast, plus the researcher's context—as Bakhtin would have it—always mediates the material, notwithstanding the efforts to give voice to the research object(s). However, on the other hand, it provides an extra layer of information and nuance to a study as it shifts attention away from *what identity* to *how identity* is enacted. Another difficulty consists in, as the latest work of one of the leading practice theorists suggests, the removal of the moment of "interaction" from meaning-making. This can be seen as a handicap in deciphering a practice:

> She [Knorr Cetina] points out that practice theory provides an alternative understanding to the interactionist understanding of knowledge generation. Instead of interaction, practice theory focuses on the level of the mundane functioning and everyday maintenance of orders of knowledge. (Bueger 2015, 4)

This work maintains that in order to grasp what a certain practice means, one essentially needs to subject it to a dialogical approach *à la* Bakhtin. It can mean something only in relation to a number of other practices/discourses, and here the crux of the matter is the question of the entry-point, i.e. how do we learn from practices? Discussing methodological avenues for practice theory, Bueger makes a somewhat crude assumption when he suggests that practices are ontologically prior and discourses as such are secondary, in fact, he reduces discourses to data access-points for practices (2014, 386–388). Both entry-points—i.e. discourses and practices (as far as one can draw a line between them)—need to be subject to a dialogical approach; otherwise it might be that the researcher's context overshadows that of the research object's.

Owing to the above incisions into the body of discursively and practically oriented approaches to IR and beyond, it should be underlined that both approaches are at their weakest when they overemphasise, respectively, the other's commitment to either discourse or practice. When this is the case, particular definitions of discourse and practice emerge. Of course, as practice theorists are just beginning to chart their ground, this debate is only gaining pace.

Problematising the Discourse/Practice Dichotomy

This is an attempt to (re)problematise the relationship between discourse and practice—to rethink the conceptual divide between linguistic and practice turns. The reason for this exercise is to understand the merits and pitfalls of both approaches, and to see whether these perspectives are exclusive or possibly mutually accommodating. According to practice theorists Bueger and Villumsen, the key difference between linguistic and practice imaginaries is where they locate shared knowledge: the former locate it "in intersubjective symbolic orders (or discourses)", while "practice approaches locate it in practice, in practical activities and its representations" (2007, 425; Bueger 2014). In this work, I maintain that the shared systems of meaning that guide the actor in its daily activities do not have to be limited to discourses or practices, i.e. they do not have to be imagined in either/or way.

In the first part of this section, the focus is on the two turns: linguistic and practice. In order to better grasp the conceptual apparatus of both sides, I offer a brief delineation of each. In particular, the relationship between discourse and practice will be investigated. This relationship will be studied by zooming in on how the respective turns make sense of discourse and practice, but also on the ontological and epistemological commitments of both, the extent to which these differ and the consequences of these differences. The caveat is that although I discuss these approaches separately, I surmise that there is a lot of room for debate and difference inside each approach as well as between discourse and practice approaches—where there are different but also similar dynamics at play.

Probing the terrains of both turns provides the necessary background for considering the concepts of telling and acting, which gain a lot of conceptual vigour from both turns. Within this work, telling and acting, responding loosely to the notions of discourse and practice respectively, are separated diachronically, which means that essentially, as Van Leeuwen (2008, 6) puts it, doing something and talking about it are separate phenomena in social reality. Note that the distinction/dichotomy or complementarity is maintained in the approaches of both turns—the question is whether it is possible to capture the "social" without creating space for the other turn in a meaningful way. However, apart from being able to draw a diachronic distinction between the two social phenomena, it is excruciatingly difficult to separate the two as they are interwoven with one another, in that they refer to particular *modus operandi* of how actors express themselves, and thus also to the infinite process of becoming these actors. Therefore, it is not the separating line between them that directs this work, but rather the process by which the "two stages" inform us of the social reality.[8]

The Linguistic Turn and Its Premises

Speaking is an activity with normative consequences. (Onuf, quoted in Debrix 2003, 12)

I begin by briefly discussing some of the key ideas offered by the representatives of the so-called linguistic turn.[9] This is a necessary step in order to provide a background against which to unfold my own model of telling and acting identity, combining elements of both linguistic and practice turns.

According to François Debrix (2003, 23), the starting point for post-positivist IR scholarship—which represents the linguistic turn—is the analysis of the *place*, *role* and *use* of language in IR. Furthermore, the overarching idea intrinsic to this turn argues that the social can be conceived as a discursive space (Laclau and Mouffe 2001). Debrix insists that it is necessary to make a distinction between different movements that have gathered their theoretical energies from the linguistic turn, namely constructivism and poststructuralism, since they have a slightly different take on language. Thus, below I present the main premises of linguistic turn *qua* constructivist and poststructuralist tenets in relation to their different conceptualisations of the relationships between discourse, practice and action.

Karin Fierke's Work: An Example of Constructivist Thought

To illustrate (critical/thick) constructivist thought, I turn to Karin Fierke, as one of the notable scholars underlining the prominent place of language in making sense of our social reality.[10] Here, I will focus on deciphering the relationship between discourse and practice—how and in what ways do they relate to each other?

Relying on Wittgenstein's thought, Fierke argues that one of the key things to focus on is meaning in use, i.e. "rather than seeking an external cause or trying to look inside the minds of individuals, the focus shifts squarely to the question of meaning in use" (2010, 86). This boils down to investigating the public language that offers reasons for any given action (cf. ibid., 87). Language in constructivist vocabulary, including Fierke's approach, means that it is seen as "a form of life" (Debrix 2003, 8); language is said to equal social action, i.e. it communicates what is supposed to be done (ibid.). Taking cue from Wittgenstein, Fierke employs the concept of a language game to illustrate how language is used by a certain actor:

> language user is embedded in a context and constrained by its rules, yet may, through her choices and actions, shape that context, much as the chess player, while embedded in the rules of the game, exercises choice in moving from any particular space. (2002, 101)

She elaborates further that "rules are patterns that constitute who we are and how we act in relation to specified others" (ibid., 102). With these images, Fierke eloquently portrays the structure (rules) and agency problematique as understood by constructivists. It is crucial to note that for Fierke, language acts as conduit for meaning—a tool through which we are able to make sense of our surroundings (cf. 1996, 480). Importantly, Fierke (1996, 493) underlines the inescapable place of language in IR by referring to the necessity for policies to have a "linguistic component" since "you cannot have certain policies secretly", e.g. "making a threat needs to be uttered".

The nexus of language, practice and action—though not an explicit point of departure—figures in Fierke's work. With the following quote from Wittgenstein (1973, paras. 206, 219, quoted in Fierke 2010, 89),

Fierke aptly captures the close relations between language-practice: "the *rules* [language games] are like *habits*, insofar as we often forget, through repeatedly following them, that they rest on rules" (emphasis added).[11] This indicates that language carries meaning and, at times, language equals daily know-how. Consequently, language is seen to have this habitual component that is characteristic of practice approaches. Moreover, practices (as they are understood by practice theorists and perhaps not sufficiently problematised in constructivist writings) occupy a relatively implicit position: if one follows the linguistic turn authors, there is a linear relationship where language precedes practice and action (where the latter two are not really distinguishable from another). The connection with action is revealed when Fierke elaborates on the above idea: "the rules constitute a practice that is replicated in the acts of multiple participants, who may never know one another, and they *regulate* action insofar as deviations from the rules may be sanctioned" (ibid., 89). In sum, although Fierke—taking a lot of creative energy from Wittgenstein—centred on the role of language, she also touched upon a number of other aspects (though perhaps not so ardently underlined) that need to be considered when thinking about "human activity". In this sense, Fierke points out that one of the key ideas that Wittgenstein communicates is that we can talk about "rule-guided action, informed by human traditions, customs and practices" (ibid., 90). Therefore, for thick constructivism, albeit practices are not elaborated in such great detail, they might be understood to be part of the rules. On balance, however, practices as such do not receive much coverage, the main division being between words and deeds (or actions). Debrix (2003, 9–10) illustrates this by referring to Onuf, who summarises the constructivist rationale: (i) "people use words to represent deeds" and moreover, "without the support of language, the deed could not be realised". Secondly (ii), Onuf claims that "language makes the deed by re-presenting and actualising it", referring to the speech act logic that serves as a mainstay in constructivist works more generally.

In her recent work, Fierke (2013a) reviews the work of critical scholars to enquire about the role of language in security studies. The paper commences rather provocatively by asking "is there life beyond language?" (ibid.). Although she does not refer to practice theorists, the problematique of the body (*à la* Hansen 2000 and Butler 2011) and the material turn (*à la* Aradau 2010) are discussed. This excursion is of significance since it attempts to do away with the language versus body dichotomy, but in a way that does not banish language or discourse from the forefront, rather rethinking its workings (and making it more relevant for the "reality out there"). Two key openings for approaches taking language seriously are made: firstly, Fierke notes that Butler's approach "makes it possible to deal with non-verbal communication, both visual and bodily, which, [it is] argue[d], the Copenhagen School has not addressed" (2013a, 8). Secondly, with reference to both Hansen and Aradau (who goes even further with the material turn than Butler or Hansen), it is possible to see the subject under scrutiny in a much wider sense (than before), "as a speaking, feeling, acting subject who occupies a body which may be subject to pain, suffering or pleasure" (ibid., 13–14). Thus, Fierke ends up with talking about "embodied security" which "is not isolated from a material context but fundamentally bound up in the intraction [*sic*] between humans and their material environment, both of which are constituted in and through language" (ibid., 16).[12]

Though this is a relatively sketchy overview of what the "constructivist party" of the linguistic turn has to offer, I believe that the main arguments are there. Language is not merely a mirror of the world, one should focus on language/meaning in use, as the nexus of language-practice-action. One of the things to bear in mind is that there is no single and homogeneous group of IR theorists that describe themselves as representatives of the linguistic turn. Thus, I believe that the linguistic turn offers a critical mindset but not a theory/school per se. Probably the key questions here are how the scholars subscribing to (some) tenets of the linguistic turn have defined and employed the concept of discourse, and whether they have given thought to practice(s) and action, and consequently on the methodology/methods apposite to their ontological/epistemological commitments. All in all, critical constructivists reserve a central role and place for language, and other concepts/phenomena (such as practice/action)—as far as these are conceptualised—are subordinated to language or depend on it in one way or another.

Lene Hansen's Work: Epitomising Poststructuralist Grammar

In contrast to Fierke and constructivists in general, poststructuralists adopt a somewhat different approach to language. Debrix (2003, 6–7) demonstrates this well when he remarks that on the one side, constructivists refer to the "normative aspects of language", whereas on the other side, poststructuralists "cannot go beyond the recognition that language is generally performative". Owing to this, the major fault line lies in how *performativ-*

ity is understood. In the case of constructivists, "the speaker of the word is the performer. … language remains the performer's tool"—versus poststructuralists who maintain that "language itself is the performance". He further explains that for poststructuralists, "social reality is already within text" (a well-known Derridean stance) (ibid., 13). What poststructuralists highlight is that language transcends the spoken word, plurality and messiness of meaning in texts (again Derrida and the postponement of meaning), and the importance of the discourse-power nexus (ibid., 13–16). Another division characteristic of constructivist and poststructuralist theorising is the status of shared meaning. While the former sees this as a relatively stable entity, the latter takes issue with this pronounced universality, rather stressing the uneasy particularity that undermines the consistency and generalisability of the "shared" rules (see Epstein 2013).

Lene Hansen maintains that for poststructuralists, language—or better discourse as the space in which expression, meaning-generation occurs—is political, which means that it is "a site for the production and reproduction of particular subjectivities and identities while others are simultaneously excluded" (2006, 18). For poststructuralists, discourse is "everything", in that, the material is always discursively mediated (ibid., 25). While constructivists focus on the constitutive/constructed character of language—seen as an instrument of the subject—poststructuralists do not take the subject as an autonomous category; instead they talk about subject positions. Thus, for example, Doty argues that "agency is not understood as an inherent quality of individual human beings qua human beings, but rather as a positioning of subjects that occurs through practices, practices which are inherently discursive and ultimately undecidable" (1997, 383–384).

This observation conveniently leads to the issue of the understanding of practices (often discursive practices) that poststructuralists adopt. In fact, practices are not elaborated upon apart from when they are invoked in connection with the inescapable performativity that discourses signify (thus, they provide a characteristic of discourses). An apposite example of the way poststructuralists use the concepts of discourse and practice interchangeably (or together) is the following excerpt from Foucault:

> Discursive practices are characterized by the delimitation of a field of objects, the definition of a legitimate perspective for the agent of knowledge, and the fixing of norms for the elaboration of concepts and theories. … each discursive practice implies a play of prescriptions that designate its exclusions and choices. (1997a, 199)

Thus, practice and action are not really conceptualised in detail, further-more, they do not have a prominent place in either constructivist or poststructuralist writings. For poststructuralists, discourses provide the direction for actions (cf. Hansen 2006, 21), and in that sense they are inherently performative.

In her recent work, Hansen (2011) constructively engages with the practice turn and offers a vision of what a poststructuralist practice approach would look like. Importantly (ibid., 281), she notes that the significance of considering practices within "a traditional poststructuralist textual method-ology" opens up "the space between texts and 'doings.'" In particular, its value lies in its consideration of action that is not exclusively textual. Thus, while Hansen takes practices seriously, her concern is "with the public and discursive 'practice performances' of central actors during times of cri-sis" (ibid., 282). In her framework, practices acquire a somewhat different meaning, they do no only refer to practical knowledge—that is, they are not always routine—but they can also be unstable, and contested (see Hansen 2011, 281). In her framework, then, the epistemological and methodolog-ical focus is on discursive practices. Hansen's approach and poststructural-ism more generally lay bare the role discourses play in meaning-making and how this process is inherently unstable.

The Practice Turn and Its Premises

According to Adler and Pouliot (2011, 3), the recent practice turn[13] in social theory "takes competent performances as its main entry point in the study of world politics". Importantly, their work emphasises that the practice approach does not offer a grand theory but rather encourages to take practices seriously.[14] Thus, practice theorists enrich the ontological considerations of (IR) scholars (ibid., 4, 11). A number of works by prac-tice theorists contend that there is no one uniform practice approach, but different takes on it. My considerations below will try to tease out some arguments that are relevant to making sense of the practice-discourse rela-tionship.

Adler and Pouliot define practices as follows:

> practices are competent performances. More precisely, practices are socially meaningful patterns of action which, in being performed more or less compe-tently, simultaneously embody, act out, and possibly reify background knowl-edge and discourse in and on the material world. (2011, 6)

They note a difference between the concepts of behaviour, action and practice (cf. 2011, 6), where the key divergence lies in seeing practices as *patterned deeds*. The main distinction introduced between discourses and practices is the idea that qualitatively they do not denote the same *form of action*. In their taking stock of what practices entail, the two authors refer to five typical characteristics of practices:

(i) practice is a performance

(ii) practice tends to be patterned

(iii) practice is more or less competent

(iv) practice rests on background knowledge

(v) practice weaves together the discursive and material worlds. (Adler and Pouliot 2011, 7–8; cf. Bueger and Gadinger 2015)

The fifth characteristic is of particular importance as it demonstrates how the practice approach relates to discourse/language. The way practice and discourse relate to one another is via meaning, namely language is the conduit of meaning (constructivists and poststructuralist nod). This is well illustrated by Bueger and Gadinger who argue: "that practices are composed of both sayings and doings entails that analysis is concerned about both *practical activity* and *its representation*" (2007, 10; emphases added). Adler and Pouliot (2011) refer to discourse/language as the medium through which practices acquire meaning. They maintain that "in order for practices to make sense, then, practitioners must establish (contest, negotiate, communicate) their significance" (2011, 14). Elaborating on this suggestion, they maintain that practices *lean on language* in two senses: firstly, "as accounts of lived practices [that] are textually constituted" (as suggested a few lines above), and secondly, "the competence of routinely doing something socially meaningful often relies on discourse", in the sense that language is a speech act (ibid., 13–14).

In this sense, it is crucial to ask, what are the ways in which a researcher can gain knowledge from discourses and practices?[15] The latter is something that needs more attention.[16] For instance, Neumann (2002, 628) asks "how best to analyse social life given that social life can only play itself out in discourse". To his mind, a proper analysis should also engage with "contextual data from the field" (ibid., 628) and not just "text-based analyses of global politics". The latter point is crucial as it exposes the limits of both discourses and practices, in that not all discourses and/or practices speak (e.g. consider Hansen 2000; De Certeau 1988; also Fierke 2013b). Another issue that one should be wary of is the power/politics of naming something habitual (succinctly pointed out by Kratochwil 2011, 53) and the consequences of that. Is it possible to ascertain always that something is routine, and how do practice approaches deal with the non-routine? Also, certain methodological problems arise in interpreting practices: who performs the observation (outsider to a certain practice?), and is observation the sole method of registering practices?[17] This is further complicated by the issue of whether discourses—in addition to their representational and speech act-like characters—also inevitably precede practices/action (cf. Neumann 2002), and if so, what are the implications of seeing the discourse-practice relationship in this way?

Telling and Acting Identity

I argue that an actor's identity is composed of both processes—telling and acting—and that either process involves both *speaking* and *doing*, albeit in different ways and to different degrees, and sometimes, as De Certeau suggests, they just do not (yet) speak (1988, 61), or do. Thus, while practice theorists argue that practices—implicit knowledge and meaning—are ontologically prior (Bueger 2014, 386) and discourses—for example, explicit knowledge (such as norms and rules)—secondary, the approach taken here offers a somewhat different logic though it comprises elements of both "turns", especially given their reliance on one another.[18] This task is worthwhile since a detailed understanding of how telling and acting operate can enable a better understanding of an actor's identity and its effects. The aim is to zoom in on the different logics that the processes of telling and acting can follow.

In the next section, I will attempt to clarify what the concepts of telling and acting stand for and how they function as locales of identity.

Telling and Acting as the Sites of Identity

My theoretical approach to *identity* takes its cue from a mainly postpositivist platform that highlights, most importantly, the dialogical quality of an actor's identity. This means that identity cannot but contain contextual cues and responses to its others. While the previous sections addressed some of the aspects and dynamics of identity construction process, here the discussion turns to the two key sites of identity. In this, I found Lebow's work an inspiration since it does not erect neat divisions between various approaches to identity (2012). In fact, he seems to find it impossible to just follow one understanding of identity. He subscribes to what he calls the thicker formulations of identity (see Lebow 2012, 30–39). As Lebow (ibid., 36) elaborates, scholars supporting thick formulations of self "are less interested in the self as an abstract concept and more in how ordinary people understand themselves" and the ethical or behavioural consequences of these conceptions of the self. It is worthwhile to quote Lebow at some length as he aptly summarises the essence of the different approaches (ibid.):

> The *narrative self* emphasizes the role of stories as vehicles for constructing and propagating individual and collective identities. The *pragmatic self* emphasizes the importance of behavior, especially habitual behavior, and the ways in which our actions and reflections about it determine our understanding of who we are. The *social and postmodernist selves* – one bleeds into the other – stress the social nature of identity even more than the narrative and pragmatic selves. They draw our attention to the constraining effects of linguistic structures, discourses and social and economic practices. Postmodern selves are also appealing in their understanding of identities as multiple, inconsistent and fragile and a source of psychological angst. (emphases mine)

The difficulty, as Lebow suggests, lies in choosing *within* and *between* these approaches. Each of them highlights a particular aspect of the practice of identity (see the quote above). A common theme uniting most of these thick formulations is the understanding of identity "as the product of interaction between individuals and their societies" (2012, 37). In the light of this, Lebow situates his approach within thick approaches to identity and argues that "identities are created, transmitted, revised and undermined through narratives and practices" (ibid., 46). The meaning of these mediums of identity is captured in the above quote (see Lebow 2012, Introduction, Ch. 1). The crux of the matter lies in the fact that the relationship between narratives and practices is still poorly understood (ibid., 47; Goff and Dunn 2004, Ch. 14). There is no one formula of how narratives and practices interact that can apply to all cases. Furthermore, as Lebow notes, "the boundaries between text and practice are blurred and there is considerable overlap" (2012, 47). Note that, despite raising this issue, he does not sufficiently tackle it in his work. The degree to which this remains a problem for linguistic and practice turn authors can be gleaned from my analysis.

My approach does not claim to definitively trump all others, but seeks to provide just one possible, and so far overlooked, configuration of the interaction between discourses and practices. As my work follows in post-positivist footsteps, it takes it cues from critical constructivism (as defined, e.g. by Fierke and Jørgensen 2001; Pouliot 2007), poststructuralism (see esp. Hansen 2006) and postcolonialism and is explicitly normative (Erskine 2010). The constructivist lens is most potent when it comes to acknowledging that, on the metatheoretical level, both knowledge and social reality are not only constructed, but also mutually constitutive (see Pouliot 2007). A crucial methodological implication, according to Pouliot (ibid., 364), is the fact that "research must begin with what it is that social agents, as opposed to analysts, believe to be real".

In my work, this is a weighty proposition, as partly, the analytical division into telling and acting stems from the EU's firm belief in the possibility of neatly differentiating between telling and acting (though in reality one can see how these categories collapse into one another). The poststructuralist lens contributes to the investigations of language uses: it hints at the complex and arbitrary process of conveying meaning and puts emphasis on (power) relations that are the *sine qua non* of our social space. Postcolonial and normative lenses refer to the inherently relational and ethical states of being in the world. For example, Barkawi and Laffey (2006, 349) point out that "relational thinking provides inherent defences against Eurocentrism because it begins with the assumption that the social world is composed of relations rather than separate objects, like great powers or 'the West'"; normative commitments underline the importance of seeing actors on the international arena as moral agents with responsibility. In that, how to act in relation to others is crucial if one is to take ethics seriously (see Zehfuss 2009).

The processes of telling and acting (explained below) provide the ground for interrogating identity (cf. Lebow 2012, 46–49). In this work, identity is conceptualised as a contextually and dialogically shaped self-understanding/representation, which is dependent on a particular constellation of the processes of telling and acting (cf. Guillaume 2011, 35, 50). Identity needs to be understood in a processual manner, meaning that identity formation can be seen as a politics of both becoming (Mälk-soo 2010, 26) and co-being (in a Bakhtinian sense). Owing to this it is crucial, firstly, to account for the moments of telling and acting. Secondly, on a more minute level, identity dynamics comprise "an identity's expression, its contextuality and its relations to different and/or alternative self-understandings/representations" (Guillaume 2011, 50). It is possible to map both *who* and *what* are the chief constituting influences for an actor's identity formation—especially given that there is always a measure of dialogue in an actor's speech (Bakhtin, quoted in Todorov 1998, 60). Thus an actor's discourse features a multitude of speakers and addressees to/with/on behalf of whom the actor is speaking (cf. the previous discussion of dialogue/dialogism).

In this work, discourse and practice are separated diachronically—in a way operating on different time tracks—(cf. Neumann 2002, 631) which means that although knowledge from actual experience is mirrored in language, these processes (i.e. telling and acting) are separate phenomena in social reality (cf. Van Leeuwen 2008, 6). Telling refers to discourse ("as articulated in written and spoken text"; Hansen 2006, 2), which can be seen as the pre-deployment stage. Although distinct from action, discourse is understood in poststructuralist terms, as being equipped with performative power/capacity (see Butler 2011).[19] Acting, in turn, refers to the social practices ("socially [un]regulated ways of doing something", Van Leeuwen 2008, 6), or the moment of implementation (e.g. the CSDP mission on the ground).[20] Crucially, both the telling and acting stages are discursively performative. The significance of acting, with reference to a dialogical moment in identity construction, is well captured by Fierke's (2013b) notion of "the act of speech". A peace operation unfolding on the ground is made sense of through the acts of speech, that is, by providing representations of what acting constitutes.

Furthermore, action can be understood as the materialisation of the frames conveyed by telling, i.e. the extent to which rhetoric is actualised, yet it does not imply a one-to-one relationship between telling and acting (cf. Chilton and Schäffner 2002, 11), but rather that telling creates a pool of possibilities in which more than one course of action is rendered possible. Here the difference between behaviour-action-practice is not maintained as strictly as in some of the practice approaches; rather, it is argued that whether something is a practice (as defined by the practice theorists) or not depends on the empirical case at hand. For instance, when talking about the EU's CSDP operations, one needs to be careful not to impose an understanding of actions as "practice" where there might not be a stable practice in place.

The telling–acting model is useful as it allows for a nuanced study of an actor's identity. In this sense, telling and acting sites of identity are not a priori invested with meaning; on the contrary, their significance unfolds when they are studied in deep complementarity, as they are contingent on one another but also on *who speaks* (see esp. Epstein 2010). For analytical purposes, the study of an actor's discourse on a given subject is separated into telling and acting stages of discourse in order to problematise the often-spotted gap between the two. Discourses open a certain contingency framework (cf. Foucault 2002, 54), yet this should be seen on a scale from the more rhetorical (performatively less-charged/empty) to the more speech act (performative) related results. However, it is not just the gap between the two that directs this work but rather the construction of this gap in the first place. With this in mind, I attempt to be reflective about both the analytical move I make and the loci these sites acquire in the course of my empirical case studies. This said, I intend my approach to be seen as a debate opener, in that the possibilities offered by studying identity through the sites of telling and acting are not exhausted within this work—rather a particular reading is offered, in a tone that will hopefully spark discussion.

The dynamics and issues that arise from differentiating between these two moments—telling and acting—are numerous. To start with, it is crucial to ponder the consequences of utilising these concepts. If telling and acting are qualitatively different things in social reality (as a minimum referring to a temporal difference), does it not shift our attention to the *res, non verba* logic that the EU itself also subscribes to, and if so, to what effect?[21] Secondly, the issue of consistency between telling and acting comes to the fore. The model introduced here does not take for granted that telling equals acting, or that one process wholly decides the other; furthermore, it asks whether they have to match for the actor to succeed. Also, the question of whether these processes have different functions arises: to what extent do their roles/functions differ, and—perhaps more importantly—who are the "authors" of these processes (there is not a complete overlap, esp. when dealing with the EU)?[22] Another question relates to the ways in which we can learn about these processes and the consequences of that. Thus, ultimately, the greatest tension emerges from the fact that telling and acting simultaneously differ and overlap.

The weighty reasons for considering both moments of an actor's expressive realm are that not to do so unnecessarily restricts the scope of both the relevant material and questions to be asked. To study the EU's discourse on CSDP without considering the ways in which the CSDP operations are conducted/implemented on the ground, for example, leaves one with only a piece of the puzzle (i.e. the telling part). Or, as acting goes beyond the representation of patterned actions (i.e. the habitual), considering both telling and doing allows for engaging with deeds of all kinds without inserting an a priori need for a pattern to contemplate actions as practices. It also makes it possible to enquire what happens if the telling and acting do not match—that is, to detail the inherent performativity of discourses. This theoretical exercise does not aim to stabilise the categories of telling and acting, but rather to open up the debate.

Deciphering the Telling and Acting of the EU

> Being able to define the 'real' in political discourse is the first step towards getting to define the solution. (Zehfuss 2002, 246)

> the ESS should encapsulate both "the first comprehensive review, not only of the threats but also *how* we can best respond to them." (Solana 2003, November 26)

This work focuses on how the EU both tells and acts its identity. This focus, in a deeply contextual and diachronic manner, enables a processual account of identity. Both of these processes or stages—telling and acting—of identity construction are comprised of discourses that convey meanings about how to address conflicts. Discourses are the key to investigating the notion of simultaneously being and becoming a particular subject and thus practising certain ways to build peace (cf. Buckley-Zistel 2006; Doty 1996; Escobar 1995; Hansen 2006, esp. Ch. 2). This chapter starts by introducing a particular vocabulary of discourse analysis (DA) that will be used to investigate how, by subscribing to particular understandings of peace and conflict, a specific approach towards conflicts is promoted. This book is concerned mainly with the EU's discourse on CSDP, yet it tries to offer other stories as well, to avoid the danger of a single story (Adichie 2009; see also Prashad 2014). This danger materialises if one does not take seriously the power relations embedded in telling a story, or the position of the author of a story. Further, I will introduce the discursive material used within this work.

Utilising DA allows me to openly question the "common sense" of the EU's CSDP. This is because the EU's CSDP is expressed in discourses advancing particular meanings, leading to particular dialogues between the self and its others. These meanings convey a certain relation to the world. Concomitantly, these meanings guide the actor in making sense of its surroundings, but through the recourse to these meanings, the actor also participates in (re)producing or reinforcing its surroundings as well as their particular interpretations.[23] Taking her cue from poststructuralist DA, Lene Hansen (2006, 21; see also Epstein 2008) points out how discourses not only construct problems but also offer particular solutions to the problems they purport to spot. Of course, the actor does not start from a blank canvas, being always immersed in a specific context. These contextual cues become evident in the discourses, as they are inescapably dialogical (see Chapter 1 of this book). The dialogical aspect of discourse is captured in this book by canvassing the contextual dynamics surrounding the EU's missions, studying the main topics, the representation of its multiple others, and finally providing a close-up of how the EU tells and acts its peace missions. The chief influence in adopting this approach comes from the third generation of discourse theory (see Torfing 2005, 1–28), which in IR is exemplified by Doty (1996), Hansen (2006), and Epstein (2008).[24]

Owing to the intricate relationship between discourse and power, the discussion below will be built around the concept of *power* and how it partners up with discourse in both meaning- and world-making (see esp. Doty 1996, Conclusion). Power, as Foucault contends (1997b, 167), is relational and has a myriad of functions, both repressive and productive. It is maintained here that the functions of power need to be further problematised, in that particular constellations of power dynamics—the degrees to which it is repressive and productive—vary depending on the context. For example, "some discourses are more powerful than others because they are articulated to, and partake of, institutional power" (Laffey and Weldes 2004, 29; Foucault 1997b, 169). Thus, in a discursive struggle, apropos Foucault,

> not all the positions of the subject, all the types of coexistence between statements, all the discursive strategies, are equally possible, but *only those authorised by anterior levels*, given for example, the system of formation that governed. (2002, 81; emphasis added)

This state of affairs points to the thorny question of agency: i.e. agency is always contextually rooted, mediating the discursive terrain inhabited by nodal points—that is, the "privileged discursive points" which "partially fix meaning" (Laclau and Mouffe 2001, 112–113)—and the resistance that challenges these nodal points. Hence, as Laclau and Mouffe maintain (ibid., xvi), it is crucial to think in terms of hegemonic relations. Wodak (2009, 35–36), following Holzscheiter (2005), provides a succinct framework to register the different ways of exercising power, integrating micro- and macro-levels of analysis:

(i) *power in discourse*: actors' struggles over different interpretations of meaning;

(ii) *power over discourse*: privileged access in macro and micro contexts;

(iii) *power of discourse* (see Foucault above): regulate what can or cannot be said in a broader macro-structure of meaning.

Bearing in mind the described issues, I will survey the fluid power dynamics characteristic of the common sense of the EU's CSDP. This involves the three fundamental elements that any experience, according to Foucault, is concerned with, namely "a game of truth, relations of power, and forms of relation to oneself and to others" (1997c, 116–117). Within this work, the emphasis is set on the EU's discourse, in order to investigate how this particular discourse sees and interprets peace and conflict, as well as acts upon them. It takes its cue from institutional ethnography (see Escobar 1995, 107) that rivets on professional discourse and how it participates in "structuring the conditions under which people think and live their lives". Focusing on the institutional apparatus becomes especially crucial when previous evidence suggests that the prevalent mode of peacebuilding affects significantly how conflicts are understood and, in turn, how responses to conflicts thus understood are formulated/enacted (see, e.g., Viktorova Milne 2009, esp. Ch. 4; Autesserre 2014; Hellmüller 2013).

Taking into account the precepts introduced above, the empirical analysis of the EU's self-representation will centre on the way its role in peacebuilding is represented through telling and acting peace missions. Besides drawing on the techniques introduced by the poststructuralist DA (Doty 1996; Hansen 2006), my analysis makes use of some elements in the toolbox of the Discourse-Historical Approach (DHA). For example, I cover three techniques in more detail: mapping the key topics of discourses, mapping social actors (i.e. the representation of the multiple/significant others) and the discursive strategies deployed (Reisigl and Wodak 2009; Wodak 2009).

The specific techniques used to analyse discourse make the logic of telling and acting manifest by paying attention to the contextual specifics of the discourses under scrutiny. In this way, the analysis of the EU's discourses on peacebuilding is divided into two or three phases, which capture the life cycle of the EU's peace missions. These phases, roughly speaking, correspond to the EU's discourses before, during and after deployment. Furthermore, within these phases I trace the meanings that the studied discourses communicate, bearing in mind the integrally dialogical nature of these meanings (refer back to the first part of this chapter). I have highlighted three themes present in these discourses: primary topics, primary dialogue partners (i.e. the multiple and significant others) and the discursive strategies. The dialogical approach together with the post-positivist lens foregrounds the relational and deeply contextual aspects of discourses. I pay attention to how, within the particular phase the discourse is gleaned from, the EU frames the situation it finds itself in, the key themes, events, actors; how it argues for certain policies and legitimises the taken course of action. In order to make sense of these discourses, I rely on the meaning structures presented in this chapter. I cannot transcend the spatio-temporal specifics of discussions about peace: in order to analyse discourses, I not only rely on the problem-solving and critical literature on peace and conflict studies, but also the particular discourses that either do or do not link with the above literature, but regardless of that are concerned with peace. Therefore, I always situate the EU's discourses in relation to other actors' discourses, to preserve the contextual diversity of a specific phase under scrutiny.

THE EU's DISCOURSE ON THE CSDP

This section explores the sources of the official and public discourse of the key articulators of the CSDP identity. The objective is not to delve into the discursive struggle over the CSDP within the EU, but rather to investigate the official line of this policy, in order to understand its overall rationale (cf. Kuus 2014).

One of the crucial reference points for this study is the discourse of the High Representative (HR) for the Common Foreign and Security Policy (CFSP), Javier Solana (and later Catherine Ashton),[25] as their discourse largely shapes the CSDP (Kurowska 2008, 2012; Bono 2006). This is coupled with the discourse of other actors which participate in communicating the CSDP to the outside world. Therefore, the discourse of the Council of the European Union and the Presidency in all their different forms, such as statements, conclusions and newsletters, is also explored in this study. For contextual purposes, I have also examined the positions of the European Commission (Commission) and the debates of the European Parliament (EP) surrounding the Union's CSDP activities, albeit to a lesser degree. In the following analysis, the chosen discourses represent different political genres on the scale from more to less official.[26] With regard to the acting stage of discourse, I have tried to tap into the discourse of the on-the-ground missions' staff. In addition to the EU scripts, all the case study chapters explore non-EU discourses, in order to provide contextual nuance. Furthermore, with regard to the missions in the Balkans, I conducted 25 interviews in Sarajevo between 13 and 24 August 2012, and in Pristina between 25 November and 1 December 2012. These interviews were all conducted in English, and they do not include some of the personal conversations I had with the locals during my stay. I managed to create a balance between my interviewees, so that roughly half of them represented the outside actors and half the locals.

There are a number of vital clarifications to make: the local setting I tapped into was for the most part relatively "official", in the sense that I mostly talked with local NGO people. This means that I cannot claim to be able—relying solely on the interviews—to represent the local moods in their diversity. However, coupling these discourses with all the secondary material about the Balkans provided me with the necessary (counter-)discourses to achieve a deeper degree of contextuality. I used the format of a semi-structured interview in order to both tease out the themes I had not thought about beforehand, and to respond to the topics raised during the interviews and avoid—as much as possible—directing the course of interviews (see Silverman 2013). Furthermore, owing to, on the one hand, some practical constraints to do with the availability of resources to conduct more on-site research, and, on the other side, the chosen scope of the research design that aimed at portraying the larger frames of telling and acting, it is important to acknowledge the perimeter of my findings. Therefore, I openly recognise that the chosen methods allow to capture the EU's wider frame of reference, whereas the minutiae of telling and acting peace would have required a more bottom-up research design.

Altogether, the examined EU discourses embody the overarching identity script that represents and communicates an array of different voices captured, to different degrees, in hybrid statements (see dialogism as discussed in Todorov 1998).[27] The ideas that do get published, so to speak, are of interest for this research, since these are created by the discourses that openly claim to speak for the CSDP. Through the analytical move of slicing the discourse up into the telling and acting stages I am not only able to follow in detail how the EU makes sense of its CSDP—and, more broadly, peace and conflict—but also query the relational puzzle in which the EU finds itself. In this way, the fluid *dramatis personae* of the selves-and-others materialise in the act of the EU's telling and acting the CSDP. This also means that the discourses under scrutiny are sensitive to the locales they are gleaned from.

Fundamentally, despite working out the specifics of authorship of the CSDP identity, it is imperative to note that the officially communicated policy has real effects. The EU's telling and acting of its peace missions matters to the conflict theatres, as it clearly influences the locals' aspirations for peace. Relatedly, as I have stated before, the case selection is primarily premised on the idea that despite the size, length, nature, comparability or any other criteria, the EU peace missions on the ground affect the conflict theatre. At the same time, the choice of cases hits at the core of the CSDP as I have chosen to study the EU's most vaunted CSDP missions. In this sense, these operations have played a weighty role in the narration of the EU as a peacebuilder, in that, their purported success (sometimes touted as successful only after the launch of the mission, see Chapter 4) is equated with the success of the entire CSDP.

FINALE

The aim of this chapter was to explore the debate between the practice approaches and the manifold perspectives that take discourse as their leading concept in the study of identity. What emerged from this analysis is that this debate is as yet not really there, and thus both approaches separately define the perimeters of the other—so in Bakhtin's terms, there is dialogue, but it is of the monologic version (note Bakhtin's idea that there is always a degree of dialogue—1986, 89–92). This chapter by no means resolved this debate, but rather set the parameters to open it in earnest, as a necessary setting for the theoretical framework adopted here. Equally, the aim was to introduce my approach to identity, which relies on a diverse post-positivist platform and sees as its overarching principle Bakhtin's dialogism. This was based on a critical excursion into the discourse and practice "turns" in International Relations and beyond, which explored the various ways of conceiving the relationship between discourse and practice: for example, the fact that traditionally for poststructuralists discourse equals performance, and thus the prominence of discourse is maintained, while constructivists stay true (for the most part) to the speech act formula. Given such predominant emphasis on discourse, the introduction of a particular take on practice approaches allowed me to broaden the ontological ground. It also raised a number of questions—unfortunately not all can be effectively dealt with here—that prove vital to future attempts of conceptualising the various logics of relationship between discourse and practice. I draw on the concepts of telling and acting to propose one way of making sense of this relationship.

The second part of this chapter discussed the methodological choices of my work and made clear that this book subscribes to key interpretivist/postpositivist methodological claims. In this way, the primary assumptions of a constructivist-interpretivist methodology were reflected on: the focus on meaning and its contextuality (its spatio-temporal specificity) and relationality (multiple and significant others' dynamic). Above all, the methodological apparatus espoused is a manifestation of the interpretivist logic: it makes a convincing case why the main method is discourse analysis as it is able to explore the meaning- and world-making role that discourses play.

NOTES

1. The label "ir" ("international relations") refers to world politics, whereas "IR" (International Relations") refers to the discipline that engages with world politics as its subject matter.
2. Appositely, Badiou's pondering on ethics shines further light on the logic of these "standards". In his essay, he stresses the importance of singularity of situations and the danger of totalising tendencies when approaching ethics, and the implications of the latter, i.e. "become like me and I will respect your difference" (2012, Ch. 2).
3. Note that the challenge that the concept of identity poses for positivist approaches is appositely captured in Zalewski and Enloe's work (1995, esp. 294–305).
4. This approach is in line with the august body of work in relational sociology (Dépelteau 2018) that offers different ways how to study relations rather than substances. As Dépelteau suggests, "relational thinking is much more than a call for studying relations. It is a worldview insisting on our interdependency rather than our independence" (ibid., 11). Two particularly

insightful chapters in the edited volume are Selg and Go's as they capture the strength of doing relational research by underlying power relations and the importance of postcolonial relationalism (see Dépelteau 2018).

5. Note that not all of these will be adumbrated here, for further debate see, e.g., Special Issue: Out of the Ivory Tower (2012).

6. For instance, as I have observed within the EU's discourse (mainly regarding its CSDP policy but also beyond) the telling and acting moments are crucial and used strategically to muster support for its foreign policy. To illustrate this, I present one of the oft-repeated thoughts by the EU, here via Solana: "The good news is that we have made significant progress in the last 10 years in building the beginnings of a credible foreign policy. Like a person, we have developed. From talking about problems to writing communiqués to taking action in crisis zones helping people" (2009, July 11); or "We have come a long way in developing ESDP as a tool enabling Europe to project itself through action in response to crises" (2009, July 28; cf. Ashton 2010, March 10).

7. This question is dealt with in more detail in the empirical part of this work.

8. Making a case for visual studies of visual material Yanow succinctly captures what a well-rounded analysis of the social means: "things visual do not have lives *independent of other senses*, other acts, other language. Whereas breaking out of our logocentrism is a welcome move, we should be admitting all of our sense observations into the realm of scientific inquiry. Meaning-making and its communication are multi-modal; and we would not be advancing our research processes in isolating and privileging the visual while ignoring its concomitant modalities. I hope we can add visual materials and methods to our analytic repertoire without losing the others" (Yanow 2014, 182). The truth of the matter is that we are not able always to grasp this entirety of the social that our senses offer but perhaps if we openly see the value in different ways of "looking" at a problem there is more modesty when we claim that one medium is able to trump all others and/or capture the entirety of the social by itself.

9. A good overview of the linguistic turn is given in Debrix (2003).

10. See Fierke and Jørgensen (2001) for a discussion on the difference between "thick" and "thin" constructivism.

11. Cf. Taylor (1993, 56–58) who underlines the reciprocal relation between rule and action, noting that "rule lies in the practice".

12. A good example of how discourse and practice can work under different logics is Fierke's recent book where she investigates how contextually specific meanings can shape acts of political self-sacrifice. She argues that "self-sacrifice, rather than being a substitution, is an 'act of speech' in which the suffering body communicates the injustice experienced by a community to a larger audience" (2013b, 37).

13. For a good overview of scholars who have shifted their focus to practice, see Adler and Pouliot (2011, 4; Bueger and Gadinger 2014).
14. According to Bueger and Gadinger (2007, 4), "practice theories understand themselves as neither post-structuralist nor as constructivist theories … Rather, practice theories attempt to work in an ontological in-between".
15. The "how to conduct practice research" has been addressed by e.g. Bueger (2014).
16. For example, Adler and Pouliot (2011, 21) note that practice approaches welcome a pluralistic methodology, yet the different options are not discussed. The possible method choices of practice "theorists" are discussed in more detail in Bueger's work (see Bueger 2014; also Bueger and Gadinger 2014).
17. As the practice turn is only just gaining momentum (at least in IR circles), its internal divides, multiplicity of methods and other issues are not comprehensively covered here. For a detailed and accessible overview of both the shared commitments of practice theory as well as its divergences consult Bueger and Gadinger (2014).
18. At one point, they do make references to one another and even collapse into one another.
19. Referring to the importance of meaning-making, Butler (2011, 185) notes: "the effects of performatives, understood as discursive productions, do not conclude at the terminus of a given statement or utterance, the passing of legislation, the announcement of birth. The reach of their signifiability cannot be controlled by the one who utters or writes, since such productions are not owned by the one who utters them. They continue to signify in spite of their authors, and sometimes against their authors' most precious intentions".
20. Kurikkala suggests that performance "seeks to fulfill in practice the 'promise' of naming" (2003, 57). This is just one logic that the telling and acting relationship can follow.
21. Consider at this juncture the problematic of the "expectations-capability" gap and the considerably larger importance attached to the acting stage (i.e. performance) by academics and policy-makers alike.
22. Perhaps here the multiplicity of actors within, and in response to, these processes is best problematised, as the processes of telling and acting are always directed *towards* somebody, which brings to light the element of contestation over them.
23. Works that specify the post-positivist/interpretivist research design in more detail and complement the sources covered in my book: Schwartz-Shea and Yanow (2012) and Lynch (2014).
24. For good overviews of the different DA approaches, consult, e.g. Glynos et al. (2009) and Torfing (2005). For an elaborate and interesting take on how culture as a concept can be applied to studying conflict and its

resolution, see Viktorova Milne (2009). In her work, "culture" functions as a framework of analysing the logic of meaning-generation and world-making that is part of our everyday life.

25. Javier Solana was in office from 1999 to 2009 and Catherine Ashton's term lasted from 2009 to 2014.
26. Genres refer to different kinds of texts, e.g. speeches, statements, etc. (see Reisigl and Wodak 2009, 89–90).
27. I am indebted to Jevgenia Milne for pointing out to me that by subscribing to a specific approach, an actor simultaneously re-negotiates it.

References

Adichie, Chimamanda Ngozi. 2009. "Chimamanda Ngozi Adichie: The Danger of a Single Story." TEDGlobal Conference. https://www.ted.com/talks/chimamanda_adichie_the_danger_of_a_single_story/transcript?language=en.

Adler, Emanuel, and Vincent Pouliot, eds. 2011. *International Practices*. Cambridge: Cambridge University Press.

Aradau, Claudia. 2010. "Security That Matters: Critical Infrastructure and Objects of Protection." *Security Dialogue* 41 (5): 491–514. https://doi.org/10.1177/0967010610382687.

Arendt, Hannah. 1998. *The Human Condition*. 2nd ed. Chicago: University of Chicago Press.

Ashton, Catherine. 2010. "Address by Catherine Ashton at the Joint Debate on Foreign and Security Policy—European Parliament Plenary." Strasbourg. In *EU Security and Defence: Core Documents 2010*, vol. XI, March 10, compiled by Catherine Glière. Paris: EUISS. https://www.iss.europa.eu/content/european-union-security-and-defence-core-documents-2010.

Autesserre, Séverine. 2014. *Peaceland: Conflict Resolution and the Everyday Politics of International Intervention*. New York, NY: Cambridge University Press.

Badiou, Alain. 2012. *Ethics: An Essay on the Understanding of Evil*. Translated and introduced by Peter Hallward. London: Verso. Kindle edition.

Bakhtin, M. M. 1981. *The Dialogic Imagination: Four Essays by M. M. Bakhtin*. Edited by Michael Holquist. Translated by Caryl Emerson and Michael Holquist. Austin: University of Texas Press.

Bakhtin, M. M. 1986. *Speech Genres and Other Late Essays*. Edited by Caryl Emerson and Michael Holquist. Translated by Vern W. McGee. Austin: University of Texas Press.

Barkawi, Tarak, and Mark Laffey. 2006. "The Postcolonial Moment in Security Studies." *Review of International Studies* 32 (2): 329–352. https://doi.org/10.1017/s0260210506007054.

Bono, Giovanna. 2006. "The Perils of Conceiving of EU Foreign Policy as a 'Civilising Force.'" *Internationale Politik und Gesellschaft* 1: 150–163. http://library.fes.de/pdf-files/id/ipg/03647.pdf.

Bourdieu, Pierre. 1989. "Social Space and Symbolic Power." *Sociological Theory* 7 (1): 14–25.

Buckley-Zistel, Susanne. 2006. "In-Between War and Peace: Identities, Boundaries and Change After Violent Conflict." *Millennium: Journal of International Studies* 35 (1): 3–21. https://doi.org/10.1177/03058298060350010101.

Bueger, Christian. 2014. "Pathways to Practice: Praxiography and IR." *European Political Science Review* 6 (3): 383–406. http://dx.doi.org/10.1017/S1755773913000167.

Bueger, Christian. 2015. "Making Things Known: Epistemic Practice, the United Nations and the Translation of Piracy." *International Political Sociology* 9 (1): 1–18. https://doi.org/10.1111/ips.12073.

Bueger, Christian, and Frank Gadinger. 2007. "Culture, Terror and Practice in International Relations: An Invitation to Practice Theory." Paper Prepared for the Workshop "The (Re-)turn to Practice: Thinking Practices in International Relations and Security Studies," May 18–19. Florence: European University Institute.

Bueger, Christian, and Frank Gadinger. 2014. *International Practice Theory*. Basingstoke: Palgrave Macmillan.

Bueger, Christian, and Frank Gadinger. 2015. "The Play of International Practice." *International Studies Quarterly* 59 (3): 449–460. https://doi.org/10.1111/isqu.12202.

Bueger, Christian, and Trine Villumsen. 2007. "Beyond the Gap: Relevance, Fields of Practice and the Securitising Consequences of (Democratic Peace) Research." *Journal of International Relations and Development* 10 (4): 417–448. https://doi.org/10.1057/palgrave.jird.1800136.

Butler, Judith. 1992. "Contingent Foundations: Feminism and the Question of 'Postmodernism.'" In *Feminists Theorise the Political*, edited by Judith Butler and Joan W. Scott, 3–21. New York: Routledge.

Butler, Judith. 2004. *Precarious Life: The Powers of Mourning and Violence*. London: Verso.

Butler, Judith. 2011. *Bodies that Matter: On the Discursive Limits of Sex*. London: Routledge Classics.

Cebeci, Münevver. 2012. "European Foreign Policy Research Reconsidered: Constructing an 'Ideal Power Europe' Through Theory?" *Millennium: Journal of International Studies* 40 (3): 563–583. https://doi.org/10.1177/0305829812442235.

Chilton, Paul A., and Christina Schäffner. 2002. "Introduction: Themes and Principles in the Analysis of Political Discourse." In *Politics as Text and Talk: Ana-*

lytic Approaches to Political Discourse, edited by Paul A. Chilton and Christina Schäffner, 1–41. Amsterdam: John Benjamins.

Debrix, François, ed. 2003. Language, Agency, and Politics in a Constructed World. New York: M. E. Sharpe.

De Certeau, Michel. 1988. The Practice of Everyday Life. Berkeley: University of California Press.

Dépelteau, François, ed. 2018. The Palgrave Handbook of Relational Sociology. Switzerland: Palgrave Macmillan.

Diez, Thomas. 2005. "Constructing the Self and Changing Others: Reconsidering 'Normative Power Europe.'" Millennium: Journal of International Studies 33 (3): 613–636. https://doi.org/10.1177/03058298050330031701.

Doty, Roxanne. 1996. Imperial Encounters: The Politics of Representation in North-South Relations. Minneapolis: University of Minnesota Press.

Doty, Roxanne. 1997. "Aporia: A Critical Exploration of the Agent-Structure Problematique in International Relations Theory." European Journal of International Relations 3 (3): 365–392. https://doi.org/10.1177/1354066197003003004.

Epstein, Charlotte. 2008. The Power of Words in International Relations: Birth of an Anti-whaling Discourse. Cambridge: MIT Press.

Epstein, Charlotte. 2010. "Who Speaks? Discourse, the Subject and the Study of Identity in International Politics." European Journal of International Relations 17 (2): 327–350. https://doi.org/10.1177/1354066109350055.

Epstein, Charlotte. 2013. "Constructivism or the Eternal Return of Universals in International Relations: Why Returning to Language Is Vital for Prolonging the Owl's Flight." European Journal of International Relations 19 (3): 499–519. https://doi.org/10.1177/1354066113494669.

Erskine, Toni. 2010. "Normative IR Theory." In International Relations Theories: Discipline and Diversity, edited by Tim Dunne, Milja Kurki, and Steve Smith, 2nd ed., 36–58. Oxford: Oxford University Press.

Escobar, Arturo. 1995. Encountering Development: The Making and Unmaking of the Third World. Princeton, NJ: Princeton University Press.

Fierke, Karin. 1996. "Multiple Identities, Interfacing Games: The Social Construction of Western Action in Bosnia." European Journal of International Relations 2 (4): 467–497. https://doi.org/10.1177/1354066196002004003.

Fierke, Karin. 2002. "Links Across the Abyss: Language and Logic in IR." International Studies Quarterly 46 (3): 331–354. https://doi.org/10.1111/1468-2478.00236.

Fierke, Karin. 2010. "Wittgenstein and International Relations Theory." In International Relations Theory and Philosophy: Interpretive Dialogues, edited by Cerwyn Moore and Chris Farrands, 83–94. Oxon: Routledge.

Fierke, Karin. 2013a. "Is There Life Beyond Language? Discourses of Security." Paper Presented at the ISA Annual Conference, San Francisco.

Fierke, Karin. 2013b. *Political Self-Sacrifice: Agency, Body and Emotion in International Relations.* Cambridge: Cambridge University Press.

Fierke, Karin, and Knud E. Jørgensen. 2001. *Constructing IR: The Next Generation.* New York: M. E. Sharpe.

Foucault, Michel. 1997a. "History of Systems of Thought." In *Michel Foucault: Language, Counter-Memory, Practice: Selected Essays and Interviews*, edited by Donald F. Bouchard, 199–204. Oxford: Blackwell.

Foucault, Michel. 1997b. "Sex, Power, and the Politics of Identity." In *Ethics: Subjectivity and Truth by Michel Foucault: The Essential Works of Michel Foucault 1954–1984*, edited by Paul Rabinow, vol. 1, 163–173. New York: The New Press.

Foucault, Michel. 1997c. "Polemics, Politics, and Problematisations." In *Ethics: Subjectivity and Truth by Michel Foucault: The Essential Works of Michel Foucault 1954–1984*, edited by Paul Rabinow, vol. 1, 111–119. New York: The New Press.

Foucault, Michel. 2002. *The Archaeology of Knowledge.* Translated by A. M. Sheridan Smith. London: Routledge Classics.

Frueh, Jamie. 2004. "Studying Continuity and Change in South African Political Identity." In *Identity and Global Politics: Empirical and Theoretical Elaborations*, edited by Patricia M. Goff and Kevin C. Dunn, 63–78. New York: Palgrave Macmillan.

Glynos, Jason, David Howarth, Aletta Norval, and Ewen Speed. 2009. "Discourse Analysis: Varieties and Methods." Working Paper. National Centre for Research Methods. http://eprints.ncrm.ac.uk/796/.

Goff, Patricia M., and Kevin C. Dunn, eds. 2004. *Identity and Global Politics: Empirical and Theoretical Elaborations.* New York: Palgrave Macmillan.

Guillaume, Xavier. 2011. *International Relations and Identity: A Dialogical Approach.* London: Routledge.

Hamati-Ataya, Inanna. 2010. "Knowing and Judging in International Relations Theory: Realism and the Reflexive Challenge." *Review of International Studies* 36 (4): 1079–1101. https://doi.org/10.1017/s0260210510000550.

Hamati-Ataya, Inanna. 2012. "Reflectivity, Reflexivity, Reflexivism: IR's 'Reflexive Turn'—and Beyond." *European Journal of International Relations* 19 (4): 669–694. https://doi.org/10.1177/1354066112437770.

Hamati-Ataya, Inanna. 2014. "Outline of a Reflexive Epistemology." *Epistemology & Philosophy of Science* 42 (4): 46–66. https://doi.org/10.5840/eps201442470.

Hansen, Lene. 2000. "The Little Mermaid's Silent Security Dilemma and the Absence of Gender in the Copenhagen School." *Millennium: Journal of International Studies* 29 (2): 285–306. https://doi.org/10.1177/03058298000290020501.

Hansen, Lene. 2006. *Security as a Practice: Discourse Analysis and the Bosnian War*. London: Routledge.

Hansen, Lene. 2011. "Performing Practices: A Poststructuralist Analysis of the Muhammad Cartoon Crisis." In *International Practices*, edited by Emanuel Adler and Vincent Pouliot, 280–309. Cambridge: Cambridge University Press.

Hellmüller, Sara. 2013. "The Power of Perceptions: Localising International Peacebuilding Approaches." *International Peacekeeping* 20 (2): 219–232. https://doi.org/10.1080/13533312.2013.791570.

Hobson, John M. 2012. *The Eurocentric Conception of World Politics: Western International Theory, 1760–2010*. Cambridge: Cambridge University Press.

Hobson, John M., and Alina Sajed. 2017. "Navigating Beyond the Eurofetishist Frontier of Critical IR Theory: Exploring the Complex Landscapes of Non-Western Agency." *International Studies Review* 19 (4): 1–26. https://doi.org/10.1093/isr/vix013.

Holquist, Michael. 2002. *Dialogism: Bakhtin and His World*. 2nd ed. London: Routledge.

Jackson, Patrick T. 2004. "Whose Identity? Rhetorical Commonplaces in 'American' Wartime Foreign Policy." In *Identity and Global Politics: Empirical and Theoretical Elaborations*, edited by Patricia M. Goff and Kevin C. Dunn, 169–189. New York: Palgrave Macmillan.

Jackson, Patrick T. 2011. *The Conduct of Inquiry in International Relations: Philosophy of Science and Its Implications for the Study of World Politics*. Abingdon: Routledge.

Khalili, Laleh. 2010. "The Ethics of Social Science Research." In *Critical Research in the Social Sciences: A Transdisciplinary East-West Handbook*, edited by Roger Heacock and Edouard Conte, 65–82. Ramallah: Birzeit University.

Kratochwil, Friedrich. 2011. "Making Sense of 'International Practices'." In *International Practices*, edited by Emanuel Adler and Vincent Pouliot, 36–61. Cambridge: Cambridge University Press.

Kurikkala, Flora. 2003. "Representation of the Changing Self: An EU Performance in the Middle East." PhD diss., University of Tampere.

Kurowska, Xymena. 2008. "The Role of ESDP Operations." In *European Security and Defence Policy: An Implementation Perspective*, edited by Michael Merlingen and Rasa Ostrauskaite, 25–42. London: Routledge.

Kurowska, Xymena. 2012. "Introduction: The Role of Theory in Research on Common Security and Defence Policy." In *Explaining the EU's Common Security and Defence Policy: Theory in Action*, edited by Xymena Kurowska and Fabian Breuer, 1–15. New York: Palgrave Macmillan.

Kuus, Merje. 2014. *Geopolitics and Experience: Knowledge and Authority in European Diplomacy*. Chichester: Wiley.

Laclau, Ernesto, and Chantal Mouffe. 2001. *Hegemony and Socialist Strategy: Towards a Radical Democratic Politics*. London: Verso.

Laffey, Mark, and Jutta Weldes. 2004. "Methodological Reflections on Discourse Analysis." *Qualitative Methods* 2 (1): 28–30.

Lebow, Richard Ned. 2012. *The Politics and Ethics of Identity: In Search of Ourselves.* Cambridge: Cambridge University Press.

Lynch, Cecelia. 2014. *Interpreting International Politics.* New York: Routledge.

Mälksoo, Maria. 2010. *The Politics of Becoming European: A Study of Polish and Baltic Post-Cold War Security Imaginaries.* London: Routledge.

Neumann, Iver B. 2002. "Returning Practice to the Linguistic Turn: The Case of Diplomacy." *Journal of International Studies* 31 (3): 627–651. https://doi.org/10.1177/03058298020310031201.

Pin-Fat, Véronique. 2010. *Universality, Ethics and International Relations: A Grammatical Reading.* Abingdon: Routledge.

Pouliot, Vincent. 2007. "'Sobjectivism': Toward a Constructivist Methodology." *International Relations Quarterly* 51 (2): 359–384. https://doi.org/10.1111/j.1468-2478.2007.00455.x.

Prashad, Vijay. 2014. *The Poorer Nations: A Possible History of the Global South.* London: Verso.

Reisigl, Martin, and Ruth Wodak. 2009. "The Discourse-Historical Approach (DHA)." In *Methods of Critical Discourse Analysis*, edited by Ruth Wodak and Michael Meyer, 87–121. London: Sage.

Rowley, Christina, and Jutta Weldes. 2012. "The Evolution of International Security Studies and the Everyday: Suggestions from the Buffyverse." *Security Dialogue* 43 (6): 513–530. https://doi.org/10.1177/0967010612463490.

Schwartz-Shea, Peregrine, and Dvora Yanow. 2012. *Interpretive Research Design: Concepts and Processes.* New York: Routledge.

Shapiro, Michael J. 1984. "Introduction." In *Language and Politics*, edited by Michael J. Shapiro, 1–12. New York: New York University Press.

Silverman, David. 2013. *Doing Qualitative Research.* 4th ed. London: Sage.

Solana, Javier. 2003. "'The Voice of Europe on Security Matters': Summary of the Address to the Royal Institute for International Relations." November 26. https://www.consilium.europa.eu/uedocs/cms_data/docs/pressdata/en/discours/78071.pdf.

Solana, Javier. 2009. "Europe's Global Role—What Next Steps? (Ditchley Foundation Lecture)." July 11. London. https://www.consilium.europa.eu/uedocs/cms_data/docs/pressdata/en/discours/109193.pdf.

Solana, Javier. 2009. "ESDP at 10: What Lessons for the Future?" July 28. Brussels. http://www.consilium.europa.eu/uedocs/cms_data/docs/pressdata/en/discours/109453.pdf.

Special Issue: Out of the Ivory Tower. 2012. *Millenium: Journal of International Studies* 40 (3). https://journals.sagepub.com/toc/mil/40/3.

Taylor, Charles. 1993. "To Follow a Rule ...." In *Bourdieu: Critical Perspectives*, edited by Craig Calhoun, Edward LiPuma, and Moishe Postone, 45–60. Chicago: University of Chicago Press.

Todorov, Tzvetan. 1998. *Mikhail Bakhtin: The Dialogical Principle*. Translated by Wlad Godzich. Minneapolis: University of Minnesota Press.

Torfing, Jacob. 2005. "Discourse Theory: Achievements, Arguments, and Challenges." In *Discourse Theory in European Politics: Identity, Policy and Governance*, edited by David Howarth and Jacob Torfing, 1–32. Houndmills: Palgrave Macmillan.

Van Leeuwen, Theo. 2008. *Discourse and Practice: New Tools for Critical Discourse Analysis*. New York: Oxford University Press.

Viktorova Milne, Jevgenia. 2009. "Returning Culture to Peacebuilding: Contesting the Liberal Peace in Sierra Leone." PhD diss., University of St Andrews.

Vrasti, Wanda. 2008. "The Strange Case of Ethnography and International Relations." *Millennium: Journal of International Studies* 37 (2): 279–301. https://doi.org/10.1177/0305829808097641.

Wodak, Ruth. 2009. *The Discourse of Politics in Action: Politics as Usual*. Basingstoke: Palgrave Macmillan.

Yanow, Dvora. 2014. "Methodological Ways of Seeing and Knowing." In *The Routledge Companion to Visual Organisation*, edited by Emma Bell, Samantha Warren, and Jonathan E. Schroeder, 167–189. Abingdon: Routledge.

Zalewski, Marysia, and Cynthia Enloe. 1995. "Questions About Identity in International Relations." In *International Relations Theory Today*, edited by Ken Booth and Steve Smith, 279–305. Cambridge: Polity Press.

Zehfuss, Maja. 2002. "The Politics of Reality: Derrida's Subversions, Constructivism and German Military Involvement Abroad." In *Constructivism in International Relations: The Politics of Reality*, edited by Maja Zehfuss, 196–249. Cambridge: Cambridge University Press.

Zehfuss, Maja. 2009. "Poststructuralism." In *The Ashgate Research Companion to Ethics and International Relations*, edited by Patrick Hayden, 97–111. Farnham: Ashgate.

CHAPTER 3

A Way to *Just Peace?*

All approaches to peacebuilding have a particular ethic or an underpinning leitmotif that sets the parameters of what is or is not peace and of acceptable means of achieving peace. (Mac Ginty 2011, 67)

But the most striking manifestation – and *raison d'être* – of this policy [CSDP] is our capacity to back our diplomacy by action on the ground, i.e. our crisis management operations. (Solana 2005, December)

This chapter is intended as a lens through which the EU's CSDP missions will be interpreted; therefore, it offers certain basic assumptions, arguments and ideas—a critical frame—which allow for a meaningful analysis of the "goods" the CSDP missions claim to deliver. The previous chapter set the overall theoretical *modus operandi*—arguing that the EU's identity becomes substantiated in the contextually specific instances of telling it and acting it out. Here the focus is set on the concept of peacebuilding. I inspect the commonsense framing of peace(building) that the EU practices in the context of CSDP. The importance of a critical lens lies in the fact that it gives the tools to foreground the deep contextuality of peace. Subsequently, this work draws on several critical approaches[1] to peace that probe the self-evidence of the dominant understandings (e.g. questioning commonsensical terminology of peace missions), "seek to uncover power and its workings" (Richmond 2014a, 19), attempt to go beyond negative peace (Galtung 1969; Boulding 1999), contextualise and thus underline the flu-

© The Author(s) 2020
B. Poopuu, *The European Union's Brand of Peacebuilding*,
Rethinking Peace and Conflict Studies,
https://doi.org/10.1007/978-3-030-19890-9_3

idity of peace (see esp. Higate and Henry 2013; Wibben et al. 2018).[2] At the centre of the critical strand of literature on peace lies the recognition that there is no univocal understanding of peace (Richmond 2007, 251, 264; Pugh 2013) and that local actors are not just well placed but also instrumental in informing ideas and actions for peace (esp. Firchow 2018; Richmond 2014b).

Taking a cue from the critical approach, the emphasis is on how the EU's CSDP missions understand peace, focusing on questions *what peace is, who it is for* and *who can script peace.*[3] The work of Amartya Sen provides an inspirational framework for tackling the respective issues. Given that the more critical takes on peace underline the significance of peace being anchored to people's everyday lives (Mac Ginty 2008), Sen's approach seems particularly suitable for enriching the critical vocabulary on peace(building). As Aggestam and Björkdahl (2013, 2, relying on Hoppe 2007, 71) point out, "the use of 'just' serves to measure the ethical quality and durability of peace as well as the realisation of justice demands". In this, their thoughts on just peace correlate closely with Sen's ideas on justice. Sen's approach underscores the importance of justice being about "the way people's lives go" (2010, x), and that they have a say in how their lives are organised (Sen 1999, 31–33), emphasising the need for contextually sensitive understandings of peace. Since many critical approaches "see peace as connected to social justice and emancipation, meaning human rights, equality, solidarity, and sustainability" (Richmond 2014a, 18), justice and peace cannot but be seen as intimately connected.

This chapter will discuss some of the key points made by Sen and the critical strand of literature in peace and conflict studies, in order to make explicit the lens through which the CSDP missions will be interpreted. The following sections raise a number of issues. Firstly, peacebuilders tend to be preoccupied with the argument (the logical fallacy, as pointed out by Viktorova Milne [2009, 97–98], aside) that what they offer is both the only and the best solution. Sen in this context makes two valuable claims: to advance justice, we are not in need of a transcendental approach capable of identifying a perfectly just society; rather, what is required is a comparative take on justice that centres on alleviating contextually specific injustices. The EU labels its own approach as unique—while subscribing to the only and best approach of the UN—by pointing to the fact that it has at its disposal both the civilian and military instruments of crisis management. While this issue will surface in the case studies, it is paramount to point out the weak logic of this claim. The latter claim focuses squarely on the EU's point of view; without due diligence, the EU-introduced logic directs one's focus from the substance of its approach to peacebuilding to the existence of capabilities. Furthermore, justice is an ongoing process, not something fixed once and for all. In a way, the discourse of standards promoted by the international community skirts around this issue when it comes to their positionality as norm promoters. Secondly, interveners are keen to focus on institutions rather than people. Sen, while not denying the importance that institutions can play, stresses that we need to go beyond just institutions and concentrate on the lives people actually lead. Thirdly, it is indefensible to make a case for a neutral/technocratic approach to peacebuilding. It is people's lives that are at stake, and the choices made about them are intensely embedded in the socio-economic and political vistas of a prevalent context. Sen has illustrated this by referring to the capabilities approach (1999), which underlines both the multiplicity and contextuality of different capabilities.

Approaches to Justice[4]

In situating his approach, Sen refers to two main lines of reasoning about justice—the contractarian and the comparative (Sen 2010, xv–xvii, 5–10). The first of these concentrates on "identifying perfectly just social arrangements" (ibid., xvi), whereas the latter focuses on "making comparisons between different ways in which people's lives may be lead, influenced by institutions but also by people's actual behaviour, social interactions and other significant determinants" (ibid., xvi). Importantly, these two currents of thought have some commonality; for example, both rely on "reasoning and the invoking of the demands of public discussion" (ibid., xvii). Possibly the best way to grasp what reasoning involves is, by way of its other, unreason. As Sen argues, "unreason is mostly not the practice of doing without reasoning altogether, but of relying on very primitive and very defective reasoning" (ibid., xviii). This indicates that reasoning is not an ideological position per se but rather an invitation to discuss (important) matters—it does not necessarily define the right behaviour, but is rather a tool or a format of engagement. If the contractarian position promotes a single premise on which just institutions are modelled, then Sen—identifying more with the second group—argues for the plurality of values and voices in a social space in which there is no inherent hierarchy between them (ibid., 12–15). Moreover, referring to Williams (1985, 133 cited in Sen 2010, 14), Sen underlines the constructive and constitutive moment of disagreement, arguing that it does not necessarily need to be overcome and at times even cannot be wholly overcome (see his ideas on partial rankings, e.g. 2010, 396–400). Yet, crucially, as Kapoor demonstrates, hailing the value of pluralism and bearing in mind the fact that not everyone has equal access to the public sphere to voice their (dis)agreement are two separate things, both of which need to be considered (2008).[5]

PROBLEMS WITH PERFECTLY JUST SOCIAL ARRANGEMENTS

Sen identifies two major problems with the contractarian (or "transcendental institutionalism") approach: firstly, there might not be a unified position on the nature of a just society (2010, 9, Introduction). Secondly, he points to the fact that concentration on the lives people actually live makes the "identification of a possibly unavailable perfect situation" redundant (ibid.). In an important third point stressing the role of contextual dynamics, Andrieu argues that Rawls' political liberalism does not match the reality of post-conflict societies, in that it is not able to deal with their vulnerability (2014, 100). The first issue would be especially ruinous for the contractarian approach—or, more specifically, to Rawls, with whose position Sen takes issue the most—as it leaves unaddressed a situation in which there are competing principles of justice, which begs the question of how then "a particular set of institutions would be chosen" (Sen 2010, 12).[6] The second point of criticism is crucial, as it points to the age-old debate in philosophy—that of distance/closeness to people's everyday life. Sen offers a succinct example about the unhelpfulness of the knowledge that *Mona Lisa* is the ideal picture in a world where one needs to make a choice between a Dali and a Picasso (16). In similar terms, it is not possible to export the Swedish peace—if that were labelled as the ideal model of peace—to Kosovo, since these countries do not share the same people, history, culture and so on. Peace cannot be instituted relying solely on imitation, rather peace needs to be negotiated (Sen's open-debate requirement is useful here, as explained below). Also, and perhaps more pressingly, there is no need to identify *the* perfect peace in order to have peace. Ultimately, as Gandhi and a number of others have suggested, there can be no durable peace if those for whom the peace is meant are not in the lead (Brown 2008, 156). If one asks how peace(building) should be evaluated, then the answer of the critical literature is that the key lies in local legitimacy. As Tadjbakhsh (2010, 128) holds, "in post-conflict situations, the ethical focus is based on what those who have suffered perceive as morally valuable instead of the cost/benefit rationale made by external Peacebuilding". In a similar vein, Autesserre (2014, Ch. 1) contends that intervention efforts should be evaluated by keeping in mind a situation-specific definition of effectiveness, which translates into something quite akin to Sen's propositions (discussed further below). Autesserre views a peacebuilding project as effective "when a large majority of the people involved in it views it as such". She further clarifies that

> the initiatives I present as effective are programs or projects that, during interviews or informal discussions, both implementers (international interveners and local peacebuilders) and intended beneficiaries (including local elite and ordinary citizens) presented as having promoted peace in the area of intervention. (ibid.)

This measuring rod for success/failure of a peace operation is exacting, and something that many implementers/evaluators fail to offer.[7]

MOVING AWAY FROM THE ONLY AND BEST SOLUTION

> The idea that there is only one kind of just society – a liberal society defined by principles set out in Rawls's model – and that all others represent a falling off from this ideal does not seem a plausible response to the pluralism that undoubtedly exists in the modern world. (Brown 2010, 6)[8]

Central to Sen's argument throughout the book—i.e. the need for an accomplishment-based understanding of justice—is the idea that "justice cannot be indifferent to the lives that people actually live" (2010, 18). In advocating this view, Sen provides the readers with an apt example that calls for betterment rather than a perfectly just society:

> When people agitated for the abolition of slavery in the eighteenth and nineteenth centuries, they were not laboring under the illusion that the abolition of slavery would make the world perfectly just. (ibid., 21)

The above example underlines the significance of context and the fact that whatever the good/value that is debated over needs to be as meaningful as possible to those who later have to live with it.

Probably the biggest problem Sen has with Rawls has to do with the concept of original position, which is the basis of Rawls' definition of fairness.[9] Sen doubts whether it is possible to create an imaginary zero-point with people involved having no interests (2010, 54). The impossibility of this zero-point resides in the idea that meanings (or interests in this case) cannot be divorced from the social context, since "our very understanding of the external world is so moored in our experiences and thinking that the possibility of going entirely beyond them may be rather limited" (Sen 2010, 170; Skinner 2002, 87). Moreover, Sen is not at all convinced about the idea nor possibility of a unique set of principles on which just institutions are built (2010, 57). Another point of concern for Sen is that actual behaviour is not really accounted for in Rawls' theory of justice. Rawls argues that people in the original position come up with a "political conception" of justice that all accept and agree to follow; however, Sen does not believe that this means that in reality people's actual patterns of behaviour would conform to that (ibid., 68). Furthermore, what Rawls imagines is—as has been mentioned before—an ideal (utopian) reality, in which reasonable behaviour/persons is a neat category, and which basically amounts to disregarding self-interest after the social contract has been agreed upon (ibid., 79). To Sen's mind, self-interest (Sen 1977) is not a problem per se. People are not only (if at all), as Sen reasons, guided by self-interest. The problem arises when one considers the limited vocabulary of Rawls, which prescribes that people are self-interested in the same sense, meaning that they would understand justice exactly in the same way. Consider Rawls' definition of reasonable vs. unreasonable persons, which is largely based on being vs. not being self-interested, and the fact that reasonableness is defined as an utterly homogeneous category (Sen 2010, 79; Fierke 2013, Ch. 2).

Sen ponders whether the transcendental approach is necessary, i.e. should come before we delve into the comparative approach. "It is not at all obvious", Sen maintains, "why in making the judgement that some social arrangement X is better than an alternative arrangement Y, we have to invoke the identification that some quite different alternative, say Z, is the very 'best' (or absolutely 'right') social arrangement" (2010, 101). Another important question he raises is whether comparatives should identify with transcendence (i.e. the one and only right way)? According to Sen, having this one right reference from which the comparatives can take their departure point is not that credible a thought when one thinks about "unbridgeable gaps in information, and judgemental unresolvability involving disparate considerations" (ibid., 103).

While Rawls' analysis ends with the identification of just institutions which unequivocally bring about a just society (i.e. establishing just institutions is seen as an end in itself), Sen argues that "we have to seek institutions that promote justice" (ibid., 82), meaning that we need to take into account the actual consequences that the agreed institutions generate (ibid., 83, 85). In sum, Sen is advocating an approach that does not believe that justice can be reached once and for all; rather he suggests that there needs to be a continuous review over the state of affairs: "to ask how things are going and whether they can be improved is a constant and inescapable part of the pursuit of justice" (ibid., 86).

Key to Justice: Reasoning That Creates Room for Multiple Others

In order to understand how Sen advises one to make sense of justice, it is necessary to grasp how he defines reasoning. He rebuffs the idea that reason is more akin to some worldviews or positions than others and asserts that instead reason "helps to scrutinise ideology and blind belief" (2010, 35). In this way, simply referring to European/international standards as the vanguard of development, as the EU tends to reason, would not bear scrutiny. Sen bolsters his arguments by referring to different authors; for instance, he mentions Akbar who "argued for the need for everyone to subject their inherited beliefs and priorities to critical scrutiny" (ibid., 38). In support of this view, Sen notes Akbar's view of reason as supreme, "since even in disputing reason we would have to give reasons for that disputation" (ibid., 39).

It is important to bear in mind that Sen is not making any truth claims with the promise of relying on reason; rather, as he puts it, "the case for reasoned scrutiny lies not in any sure-fire way of getting things exactly right (no such way may exist), but on being as objective as we reasonably can" (2010, 40). In an exercise to pin down reasoning, Sen comes across other heavily laden concepts, such as objectivity. In starting to think about this quality of reasoning, he refers to one of its essential applications, public reasoning:

> In seeking resolution by public reasoning, there is clearly a strong case for not leaving out the perspectives and reasonings presented by anyone whose assessments are relevant, either because their interests are involved, or because their ways of thinking about these issues throw light on particular judgements

– a light that might be missed in the absence of giving those perspectives an opportunity to be aired. (ibid., 44)

Further elaborating on this topic, Sen relies on Smith's counterfactual: "what would an impartial spectator from a distance say about that?" (ibid., 45). The valuable quality that Smith advocates—and Sen subscribes to—is the quality of inclusive discussion—avoiding both local parochialism and outside-in export.[10] In the context of devising peace operations or evaluating them, I believe the single most important principle would be to make sure that "objectivity is linked, directly or indirectly, ... to the ability to survive challenges from informed scrutiny from different perspectives to be an essential part of the demands of objectivity for ethical and political convictions" (ibid., 45).[11] In other words, if a particular entity claims that a particular approach they have adopted is objective, this has to be convincingly proved, and the process through which this (objective) standpoint was reached should be made transparent. It also demonstrates that objectivity cannot be something fixed, rigid or universal; in fact, it needs flexibility to survive and to matter in the everyday life of ordinary people. Though Sen does not explicitly discuss the power relations involved, it is apparent that he reinforces inclusiveness by making a case for the not-so-powerful (i.e. to go beyond the voices of the elite/dominant power):

> there is also the need, in any country, to go beyond the voices of governments, military leaders, business tycoons and others in commanding positions, who tend to get an easy hearing across borders, and to pay attention to the civil societies and less powerful people in different countries around the world. (2010, 409; cf. Harding 1991, esp. Chs. 6, 11)

The above discussion about reasoning and objectivity dovetails well with feminist writings on "strong objectivity" that stress how our knowledge claims are rooted in our social position. Importantly, bearing this in mind helps us to understand the locations from which a certain better world is envisaged and how empirically the world-as-it-is is interpreted (see Harding 1991).

The strength of Sen's arguments comes from the ability to question his route of reasoning every step of the way. Thus, for instance, he considers the possible position that the critics of reasoning might take. In other words, Sen spells out the critics' concern that "some people are easily over-convinced by their own reasoning, and ignore counter-arguments and other grounds that may yield the opposite conclusion" (2010, 48). The way out of this is seen in "better reasoning", which in a simplified manner translates into taking note of the multiple others. Hannah Arendt beautifully captures the latter idea when she pens: "to think with an enlarged mentality means that one trains one's imagination to go visiting" (quoted in Topper 2011, 369). The kernel of this discussion is the thought that no one actor can monopolise the label of reason, since reason is as much about putting forth arguments as it is about listening, reassessment and caution.

Sen's Approach to Justice

In opening, the space for different visions of justice, Sen draws on social choice theory[12] of justice because "the outcomes of the social choice procedure take the form of ranking different states of affairs from a 'social point of view,' in the light of the assessments of the people involved" (2010, 95). In contrast, the mainstream theories (from Hobbes to Rawls and Nozick [ibid., 96]) are concerned with the supreme alternative.

Below I will briefly consider the key features of SCT that have a bearing on the theory of justice (see Sen 2010, 107–111). The focus needs to be on the comparative, not just the transcendental. A theory of justice, according to Sen, "must have something to say about the choices that are actually on offer, and not just keep us engrossed in an imagined and implausible world of unbeatable magnificence" (ibid., 106). Crucially, in this context it is worth pointing to Mitchell's work (2011) where the dynamics of *quality* and *control,* as characteristics of the everyday life and peacebuilding practices, are debated. One of her findings is that these dynamics cannot be neatly sequestered or a priori tied to an entity (whether the local actors or "outsiders"); also these dynamics can coexist. The evidential bases of her article demonstrate that cultivating quality can have perverse effects, especially when context sensitivity is sacrificed in the name of some ideal, one and only solution; e.g. the discourse on joining the EU fits this description, as utopian progress and prosperity is promised in the future if a particular EU-proposed *modus operandi* is followed (see the author's examples on this as well [ibid., 1641]). Second, issues of social justice inescapably involve plurality of competing principles (a feature that has received some coverage already). Third, it is crucial to make room for reassessment and further scrutiny (a much needed quality in case of evaluating peace operations beyond the internal assessments). Fourth, and in close connection to the second point, SCT is open to imperfect or partial resolutions, which occur because of incompleteness which goes hand in hand with the idea of justice. Fifth, it welcomes a diversity of voices (both because they are enlightening and/or the person/party is directly involved). Sixth, explicitness (clearness) of expression and reasoning is promoted and valued, as only then can there be a meaningful discussion. Furthermore, it champions public reasoning, "involving arguments coming from different quarters and divergent perspectives" (Sen 2010, 392). And finally, it sees as important to devote energy to social realisations (i.e. "resulting from actual institutions, behaviour and other influences" [ibid., 7]). This idea of social realisations "demands that outcomes be seen in these broader terms, taking note of actions, relations and agencies" (ibid., 217). For Sen, importance does need to be attached not only to the outcome but also to the whole process (ibid., 215). For instance, it would be entirely misleading to focus only on the quarterly (or annual, etc.) reports of different international organisations on their activities in conflict regions—which mostly contain avalanches of statistics on how they have succeeded—without taking note of their everyday activities in situ, or of NGO reports of their activities, which more often than not draw a completely different picture of the "success" of the operation.

The SCT should be coupled with rational choice, since it functions as a necessary component to the application of SCT.[13] The key to rational choice is not to argue that rational choice demands self-interested behaviour, but rather that it demands "subjecting one's choices ... to reasoned scrutiny" (Sen 2010, 180, Ch. 8). This means that "*the grounds of choice have to survive investigation* based on close reasoning (with adequate reflection and, when necessary, dialogue with others), taking note of more information if and when it is relevant and accessible" (ibid., 180; emphasis added). It is crucial to note that (rational) choice in Sen's terms seems to invoke Arendt's *amor mundi*—the idea of concern, care and responsibility (see Kattago 2013). His notion of the "willingness to consider an argument proposed elsewhere" and the promise to make room for "pervasive plurality" in which we live cannot but demand an inclusive existence (Sen 2010, 407, 309).

It is suggested that any theory of justice "has to choose an informational focus, that is, it has to decide which features of the world we should concentrate on in judging a society and in assessing justice and injustice" (Sen 2010, 231). In answering this question, Sen subscribes to the freedom-based capability approach: "in contrast with the utility-based or resource-based lines of thinking, individual advantage is judged in the capability approach by a person's capability to do things he or she has reason to value" (ibid., 231). The capability approach "focuses on human life, and not just on some detached objects of convenience, such as incomes or commodities that a person may possess, which are often taken especially in economic analysis, to be the main criteria of human success" (ibid., 233). This freedom-based approach is valuable because it draws attention to both an actor's agency as well as well-being. This perspective does not offer a hierarchical ranking, as Sen believes that we cannot limit justice to a fixed blueprint; contextuality is the key.

Andrieu's work on transitional justice seems to echo many of Sen's criteria set out with respect to social choice theory. In addition to being explicit about the choice of the informational basis of justice, Andrieu's work proves illuminating as she comments on the politics of this choice. Fittingly, Andrieu (2010, 2014) problematises the means (transitional justice, as one component of the peacebuilding enterprise) and end goals of achieving peace (transition to a functioning democracy) (2014, 97). She counterpoises transitional justice with political liberalism of John Rawls, critiquing both "parties" to this equation in one another's light (Andrieu 2014). In this way Andrieu suggests, firstly, that in order for transitional justice to cohere with its *telos* (transition to democracy), it needs to concentrate more on providing the means—here the author emphasises the value of restoring the channels of communication (98)—rather than the script of transition: "it must assume that truth and reconciliation are tentative at best, and are better sought through conflict and controversy than through the manufacturing of a politically authorised consensus" (2014, 99). Secondly, this *telos* should be reacquainted with its ethical purpose. Having this in mind, the author refers to the fact that Rawls' end goals are too thin for the purposes of transitional justice, which sees its ethical purpose as human well-being (100–101; see Sen 2010; Nussbaum 2011).

It is important to take from this section the understanding that justice is deeply contextual, and that to avoid imposition, discussions of it should be inclusive of different voices. The above section highlighted that both the approach to and informational basis of justice are far from neutral; therefore, justice cannot be approached in a cookie-cutter manner.

MEANINGS OF (JUST) PEACE

The thinking about peace continues to be problematised: the debate about peace has been opened, and it has been suggested that it should remain open, rather than being resolved into any limited conception of peace (see Richmond 2007). This opening calls not only for an actual debate, but also for a problematisation of *who authors peace*, with emphases placed on *postionality, contextuality* and *legitimacy* of the vocabulary of peace (see Prashad 2007; Khalili 2013; Mac Ginty and Richmond 2014; Sabaratnam 2017; Firchow 2018). Oliver Richmond has been at the forefront of a critical thinking on peace, arguing that "peace always has a time and a place, as well as representatives and protagonists in diplomatic, military, or civilian guise, and [it] exists in multiple forms in overlapping spaces of influence" (2007, 264).

The advantage of a critical perspective in attempting to problematise peace lies in the fact that this perspective equips me with tools to contest different conceptualisations of peace. A critical approach enables to recognise the power relationships, time, place and different parties to peace: it allows for interrogating the numerous other categories that the problem-solving approach habitually ignores, such as ethics, norms and politics—i.e. aspects that to a critical enquiry are part and parcel of peace operations. I share the assumption that *context* colours our existence (see Flyvbjerg 2001, 71). A problem-solving approach with its commitment of universality/homogeneity tries to mask its context and rob others of theirs. Accordingly, the often-made appeals to cosmopolitanism—in the name of moral authority and legitimacy—need to be studied rather than accepted a priori, since labels are often abused in the name of rather unpleasant agendas. The concept of *mission civilisatrice* refers to one of the instances in which cosmopolitanism is masquerading as a universal, but is in essence strikingly particular (for a good discussion, see Appiah 2005, Ch. 6).

In general, debates about peace tend to revolve around a simplistic realist–idealist axis, which translates into either a pessimistic vision of the slim chances of peace (or, if peace, then a bare minimum—i.e. negative peace), or peace seen in relatively utopian terms (as an unattainable goal) (see Richmond 2007, 251). Both of the visions have an overarching similarity, in that peace is seen as a commonsensical notion (e.g. peace is peace), relying on the use of empty signifiers (i.e. we all have an innate notion of what peace is, so there is no need to elaborate on it). Crudely put, the largely unproblematic take on peace described above is widespread in the peace and conflict studies circles as the epitome of a problem-solving approach. A critical take on peace, however, understands peace not as a neutral, taken-for-granted state, but *an imagined state* where one cannot get around the questions such as *for whom* peace is, *how* peace is built/imagined and *what* peace is.

It is widely accepted now that the liberal peace (taking the problem-solving route) is the dominant way of building peace:[14]

> The most widely recognised conceptualisation of peace, which has now entered into the consciousness of policymakers and academics, rests upon the various formulations of liberal-internationalist and liberal-institutionalist debates about governance. (Richmond 2007, 263; also Mac Ginty 2011, 20)

Attention should be paid to the governance aspect of this trend, as many of these "liberal" endeavours have a very intrusive and top-down attitude (see Mac Ginty 2011, 30–31). In order to avoid exporting a single model of peace (devoid of scrutiny), Richmond and many others who see the value in subjecting peace to a critical gaze have argued that perhaps in thinking about peace one should jump off the beaten track and see what "the margins" of IR and other perspectives have to offer (see esp. Richmond 2008). Thus, for example, Richmond promotes critically inclined theories such as poststructuralism that, although "not offer[ing] an explicit theory, approach, or concept of peace", does imply "its [peace's] multiplicity and hybridity" (Richmond 2008, 455). Exemplary work in this regard has been done by Sabaratnam (2017) and Firchow (2018) who have in diverse ways interrogated received wisdom of peace(building). Both start from and value peoples' experiences and thus exhibit what it means to start from local understandings of peace. For instance, Sabaratnam has convincingly argued that by contextualising our standpoint it becomes evident that received wisdom always emerges from a particular site and is thus testament to a particular logic of relations. The issues and questions raised in these works speak to the importance of contextualising peace, and therefore, they help to safeguard against ahistorical accounts of peace.

Many critically inclined authors demand that the centre stage in thinking about peace is given to the local aspirations for peace (Mac Ginty and Richmond 2013; cf. Sabaratnam 2017, and Firchow 2018). It is worth quoting the ideas Richmond introduces at length here:

> Any version of peace should cumulatively engage with everyday life as well as institutions from the bottom up. It should rest on uncovering an ontology, perhaps indigenous, on empathy and emancipation, and recognise the fluidity of peace as a process, as well as the constant renegotiation of 'international' norms of peace. Agents of peace should endeavour to see themselves as mediatory agents of empathetic emancipation, whereby their role is to mediate the global norm or institution with the local before it is constructed. This

involves an exploration of different and hybrid ontologies of peace. (2008, 463; see also Richmond 2014a, b)

Sen and Richmond introduce ideas of peace and justice that, read together, envisage a more sustainable path to *just peace*. In the concluding section, I will summarise how Sen's ideas can contribute to a more inclusive understanding of peace in the already very noteworthy critical endeavour.

A Promising Path to (Just) Peace?

The questions guiding my work—*what* peace, *how* peace, peace *for whom*—will be asked with reference to the specific contexts of the three case studies. These questions together with the debates this chapter has introduced will structure my analysis of the EU's CSDP operations and sketch out the process of EU's becoming a distinct actor in peacebuilding. The chief task of this chapter was to introduce Sen's ideas on justice and the critical literature on peace in order to create a point of departure for my analysis. The originality of this quest resides in the fact that Sen's ideas have not been incorporated into the peace and conflict literature to such an extent before. Below, I will focus on some of the major insights gathered from the above discussion.

Firstly, Sen's ideas on justice provide a particularly elaborate understanding of one of the key goals of positive peace: social justice. He argues for an idea of justice that is responsive to the context—and not as something that exists on an abstract level, i.e. *perfect justice*. Justice, then, similarly to peace, is very much rooted in everyday life. Thus, it can be both particular and universal. Secondly, both Sen's approach and the critical strand of peace and conflict studies point to the importance of spatio-temporality and thus to the fluidity of justice/peace, indicating that they cannot be approached in a static manner or resolved *once-and-for-all*, but need to be seen as movable entities and open categories that are not fixed in stone. Thirdly, Sen places a premium on (public) reasoning as a *modus operandi* for locating justice and hence subjecting one's ideas of justice to scrutiny. This insight is valuable both when thinking about devising a response to a conflict and criteria for evaluating peace operations. There is considerable momentum attached to peace and justice being subject to debate, and hence notions of transparency and accountability become ineluctable. Fourthly, perhaps the element that is most valuable in the critical approaches to peace(building) is their ability to see beyond the status quo and to critically interrogate the vocabulary of peace support operations.

Sen's work is refreshing because it transcends the ingrained limitations that certain theoretical perspectives have created in our perception of the world. Thus, in applying the lessons learned from Sen to the thinking about peace, two seminal points should be added: one about human nature and the other about the axis of local-global.

Human nature, for Sen, is not confined to self-interested behaviour; rather there is a much more complex system of triggers that prompt certain behaviour/decisions. Thus, his vision of what justice is and could be is much more open-ended, in contrast to some Hobbes-inspired scholars who, owing to their view of human nature, limit their ideas about justice. "What we owe to each other", Sen believes, taking cue from Thomas Scanlon,

> is an important subject for intelligent reflection. That reflection can take us beyond the pursuit of a very narrow view of self-interest, and we can even find that our own well-reflected goals demand that we cross the narrow boundaries of exclusive self-seeking altogether. (2010, 32–33)

If the above vision is predicated on the idea that global justice is only possible if/when we have a global government, then we are facing another imaginary limit that hampers us from thinking about the possibility of global justice. There are two problems with this self-inflicted limited vision of the world: first, it relies more on the technical issues than substantive ones (the elevated position granted to institutions); second, it imposes on the world too strict an ontology (states are bounded, and this system of states has prevailed and will in the future). Sen counters this pessimism by stating that "the relevance and influence of global discussions are not conditional on the existence of a global state, or even of a well-organised planetary forum for gigantic institutional agreements" (2010, 141). He believes that justice cannot be a neatly bounded question, since in the current state of affairs people are affected by developments far and near—but perhaps most importantly, Sen's plea for open debate cannot be satisfied if we resort to bounded categories in talking about justice.

Why is global justice especially relevant for the topic of just peace? By way of an answer, global justice allows for pursuing new avenues in thinking about interventions of different kinds. For instance, Sen does not see a problem in establishing a global democracy, which would be much needed to hold the large enterprise of peacebuilding accountable. This is crucial as the current system is built (because of the limited visions of different actors) upon an enormous power asymmetry. Illuminatingly, Sen proposes that "active public agitation, news commentary and open discussion are among the ways in which global democracy can be pursued, even without waiting for the global state" (2010, 409–410). Global justice is needed to guarantee an open and inclusive debate that keeps at bay both global imposition and local parochialism (ibid., 402–407). Also, "the evaluation needed for the assessment of justice", as Sen argues, "is not just a solitary exercise but one that is inescapably discursive" (2010, 337). This idea can be contrasted with the international community's overwhelming trend of technocratic reasoning (using labels such as neutrality, efficiency, apolitical, etc.), in order to place their responses to conflicts beyond debate. As their argument goes, they are just providing technical fixes devoid of agendas, which allows them, in turn, to state that the offered help does not need to be discussed or problematised because it is per se concerned with the *technical* [read: innocuous] (cf. Mac Ginty et al. 2012).

Adopting these insights from Sen as a starting point for a discussion about peace will make it more fruitful and elevate our imagining of peace above their current limitations. The single most crucial point in Sen's book—though not entirely revelatory in the context of peace and conflict studies—is his plea that justice has to be about the lives that people actually lead (e.g. 2010, 21). Thus, the everyday lives of people matter for any conception of peace/justice. It follows that, in order to attain these twin goals, there needs to be a genuine and direct engagement with all those parties whose lives they affect. Peace and conflict studies do take note of the idea of local ownership, but policy circles largely see it as a tactic to win hearts and minds (which often translates into local ownership on paper). In contrast, the critical scholars favour the term "local agency" and stress the need for the locals' active role in shaping peace (see Mac Ginty and Richmond 2013, 2014). In this context, Sen's perspective proves useful, as it promotes hybrid ownership of peace. To an extent, hybrid peace is nothing new, but usually in the field of peace and conflict it is imagined as being strictly between the peace agents involved (both local and global)—not the wider audience, as envisaged by Sen. Sen's approach empowers the individual in terms of promoting his/her capabilities and freedoms, rather than viewing people as mere "statistics" in "measuring" justice. All in all, it is of consequence to acknowledge that Sen does not promote a static definition of justice, but rather argues for particular processes (e.g. open debate with the widest access and participation, paying attention to the human life—not bare numbers, and so forth) that have the potential to bring about the best possible solution in any given situation.

NOTES

1. See Pugh for a detailed discussion of the prevailing camps of thought on peacebuilding, i.e. the problem-solving and the paradigm critique (2013).
2. Negative peace, according to Fetherston, "refers to a situation that is 'not war' but where structural violence exists, whereas positive peace is a situation where human beings are not impeded from fully developing and living out their life-span – a situation sometimes referred to as peace with justice" (2000, 202).
3. This way of framing the issue draws on Tadjbakhsh's work (2010) problematising the values and goods a peacebuilding mission *is for*, in order to stop and contemplate the legitimacy of those goods and the implications of a particular portrayal of these goods.
4. My intention is not to offer a detailed review of different approaches to justice but rather to provide an initial contextual note for Sen's perspective. for a more thorough engagement with different approaches to justice, Sen's book (2010) is an excellent starting point as he enters into *a meaningful dialogue* with so many.
5. See esp. Ch. 6 of his work where this issue is aptly demonstrated by interrogating Habermas–Mouffe debate on radical democracy.
6. See Sen (2010, 11–12) where he brings out this puzzle.
7. See Everyday Peace Indicators project (https://everydaypeaceindicators. org).
8. In a similar manner, Sen argues that it is illusory to imagine a world *à la* Huntington, where people fit one-sized boxes with clearly bounded identities. Perhaps even more importantly, he brings out the destructiveness of seeing the world through one-dimensionality as "many of the conflicts and barbarities in the world are sustained through the illusion of a unique and choiceless identity" (2006, xv).
9. Relying on contractarian reasoning, Rawls invokes the idea of the original position signifying a time when all people (unencumbered by self-interest) can unanimously agree on a social contract (Sen 2010, 52–74).
10. See especially Ch. 6, where open and closed impartialities are discussed (Sen 2010).
11. At this juncture, the idea of countervailing power proves useful. Referring to Galbraith (1952), Sen argues that in order to avoid a situation of one voice dominating (e.g. one-party states), there should be a number of institutions that "exercise 'countervailing power' over each other" (2010, 81).

However, this principle does not necessarily have to be confined to institutions—it can also mean other parties (NGOs, civil society in different configurations, etc.) that are crucial to a given debate. This argument is in many ways akin to the impartial spectator idea introduced above.

12. Hereafter SCT.
13. Not to be confused with Rational Choice Theory (see Sen 2010, 178–183).
14. Although the critiques directed against the prevailing way of building peace have been numerous, Pugh appositely sums up the chief lines of critique: "[liberal peace] merges security and development; 'romanticises the local' as victims or illiberal; builds hollow institutions; designs economic life to reproduce assertive capitalism; equates peace with state-building; and assumes the interveners have privileged knowledge and that liberalisation is the only system available" (2012, 411; cf. Campbell et al. 2011).

References

Aggestam, Karin, and Annika Björkdahl. 2013. "Introduction: The Study of Just and Durable Peace." In *Rethinking Peacebuilding: The Quest for Just Peace in the Middle East and the Western Balkans*, edited by Karin Aggestam and Annika Björkdahl, 1–15. London: Routledge.

Andrieu, Kora. 2010. "Civilising Peacebuilding: Transitional Justice, Civil Society and the Liberal Paradigm." *Security Dialogue* 41 (5): 537–558. https://doi.org/10.1177/0967010610382109.

Andrieu, Kora. 2014. "Political Liberalism After Mass Violence: John Rawls and a 'Theory' of Transitional Justice." In *Transitional Justice Theories*, edited by Susanne Buckley-Zistel et al., 85–104. Abingdon: Routledge.

Appiah, Kwame Anthony. 2005. *The Ethics of Identity*. Princeton: Princeton University Press.

Autesserre, Séverine. 2014. *Peaceland: Conflict Resolution and the Everyday Politics of International Intervention*. New York, NY: Cambridge University Press.

Boulding, Elise. 1999. "Peace Culture." In *Encyclopedia of Violence, Peace & Conflict*, vol. 2, edited by Lester Kurtz, 653–667. San Diego: Academic Press.

Brown, Chris. 2010. "On Amartya Sen and *The Idea of Justice*." *Ethics and International Affairs* 24 (3): 309–318. https://doi.org/10.1111/j.1747-7093.2010.00269.x.

Brown, Judith M., ed. 2008. *Mahatma Gandhi: The Essential Writings*. Oxford: Oxford University Press.

Campbell, Susanna, David Chandler, and Meera Sabaratnam, eds. 2011. *A Liberal Peace? The Problems and Practices of Peacebuilding*. London: Zed Books.

Fetherston, A. B. 2000. "Peacekeeping, Conflict Resolution and Peacebuilding: A Reconsideration of Theoretical Frameworks." In *Peacekeeping and Conflict Resolution*, edited by Tom Woodhouse and Oliver Ramsbotham, 190–218. London: Frank Cass.

Fierke, Karin. 2013. *Political Self-Sacrifice: Agency, Body and Emotion in International Relations.* Cambridge: Cambridge University Press.

Firchow, Pamina. 2018. *Reclaiming Everyday Peace: Local Voices in Measurement and Evaluation After War.* Cambridge: Cambridge University Press.

Flyvbjerg, Bent. 2001. *Making Social Science Matter: Why Social Inquiry Fails and How It Can Succeed Again.* Translated by Steven Sampson. Cambridge: Cambridge University Press.

Galtung, Johan. 1969. "Violence, Peace and Peace Research." *Journal of Peace Research* 6 (3): 167–191. https://doi.org/10.1177/002234336900600301.

Harding, Sandra. 1991. *Whose Science? Whose Knowledge? Thinking from Women's Lives.* Ithaca, NY: Cornell University Press.

Higate, Paul, and Marsha Henry. 2013. *Insecure Spaces: Peacekeeping, Power and Performance in Haiti, Kosovo and Liberia.* London: Zed Books. Kindle.

Kapoor, Ilan. 2008. *The Postcolonial Politics of Development.* Abingdon: Routledge.

Kattago, Siobhan. 2013. "Why the World Matters: Hannah Arendt's Philosophy of New Beginnings." *The European Legacy: Toward New Paradigms* 18 (2): 170–184. https://doi.org/10.1080/10848770.2013.772362.

Khalili, Laleh. 2013. *Time in the Shadows: Confinement in Counterinsurgencies.* Stanford: Stanford University Press.

Mac Ginty, Roger. 2008. *No War, No Peace: The Rejuvenation of Stalled Peace Processes and Peace Accords.* Basingstoke: Palgrave Macmillan.

Mac Ginty, Roger. 2011. *International Peacebuilding and Local Resistance: Hybrid Forms of Peace.* London: Palgrave Macmillan.

Mac Ginty, Roger, and Oliver P. Richmond. 2013. "The Local Turn in Peace Building: A Critical Agenda for Peace." *Third World Quarterly* 34 (5): 763–783. https://doi.org/10.1080/01436597.2013.800750.

Mac Ginty, Roger, and Oliver P. Richmond. 2014. "Where Now for the Critique of the Liberal Peace?" *Cooperation and Conflict* (OnlineFirst version). https://doi.org/10.1177/0010836714545691.

Mac Ginty, Roger, Sandra Pogodda, Oliver P. Richmond, and Birte Vogel. 2012. "Technocracy, Governance and Conflict Resolution." In *Norms and Premises of Peace Governance: Socio-Cultural Commonalities and Differences in Europe and India* (Berghof Occasional Paper No. 32), edited by Janel B. Galvanek, Hans J. Giessmann, and Mir Mubashir, 37–43. Berlin: Berghof Foundation.

Mitchell, Audra. 2011. "Quality/Control: International Peace Interventions and 'the Everyday'." *Review of International Studies* 37 (4): 1623–1645. https://doi.org/10.1017/s0260210511000180.

Nussbaum, Martha C. 2011. *Creating Capabilities: The Human Development Approach.* Cambridge: Harvard University Press.

Prashad, Vijay. 2007. *The Darker Nations: A People's History of the Third World.* New York: The New Press.

Pugh, Michael. 2012. "Reflections on Aggressive Peace." *International Peacekeeping* 19 (4): 410–425. https://doi.org/10.1080/13533312.2012.709749.

Pugh, Michael. 2013. "The Problem-Solving and Critical Paradigms." In *Routledge Handbook of Peacebuilding*, edited by Roger Mac Ginty, 11–24. Abingdon: Routledge.

Richmond, Oliver P. 2007. "Critical Research Agendas for Peace: The Missing Link in the Study of International Relations." *Alternatives: Global, Local, Political* 32 (2): 247–274. https://doi.org/10.1177/030437540703200205.

Richmond, Oliver P. 2008. "Reclaiming Peace in International Relations." *Millennium: Journal of International Studies* 36 (3): 439–470. https://doi.org/10.1177/03058298080360030401.

Richmond, Oliver P. 2014a. *Peace: A Very Short Introduction*. Oxford: Oxford University Press. Kindle.

Richmond, Oliver P. 2014b. *Failed Statebuilding: Intervention and the Dynamics of Peace Formation*. New Haven: Yale University Press.

Sabaratnam, Meera. 2017. *Decolonising Intervention: International Statebuilding in Mozambique*. London: Rowman & Littlefield.

Sen, Amartya. 1977. "Rational Fools: A Critique of the Behavioral Foundations of Economic Theory." *Philosophy and Public Affairs* 6 (4): 317–344. http://www.jstor.org/stable/2264946.

Sen, Amartya. 1999. *Development as Freedom*. New York: Alfred A. Knopf.

Sen, Amartya. 2006. *Identity and Violence: The Illusion of Destiny*. New York: W. W. Norton.

Sen, Amartya. 2010. *The Idea of Justice*. London: Penguin Books.

Skinner, Quentin. 2002. "Meaning and Understanding in the History of Ideas." In *Visions of Politics, vol. 1: Regarding Method*, 57–92. Cambridge: Cambridge University Press.

Solana, Javier. 2005. "Foreword." *ESDP Newsletter*, December, Issue 1. https://www.iss.europa.eu/sites/default/files/EUISSFiles/ESDP_newsletter_001_0.pdf.

Tadjbakhsh, Shahrbanou. 2010. "Human Security and the Legitimisation of Peacebuilding." In *Palgrave Advances in Peacebuilding: Critical Developments and Approaches*, edited by Oliver P. Richmond, 116–136. Basingstoke: Palgrave Macmillan.

Topper, Keith. 2011. "Arendt and Bourdieu Between Word and Deed." *Political Theory* 39 (3): 352–377. https://doi.org/10.1177/0090591711400028.

Viktorova Milne, Jevgenia. 2009. "Returning Culture to Peacebuilding: Contesting the Liberal Peace in Sierra Leone." PhD diss., University of St Andrews.

Wibben, Annick T. R., Catia Cecilia Confortini, Sanam Roohi, Sarai B. Aharoni, Leena Vastapuu, and Tiina Vaittinen. 2018. "Collective Discussion: Piecing-Up Feminist Peace Research." *International Political Sociology* (OnlineFirst version). https://doi.org/10.1093/ips/oly034.

CHAPTER 4

Artemis in the Democratic Republic of the Congo: A Necessary "Success Story"

CSDP operations do not just represent crisis management tools, they serve as "important building blocks in the construction of an EU security policy"; moreover, they function as an opening onto the international field (Kurowska 2008, 25–26). Indeed, this is very topical for the context of the EU's first autonomous military operation—code-named Artemis—in the Democratic Republic of the Congo (DRC). The EU's situation in 2003 was definitely characterised by an air of urgency (Kurowska and Seitz 2011, 21), as the 1990s presented a number of advances in defining the CSDP but no concrete actions.[1] This urgency gained momentum after the deployment of the EU Police Mission in Bosnia (January 2003) and Operation Concordia in Macedonia (March 2003). However, since these operations still fell short of the label "autonomous", there was a pronounced call for *action* to demonstrate the EU's credibility. Adding to the contextual scenery were frequent calls (e.g. the summit in Le Touquet) for the EU to demonstrate a global profile (Ulriksen et al. 2004).

The aim of this chapter is to critically interrogate who Artemis was for, by delving into the discursive vehicles representing Artemis and, by extension, the CSDP as a whole. Throughout the analysis, the conceptualisation of Artemis is problematised, relying on the conceptual framework (presented in Ch. 2 and 3) in order to enquire into the *modus operandi* of the CSDP. The script on Artemis, and by extension the CSDP, is probed by: (i) locating the key topics that surround the operation; (ii) shedding light on the EU's conceptualisation of its manifold others; and (iii) placing under scrutiny the

© The Author(s) 2020   71
B. Poopuu, *The European Union's Brand of Peacebuilding*,
Rethinking Peace and Conflict Studies,
https://doi.org/10.1007/978-3-030-19890-9_4

telling and acting of Artemis. This way of analysing Artemis demonstrates well how the EU's conceptualisation of Artemis goes hand in hand with articulating "the problem"—here understood both as the particular conflict at hand, and as the larger scope of the CSDP's concerns—that the operation is supposed to tackle (see esp. Escobar 1995; Autesserre 2010).

SETTING THE STAGE IN THE DEMOCRATIC REPUBLIC OF THE CONGO: ENTER ARTEMIS

A UN peacekeeper, originally from North Africa, lectured me [Autesserre] once on how to understand the situation in the Congo. In essence, he warned: Do not come here with your European sensibilities and your European ideas. Violence and corporal punishments are a part of life here. The Congolese are used to it. Whipping people is the way of the Congo. The Congolese do not feel it the same way we do, he explained. A Western diplomat to whom I relayed this story found such normalisation of violence a quite 'legitimate' phenomenon. 'It's a human tragedy,' he said, 'but ... it is a country that has been through, certainly since 1996, a decade of pretty serious ongoing violence, and people become somewhat numb to that, such as the level of shooting [in a large US city] would seem intolerable in Tokyo, but [in that US city] it is part of the background'. (Autesserre 2010, 74–75)

This short section cannot endeavour to give a comprehensive overview of the contextual dynamics of the DRC before the EU entered the stage. However, it does sketch out a number of key understandings of the Congo wars harboured by the international community, and how those understandings in turn shaped their responses in the DRC.[2] The latter will provide a particularly useful reference point when considering the appearance of the EU operation on the scene.

In all important respects, the stage was set before the EU deployed its operation in the DRC. This is to say that the dominant international peacebuilding culture had already developed an understanding of the DRC conflicts that informed the EU's policy. In this sense, while it cannot be denied that certain specific events took place, the attachment of meaning to them and the subsequent arrangement of the contextual dynamics bring out the performative force present in the discourses that name the DRC a particular place and thus prescribe strategies to approach it.[3] In other words, as Autesserre suggests, "the dominant culture shapes the international understanding of the causes of violence and of the interveners' role, thus allowing for certain actions while precluding others" (2010, 22; see also Jabri 2007, 29–30, 40).

The chief element that was absent from the international peacebuilders' accounts of the conflict in the DRC was its distinctly local character—in addition to the regional and national dynamics that also carried significance. In this way, the prime causes of the DRC wars were located on the national and regional levels, with the overarching theme being that of state failure. The top-down understanding of the problematique meant that in the aftermath of the Congo wars in the 1990s, the response of the international community was centred on statebuilding (see Autesserre 2010; Hellmüller 2013). This is not to suggest that the national and regional issues did not matter in the dynamics of the conflicts, but rather that the local level issues played a considerable (albeit largely neglected) role as well.

In order to avoid rehearsing the extensive work done on this matter, the following discussion touches upon a couple of prevalent discursive frames that surrounded the responses to the Congo wars.[4] After the two Congo wars, a ceasefire agreement was reached in Lusaka in 1999.[5] This agreement was prefaced by the UNSC resolution 1234 in April 1999, which envisaged elections as a remedy to the "state failure", which exemplified as a widely shared approach to understanding the DRC context (Hellmüller 2013, 221). The UN deployed a peacekeeping mission, MONUC (the United Nations Observer Mission in the Democratic Republic of the Congo), to monitor the implementation of the Lusaka agreement. The agreement was seen by the international community as the most feasible basis for the resolution of the conflict in the DRC (UNSC 1999, November 30; Council 2003, May 8). The key objective of the agreement was to put an end to hostilities in order to move towards rebuilding the state. However, the underlying causes of the conflict—in particular those below the regional-national levels—remained unaccounted for, and thus the approach to security included only a very traditional reading that was out of touch with the local security needs (Hellmüller 2013), focusing instead on state security, the security of the DRC and its neighbouring countries (see esp. Ch. 12 of the agreement) (Rogier 2004b). Not only was the Lusaka Accord already geared towards building up state institutions, the numerous UNSC resolutions were also primarily concerned with activities on the national and regional levels (Autesserre 2010, 92). The Lusaka Accord paved the way for a national dialogue—known as the Inter-Congolese Dialogue—an enormously promising endeavour if one looks at the diversity of parties included; however, by scrutinising its general direction, it is possible to discern that statebuilding concerns hijacked its agenda (Rogier 2004a, b). The fact that the ceasefire did not manage to introduce a break from fighting did not alarm the international community. Subsequently, the peace process—with the signing of a flurry of ceasefires—went hand in hand with fighting and continued violence, especially in many parts of the eastern DRC. This period of consecutive agreements culminated with the Global and All Inclusive Agreement in December 2002. This agreement, which marked the finalisation of the Inter-Congolese Dialogue, similarly to the Lusaka ceasefire did not attend to the causes of the conflict. Rather, it was driven by the setting up of transitional administrative structures to prepare the country for elections, which the international community saw as a panacea for the DRC's troubles (Autesserre 2010, Ch. 2–3). By and large, the above focal points in responding to the wars in the DRC demonstrate that the international community—with the UN at the helm—was much more concerned with statebuilding, whereas conflict resolution activities, especially ones dealing with local issues, were underplayed (Vircoulon 2010).

The Global accord marked for the international community (IC) the genesis of a transition from war to peace.[6] In this way, the signing of peace agreements heralded for the IC a change in the conflict theatre. Hence, from late 2002 onwards, the IC saw the DRC overwhelmingly as a post-conflict situation (Autesserre 2010, 65), despite the fact that "throughout the transition [2003-2006]", the state of affairs in the DRC was extremely precarious. As Autesserre recounts:

> unremitting clashes between various armed groups and militias, frequent massacres of civilians, massive population displacements, and appalling human rights violations, including widespread sexual violence, persisted in the provinces of North Kivu, South Kivu, North Katanga, and in Oriental Province's Ituri district. (ibid., 4)

Autesserre brings our attention to the fact that this localised violence continued—and greatly deteriorated—during the postelection period. In cases where localised violence turned up on the radar of the internationals, it was depicted as private and criminal; furthermore, and very problematically, violence was seen as inherent to the Congo, and the lack of state authority was understood as the chief reason for it (Autesserre 2010, 68–80). It is notable that, in their depiction of the DRC as inherently violent, the internationals exclude the colonial moment. That is, "about 10 million Congolese died of forced labour, massacres, burned villages, malnutrition, and the chicotte under colonial rule" (Hochschild 1998 quoted in Autesserre 2010, 76; see also Prashad 2007). This is not to deny that there has been extreme and horrific violence in the postcolonial Congo, but rather to acknowledge the undefendable argument that treats violence as somehow more characteristic of the DRC than of *other* places. It also serves to point out the powerful performative effects of naming the Congo as particularly violent, even barbaric, and the consequences of this; for example, the recurrent reiteration of violence as "normal" in the DRC puts in place a particular policy focus.

Since the local causes of violence and conflict were either overlooked in the top-down logic of engagement—or misinterpreted—the attention towards the eastern Congo was lukewarm until the fighting intensified in late 2002 and 2003.[7] Even when the UN finally gazed towards the eastern part of the Congo, though limiting itself to Ituri (Autesserre 2007, 265–266), it failed to address the chief causes of violence and conflict there, which were to do mainly with land disputes (see Vircoulon 2010; Autesserre 2010, Ch. 4; Hellmüller 2013, 2014a). The logic of intervention that the international community championed during the transition was acutely paradoxical; to illustrate this I turn to Autesserre who beautifully captures this tension (2010, 97):

> During the Congolese transition, UN actors and diplomats interpreted the prohibition of international interference in the domestic affairs of states as forbidding action at the subnational level. According to most UN, diplomatic, and nongovernmental interviewees, such subnational intervention would be a paternalist, neocolonial, or neoimperial endeavour. In contrast, international actors considered interference legitimate as long as they worked with, and filtered their demands through, national representatives. For example, the diplomats and UN staff I interviewed did not perceive their efforts to influence the Congolese constitution as paternalist, neocolonial, or neoimperial, even though they put tremendous pressure on the transitional representatives, wrote part of the constitution, and then threatened to cut funding if the parliament did not adopt a document satisfactory to Western powers.

Such justification, coupled with how the conflict was understood, meant that MONUC left the resolution of the land issues to the Congolese authorities. In this way, MONUC's mandate exclusively focused on issues that were understood to be vital for peace from its own position, notwithstanding the mismatch with the locals' perspective, concerned with resolving the land issues and peaceful cohabitation with neighbours (see esp. Hellmüller 2013, 222–223, 225–227). As a result, although security, together with elections, was the primary focus of the MONUC mandate (UNSC 2000), it did not manage to deliver security for the locals, concerned as it was with creating a safe environment for the elections.

The EU's military operation, deployed to the Ituri capital Bunia from June to September 2003 at the request of the UN, subscribed to the overarching international narrative of the conflict.[8] In this way, the primary narratives of the peacebuilding apparatus in place in the DRC where upheld, i.e. that the primary contribution to the peace process occurs on the national level, and that the peacebuilding activities facilitate the establishment of the transitional government in the DRC (UNSC 2003).

Key Themes of Artemis

Congo is a jungle where people behave like animals and where only the law of the jungle applies. … The last shred of civilisation has left Congo. Even animals do not behave like this towards each other in the animal world. … Without drastic reforms, without an actual, working state structure, the Congolese population is at the mercy of the wild animals among people, and only the rule of the jungle applies. (Van den Bos, EP debate 2003, May 15)[9]

Common European values have grown out of common historical experience, which in extreme cases can provide a justification for armed intervention. For a postmodern state [which the EU is (becoming), according to Cooper] there is a difficulty. It needs to get used to the idea of double standards. Among themselves, the postmodern states operate on the basis of laws and open co-operative security. But when dealing with more old-fashioned kinds of state outside of the postmodern limits, Europeans need to revert to the rougher methods of an earlier era – force, pre-emptive attack, deception, whatever is necessary for those who still live in the 19th century world of every state for itself. In the jungle, one must use the laws of the jungle. In this period of peace in Europe, there is a temptation to neglect defences, both physical and psychological. (Cooper 2003, 61–62, quoted in Kurowska 2008, 32)

Apart from certain essentialist voices amid different EU actors, the renditions of the DRC conflict and correspondingly the responses imagined to it showed signs of different ways of seeing conflicts and consequently offered different "cures".[10] Yet, for the most part, a top-down approach to peace prevailed, where "building up the state so that peace can trickle down" mindset was a mainstay. It is crucial to note that there is an overwhelming trend of *Huntingtonian* attitudes—a rigid and primordialist way of approaching identity (see Kuus 2012)—among the international community which, at their extremes, advance views not dissimilar to the assertions captured in the epigraph.[11] Below I map the main topics communicated by the CSDP articulators to comment further on the EU's understanding of peacebuilding. This by no means is an exhaustive endeavour; rather, my aim is to focus on the themes that prove relevant in the context of the CSDP. It should be kept in mind that the period from 1999 to 2003 was characteristic of the capability-driven approach to the CSDP, which meant that while crisis management procedures were in place, conceptual work, such as a strategy or a doctrine, was largely missing (see Bono 2004).

On balance, the discourses on CSDP consisted of two main discourses that overshadowed other issues. The first discourse centred on the role of capabilities. In fact, as noted above, the CSDP was, for the most part, defined through capabilities. The other recurrent discourse emphasised the establishment and development of relations with other international organisations, i.e. the dynamic of cooperation/coordination.

To start with, the overall progress of the CSDP is measured by the development of both military and civilian capabilities. The latter two aspects definitely sit at the centre of discussions about the CSDP (e.g. Presidency 2003, June 20). Moreover, the CSDP is framed through the capabilities question to such an extent that it suggests that the content side of the debate is regarded as a common-sense issue, or that the contents are just assumed to follow automatically with no thought given to them at all. This "technicist orientation" (see Viktorova Milne 2009, Ch. 4) is further demonstrated by the prioritisation of developing procedures of crisis management to the detriment of a strategy; and hence it is pointing to the problem-solving mindset at work. Aside from prioritising the instruments of the CSDP, a great deal of stress is placed on "acting". The principle *res, non verba* is often reiterated to varying degrees, implying that defence should not be "only about rhetoric, but about resources" (Solana 2003, April 28; EP debate 2003, June 18). There is a marked link between capabilities and action: "we need to be able to act. And that means having military capabilities" (Solana 1999, quoted in Kurowska 2008, 31). Peculiarly, this overarching idea that actions speak louder than words translates into the repeated calls by Solana for the EU to acquire the necessary military capabilities. Fundamentally, as the argument goes, being an actor in peacebuilding means having military capabilities in addition to civilian ones (e.g. Solana 2003, March 24; Solana

2003, March 26). Closely tied to this logic is the development of operational capability, that is, the deployment of CSDP operations, meaning that EU missions are seen as proof of the EU's actorness, and that the EU has proved its agency by deploying missions (Presidency 2003, June 19–20).

Owing to this focus on the development of capabilities (which of course merits debate, but not to the detriment of other issues), the conceptual premises of the CSDP have been silenced; that is, they have acquired a self-evident status. As a result, the approach the EU advances rests on the belief that peacebuilding is a neutral, technical and apolitical endeavour (see Bellamy and Williams 2004). In keeping with the problem-solving mindset which guides peace operations, the main components of dealing with conflicts are seen as if corresponding to a mathematical equation: the rule of law and effective state-level structures; multilateralism (e.g. Solana 2003, January 15, 2003, February 26); a stable, durable and peaceful liberal democracy[12] (Solana 2003, May 7; cf. EP debate 2003, May 15). Similarly to other proponents of liberal peace, for the EU, the outcome of this logic is to present peacebuilding as an authorless endeavour—that is, a universal undertaking rather than a particular experiment. However, despite this image of peacebuilding as a universal undertaking, the particular quality of its instances becomes manifest as soon as its logic is interrogated. Below, I use three separate topics (multilateralism, security, responsibility) of the EU's discourse to illustrate this hidden particularity.

The promotion of multilateralism serves two objectives. On the one hand, there is a practical aim of enhancing cooperation with other international organisations, not necessarily with regard to conceptual issues, on the procedural level (Joint UN-EU Declaration 2003, September 24). On the other hand, the EU showcases multilateralism in order to counter the possibility of a unilateralist international arena. Accordingly, the mantra that "nobody alone can resolve these complicated problems that we are facing now" (Solana 2003, April 3) is recurrently invoked. However, the "we" of the multilateralist order is a very specific group of actors, and their norms and rules also emanate from specific sources, and it is these rules that are being reinforced through multilateral action: "that we act together to sustain and strengthen a world based on rules" (Solana 2003, April 7). Furthermore, it is explicitly stated that the UN is seen as the authority on war and peace. For instance, "questions pertaining to war and peace are treated there [at the UN]" (Solana 2003, February 24; Presidency 2003, March 20–21); "the UN should continue to be the centre of gravity of the solution to the post-conflict" (Solana 2003, March 20). Crucially, the politics of multilateralism becomes evident in how the contents of such form of togetherness are formulated (see below the sections about the significant and multiple others).

In defining what the new security environment holds, two topics emerge: the borders of security/insecurity and the naming/roles of security providers/recipients. Namely it is envisaged that insecurity reigns outside the EU's borders, and thus there is a constant positioning of the security providers and the recipients of security as located on opposite sides of the EU border. The perception that new security threats and risks are "more diverse, less visible and less predictable" (Solana 2003, June 18) than before leads to the construction of the "outside" realm as inherently insecure. The inside realm acquires even clearer borders when one considers Solana's statements about the EU-US relationship: "ours is a partnership of democracies, for democracy" (2003a, July 10). The basis of separation into the inside and outside is well outlined by Solana when he states that "our common mission [the EU's and the US'] is to defend and expand the boundaries of a stable, durable and peaceful liberal democracy; *to share with others* the rights and opportunities we enjoy" (2003b, July 10, emphasis added). Bono claims that the way threats are presented in the ESS corresponds to their reading by the Bush administration. Critically, she underlines that if insecurity is understood solely in a hermetically sealed-off manner—such as when the causes of poverty are linked to the "internal structural problems of the developing countries"—then the wider structural issues—for instance, the international economic system and/or the interventionism of some Western governments—are by default suspended from discussion (2006, 158).

The responsibility to become a global actor is a prominent discourse reiterated by Solana. For example, "now that we have constructed a European Union *we have to be a player in the international field*, the international arena and for that we have to have diplomatic capabilities, crisis management capabilities, trade capabilities, economic capabilities and also military capabilities" (Solana 2003, February 24). Or: "our publics and our global partners *expect us* to have an effective and clear policy on issues of international importance" (Solana 2003, March 24), and "we have to organise our defense not to be independent of, but because we have responsibilities" (Solana 2003, April 28). In articulating the EU's global role, a particular vision is advanced: "globalisation brings more freedom and wealth, but *if not properly managed* it can also generate new frustrations. This new context underlines the need for more effective collective security through a common appreciation of the major challenges facing us" (Solana 2003, November 12; emphasis added); "we have a duty to assume our responsibilities for security – to our citizens, to our neighbours and, more widely for global security" (Solana 2003, November 26). These examples illustrate how responsibility to become a global actor stems from "the voices of the self" as opposed to "the voices of others" (see Muppidi 2004, 60). In this sense, one of the largest structural imbalances—portrayed as a natural state of affairs—becomes the present ordering of the global arena, where the role of "a proper manager" of the international field is the prerogative of a spatio-temporally sensitive "we" (see Rengger 2000, 127).

In sum, the discursive backbone surrounding operation Artemis conveys a conceptualisation of the CSDP that is dominated by concerns about the tools and coordination dynamics of peacebuilding, whereas the philosophy of peacebuilding is both muted and taken for granted. But also, and very importantly, it becomes evident how (the substance of) peacebuilding is a matter for a specific group of actors, while those undergoing it are portrayed as passive recipients.

Multiple Others

In the EU's discourse, the local actors[13] with whom the EU engages are more often than not seen in an undifferentiated and largely unproblematic way. For example, one of the main interlocutors on the ground is envisaged as follows:

> The missions [ESDP in the field] aim to help the authorities on the ground to deal with problems themselves. They are designed and implemented in a spirit of partnership and are aimed at ensuring *that eventually these communities* take responsibility for their own security. (Solana 2003, May 7; emphasis added)

In this way, Solana identifies the main partners for the EU in conducting CSDP missions and places the final "burden" of their success on their shoulders. It is imperative to register that when Solana refers to the partners on the ground, he predominantly refers to the authorities (i.e. the elite). This indicates that the social contract is perceived in rather idealistic terms, which is very problematic, as in the states where conflict has ruptured the relationship between the state apparatus and the people, it should not be seen as a priori functioning.[14]

Beyond representing the local as the elite, the local is "silenced" and more often than not conveyed as the whole standing for a part (*totum pro parte*), whereby the distinctness of different actors might be destroyed: e.g. as ordinary people (Solana 2003, January 15) or as innocent people (Solana 2003, March 18). The instances when this portrayal appears in more variegated registers are usually related to imminent deployment albeit even then to a limited degree. The key distinction that is made in the EU's discourse is between the generic and the vulnerable others. The generic other is the one who is the perpetrator of new risks and threats. To a large extent, the CSDP was not about making peace with/for others, it was about securing peace *for* the EU and Europe. This is perceptible from the way the strategic objectives within the draft ESS are set (see Solana 2003, June 18; Solana 2003, June 20). The other group inhabiting the imagined "outside" of the EU/Europe is named as the vulnerable group (i.e. the victims who need help). In a number of instances, a crude division is made that associates the ability to help, or envisage solutions exclusively with the international community (*yang*), whereas the *yin* of this equation are the developing countries/conflict-affected societies, who are portrayed in rather simplistic and passive overtones. For instance:

> Chris Patten and I have worked to achieve a comprehensive approach to security in the Western Balkans. Our approach links the Stability and Association Agreements, trade, and development, with judicial, police and military instruments *to rebuild peaceful and stable societies.* (Solana 2003, May 21; emphasis mine)

The nub of the problem lies in the overly dichotomous and hermetic portrayal of the imagined *us* vs. *them*, which effectively forecloses any discussion about the structure of the international system and the part it plays in a particular state of affairs. Further, the simplistic treatment of various local actors is strikingly revealed in Solana's address at a public meeting of the UN Security Council, when he refers to two groups on the local level as: (i) "negative forces/warring factions/enemies of peace", i.e. spoilers of the peace effort; and (ii) the Congolese people and their leaders who want peace (2003, July 18). Occasionally, other local actors are mentioned, but usually this is done as part of the CSDP's success narrative, that is, by referring to the ways in which these actors (e.g. NGOs) have been enabled/assisted.[15]

As a concluding thought, the script for peace that is put forth argues that "the best protection for our security is a world of well-governed democratic states" (ESS 2003, 10). This threadbare argument has a tendency to evaporate, since the "grand recipe" that defines it is highly contested and, if closely investigated, opens the door to many problems (incl. ethico-political) that do not render themselves to an easy solution. This is so because the path to "well-governed democratic states" tends to be authored by the IC (see the above examples) and thus is (i) limited to its view (which is introduced as unquestionable), and (ii) based on certain assumptions which, although seemingly law-like, are extensively debated in the field of peace and conflict studies since they do not easily render themselves to one right answer. As has been illustrated throughout this analysis, there are a number of inconsistencies in the EU's discourse that potently explain why this is the case. For instance, the fact that the relationship between the EU and the recipient state is painted in unequal terms implies that the substance of democracy is hardly locally owned, but imported in a way the EU sees right. This is especially clear when the EU's arguments take an array of conflictive/inconsistent routes: e.g. "we will bring peace", yet the final responsibility rests with the local actors. It seems that there is a fine line between saving strangers and eradicating strangeness, which is not easy to mediate, as demonstrated by the EU. Especially when democracy is conveyed with the words "to stabilise" and "normalise", which indicate that rather than democracy, the interventions aim to achieve a state of sta-bility (i.e. putting a stop to physical violence). Importantly, this stance is very similar to the findings of Pace with regard to the Commission pro-grammes (2009, 42) where the end state is not democracy but "stability and [economic] prosperity". Crucially, this begs the oft-raised question: for whom are these interventions conceived? As Pace argues, in the case of the Commission, "the ultimate objective of these initiatives [e.g., the ENP] is securing the EU's own concerns about (in)migration, security, and stability rather than 'transformation' in the MENA" (2009, 45). A similar logic seems to reverberate through the ESS and more generally the CSDP discourse.

Significant Others

For the most part, Solana's discourse is directed to its significant others, who are seen as key figures in recognising the proposed new role for the EU, i.e. its *becoming* of an actor that is able, similarly to the UN and NATO, to offer peace support operations (PSOs). Consequently, this part sets out to query how these actors are envisaged and the importance of that to the EU's self-image. Interestingly, the extent to which the EU adopts certain principles of other actors is important, yet perhaps even more intriguing is the fact that by subscribing to certain approaches, the EU inevitably renegotiates them, creating hybridisation on this level. Thus, it is interesting to enquire to what extent the international consensus on peacebuilding exists.

In generic terms, the EU constructs the entity of international community with which the EU identifies. Solana asserts on a number of occasions that it is the EU's responsibility to contribute to the international community's efforts (2003, March 20). This notion is used very loosely to label the efforts of a varied bunch of actors on international/regional levels, with the assumption that these actors share a common understanding of peacebuilding and work in tandem with one another without any problems. Thus, the label "international community" is used strategically as a legitimising clause—carrying the overtone of "might is right". However, once this category is disaggregated, it is possible to take note of how the international community becomes a diverse and contested reference point.

The biggest authority, in the EU's eyes, on the subject of building peace is the UN, as becomes evident from recurrent references to it. For example, "strengthening the United Nations, equipping it to fulfil its responsibilities and to act effectively, must be a European priority" (Solana 2003, June 18; Solana 2003, June 20; GAERC 2003, July 21) and is seen as one of the primary tasks for the EU. Moreover, Solana underscores that "the fundamental framework of international relations is the UN Charter" (2003, June 18). The result is that the UN is granted an unquestioned and a largely omnipotent character (see esp. Solana 2003, April 20). Equally, it appears that constant references to the UN function as an attempt to legitimise the EU's new international agency. To be seen having military capabilities is a fairly big step for the EU as a formerly purportedly civilian power, so adherence to the UN rules (supposedly embodying a widespread consensus) is a safeguard against possible accusations of aggression, imperialism, etc. Simultaneously, the EU is arguing for a broad multilateral cooperation, which introduces the dynamic of creating peace together. According to Solana, "even a strengthened MONUC cannot do all that is required in Bunia, alone and without assistance" (2003, July 21). Thus, though there is an explicit deference to the UN's authority on the matter of peacebuilding, there also seems to be, in parallel, a wish to re-negotiate this authority into *co*-authority.[16]

One of the central dialogue partners that the EU discourses reveal is its former self, meaning that the EU is engaging in what Diez calls "temporal othering that is self-reflexive: it does not represent another group as a threat, but the self's own past" (2004, 320). However, the EU does not treat its former self as a threat per se, rather seeing it as an impetus for change, and that functions as a constant point of reference. The story of the present self is largely seen in progressive terms. The identity debate with the EU's past—however immediate that past might be—is captured in Solana's comments on the discord caused by the debate over Iraq: "I have the very profound sentiment that whatever has happened in the *last few days, the EU will reconstruct* not only the human relations between the leaders and more importantly the project that we have. And the project of the EU is a project of peace, the project for the stabilisation of the world" (2003, March 18; cf. Solana 2003, March 24).

By and large Solana adopts the label "we", or the institutional reference of "the EU" to talk about the CSDP efforts. This is a strategic move to construct a united and common stand of the EU in its CSDP activities— "the EU is more than the sum of its parts" (Solana 2003, May 7).[17] In a similar sense, Solana asserts the actorness of the EU by saying that "the EU is going to continue working with determination in order to make possible stability in the world" (2003, March 18). Apart from using the label "we" to communicate the common policy of the EU, and thus construct a common identity, for Solana this has another relevance. Drew and Sorjonen (1997) identify what they call person references as a means of enacting institutional identity: "participants may display their orientation to their acting as incumbents of an institutional role ... by using a personal pronoun which indexes their institutional identity rather than their personal identity" (quoted in Benwell and Stokoe 2006, 94). The most common forms of person references are the first person plurals "we" and "us" (ibid.). Referring back to the Iraqi question and the rift that had caused between the EU member states, a number of Solana's "we-s" are an attempt to suture together the common in the EU. Thus, it is not a pronouncement of a state of affairs—rather it is a rhetorical construction project in progress.

The member states of the EU are mentioned strategically either (i) to carve out the reasons for acting together and the pressing need to do so (e.g. "today's complex problems cannot be tackled by any single country" [Solana 2003, June 18]) or (ii) to maintain that the EU is acting as one (e.g. the EU is more than the sum of its parts [Solana 2003a, July 10]), although this is often nothing more than a misnomer for a call to become an entity that is able to speak more successfully with one voice. The most interesting aspect of Solana's discourse about the EU and/or member states is the consistency with which the argument for more action, more responsibility on the EU's part is advanced. To make this discursive trap (see Schimmelfennig 2001) more pressing, Solana refers to multiple instances that appear to demand more action, new roles, a unified voice, as in this abstract argument that "we have to do more if we are to be an important player" (Solana 2003, July 11), or that it is the "citizens of this continent" who demand a more capable Europe/the EU (ibid.), while "non-European countries" are also calling on the EU. In addition, Solana refers to the American criticism of Europe as not doing enough on defence (2003a, July 10). Furthermore, Solana argues that because the world has become more globalised, we have global problems and those need "common solutions" (ibid.), by way of reinforcing the international community and especially the UN: "effective alliances and partnerships need effective capabilities, to which all members contribute" (Solana 2003b, July 10).[18] Notice that with these reasons Solana is carving out a place for the EU within the IC ranks.

The United States (US) is referred to as the key authority speaking on behalf of the transatlantic relationship. Owing to that, Solana makes great efforts to reconcile and reassure the EU-US relationship that due to the Iraqi issue brought about a difference of perspective among some member states and the US. This instance made explicit the *punctuated* equilibrium that exists between the two camps, i.e. the US and the EU but also among the member states' allegiances vis-à-vis the US and the EU approach. Thus, for the most part Solana engages in a prudent tactic of convincing the audience of a revived and unproblematic partnership. For instance, the following idea is a leitmotif of the discourse on the US: "acting together the US and Europe remain the most powerful alliance for progress towards a more secure and just world" (2003, June 30). In terms similar to drawing the UN into the effective multilateralism discourse, the US also becomes part of the same discursive trap (cf. Schimmelfennig 2001). Although Solana emphasises the importance of common purpose, he does not believe that one can just assimilate two different mindsets that easily, hinting that "we have also to be able to accept that in some cases we can have honest disagreements" (Solana 2003, June 30). Importantly, by reiterating the commitment to common purpose, Solana engages in reframing the relationship. This is clearly the case when Solana argues that "what we [the US and the EU/Europe] were split over was not the disarming of

Saddam but *how to* achieve it" (2003, July 11). In an earlier statement, a similar position is put forth: "our differences [between the EU and the US] have often been sharpest over the question of using force" (Solana 2003a, July 10). The way Solana represents the issue, however, raises the question whether *how to* intervene is just a technical issue and not as important as the question of whether to intervene in the first place.

NATO is mentioned mostly in passing, as in the ESS draft: "NATO is an important expression of this [transatlantic] relationship" (Solana 2003, June 20). It seems that NATO's name comes up in very functional ways: i.e. when Solana refers to the EU's main achievements (see Solana 2003, June 30) where NATO's input was useful. Importantly, the relationship between NATO and the EU is defined in pragmatic terms: "no one questions the fact that NATO is the forum for our common security. Within it, our role is defined by operations for the handling of crises, not directed towards war but towards the attempt to guarantee peace" (Solana 2003, July 11).

In sum, the most easily distinguishable entities that resurface constantly in Solana's discourse are the multitude of *we*-s and the international community; however, they appear to mean and include/exclude different actors at any given time. In most cases, "we" is employed when Solana talks about the EU. If this "we" is extended beyond the EU, it is used in contexts where it also comprises either the Europeans and/or the "significant others" (e.g. the US, NATO, the UN). Thus, all in all, the "we" refers to the Western actors, with the effect of ironing out the differences these actors may have, and simultaneously circumscribing the silenced "them" that do not seem to fit into the "we".

TELLING AND ACTING ARTEMIS

to save strangers but not to cure their 'strangeness'. (Pugh 2012)

Whatever ethics is precisely, it is a discourse that articulates what we should do.

The challenge is to acknowledge the other as other and not to, implicitly or explicitly, in the very act of recognition, make them conform to our expectations of what are acceptable ways to life. (Zehfuss 2009, 99, 105, respectively)

To utilise the telling and acting analytical model, the EU's discourses on peacebuilding are further divided loosely into three groups: (i) discourses before deployment (as a representation of telling), (ii) discourses during deployment (as a representation of acting), and (iii) discourses after deployment (a return to telling). The aim of this endeavour is to provide a more nuanced picture of how the identity construction process works and to probe the (in)consistencies of the telling–acting relationship. Discourses on peacebuilding are linked to the academic debates about different ways of approaching responses to conflicts. In crude terms, these are polarised between the problem-solving and the critical approaches, thus creating two opposing semantic fields concerned with peacebuilding.[19] The difference between them lies in the move from descriptive accounts (Bellamy et al. 2004) to more critical accounts problematising, inter alia, the questions of who does peacebuilding and how, for whom peace is designed or intended (see Richmond 2011, 15).

(i). Before Deployment

Interviewer: What do you understand by global responsibility?

Solana: So we have long been a global power. What we just have not been hitherto, however, is a military player. But this is what we must become, if we wish to defend our values (2003, June 12).

The idea of this section is not to provide an exhaustive list of activities or values that underpin the CSDP, but rather to critically discuss both the elements and the nature of peacebuilding that Solana et al. introduce in the context of Artemis.

Artemis, following Solana (2003, June 4), identifies three core activities that constitute the EU's first autonomous military operation. These three elements, if further contextualised, offer revealing insights. First, it is stated that "the atrocities perpetrated in the region" constituted "one of the main reasons of our [the EU's] quick reaction to the request of Kofi Annan" (ibid.). It is further argued that "we [the general audience Solana is addressing] are facing a humanitarian crisis", and that "*time is therefore of essence*" (ibid.; emphasis added). The way Solana frames the situation and subsequently the EU's reaction to the crisis leaves an impression that it was indeed a timely response, whereas in "reality", the only things timely about the EU's reaction were responding (in the affirmative) to the UN's request and the rapid deployment (Howorth 2007, 233–234). According to some NGO reports about the state of affairs on the ground, although there was an extremely precarious situation at the time of speaking, the situation did in fact require attention much earlier than it received any discursive coverage.[20] Thus, acting timely needs to be qualified with the question "timely for whom?"

Secondly, another argument for intervention rests on the more persistent urge of the EU, as envisaged by Solana, to become militarily capable. This need is given significantly more attention in the EU's discourses on peacebuilding than any other theme. The development of military capabilities needs to be qualified with the question of who benefits from their deployment. For instance, the Human Rights Watch (HRW) reports that "until mid-2002, the European Union (EU) proved largely ineffective in influencing developments in DRC because leading member states were divided over which side to support" (2003). In a similar vein, Turner argues that one of the "lessons" of Artemis was that "France is willing to practice geopolitics behind a screen of humanitarianism. That is, its motivation apparently was in part to consolidate its influence in Kinshasa rather than helping war victims in Ituri" (2007, 159). Trenchantly, a number of authors reached the conclusion that Artemis served the EU's own interests (or its member states') rather than benefitting anyone else (see, e.g., Olsen 2009, 245–246).

Thirdly, although one of the stated goals of Artemis was to improve the humanitarian situation, the starting point for that was the commonplace acknowledgement that the political elite represented the views of the locals. This clearly reflects that the EU understands peacebuilding in its more traditional sense, as described by Bellamy et al. (2004). Yet, ostensibly this operation differs from the traditional peacekeeping efforts of the Cold War era in the sense that it alludes to the concept of "responsibility to protect" (R2P),[21] with one of the cited reasons for intervention being the grave humanitarian situation (see the discussion above). However, in this case it can be argued that humanitarianism serves as a veneer that "has mainly emblematic status as a legitimising principle attached to PSOs [peace support operations]" (see Pugh 2005, 49–50).

Solana emphasises the limited character of the operation (2003, June 4), and that it should not be seen as a full-fledged operation in its own right (e.g. "the EU force is not going to substitute the MONUC, it will provide a bridging element", ibid.). Framing it in this way is a prudent move, for if Artemis creates an impression of a stopgap measure, this is entirely justified because it was intended as such from the beginning. However, this logic seems to be misguided in view of the question of *who peace is for*. It seems that a number of authors assess the EU's efforts in terms of the EU's internal developments, forgetting that these do have an effect on the ground. Thus, from a more critical perspective, this criterion for assessing missions seems to be entirely flawed and tautological—something that escapes the attention of less critically minded analysts. For example, Howorth echoes the internal logic of assessing Artemis as follows: "an *impartial* assessment suggests that the mission, which involved rapid force projection to a distance of 6500 kilometres into unknown and non-permissive terrain, was a success" (2007, 233; emphasis added). In relation to the external dimension of evaluation (i.e. asking "who peace is for?") and to the NGO reports that castigated Artemis, Howorth responds (2007, 234): "these criticisms, which were also aimed at the UN itself, are based, to some extent on a misunderstanding of the terms of reference of the mission, whose mandate was strictly limited to the area around Bunia".

The three articulated reasons for embarking on operation Artemis—the humanitarian argument, the supporting the UN argument and the argument that the EU should become a military power—beg the question of who Artemis was for: the EU's institutional purposes or the people of the DRC? If it was for the people, then was it for the locals or the elites? Although the EU did moderately improve the situation on the ground, it becomes apparent, once this discourse of limited progress is contextualised and the common-sense categories of legitimate responses investigated—also keeping in mind the subject position of the speaker—that the EU's contribution was rather meagre indeed. It does offer a more sophisticated response to conflicts than the traditional peacekeeping paradigm, although some elements of the first generation can be detected easily, i.e. the unproblematic relationship envisaged between the elite and the locals, or the stabilisation discourse that offers to place a temporary lid on the conflict for three months and then hands it over to the UN to come up with more long-term solutions.

Although the presented analysis already portrays an array of argumentative strategies, it is still crucial to reiterate them here to exemplify both how certain avenues of activities get legitimised, and the meanings these argumentative strategies carry. Firstly, Solana argues that "now that we have constructed a European Union we have to be a player in the international field ... and for that we have to have diplomatic capabilities, trade capabilities, economic capabilities and also military capabilities and that's what we are trying to do" (2003, February 24). The latter signifies a logic that is essentialist by its nature: (i) the existence of the EU presupposes an international role and, perhaps more importantly, and (ii) this role is not something that emerges from its actual needs but rather from a preconceived definition of what an international player is/ought to be like.[22] In other words, the EU's response to the outside is mechanical and predetermined, i.e. rather than the EU understanding the needs of its context, the context should comply with the needs of the EU. Secondly, this logic of "because the EU, there should be x, y, and z" is supplemented by the argument that the EU aspires for an "effective and clear policy on issues of international importance" (Solana 2003, March 24) because it is expected by its peers and its publics. Thirdly, this aspired role of the EU is also needed because "nobody alone can resolve these complicated problems that we are facing now" (Solana 2003, April 3)—not even the US with its more unilateralist approach (Solana 2003, February 24). Thus, regrettably, "the question of what peace might be expected to look like from the inside (from within the conflict environment) is given less credence than the way the international community and its organisations and actors desire to see it from the outside" (Richmond 2005, 91). Albeit this section offered only a cross-section of the argumentative techniques used by the EU to legitimise the process of becoming a peacebuilder, it is a telling one, as it provides an insight to the EU's displayed mindset, which seems to be of an instrumental, context-distant and technical kind.

(ii) During Deployment

The aim of this section is to map the way the EU has represented its actions on the ground through discourses. In other words, I will enquire *what the EU said it did* versus *what the EU said it would do* (the telling part) in the frames of Artemis. This is a worthwhile venture as it problematises the link between telling and acting by asking: How can one gain knowledge from these two stages of telling and acting, and in what ways do these different knowledges matter; to what extent do discourses get materialised, and if they do not, how is that dealt with (e.g. is it ironed out, silenced, explained?), and finally, what are the consequences of this all to the multiple and significant others? The above questions prove particularly salient as it has been noted that the way actors understand conflicts, and how they deploy particular discursive frames to voice those understandings has a direct correlation to their subsequent responses (e.g. Autesserre 2010).

Investigating the relationship between telling and acting here reveals that most of the activities that are reported in this stage are connected to what was promised earlier.[23] However, the importance of telling–acting resurfaces if one enquires who does the speaking: i.e. who represents actions. From different sources, one can receive varied narratives on what/how something was done. It seems that the consistent EU narrative on the equilibrium between words and deeds is disrupted as soon as one engages with a variety of sources. In case of the EU's own narrative, the inconsistencies are minor compared to those revealed in other external sources, such as the UN, various NGO reports and various secondary accounts (e.g. Autesserre's work); therefore, in order to offer a thorough account of the relationship between telling and doing, it is necessary to go beyond the official discourse dominating the EU's semantic field.[24] On a more general level, the words-deeds relationship can be and is disrupted once the approach behind the presented discourse is explored, thus disruptions may be found between different problem-solving approaches, and between different critical approaches, although most likely the gap between the problem-solving and more critical approaches is the widest.

Below I will probe the ways in which the words-deeds relationship is addressed by the EU's official actors and assess the implications of that. There is a considerable effort to frame Artemis as a success story—e.g. the deployment of Artemis "confirms the European resolve to act" (Solana 2003, June 30). For instance, in mid-June Solana was already arguing that the launching of Artemis was a success; moreover, he said that the decision in itself was an indication of success (2003, June 18). Thus, at this stage as well, it seems that the EU's evaluation of Artemis was based on internal concerns—i.e. the fact that it was able to launch an operation in Africa and on such short notice, that this was the EU's first autonomous operation (without reliance on NATO's resources); that the EU is, after all, a global power. Other categories (e.g. the external dimension) of the evaluation seem to have been largely sidelined.

The remainder of this section investigates how and what is reported as being done in the frames of Artemis. The recurrent motif that precedes almost every investigation into the evaluation of Artemis is the lack of intention to pacify the whole region—that the EU's mandate was limited in both time and scope (see, e.g., Solana 2003, June 18). In addition, the main tenets of traditional peacekeeping are addressed (see Bellamy et al. 2004), such as getting consent for the intervention from conflict parties: Solana reports having consulted the presidents of the countries involved and confirmed their intent to cooperate (Solana 2003, June 18). Further-more, Solana argues that the stabilisation of Ituri rests on the wider peace efforts in the DRC and the establishment of relevant institutions (ibid.). Note how Solana evades the responsibility of Artemis by representing "the road to peace" in this way. Overall in 2003, it appears that the CSDP is framed as an aspect of the EU's and other actors' wider effort, which is telling, as it seems to be used strategically to diffuse responsibility. Another aspect of this "wider effort" frame is the articulation of the CSDP as an *aspect of the wider effort* of the EU (see, e.g., Solana 2003, January 15). Gourlay (2004) argues that despite the many rhetorical assertions about this integrated approach, the state of affairs shows a discernible divorce (mostly in terms of coordination) between the Commission and CSDP tools, espe-cially when it comes to the civilian side. Finally, Artemis is framed as the first try of the EU's "CSDP Lab" (e.g. 2003, June 18)—a prudent tactic to counter the imagined critique already in its genesis.

According to Solana, Artemis "succeeded in stopping the massacres in Bunia and helped to relaunch the peace process which had stalled in Kin-shasa" (2003, July 18). Moreover, Solana reports that the "rapid deploy-ment of the European multinational force halted this dangerous downward spiral [in Ituri region] and made it possible to relaunch the negotiations which had been bogged down for weeks" (ibid.). What is evident is a gen-eral desire to present the operation as having had a positive impact, even where there are serious grounds to question that. For example, Solana argues that "after the minor incidents which marked the beginning of the operation, and which resulted in the force having to use its weapons, the situation rapidly stabilised" (ibid.).[25] However, reportedly, operation Artemis included some more serious incident(s), such as the misconduct by the French troops in the DRC that surfaced on the EU radar only in 2008 because an EU parliamentarian raised the issue.[26] In line with regard to the "achievements" reported above, Solana (2003, July 18) argues that "the improvement in security conditions is obvious" and the positive indicators for that are, as follows:

i. the humanitarian organisations are able to travel outside Bunia to visit people they could not reach before,

ii. there is a regular influx of refugees into the city (1000 to 1500 per day).

iii. and the Ituri interim administration is again able to conduct some of
   its activities.

The problem with these indicators is their stopgap nature and thus their
failure to tackle underlying problems in a meaningful way. Thus, observing
the narrative of how and what exactly was done, it becomes obvious that the
EU's actions were very myopic since they did not address any of the more
substantial issues. For example, the security envisaged is of a traditional
state-centred kind, hardly connected to human security. Hence, the actions
echo the EU's views on what needs to be done, rather than the needs of the
locals. This is particularly clear looking at how throughout the operation the
mandate remains a fixed document that is interpreted in a very minimalist
way. What is in sight is the end date—not the end state. For instance, at the
end of the operation, Solana comments "while the situation in the rest of
the province of Ituri and in other regions of the country remains a cause for
concern, in Bunia, security and living conditions for the population as well
as for the organisations which assist it have improved significantly" (2003,
September 1). This serves as another indication of creating a temporary
safe haven that collapses as soon as the EU's troops are out. Thus, the
question of what kind of peace the EU helped to create, if we take into
account that its operation was a bridging one, remains fuzzy. Clearly, it was
not well connected to the contextual realities. Perhaps it does echo Patten's
call that "the central element in any security strategy for Europe must be to
ensure that the EU itself continues to prosper and to develop" (EP debate
2003, June 18).

(iii) After Deployment

The most prominent telling technique, representation, employed after
the operation, gives rise to the overarching mobilisation discourse (with a
strong *entrapment moment* to it, à la Schimmelfennig 2001). It frames the
present state of affairs in a way that suggests urgency of becoming an actor
in peacebuilding. This involves not solely mobilising the member states, but
also actively and openly negotiating the norms of peacebuilding that are
produced by other authoritative voices. Thus, on a more general note, there
is a push towards a multilateralist order, in which the EU is envisaged to play
an equal role. Furthermore, this order is based on (the UN's) rules. The
guardians of those rules are none other than the "most powerful" players

(cf. Caplan 2005). Unilateralism is viewed with a raised eyebrow, together with a solely militarist approach; what is advocated is "paying attention to the causes of threats as to their consequences" (Solana 2003, November 26; ESS 2003, December 12). Representations of threats in the ESS (2003) address not only the significant others—there is a distinction made between security providers/recipients—but also a much wider audience, if one considers the many speech acts that Solana has issued throughout the year to mould the public opinion.[27]

It is immediately discernible that the discourse in the aftermath of the operation Artemis has grown in its self-congratulatory tone (cf. Presidency 2003, November 24). Unsurprisingly, Artemis has become a story of success.[28] The EU considers two key aspects after the end of Artemis: (i) the external dimension and (ii) the internal dimension of the operation. According to the former, Artemis achieved its goal of re-establishing security for the town of Bunia. This, in turn, has allowed for the return of refugees, the restart of economic activities, the strengthening of the authority of the Interim Ituri administration, and the widening of the scope of MONUC activities. These conditions enabled the deployment of a strengthened MONUC. Reportedly, the transition from Artemis to MONUC went smoothly (see Solana 2003, October 3–4).[29] It is also stated by Solana that the stabilisation of the situation in Bunia has had a positive impact beyond Bunia (ibid.). This list of successes on the ground is accompanied by the manifold internal success indicators, e.g. "quick decision-making and rapid deployment", "the force on the ground was genuinely multinational", etc. (ibid.). Overall, the space given to the internal indicators seems to outweigh the space for external ones. This, in turn, also points to the undue prominence given to the internal criteria for evaluating peace operations. However, perhaps even more important than the fact that the internal metrics of success are more valorised than the external, it becomes apparent that the way "problems" are framed considerably affects the response to, and attitude towards, the said problems later on. Here, in particular, one can take note of how a certain idea of security is put forward together with a certain representation of the problems.

In summary, it is possible to see how the telling and acting of operation Artemis go hand in hand in the EU's discourse, and how it is finally mobilised in the name of *credibility*. It becomes a particular self-representation governing the semantic field of security and defence and thus representing a specific kind of governance. Essentially, the discursive peak point of Artemis can be seen in the "conceptual legacy" it has bequeathed to the CSDP.

Conclusion: Building Peace vs. Building an Image

This analysis goes well beyond Artemis as it taps into the wider discourses on CSDP in 2003. On a more prominent note, this chapter offers some insight using the telling and acting model to provide a particularly comprehensive framework for a more critical take on the CSDP identity. Moreover, it ponders the issues that accompany this model (esp. the epistemological), and how the EU itself mobilises the telling–acting in its CSDP identity construction.

Below, the aim is not to summarise *in toto* the above analysis, but to focus on a couple of key moments. The question of *who* the CSDP is *for* was kept in mind throughout the analysis. Based on the forging of the CSDP identity in 2003, it seems that it is more for the EU itself, as well as the recognised partners of the EU, rather than for the local actors, or, for that matter, for the conflict theatre. Crucially, the EU seems to be in a paradoxical situation, as it sees, on the one hand, the added value of the CSDP in the fact that it can offer something different (or even unique, according to Solana), whereas on the other hand, it goes to great pains to align itself with the already established hegemonic voice(s) on peacebuilding (esp. with the UN). To muddy the waters even further, the EU's discourse both praises and subverts (in more subtle ways) the establishments of peacebuilding already in place. The EU aspires for a less militarised approach than that of the US and, by extension, NATO.

Having a more comprehensive view of the CSDP identity also sheds some light on how the EU affects/is affected by the character of the global "enterprise" of peacebuilding. As argued in the theory section, it is important to bear in mind how in subscribing to something, an actor simultaneously negotiates it. The year 2003 has seen as a proactive campaign to change how peacebuilding is imagined. For instance, the EU argued for a multilateralist world order. This, unfortunately, still largely reflects an elitist view, taking only a step (or half) away from the UN. Perhaps more energy is put into arguing against the unilateralist and forceful approaches (with the US seen as the target). In the end, this negotiation is effective in the sense that it tries to eradicate a particular unilateralism. However, the question remains whether the substitution offers much difference? In fact, the global "enterprise" of peacebuilding seems to be instituted by an international community claiming to possess a privileged knowledge on how to build peace. Note that in most cases, it is instituted for the sole purpose of legitimacy. Thus, the tensions which become most visible in the EU's dialogue with its significant others are an apposite depiction of the unease that permeates the global "enterprise" of peacebuilding.

A better understanding of the CSDP identity provides insight into how the CSDP activities fit into the EU's conceptualisation of peacebuilding. This issue has not received a conclusive treatment in the analysis presented here, yet some initial remarks made above can serve as a starting point. Here, the aim was to investigate to what extent the principles that guide the CSDP and the European Commission in peacebuilding overlap/diverge. Although during 2003, the ways in which these two entities saw one another were still being defined, the main principles guiding their behaviour were already discernible. The common thread running through their discourses was that responses to conflicts are more to do with the EU's own security than the needs on the conflict theatre with which they engage. The importance of the EU's own security notwithstanding, this sheds some light on the inherent limits of the still ongoing project of the EU's peacebuilding framework (EUPF) (cf. Björkdahl et al. 2011). Another problem with the way the EUPF is imagined by the CSDP is the strategic use of the label "wider effort". This concern arises namely because the EU has used the label to confound the debate over success. By saying that the CSDP's contribution is but an element of the whole peace effort, the EU effectively manages to evade accountability.

The significance of the operation Artemis lies in the way that it is discursively mobilised as a success story in articulating a particular, i.e. "credible", CSDP identity. In this way, this book offers both a valuable starting point for investigating the meaning(s) behind the CSDP and the ways in which the hegemonical discourse (the one analysed here) provides a particular guide for the CSDP.

NOTES

1. For an overview of the EU's security and defence field's key documents in 2003 see, e.g., Missiroli (2003).
2. This sketch draws on the research of Severine Autesserre (see also Hellmüller 2013; Vlassenroot and Raeymaekers 2004; ICG 2003, June 13).

3. This way of approaching the contextual terrain is akin to Hansen (2006), Jabri (2007), Autesserre (2007, 2010, 2014), Hellmüller (2013), Dunn (2003), and Viktorova Milne (2009).

4. Notably, the works of Autesserre (esp. 2010, 2014), Hellmüller (2013, 2014a, b).

5. For an in-depth discussion of the context and a chronology of events see Autesserre (2010, esp. Ch. 2–4, 273–278 respectively). For an overview of the peace process, see Rogier (2004a, b).

6. As a caveat, the label "IC" is used as an analytical category and should not be taken as a term designating to a homogeneous entity (see Bliesemann de Guevara and Kühn 2009). Furthermore, the discourses I tap into reveal how the actors that arguably belong to this category actively employ this label and utilise it strategically to stress unity and legitimacy.

7. "During the Congolese wars and subsequent transition", as Autesserre observed throughout her research, "international actors were still quite unfamiliar with the theories and concepts that could have enabled them to grasp bottom-up dynamics of violence" (2010, 45).

8. Ituri is a district of Oriental Province located in the northeast of the DRC. Although violence continued there despite the signing of the peace settlements, as it did in other eastern provinces, it received international attention only in 2002–2003 when developments there—previously considered as a peaceful area—caught the attention of the UN (see Autesserre 2007). For detailed background information about the deployment of Artemis consult Ulriksen et al. (2004).

9. Bob van den Bos was a member of the European Liberal Democrat and Reform (ELDR) party—as of 2012 known as Alliance of Liberals and Democrats for Europe Party (ALDE)—in the European Parliament. See Hellmüller (2014a, 191–193) who sheds light on the main concepts that influenced the international peacebuilders' readings of the crisis in Congo.

10. For a more detailed overview refer to the EP debate (2003, May 15) and to the Council *Common Positions* (2001, May 14; 2003, May 8).

11. See in this context Autesserre's work (2010, 2014), Bono (2006), Dunn (2003), and Schlag (2012).

12. It leans towards an argument well known in the peace and conflict studies' circles that institutions come first and then the substance (e.g. democracy) (Presidency 2003, July 2; GAERC 2003, January 27; Paris 2004; Cousens and Kumar 2001).

13. See Richmond (2011, 14) for the problematisation of the way locals are represented.

14. To me, this way of relating to the local has become particularly clear both from the conducted discourse analysis and from presentations by/interactions with different IOs' operations or mission staff (COST meetings, 30 November 2011, 8–9 March 2012). For instance, at the

COST meeting on 30 November 2011, the former UN Special Representative, Victor Angelo, when asked what the Chadians thought of the UN/EU interventions there, automatically referred to his talks with the president of the country, as though there is an airtight correlation between the needs of the government and the needs of the people. This indicates that attitudes and needs of the people on the ground are routinely gathered from the elite level, which is an utterly problematic way to deal with conflict-affected places (cf. Berg 2009).

15. The aim of promoting the EU trickles down to the tactical level, e.g. in case of EUFOR Chad/CAR, the EU force commander, Jean-Philippe Ganascia, indicated that (on the one side) the importance of keeping a good relationship with the NGOs lie in the fact that they are important political stakeholders as they cover the EU's actions on the ground (Skype interview 20 March 2012).

16. This portrayal of a smooth cooperation has a number of cracks in it when studied more meticulously. For instance, Morsut argues that the EU's strive to be a global actor and thus to act independently clashes with its assist-help rhetoric towards the UN (2009).

17. Solana remarks on his everyday task of constructing the common in the frames of the CSDP: "My role as European HR for the CFSP confronts me on a daily basis with the need for a single European voice and a common point of view" (2003, March 31; also Solana 2002, February 19).

18. Schimmelfennig's idea of a discursive trap refers to the actors' rhetorical commitment to doing/being something, which makes any attempt to speak/act against this "promise" riddled with problems (2001).

19. Following Krzyzanowski (2010, 87), "the investigation of semantic fields has the aim of discovering the variety of arguments and themes … which are used in relation to different social and political concepts".

20. This misconception or downplaying of the conflict dynamics was characteristic not only of the EU but also other agents of the international community (see HRW 2003; also MSF 2003; ICG 13 June 2003).

21. Bellamy et al. report that in 2000 Kofi Annan assembled a panel of experts under Lakhdar Brahimi to discuss the future direction of UN peacekeeping (2004, 75–76). The fruit of that was the widely known Responsibility to protect report (accessible at: http://www.iciss.ca/report-en.asp).

22. Consider in this context the trio of roles (model-player-instrument) outlined in Barbé, Herranz-Surrallés and Natorski's work (2015).

23. The relationship between telling and acting becomes especially pertinent in the context of CSDP if one considers one of the guiding principles of Solana's (and by extension of the EU), which according to Cristina Gallach (Solana's Spokeswoman for 14 years), was "legitimacy by action". She further adds: "action and results were and continue to be the best – if not the only – way to win legitimacy for the EU" (2011, 13).

24. The limitation of this work is the fact that it does not include local voices in their originality but is regrettably forced to rely on secondary sources.
25. The use of force by Artemis is covered by the BBC News (see the news archives in 2003).
26. See the written question by Angelika Beer (Verts/ALE) to the Council (2008). This incident was more widely covered by the Swedish national television broadcaster in 2007 (http://svt.se/2.90352/1.1101022/prisoner_tortured_at_a_swedish_military_base_in_the_congo [the link no longer functions, last accessed 10 December 2011]). See also Polgreen (2008).
27. See Wagner (2005, 14–15) for a discussion about the CSDP and public opinion.
28. Note also to the many academics contributing towards framing Artemis as a success story, e.g. Hoebeke et al. (2007, 8).
29. The UN Peacekeeping Best Practices Unit in its report (2004) provides a much more critical account; see also Ulriksen et al. (2004) and Schlag (2012).

References

Autesserre, Séverine. 2007. "D. R. Congo: Explaining Peace Building Failures, 2003–2006." *Review of African Political Economy* 34 (113): 423–441. https://doi.org/10.1080/03056240701672510.

Autesserre, Séverine. 2010. *The Trouble with the Congo: Local Violence and the Failure of International Peacebuilding.* New York, NY: Cambridge University Press.

Autesserre, Séverine. 2014. *Peaceland: Conflict Resolution and the Everyday Politics of International Intervention.* New York, NY: Cambridge University Press.

Barbé, Esther, Anna Herranz-Surrallés, and Michał Natorski. 2015. "Contending Metaphors of the European Union as a Global Actor: Norms and Power in the European Discourse on Multilateralism." *Journal of Language and Politics* 14 (1): 18–40. https://doi.org/10.1075/jlp.14.1.02bar.

Beer, Angelika. 2008. "Written Question to the Council: Misbehaviour of French ESDP Soldiers During Artemis Operation in DRC (Bunia) in 2003." E-2057/08. http://www.europarl.europa.eu/sides/getDoc.do?pubRef=-//EP//TEXT+WQ+E-2008-2057+0+DOC+XML+V0//EN.

Bellamy, Alex J., and Paul Williams. 2004. "Introduction: Thinking Anew About Peace Operations." *International Peacekeeping* 11 (1): 1–15. https://doi.org/10.1080/1353331042000228427.

Bellamy, Alex J., Stuart Griffin, and Paul Williams. 2004. *Understanding Peacekeeping.* Cambridge: Polity Press.

Benwell, Bethan, and Elizabeth Stokoe. 2006. *Discourse and Identity.* Edinburgh: Edinburgh University Press.

Berg, Patrick. 2009. "EUFOR Tchad/RCA: The EU Serving French Interests." In *The EU as a Strategic Actor in the Realm of Security and Defence? A Systematic Assessment of ESDP Missions and Operations*, edited by Muriel Asseburg and Ronja Kempin, 57–69. Berlin: German Institute for International and Security Affairs (SWP). http://www.swp-berlin.org/fileadmin/contents/products/research_papers/2009_RP14_ass_kmp_ks.pdf.

Björkdahl, Annika, Stefanie Kappler, and Oliver Richmond. 2011. "The Emerging EU Peacebuilding Framework: Confirming or Transcending Liberal Peacebuilding?" *Cambridge Review of International Affairs* 24 (3): 449–469. https://doi.org/10.1080/09557571.2011.586331.

Bliesemann de Guevara, Berit, and Florian P. Kühn. 2009. "The 'International Community'—Rhetoric or Reality? Tracing a Seemingly Well-Known Apparition." *Sicherheit und Frieden/Security and Peace* 27 (2): 73–79. http://www.sicherheit-und-frieden.nomos.de/fileadmin/suf/doc/Aufsatz_SuF_09_02.pdf.

Bono, Giovanna. 2004. "The EU's Military Doctrine: An Assessment." *International Peacekeeping* 11 (3): 439–456. https://doi.org/10.1080/1353331042000249037.

Bono, Giovanna. 2006. "The Perils of Conceiving of EU Foreign Policy as a 'Civilising Force.'" *Internationale Politik und Gesellschaft* 1: 150–163. http://library.fes.de/pdf-files/id/ipg/03647.pdf.

Caplan, Richard. 2005. "Who Guards the Guardians? International Accountability in Bosnia." *International Peacekeeping* 12 (3): 463–476. https://doi.org/10.1080/13533310500074549.

Council of the European Union (Council). 14 May 2001. "Council Common Position 2001/374/CFSP of 14 May 2001 Concerning Conflict Prevention, Management and Resolution in Africa—Statement by the Danish Delegation." *Official Journal* L 132, 3–6.

Council of the European Union. 8 May 2003. "Council Common Position 2003/319/CFSP of 8 May 2003 Concerning European Union Support for the Implementation of the Lusaka Ceasefire Agreement and the Peace Process in the Democratic Republic of Congo (DRC) and Repealing Common Position 2002/203/CFSP." *Official Journal* L 115, 87–89.

Cousens, Elizabeth M., and Chetan Kumar, eds. 2001. *Peacebuilding as Politics: Cultivating Peace in Fragile Societies*. Boulder, CO: Lynne Rienner.

Diez, Thomas. 2004. "Europe's Others and the Return of Geopolitics." *Cambridge Review of International Affairs* 17 (2): 319–335. https://doi.org/10.1080/0955757042000245924.

Dunn, Kevin C. 2003. *Imagining the Congo: International Relations of Identity*. New York: Palgrave Macmillan.

Escobar, Arturo. 1995. *Encountering Development: The Making and Unmaking of the Third World*. Princeton, NJ: Princeton University Press.

European Parliament. 15 May 2003. "Democratic Republic of Congo—The Ituri Region." http://www.europarl.europa.eu/sides/getDoc.do?pubRef=-//EP//TEXT+CRE+20030515+ITEM-007+DOC+XML+V0//EN&language=BG.

European Parliament. 18 June 2003. "Security Strategy for the European Union, Including Implementation of the UN Programme to Combat the Illegal Trade in Light Weapons." http://www.europarl.europa.eu/sides/getDoc.do?pubRef=-//EP//TEXT+CRE+20030618+ITEM-007+DOC+XML+V0//EN&language=PL.

European Security Strategy (ESS). 2003. "A Secure Europe in a Better World—The European Security Strategy." Brussels. https://www.consilium.europa.eu/en/documents-publications/publications/european-security-strategy-secure-europe-better-world/.

GAERC (General Affairs and External Relations Council). 27 Januray 2003. "2482nd Council Meeting—External Relations." Brussels. http://europa.eu/rapid/press-release_PRES-03-8_en.htm?locale=en.

GAERC. 21 July 2003. "2522nd Council Meeting—External Relations." Brussels. http://europa.eu/rapid/press-release_PRES-03-209_en.htm.

Gallach, Cristina. 2011. "Preface and Personal Remarks." In *The High Representative for the EU Foreign and Security Policy—Review and Prospects*, edited by Gisela Müller-Brandeck-Bocquet, and Carolin Rüger, 11–16. Baden-Baden: Nomos.

Gourlay, Catriona. 2004. "European Union Procedures and Resources for Crisis Management." *International Peacekeeping* 11 (3): 404–421. https://doi.org/10.1080/1353331042000249019.

Hansen, Lene. 2006. *Security as a Practice: Discourse Analysis and the Bosnian War*. London: Routledge.

Hellmüller, Sara. 2013. "The Power of Perceptions: Localising International Peace-building Approaches." *International Peacekeeping* 20 (2): 219–232. https://doi.org/10.1080/13533312.2013.791570.

Hellmüller, Sara. 2014a. "A Story of Mutual Adaptation? The Interaction Between Local and International Peacebuilding Actors in Ituri." *Peacebuilding* 2 (2): 188–201. https://doi.org/10.1080/21647259.2014.910914.

Hellmüller, Sara. 2014b. "Que Signifie la Paix en République Démocratique du Congo." *Annuaire Français de Relations Internationales* XV: 657–671. http://www.afri-ct.org/IMG/pdf/Article_Hellmuller.pdf.

Hoebeke, Hans, Stéphanie Carette, and Koen Vlassenroot. 2007. *EU Support to the Democratic Republic of Congo*. Paris: Centre d'Etudes Stratégiques. http://www.egmontinstitute.be/eu-support-to-the-democratic-republic-of-congo-rapports-et-documents-2/.

Howorth, Jolyon. 2007. *Security and Defence Policy in the European Union*. Basingstoke: Palgrave Macmillan.

HRW (Human Rights Watch). 2003. *Ituri: 'Covered in Blood' Ethnically Targeted Violence in Northeastern DR Congo.* New York: HRW. https://www.hrw.org/sites/default/files/reports/DRC0703.pdf.

ICG. 13 June 2003. "Congo Crisis: Military Intervention in Ituri." *Africa Report No. 64.* Nairobi, New York, Brussels: ICG. https://www.crisisgroup.org/africa/central-africa/democratic-republic-congo/congo-crisis-military-intervention-ituri.

Jabri, Vivienne. 2007. *War and the Transformation of Global Politics.* Basingstoke: Palgrave Macmillan.

Joint UN-EU Declaration on Cooperation in Crisis Management. 24 September 2003. New York: UN Headquarters. http://europa.eu/rapid/press-release_PRES-03-266_en.pdf.

Krzyzanowski, Michal. 2010. *The Discursive Construction of European Identities: A Multi-Level Approach to Discourse and Identity in the Transforming European Union.* Frankfurt am Main: Peter Lang.

Kurowska, Xymena. 2008. "The Role of ESDP Operations." In *European Security and Defence Policy: An Implementation Perspective,* edited by Michael Merlingen and Rasa Ostrauskaite, 25–42. London: Routledge.

Kurowska, Xymena, and Thomas Seitz. 2011. "The EU's Role in International Crisis Management: Innovative Model or Emulated Script?" In *EU Conflict Prevention and Crisis Management: Roles, Institutions and Policies,* edited by Eva Gross and Ana E. Juncos, 17–31. London: Routledge.

Kuus, Merje. 2012. "Banal Huntingtonianism: Civilizational Geopolitics in Estonia." In *The Return of Geopolitics in Europe? Social Mechanisms and Foreign Policy Identity Crises,* edited by Stefano Guzzini, 174–191. Cambridge: Cambridge University Press.

Missiroli, Antonio, ed. 2003. "From Copenhagen to Brussels: European Defence: Core Documents, Vol. IV." Chaillot Paper No. 67. Paris: EUISS. https://www.iss.europa.eu/content/copenhagen-brussels-european-defence-core-documents-volume-iv.

Morsut, Claudia. 2009. "Effective Multilateralism? EU-UN Cooperation in the DRC, 2003–2006." *International Peacekeeping* 16 (2): 261–272. https://doi.org/10.1080/13533310802685836.

MSF (Médecins Sans Frontières). 2003. "Ituri: Unkept Promises? A Pretence of Protection and Inadequate Assistance." https://doctorswithoutborders.org/sites/default/files/2018-08/drc_report_07-25-2003.pdf.

Muppidi, Himadeep. 2004. *The Politics of the Global.* Minneapolis: University of Minnesota Press.

Olsen, Gorm Rye. 2009. "The EU and Military Conflict Management in Africa: For the Good of Africa or Europe." *International Peacekeeping* 16 (2): 245–260. https://doi.org/10.1080/13533310802685828.

Pace, Michelle. 2009. "Paradoxes and Contradictions in EU Democracy Promotion in the Mediterranean: The Limits of EU Normative Power." *Democratization* 16 (1): 39–58. https://doi.org/10.1080/13510340802575809.

Paris, Roland. 2004. *At War's End*. New York: Cambridge University Press.

Polgreen, Lydia. 2008. "Investigators in Congo Check Allegations That Peacekeepers Engaged in Torture." *The New York Times*, April 3. http://www.nytimes.com/2008/04/03/world/africa/03briefs-INVESTIGATOR_BRF.html.

Prashad, Vijay. 2007. *The Darker Nations: A People's History of the Third World*. New York: The New Press.

Presidency of the Council of EU. 20–21 March 2003. "Presidency Conclusions: European Council 20 and 21 March 2003." http://europa.eu/rapid/pressReleasesAction.do?reference=PRES/03/900&format=HTML&aged=1&language=EN&guiLanguage=en.

Presidency of the Council of EU. 19–20 June 2003. "Presidency Conclusions of the Thessaloniki European Council (19 and 20 June 2003)." 11638/03. http://www.consilium.europa.eu/uedocs/cms_data/docs/pressdata/en/ec/76279.pdf.

Presidency of the Council of EU. 20 June 2003. "Presidency Report to the European Council on EU External Action in the Fight Against Terrorism (Including CFSP/ESDP)." 11638/03. http://www.consilium.europa.eu/uedocs/cms_data/docs/pressdata/en/ec/76279.pdf.

Presidency of the Council of EU. 2 July 2003. "Statement on the Formation of the Transitional Government in the Democratic Republic of the Congo." Brussels. http://eu-un.europa.eu/articles/en/article_2511_en.htm.

Presidency of the Council of EU. 24 November 2003. "EU Presidency Statement—The Situation in the Central African Region (Summary)." http://www.eu-un.europa.eu/articles/en/article_3028_en.htm.

Pugh, Michael. 2005. "Peacekeeping and Critical Theory." In *Peace Operations and Global Order*, edited by Alex J. Bellamy and Paul Williams, 39–58. London: Routledge.

Pugh, Michael. 2012. "Political Economies of Conflict and Multinational Peace Operations." At a COST IS0805 Conference titled "EU and Multilateral Peace Operations: Assessing Options and Limits." Rome, 8 March.

Rengger, Nicholas. 2000. *International Relations, Political Theory and the Problem of Order*. London: Routledge.

Richmond, Oliver P. 2005. "UN Peacebuilding Operations and the Dilemma of the Peacebuilding Consensus." In *Peace Operations and Global Order*, edited by Alex J. Bellamy and Paul Williams, 83–101. London: Routledge.

Richmond, Oliver P. 2011. *A Post-Liberal Peace*. Abingdon: Routledge.

Rogier, Emeric. 2004a. "The Inter-Congolese Dialogue: A Critical Overview." In *Challenges of Peace Implementation: The UN Mission in the Democratic Repub-*

lic of Congo, edited by João Gomes Porto and Mark Malan, 25–42. Pretoria: Institute for Security Studies.

Rogier, Emeric. 2004b. "The Labyrinthine Path to Peace in the Democratic Republic of Congo." In "The Peace Process in the DRC: A Reader," by the African Security Analysis Programme, 1–23. Pretoria: Institute for Security Studies.

Schimmelfennig, Frank. 2001. "The Community Trap: Liberal Norms, Rhetorical Action, and the Eastern Enlargement of the European Union." *International Organization* 55 (1): 47–80. http://dx.doi.org/10.1162/002081801551414.

Schlag, Gabi. 2012. "Into the 'Heart of Darkness'—EU's Civilising Mission in the DR Congo." *Journal of International Relations and Development* 15 (3): 321–344. https://doi.org/10.1057/jird.2011.17.

Solana, Javier. 19 February 2002. "Intervention by Javier Solana on the Occasion of the Launch of CER Publication by Steven Everts 'Shaping An Effective EU Foreign Policy.'" Brussels. http://www.consilium.europa.eu/uedocs/cms_data/docs/pressdata/en/discours/69508.pdf.

Solana, Javier. 15 January 2003. "Interview Published by *Nezavisne Novine*." http://www.consilium.europa.eu/uedocs/cms_data/docs/pressdata/en/sghr_int/74176.pdf.

Solana, Javier. 24 February 2003. "Interview by Jonathan Freedland." *BBC Four*. http://www.consilium.europa.eu/uedocs/cms_data/docs/pressdata/en/sghr_int/74805.pdf.

Solana, Javier. 26 February 2003. "Interview for *Nedeljni Telegraf* (Weekly Telegraph)." http://www.consilium.europa.eu/uedocs/cms_data/docs/pressdata/en/sghr_int/74732.pdf.

Solana, Javier. 18 March 2003. "Statement by Javier Solana Prior to the General Affairs and External Relations Council." Brussels. http://eu-un.europa.eu/articles/en/article_2147_en.htm.

Solana, Javier. 20 March 2003. "Remarks by Javier Solana Prior to the European Council." http://eu-un.europa.eu/articles/en/article_2157_en.htm.

Solana, Javier. 24 March 2003. "Summary of Remarks on the Occasion of the Manfred Woerner Award." Berlin. http://eu-un.europa.eu/articles/en/article_2168_en.htm.

Solana, Javier. 26 March 2003. "EU Must Be Capable of Military Action (Interview)." *Tagesspiegel*. http://www.consilium.europa.eu/uedocs/cms_data/docs/pressdata/en/sghr_int/75255.pdf.

Solana, Javier. 31 March 2003. "Remarks by Javier Solana on the Occasion of the European Foundation Leaders Summit. http://www.consilium.europa.eu/javier-solana-offline/articles.aspx?id=&bid=107&page=arch&archDate=2003&archMonth=3&lang=en [this link no longer works, last accessed 10 December 2011].

Solana, Javier. 3 April 2003. "Responding to Questions of Journalists Before the EU Meeting with US Secretary of State Colin Powell." Brussels. http://eu-un. europa.eu/articles/en/article_2210_en.htm.

Solana, Javier. 7 April 2003. "Javier Solana Address to the Kennedy School of Government, Harvard University: 'Mars and Venus Reconciled: A New Era for Transatlantic Relations.'" http://www.consilium.europa.eu/uedocs/cms_ data/docs/pressdata/en/discours/91769.pdf.

Solana, Javier. 20 April 2003. "EU's HR Solana Urges US to Act Multilaterally (Interview)." ABC. http://www.consilium.europa.eu/uedocs/cms_data/ docs/pressdata/en/sghr_int/75553.pdf.

Solana, Javier. 28 April 2003. "Interview of Javier Solana with VRT (Vlaamse Radio- en Televisieomroep)." http://www.consilium.europa.eu/uedocs/cms_ data/docs/pressdata/en/pressreview/75556.pdf.

Solana, Javier. 7 May 2003. "Speech at the Annual Dinner of the Foreign Policy Association (FPA) on 'Europe and America—Partners of Choice.'" New York. https://www.consilium.europa.eu/uedocs/cms_data/docs/pressdata/ en/discours/75674.pdf.

Solana, Javier. 21 May 2003. "Address by Javier Solana to the Institute for European Affairs." Dublin. http://www.consilium.europa.eu/uedocs/cms_data/docs/ pressdata/en/discours/75856.pdf.

Solana, Javier. 4 June 2003. "Remarks to the Press on the Preparations to Deploy a EU Military Mission in the DRC." http://eu-un.europa.eu/articles/en/ article_2395_en.htm.

Solana, Javier. 12 June 2003. "We Are Not the Africa Corps (Interview)." Die Zeit. http://www.consilium.europa.eu/uedocs/cms_data/docs/ pressdata/en/sghr_int/76153.pdf.

Solana, Javier. 18 June 2003. "Summary of the Address by Javier Solana to the EP." http://www.consilium.europa.eu/uedocs/cms_data/docs/pressdata/ en/discours/76240.pdf.

Solana, Javier. 20 June 2003. "'A Secure Europe in a Better World.'" European Council, Thessaloniki. In From Copenhagen to Brussels: European Defence: Core Documents compiled by Antonio Missiroli. Paris: EUISS. https://www.iss.europa.eu/content/copenhagen-brussels-european- defence-core-documents-volume-iv.

Solana, Javier. 30 June 2003. "Speech at the Annual Conference of the Institute for Security Studies of the EU." Paris. https://www.iss.europa.eu/content/ 2003-annual-conference-cfsp-speech-state-union-and-unions-foreign-policy- after-iraq.

Solana, Javier. 10 July 2003a. "Article by Javier Solana on 'Atlantic Drift.'" The Guardian. https://www.theguardian.com/politics/2003/jul/10/usa.eu.

Solana, Javier. 10 July 2003b. "The Future of Transatlantic Relations: Reinvention or Reform?" (Article). http://www.consilium.europa.eu/uedocs/cms_data/docs/pressdata/en/articles/76621.pdf.

Solana, Javier. 11 July 2003. "Recreating Peace Is Europe's Strength" (Interview with Ugo Tramballi for "Il Sole 24 Ore"). http://www.consilium.europa.eu/uedocs/cms_data/docs/pressdata/en/sghr_int/76745.pdf.

Solana, Javier. 18 July 2003. "EUHR Javier Solana's Intervention at the UNSC on the DRC." https://undocs.org/en/S/PV.4790.

Solana, Javier. 21 July 2003. "Summary of the Intervention of Javier Solana at the External Relations Council Debate About the Developments in the DRC." Brussels. https://www.consilium.europa.eu/uedocs/cms_data/docs/pressdata/en/discours/76770.pdf.

Solana, Javier. 1 September 2003. "Remarks at the End of the Artemis Operation in Bunia (DRC)." http://eu-un.europa.eu/articles/en/article_2675_en.htm.

Solana, Javier. 3–4 October 2003. "Remarks at the Informal Meeting of Defence Ministers." https://www.iss.europa.eu/sites/default/files/EUISSFiles/cp067e.pdf.

Solana, Javier. 12 November 2003. "'The EU Security Strategy Implications for Europe's Role in a Changing World'—Address of HR Javier Solana to the *Institut für Europäische Politik*." Berlin. http://www.consilium.europa.eu/uedocs/cms_data/docs/pressdata/en/discours/77889.pdf.

Solana, Javier. 26 November 2003. "'The Voice of Europe on Security Matters': Summary of the Address to the Royal Institute for International Relations." http://eu-un.europa.eu/articles/en/article_3050_en.htm.

Turner, Thomas. 2007. *The Congo Wars: Conflict, Myth and Reality*. London: Zed Books Ltd.

Ulriksen, Stååle, Catriona Gourlay, and Catriona Mace. 2004. "Operation Artemis: The Shape of Things to Come?" *International Peacekeeping* 11 (3): 508–525. https://doi.org/10.1080/1353331042000249073.

UN Peacekeeping Best Practices Unit. 2004. "Operation Artemis: The Lessons of the Interim Emergency Multinational Force." http://www.peacekeepingbestpractices.unlb.org/PBPS/Pages/Public/library.aspx?ot=2&scat=305&menukey=_4_2_4 (link no longer functions, last accessed 10 Dec. 2011).

UN Security Council. 30 November 1999. *Resolution 1279 (1999)*. New York: United Nations. http://www.un.org/Docs/scres/1999/sc99.htm.

UN Security Council. 2000. *Resolution 1291 (2000)*. New York: United Nations. http://unscr.com/en/resolutions/doc/1291.

UN Security Council. 2003. *Resolution 1484 (2003)*. New York: United Nations. http://unscr.com/en/resolutions/doc/1484.

Viktorova Milne, Jevgenia. 2009. "Returning Culture to Peacebuilding: Contesting the Liberal Peace in Sierra Leone." PhD diss., University of St Andrews.

Vircoulon, Thierry. 2010. "The Ituri Paradox: When Armed Groups Have a Land Policy and Peacemakers Do Not." In *The Struggle over Land in Africa: Conflicts, Politics & Change*, edited by Ward Anseeuw and Chris Alden, 209–219. Cape Town: HSRC Press.

Vlassenroot, Koen, and Timothy Raeymaekers. 2004. "The Politics of Rebellion and Intervention in Ituri: The Emergence of a New Political Complex?" *African Affairs* 103 (412): 385–412. https://doi.org/10.1093/afraf/adh066.

Wagner, Wolfgang. 2005. "The Democratic Legitimacy of European Security and Defense Policy." Occasional Paper No. 57: 1–35. Paris: EUISS. https://www.iss.europa.eu/content/democratic-legitimacy-european-security-and-defence-policy.

Zehfuss, Maja. 2009. "Poststructuralism." In *The Ashgate Research Companion to Ethics and International Relations*, edited by Patrick Hayden, 97–111. Farnham: Ashgate.

CHAPTER 5

EUFOR Althea in Bosnia: A Tiny Particle of the Peacebuilding Enterprise

This chapter maps the discourses surrounding the deployment of the EU operation Althea in Bosnia and Herzegovina (BiH). It is necessary to understand the context in which the operation was launched to get a fuller picture of the diverse meaning spaces the operation addressed—or did not address.[1] This section also serves as an introduction to the different ways in which the Bosnian context was interpreted and highlights the power that interpretation (knowing) can have on putting together a suitable "answer". Although the "right knowledge" that functions as a basis for policy-making is habitually embedded in the discourse, it can be extracted from the discourse so as to ponder its loci. This proves important since, according to Chopra and Hohe, it allows for gauging the degree to which a peacebuilding mission is participatory—whether the enterprise of peacebuilding is based on local knowledge (2004). Understanding the contextual specifics is crucial as it allows one to tap into the communicated ideas and beliefs which enabled a certain Althea and not another. Appositely, Kappler offers a solid analysis of how representations work in a peacebuilding context, and the power and agency that different actors have in representing their own and multiple others' identities (2012b). Therefore, it is absolutely crucial to contextualise as broadly as possible the event(s) one is considering. In the discussion below, I will include different contextual notes from various sources ranging from the EU's own stance to the different sources external to the EU. Perhaps with a view to the "big picture", it is crucial to bear in mind the overarching contextual tone that had captured not only the EU but also

© The Author(s) 2020
B. Poopuu, *The European Union's Brand of Peacebuilding*,
Rethinking Peace and Conflict Studies,
https://doi.org/10.1007/978-3-030-19890-9_5

the rest of the IC—the Dayton Agreement. This has created an interesting paradox for the EU, in which it experiences a locked-in-syndrome (in the spirit of the movie *Le Scaphandre et le Papillon* [Schnabel 2007]): having subscribed to the overarching peacebuilding architecture in BiH without much debate, it is now to a large extent held hostage to this reality.

Relying on manifold sources, I will divide the context into three somewhat overlapping and hybrid layers: (i) the EU/European context: incorporating the wider Commission answer to the Balkans, but also the CSDP policy line; (ii) the wider peacebuilding context: focusing, in particular, on the overarching norms guiding the so-called international community, and the NATO effort preceding the EU operation EUFOR Althea (hereafter Althea); (iii) the local setting: with a particular emphasis on the politics and governance in post-war BiH. Analysed together, these layers help illuminate the diverse frameworks that provided the setting for Althea's deployment. Additionally, this analysis aims to offer glimpses of relations between various outside actors and their local counterparts. The layers are overlapping, messy and hybrid because they do not form entirely separate spaces but are constructed, at least partly, through interaction with one another.

THE EU/EUROPEAN CONTEXT

It is crucial to bear in mind the legacy of misrepresentations that characterise the West's reaction to the break-up of Yugoslavia. According to Dunn, actors (re)act towards others based on the way they *imagine* them (2003). The way the Balkans were imagined by the member states of the EU, with the Balkans being, if put mildly, at odds with the purported European values (see Juncos 2005, 89; but also Goldsworthy 2002; Bjelić 2002), had a significant impact on the EU's activities in BiH. That is, the EU's paralysis during the conflict can, at least to a certain extent, be attributed to both divergent and superficial imaginings member states had of the conflict (parties) (see Krotz and Schild 2013, 229). Juncos notes that in the post-war period, the term "Balkans" has been increasingly substituted by "Southeastern Europe" because of the negative connotations it carries (2005, 89). However, although Juncos argues that the "old debates about the violent 'essence' of BiH – as part of the Balkans – and about the place of BiH with regard to Europe have been replaced by a firm support for a BiH strongly anchored in Europe", this support has not entirely changed the way the EU imagines BiH (2005, 91). In other words, the EU has not acknowledged the consequences of the old lesson of "imagining" in a vacuum. Although the phrase "support for BiH" is used, this "support", as succinctly argued by Chandler, is pretty much a one-sided imagining, or, as Chandler maintains, a relationship of inequality (2003). In sum, there are two aspects here worth considering: the legacy of gross misrepresentations and the question of the present way of imagining.[2]

Chandler has labelled the period of 2000–2005 in BiH as the passage to the EU "ownership" (2005, 341–345).[3] Before 2000, the EU occupied a subordinate position in the international community's involvement in former Yugoslavia, mostly in its support role to the Peace Implementation Council (PIC), which was "tasked with overseeing the implementation of Dayton" (ibid., 338–339), and seen by the Europeans as an insurance policy for having a role in the policy process (ibid., 338). Chandler argues that in 2000, "the mechanisms of regulation shifted informally from the PIC to the EU and, without the need for any formal consultation of the people of BiH, Dayton gradually was to become subordinate to the requirements for eventual EU membership" (ibid., 341). Thus, starting from 2000, the EU's overarching framework of support in BiH was the Stabilisation and Association Process (SAP). The SAP agenda, in essence, referred to extensive reforms set out in consecutive EU documents that BiH needed to meet. Two crucial questions are of consequence here, namely, what was the substance of these reforms, and what kind of relationship was imagined between the EU and BiH as parties to these reforms.

A common thread that runs through the various EU reform documents is *sustainability* (Juncos 2005, 99).[4] Although Juncos does not discuss this issue further, it definitely deserves some space as it allows for a better grasp of how the EU understands this term. To begin with, a key issue at the heart of sustainability—the Dayton Agreement—is presented in an oxymoronic manner. That is, a single document contains contradictory claims: on the one hand, it is acknowledged that the Dayton framework could prove problematic—"the complexity of the existing Dayton order could hinder BiH performance" (Commission 2003, November 18); on the other hand, one of the priorities for action identified by the Commission for BiH is to "comply with the existing conditionality and international obligations, inter alia, comply with the Dayton-Paris Peace Accords" (ibid.). Primarily, the EU uses the term "sustainability" to underline "BiH's lack of reform 'ownership'" (see ibid.). The idea of ownership, in the EU's view, refers to the ability of the BiH's politicians to materialise the EU reform package. What it does not refer to is the idea of BiH actively contributing to the actual reform agenda. This attitude is revealed in the Commission's country strategy paper for 2002–2006: "to help identify the most urgent issues, in March 2000 the Commission presented a 'Road Map' of 18 of the most pressing steps which, when implemented, will allow BiH to advance to the next stage within the SAP" (2002). Furthermore, the asymmetric relationship between the EU and BiH is not characteristic of just BiH but is ingrained structurally, in that,

> the main priorities identified for BiH relate to its capacity to meet the criteria set by the Copenhagen European Council of 1993 and the conditions set for the SAP ... . The priorities are adapted to BiH's specific needs and stage of preparation and will be updated as necessary. (Council 2004b, June 14)

Thus, largely, the EU has authored the reform agenda and BiH's role is to implement it: "BiH 'ownership' of reform was limited; in most advances, international initiative, input and pressure was key. Inadequate domestic political will and capacity inevitably have an adverse impact on the implementation of adopted reforms" (Commission 2004; see also Chandler 2005, 344; 2003 where this is discussed in more detail). The nature of the relationship that the EU suggests through its reform agenda, in particular through the European Partnership with BiH, is highly prescriptive, authoritative and asymmetrical (which is not really different from other IC actors, cf. Björkdahl et al. 2009).

Another example that exhibits the highly asymmetric relationship between the EU and BiH is the Office of the High Representative (OHR) which, as of 2002, became a double-hatted position where the OHR was also the EU Special Representative (EUSR). Before the start of Althea, Lord Paddy Ashdown was the international High Representative and EUSR to Bosnia and Herzegovina.[5] Knaus and Martin aptly pinpoint the top-down governance of both his term and more generally of the international mission to Bosnia that, in effect, took control of Bosnia's state (2003; see also Kappler 2012a, 46).[6] Chandler argues that the EUSR's power is arbitrary "in the sense of having no fixed relationship to society" (2010, 79).[7] The Commission's report (2003, November 18) demonstrates the EU's attitude towards BiH, clearly indicating that the process is not as important as the end state:

> A December meeting of the PIC gave the HR the authority to impose legally binding decisions in BiH. This has, in practice, been used in 3 ways: (i) to enact legislation, (ii) to remove officials from office and (iii) to impose

other binding decisions. Decisions taken in the context of the Bonn Powers have been instrumental in achieving reform that might otherwise have been delayed or never effected. The number and nature of these decisions reflect a persistent BiH unwillingness or inability to make progress under domestic procedure. (ibid., 10)

To conclude, it is possible to say that the EU framework together with the Dayton agenda, which even after the start of the EU's SAP remained the overarching framework of how peace was envisaged by the "outside", hijacked the peace process from BiH actors (cf. Kappler and Richmond 2011).

In the following paragraphs, I discuss the prevalent themes that surfaced in the context of the CSDP before the deployment of Althea. In the background of the Althea mission sits the report "A Human Security Doctrine for Europe", which was intended by the study group led by Kaldor to offer a substantial guide on how to implement the ESS (2004).[8] The report can be seen as a laudable attempt at equipping the ESS with a clearer strategic framework. The report, as Kaldor argues, has invited a lot of debate within the EU about human security. Unfortunately, this idea, although widely accepted within the EU, "is still not the mainstream concept of European foreign and security policy, which I see still as one focused primarily on 'crisis management'" (2010). Two things are worth commenting on in relation to this report: the much-needed conceptual energy this report brought with it, but which was utilised by the EU mainly on the rhetorical level, and the valuable constructive critique it contains, which seems not to be taken into account, as the operations to date manifest. The first theme stretches beyond the CSDP, but was one of the main ideas connected to the argument of the EU needing a more muscular approach and thus containing an implied *raison d'etre* for the CSDP. What was happening in the Balkans, according to a number of international actors, inter alia the EU, was in the EU's backyard, and thus the EU should take the initiative, especially in view of its past failings (see Rupnik 2011, 17–18) and the geographical proximity. With regard to the latter, one can refer to the Thessaloniki Summit in June 2003, where the member states confirmed that the Balkans place is in Europe and thus the Balkan region is the EU's responsibility (ibid.). Secondly, and relatedly, it was seen that the EU needs to be able to act independently from America (Black 2003), and in this connection, the significance of the CSDP was reaffirmed.

Another backdrop against which the operation in Bosnia was pursued was the widely articulated need to show that the EU had real muscle power (see ibid.). Also, concomitantly, there was the idea—very much articulated by the EU side—that Althea was an acid test for the CSDP (see Merlingen 2012, 132; but also Juncos 2005, 89; Overhaus 2009, 17). The power of this idea cannot be overlooked, since it puts a lot of pressure on the EU—albeit it is mostly self-inflicted pressure—while at the same time leaving ambiguous the purpose of the acid test, i.e. to show to other heavyweights (mainly to the USA) that it is playing its part in world affairs and has a "credible" security policy. Although there was a concern for BiH (at least rhetorically), the discourses show a much bigger concern for the EU and Europe's security. Juncos succinctly points to the logic behind the apparently altruistic drives in the EU's response in BiH[9]:

> Yet, to be sure, the EU is not an altruistic actor when promoting democracy, human rights and rule of law worldwide; it is just making short-term sacrifices to achieve long-term gains. In other words, the EU is pursuing democracy, human rights and multilateralism in order to achieve other goals (regional stability and security). Therefore, the EU's foreign policy is still a self-interested foreign policy. Even if it does appreciate the merits of these values per se, the EU is fully aware of the benefits associated with the promotion of human rights and democracy in terms of stability and security, in particular, in the European continent. (2005, 100; cf. Björkdahl et al. 2009, 7)

From a postcolonial perspective, though not exclusively, being altruistic in conducting a peace operation is *not* axiomatic.[10] From a more critical perspective (see, e.g., Björkdahl et al. 2009; Richmond 2010), the key for evaluating the altruism of any peace operation is to determine—taking into account the situation-specific definition of effectiveness (Autesserre 2014)—the extent to which the peace offered was responsive to the local people's needs and context.[11]

In addition to framing Althea as the test case for the CSDP, it was intended, according to Solana's instructions, to be "new and different", and "to make a difference" when it took over from NATO (Leakey 2006, 59). The latter argument is a mainstay in the EU's vision of what the CSDP ought to be like, and this is captured in the ESS (2003). The instructions Solana gave are considered in more detail in the following analysis of the actual deployment of operation Althea.

To sum up, the discussions in the context of the CSDP before the deployment of Althea give a number of reasons why the EU should deploy in BiH; however, the dominant theme in the discourses was the need to bolster the CSDP and to demonstrate the EU's ability to act. This section offered a schematic overview of the themes articulated in the run-up to the deployment; a more detailed analysis will be provided below.

THE WIDER PEACEBUILDING CONTEXT IN BiH

Early in the war, Vice President Gore recommended that I read something he said had helped clarify his thinking: Robert Kaplan's newly published *Balkan Ghosts*. "Whatever has happened in Beirut or elsewhere happened first, long ago, in the Balkans," Kaplan wrote, in a dangerously broad historical sweep. (Hunt 2011, xxi, 209)

There exists an array of policy- and academic-flavoured accounts that deal with the international community's peacebuilding practice in BiH.[12] My aim here is not to take stock of that literature, but rather to outline the main characteristics of the international efforts in BiH around 2004, before the deployment of Althea. Ostensibly, I will not be able to cover every aspect of this wider peacebuilding frame that Althea *became part of* at the end of 2004. As well as discussing the key characteristics of the peacebuilding enterprise in BiH, the source of knowledge and identity of the Western actors concerning BiH will be considered. In addition to providing a take on the characteristics of the international community in its entirety, I consider the narrower context of the military component of the Dayton Agreement. With reference to this, I will cast some light on the particulars of NATO's mission(s).

As Hunt reports (2011), throughout the war and afterwards (during the "peace time"), the West's knowledge about Bosnia came mostly from secondary sources, through an outsider's lens as opposed to actively engaging with the people on the ground (see, for instance, the opening quote to this section; cf. Goldsworthy 2002). Similarly, Jansen (2006) notes that many of the IC did not make an effort to familiarise themselves with the local setting, and thus, in many ways, a number of their policies were out of sync with the local moods, a case in point being the return policy. Owing to this, Hunt coins an apposite term, *worlds apart*, which sums up well the ways in which the West operated in Bosnia, but without Bosnian input (cf. Chandler 2000, 43–51):

The groups that are, in fact, most in touch with the domestic situation are NGOs. As a new diplomat, when I asked a group of fellow ambassadors how they were dealing with such organisations, they responded with a plan for "damage control." In other words, they saw these groups as adversaries. And so the insights of the NGO community – whether recording human rights abuses, exposing corruption, or setting up refugee camps – have been welcomed only rarely by officials … (2011, 217, xv)

A somewhat similar story is told by Hansen, who investigates the link between Western identity and policy in the context of the Bosnian war (2006). Analysing the prevailing texts that have guided both European and American policies in their response to the Bosnian war, she is able—although this is not her main focus—to trace the flow of the different aspects of power through the identity construction process, especially concerning the question of the source(s) of knowledge. Importantly, the many nuances of that process that are brought out by the author are also crucial in the period "after Dayton": identity politics *par excellence*, where the discursive struggle over what to do about Bosnia essentially takes place within the West. Bluntly put, the abovementioned discursive struggle translates into the following equation: the more grounded the knowledge, the more it falls upon deaf ears (e.g. following the worlds apart imagery, see Hunt 2011).[13] Perhaps most crucially, this indicates that Western knowledge does indeed count—as a Eurocentric attitude underlining the West's response (see Hobson 2012), meaning that certain kinds of knowledge are privileged and "the real power … remains in imperial capitals" (Ignatieff 2003, Introduction). Another common trait of the West was the fact that mostly, it could only approach identities as clear-cut and uniform, e.g. "a Serb is a Serb", ignoring the fact that "a large portion of contemporary Bosnians simply didn't identify themselves as belonging to one ethnicity or another. They were simply Yugoslavs. Some 40 percent of marriages in Bosnian cities were ethnically mixed" (Hunt 2011, xxiii; see also Kaldor 1999; Hansen 2006, 172).

Chandler provides a good overview of the international effort *in toto*, taking stock of the contributions of multiple others in BiH over a decade of implementing the Dayton Accords (2005). He brings out several telling characteristics of this process: for one, there is a tendency by the international community in BiH to divorce statebuilding from politics, i.e.

the international administration of BiH has excluded all but token local input in the making and implementation of policy, criticising the programmes and personnel of the main political parties and asserting that the BiH electorate is not yet to be trusted with a meaningful vote. (2005, 308)

He also notes that since Dayton, the powers of the IC have grown more interventionist (ibid.; Belloni 2007; see the point about the Bonn Powers above). Moreover, the IC mandates were extended indefinitely in December 1997 (see Chandler 2000, 51, 55). "Despite their hyper-interventionist role", as Belloni notes, "international agencies have demonstrated a strong status quo bias, preferring to preserve the current institutional and societal structures while promoting piecemeal reform" (2007, 161). This was coupled with a paradoxical lack of democracy on the journey to "western democracy": i.e. "the lack of political autonomy for Bosnian representatives, and of political accountability for Bosnian citizens" (Chandler 2005, 308). Furthermore, according to Chandler, "there would appear to be a clear international consensus that, for state-building to be a success, rule by externally-appointed bureaucrats is preferential to rule by Bosnian representatives accountable to BiH's citizens" (ibid., 309; see also Chandler 2000). As a result, Dayton represents an enormously asymmetric framework, where, as Chandler suggests (2000, 52), the Bosnian side's room for manoeuvre is extremely limited vis-à-vis the IC.[14]

Alongside these broad characteristics, it is possible to identify the chief dilemma at the heart of the international approach in Bosnia, in that the promotion of democracy, or democratisation, is done in a way that does not pay attention to the means needed to achieve it, but rather the focus is on the end goal (cf. Bieber 2006, 146). This looms large in the following statement: "the OHR remains focused on its overarching objective of ensuring that *BiH is a peaceful, viable state on course to European integration*" (Ashdown 2004a, November 3; emphasis mine). This may be a commendable objective, but it seems that the "in the meantime", or the process leading towards that goal, does not receive much attention. Instead, the IC operates according to the Dayton Agreement, which throughout the years has become the final arbiter when it comes to the question of legitimacy of the IC's actions. Thus, there is a tension between the goal of a "viable Bosnian state" versus the process of getting there, which is more reminiscent of "exporting democracy" than allowing space for Bosnian agency or democracy (cf. Chandler 2006, 478; but also Mac Ginty and Richmond 2013, 768; Bridoux and Kurki 2014). In this context, Chandler maintains that the

IC's statebuilding and democracy-promoting approach places a premium on "the regulatory role of international institutions" and concomitantly suggesting that "purely locally-derived political solutions are likely to be problematic" (2006, 478). Furthermore, if one points a finger to the limited success of the IC, then, according to Chandler the IC responds by referring to the "difficulties of bringing democracy to non-Western states" (2006, 494).

According to the ICG reports (see also Hunt 2011, 117–122), prior to 1997, the NATO-led force provided security in a very restricted manner.[15] It was risk averse, and the overarching principle directing its actions on the ground was force protection (see Hunt 2011, 120–122). It specifically avoided, apropos the ICG reports, the following actions:

> participation in civilian demining, which entailed exposure to the risk of mine strikes; escorting minority group returnees to their homes in hostile communities, which would raise the issue of safeguarding them once they were there; and above all seeking out and arresting persons who had been indicted by ICTY [International Criminal Tribunal for the former Yugoslavia], which was seen as politically entangling as well as risky. (1997, December 15, 25)

In contrast to the ICG reports, Javier Solana, the then Secretary General of NATO, tells a somewhat different story of NATO's actions on the ground (Solana 1996). In Solana's reiteration of IFOR's activities, security is given a meaning that mainly revolves around rebuilding the *physical* environment of BiH: e.g. "IFOR has repaired or rebuilt more than 60 bridges, together with more than 2,500 kilometers of main roads and many railway lines throughout Bosnia-Herzegovina" (ibid.).[16] Solana's account of IFOR's "success" clearly corresponds to the traditional security approach, whereas the ICG manages to bring in aspects of "human security" as well. It has been noted that NATO declared its BiH operation a success not because of any real improvements in the security situation, but because its interest had shifted elsewhere (Calic 2005).

This risk-averse phase of NATO's involvement needs to be foregrounded by two crucial comments: on the ground, this risk aversion came in different guises, and on a more general level, mandates do not provide concrete prescriptions, but rather broad tasks and objectives, leaving the actors on the ground with certain room for interpretation (see Autesserre 2014). In Bosnia, as Hunt argues, "sector commanders differed in how to interpret their mandate. During the next few years, IFOR troops assigned to different parts of the country assumed quite different levels of responsibility for the Bosnians around them" (2011, 230). Further elaborating on this, she brings out the varying postures these troops took:

> US military commanders came into the country with an explicit directive not to lose any troops. That, and the military's desire to avoid failure, meant that preventing "mission creep" became the goal. "Security" was applied to their own forces, rather than addressing causes of destabilisation such as hunger, fear and hopelessness. Most of the ten thousand American soldiers were thus confined to their barracks, sealed off from a country desperate for help. ... The thirteen thousand British in the northwest were much more involved in helping rebuild communities – physically reconstructing towns, getting supplies to schools, and interacting with citizens. In contrast, the French, with another ten thousand troops, oversaw the southeast sector, including Sarajevo and its airport. High-level US officials, including President Clinton, repeatedly accused them of sheltering the indicted war criminal Radovan Karadžic, foiling efforts of the war crimes tribunal to bring him to justice. (2011, 230)

In a similar fashion, the ICG reports an array of problems on the ground, pointing to "the varying agendas and policies of the SFOR contingents in Bosnia" (2001a, May 22, 11–13). Yet, the ICG team ardently suggests, notwithstanding the numerous rather alarming practices on the ground, that NATO should continue its work in BiH. Moreover, the ICG wants to see a robust NATO on the ground that is responsible for the lion's share of enforcing Dayton (see, e.g., 2001a, May 22). In contrast to the ICG's stance, Daalder is of the opinion that—worthy of quoting at some length—becoming more assertive does not necessarily solve the problem:

> Civilian implementation of Dayton has stagnated, leading the Clinton administration and others to urge SFOR to fill the gap by becoming more assertive. Although its increased assertiveness has clearly had a salutary effect – including helping to split the Bosnian Serb leadership into a hardline faction based in Pale and a seemingly more compliant faction in the north-western city of Banja Luka – these actions are unlikely to enable NATO and US forces to leave Bosnia any sooner. *There is an inverse relationship between the amount of force used to impose solutions and the extent to which peace will be self-sustaining after the foreign military presence departs. Thus, rather than enabling the timely exit of US forces, these stepped-up enforcement efforts will make peace in Bosnia more, not less, dependent on a continued military presence.* (1997, 7–8; emphasis mine)

Thus, the more robust approach of NATO does not necessarily mean a change for the better. It can, instead, result in a deepening of the dependency relationship rather than providing the grounds for sustainability. One of the most common features attached to NATO's presence was its deterrence function, yet this needs to be assessed in view of both the dependency argument and the critique that investigates the everyday practices on the ground (bearing in mind the interpretation gap, as noted by Hunt 2011).

To conclude, I want to raise a couple of issues that run through the wider peacebuilding enterprise in BiH, but also concern the efforts of NATO. Overwhelmingly, the post-war peacebuilding game is played out between the West (in all its guises) and the political elite in BiH (likewise, in all its guises). The local, beyond the various political actors with whom the numerous Dayton implementers are concerned, is imagined as a relatively passive, homogeneous entity, whose "voice" is deafeningly silent. The question is, how much "local" can be included into the enterprise of building peace, if the script used for doing that, the Dayton Agreement, does not command the popular assent. The "enforcement gap" (see, e.g., Daalder 1997, 7) is habitually pointed out as the key reason of why the peace process is sluggish. Yet if the Dayton Agreement is interpreted rigidly—as has been the case throughout its implementation phase until the present—and the Bosnian parties' role is the implementation, while the IC's is limited to "assistance" (euphemistically), then the crucial missing component is the space for (re-)negotiation and dialogue.

THE LOCAL SETTING IN BiH

> I have concluded that there are two ways I can make my decisions. One is with a tape measure, measuring the precise equidistant position between three sides. *The other is by doing what I think is right for the country as a whole. I prefer the second of these.* So when I act, I shall seek to do so in defence of the interests of all the people in Bosnia and Herzegovina, putting their priorities first. (Ashdown 2002; emphasis mine)

Ashdown's inaugural speech in May 2002 aptly exemplifies the way he— and by extension the international community, whose "representative" he believes himself to be—understood the local in Bosnia. To begin with, Ashdown juxtaposes the political parties (the "three sides"), which are not able to represent "the country as a whole", and himself, as being abler at this job. Although the whole speech is a contradiction in terms, with abundant inconsistencies (e.g. Ashdown declares himself to be the "servant of Bosnia", implying a relationship of partnership, yet simultaneously dismisses the political parties and robs the "people of BiH" of agency, assuming representation of the people of BiH without having been voted into power, thus again demonstrating the paradox of an undemocratic journey to democracy), it does communicate a certain approach towards the local context. At a stroke, the political elite are branded divisive (i.e. the problem), and the rest of the population of BiH is portrayed as the vulnerable party in the peacebuilding process, with no autonomous role given to it. If anything, the local is romanticised (Richmond 2009, 153), in that it is only—aside from the political elite—seen as a homogeneous.[17] The central tension in Ashdown's text is between *the promise of agency* and *simulating agency* (see Chandler 2010, 76). The former is captured here: "But I [Ashdown referring to himself] cannot do it for you. You have to look to yourselves. So a good motto for Bosnia and Herzegovina on the next stage of the journey would be, to paraphrase John F Kennedy, 'Do not ask what the international community can do for you. Ask first what you [the imagined homogeneous population of BiH?] can do for yourselves'" (Ashdown 2002). The latter element of the tension refers to the fact that although Ashdown is allegedly promoting the interests of BiH, the people cannot act autonomously, for their interests have to be filtered through the IC (cf. Cubitt 2013, 95–97).

The above serves as an excerpt of the predominant mode of relating to the local.[18] In order to go beyond that and grasp the local in its multiplicity (and/or homogeneity and/or anything in between), I will rely on a number of accounts of different origins (scholarly/media, outside/inside, etc.). The offered mapping will be no more than a sketch, but it enables to tease out the characteristics of the two main types of local actors that the EU engages with: the political elite and the NGOs. It should be kept in mind that the local in the IC's parlance amounts to different actors/groups, and there is no consensus or consistency as to what the local pertains to (see Kappler 2012b, 264–265). For example, Kappler (2012a, 64) argues that in the case of the EU, the concept of civil society lacks precision, and as a result "this leads to an exclusion of civil society actors when they cannot be framed in the EU's terms or when they are too difficult to deal with". Below I will consider some of the key local-level dynamics before the deployment of Althea in order to provide contextual detail, to which I can refer back later, when considering the discourses on the local surrounding Althea.

The aim here is to capture—*grosso modo*—the dialogue between the IC, the political elite and the populace. All in all, it can be said that the social contract in BiH is not between the political elite and the people of BiH, but to a large extent between the IC and the political elite. For instance, people of BiH, in general, feel that the "domestic politicians do not listen to their voters because they need to follow orders from OHR" (Kostić 2007, 313–314). The distrustful attitude towards the political elite in BiH—or politics more generally—definitely draws attention to power asymmetries that the IC further reinforces (Jansen 2013, 238–239). Nevertheless, the relationship dynamic between the three parties is much more complex. Roughly speaking, it can be placed on the continuum from acceptance to resistance (see Richmond and Mitchell 2012, 1–38). The (un)acknowledged starting point of this dialogue is that, in terms of power, the relationship is highly hierarchical, in that peacebuilding starts with the Dayton framework. According to Bieber (2006, 43, 106), the three national parties—SDA [Bosniak], HDZ [Croat] and SDS [Serb]—have dominated the political landscape of BiH largely due to the post-Dayton design of the political system. What best characterises the political system of BiH is the instrumental use of ethnic identity: that is, ethnic identity is securitised in order to mobilise the populace for certain ends.[19] Furthermore, Kostić's study offers some crucial findings in relation to the mismatch between the international vs. local ideas of peace: the IC follows a liberal peace blueprint and is thus wholeheartedly invested in both nation- and statebuilding, with a unified Bosnian state in mind. However, the IC has largely misunderstood and/or disregarded the BiH context and thus not paid attention to the salience of ethnonational identities among the three national communities and the resulting societal security dilemma that is made worse by the IC's top-down attitude (Kostić 2007).[20] "Discourses of peace and war, and the forms of power associated with them", Richmond (2013, November 28) suggests, "are produced by, and produce, socio-political relations, law, security and institutions, which go on to shape the behaviour of subjects through compliance or resistance". In view of this, even if the wider peacebuilding effort tries to bulldoze its way through BiH, it could not do so in a vacuum, without the different layers of the local context reacting with their discourses of war and peace. Here the critical question is whether the so-called ethnic markers of identity would be so conspicuous in a different structural landscape?

Secondly, Ashdown's declaration that he is a "servant of Bosnia", in reality, pinpoints the fact that the governance model in BiH is extremely complex, and there is a crisis of representation. As Krastev remarks:

> Voters are in a trap. On the one hand, they want the international community to curb corrupt politicians. On the other hand, voters want a say in making policy. International players delegitimate Balkan democracy by punishing elites who break their promises to the International Monetary Fund, while excusing or even encouraging elites who break promises to voters. (2002, 52)

This crisis of democracy promotion in BiH is underlined by an array of authors. For instance, the UNDP report (2003, 26) stresses that the participation of civil society in the policy-making process "ends the very moment the people's representatives are elected". Furthermore, it points to the already noted paradoxical mismatch between the rhetoric of sustainability (i.e. local ownership; truly autonomous civil society—see Cubitt 2013, 106) and the reality of sustaining a dependency culture (i.e. the growing powers of the IC) where the IC influence dominates the structure and content of the Bosnian state (see Chandler 2000, 60–64; Knaus and Cox 2004). Chandler (2010, 79) points out, in this context, that the EUSR's power—and by extension the wider IC's power—is arbitrary "in the sense of having no fixed or cohered relationship to society".

Thirdly, one of the key tactics in which the IC is complicit when it comes to the local beyond the political elite is the tactic of conversion—i.e. the international, wittingly or not, fashions the local in its own image. Although rhetorically, the IC has acknowledged the relevance of involving the local actors (though mainly NGOs) in the peacebuilding process, this involvement is couched in terms of conditionality, or, as Cubitt puts it, "outsiders 'cherry pick' and discriminate between local groups and tend to support those who cut across identity lines or fissures, or who are moderate and focused on issues such as democracy, civic education, women or youth" (2013, 97–98). In the majority of cases, the part of society the IC does manage to engage with is confined to the NGOs, but even then the selected local partners need to be civilised in order for them to be taken as a meaningful partners in a peacebuilding process (Belloni 2001). With reference to Belloni, there are two basic ways in which the IC conceives of the civil society (2001, 167–168). The term is usually reserved for the NGOs that are seen to inhabit the space between the individual and the state and that manage to counterbalance the state. Additionally, the term is connected to

an ideal image of a society characterised by "civility, moderation and tol-
eration". This makes the way the IC imagines the local very problematic,
since the power relationships—the overarching IC rule in Bosnia—are not
considered. The overall emphasis put on the notion of civil—explicit in the
IC's stance of developing/building NGOs (see Fagan 2005) versus genuinely listening to them—demonstrates, as stated by Hobson (2012, 27),
the vigour of international paternalism among the IC actors. "Paternalist
Eurocentrism for the most part entails", as Hobson suggests (2012, 315)
"a highly optimistic, and frequently triumphalist, 'progressive' politics".
To elaborate further, "the pioneering agency of the Europeans in conjunction with conditional Eastern agency means that not only can the former
promote the development of Eastern societies through the civilising mission, but they have a 'moral duty' to do so (i.e. the 'white man's burden')"
(ibid.). Likewise, Evans-Kent and Bleiker (2003, 104) note that NGOs in
Bosnia, more often than not, suffer from a dependency relationship, meaning that "their ability to promote and implement truly autonomous policies
is often compromised".[21] Another problematic, which these authors (ibid.,
104–105) unveil, refers to the fact that (I)NGOs claim to be authentic mirrors of the subaltern. In this way, the politics of representing and engaging
the local is problematised even further, and the authors argue that the
various (I)NGO representations do not necessarily equate with subaltern
voices on the ground (ibid.). Throughout this section, it became evident
how the structural element in peacebuilding creates such an asymmetry in
speaking peace that to overcome it the external actors have to make an
effort and listen, differently to Ashdown's strategy of further deepening
the inequality in speaking peace (see Hellmüller 2014, 200).

Capturing EUFOR Althea in BiH

Similarly to the analysis of the Artemis operation (Ch. 4), the analysis below
will follow the logic of telling and acting model as described in the theory
part. Roughly, the following section will be divided into two substantive
parts: (i) telling identity (capturing the pre-implementation phase of the
operation) and (ii) acting identity (capturing the implementation phase,
from December 2004 to roughly 2013).

Key Themes of Operation Althea

There are occasional invitations for the Europeans to take part in moulding the EU's external action, e.g. "the Strategy is a short document. It is free of jargon, clear and – I hope – accessible to all. This is how it should be. Security is everybody's business" (Solana 2004c, February 25). Despite this, the Europeans are only included in the last stage: they are mobilised as an audience that should give the final stamp of approval to the CSDP's goals. This is clearly evident in an array of statements where the causal relationship between the internal and external security is emphasised. For instance, according to Solana, "if we want to protect our citizens at home, we have to be prepared to act effectively abroad" (Solana 2004c, February 25). Two problems emerge in this context: firstly, the inclusion of the Europeans in the security debate is an illusion at best, and secondly, the support of European publics for the CSDP is questionable (Brummer 2007). Solana's reasoning is weak, since it is debatable how much say an "ordinary European", or even the political elite, can have in the EU's security policy (see Wagner 2005, 2006). His is a somewhat ambiguous and even nominal statement, as in reality there is not a way that European citizens can be directly involved in the EU's security policy; moreover, as Wagner contends (2006, see esp. 203–204; see also Bono 2006), not even the member states' executives can really control the direction in which it is going. Similarly, the report "A Human Security Doctrine for Europe" maintains that "in the area of European security policy, the well-known 'democratic-deficit' is aggravated by a lack of transparency and a 'double-deficit' in parliamentary scrutiny", which underlines the citizen-distant approach built into the policy from the start (Kaldor et al. 2004, 26).

The idea that actions count more than words—that has been the centrepiece of the EU's security policy—continues in 2004 with similar fervour. As Solana puts it:

> it is not the words but the deeds that count in international politics. The EU has now accumulated political will and resources in order to start making a difference in the field of peace and security, as it is already doing in the global market. But our ambition remains only an idea if we are not ready to put more resources behind our policies. (2004c, February 25)

Interestingly, this notion of deeds has a very particular meaning (at least most of the times)—it refers to the almost existential need to acquire the resources deemed necessary for action. To illustrate this, the ESS, as Solana argues, "is underpinned and made credible by the notion of capability" (2004a, February 17). At other times, it is used to promote the military arm of the EU's security policy. The two purposes are often intertwined; for example, as the meeting of EU defence ministers demonstrates (Solana 2004d, May 17), key emphasis with regard to the CSDP "the development of military capabilities for crisis management [that] has been a key aspect of the European Security and Defence Policy since its inception". This implies that credibility is seen more as an internal attribute versus an external one, indicating that the CSDP's role is more to build the EU's position vis-à-vis its significant others than to help with building peace. At times, it seems that capabilities, in and of themselves, mean that CSDP missions will succeed, as can be gleaned from the EU's pronouncements: e.g. Solana states that "I want to make it very clear that EUFOR will begin its operations with all the materiel and personnel that it requires – the same troop strength as SFOR. It will have what it needs to do the job" (2004i, July 15).

It is very important for the EU's *raison d'etre* to argue that its approach is different from others. For instance, "the preparation of the European Security Strategy has helped us to discover a remarkable convergence of view on security issues between EU Member States – and to uncover an authentic and uniquely European voice on security issues" (Solana 2004c, February 25).[22] This, however, runs parallel to a discourse on how the main actor in—in fact, the authority on—the international peace and security is the UN. Moreover, when convenient, the label of "international community" (seen as an unproblematic and stable category) is evoked, and then, the unique gets sidelined in favour of similarity, belonging to and subscribing to the international norms and the like.[23] In the EU's case, the use of the label "international community" is mainly reserved to cases where the EU wants to amplify its agency and legitimacy to act, based on its rightful place among the "we"; it is also a useful strategy for "sharing" responsibility and for mobilising the member states by referring to the interdependency argument (see Bliesemann de Guevara and Kühn 2009).

A theme that surfaces repeatedly in the EU's discourse is the existential imperative to become an international security actor—or to risk its own security. The following statement by Solana appears in most EU public communications: "the EU has to use this potential to create a safer and more prosperous world. This is not just a moral obligation, it is also the only path towards real security and stability within the EU's own borders" (2004j, July 27; see also the comment above about the nexus of internal–external security).

The theme of becoming/being a global actor necessitates certain common-sense actions. According to Solana, "as a global actor, we should be able to project our force wherever needed. We have to match our political decisions with the necessary capabilities" (2004l, September 17; cf. Chapter 4 of this book). Critically, the different representatives of the EU's security policy use the labels *becoming* a global actor versus *being* a global actor depending on the larger aim of their argument. When Solana "fights" for the military arm of the CSDP, he usually deploys the first label (*becoming* a global actor) (see, for example, the ESS 2003). However, if Solana is arguing for the need to intervene somewhere, he usually uses the second label (*being* a global actor), e.g. "as a global actor, we should be able to project our force wherever needed" (Solana 2004l, September 17). However, there is also some inconsistency in using the labels, as though the EU (or at least its spokesperson) is not quite certain whether or not it is in, or has completed, the process of becoming a global actor.

Another theme conveys how Althea, being part of the wider peace-building effort, will contribute towards the EU's "long term objective of a stable, viable, peaceful and multiethnic Bosnia and Herzegovina, cooperating peacefully with its neighbours and irreversibly on track towards EU membership" (Council 2004h, October 11). The latter part of this statement is one of the many hints about peace being more about the EU visions for Bosnia than a home-made and/or co-authored peace. Clearly, peacebuilding in general is not solely in the realm of altruism, yet what becomes problematic with reference to the EU in all its guises and the wider peacebuilding enterprise is the fact that, more often than not, this peace is subordinated to the peace of the peacebuilders involved. Perhaps more importantly still, this instantly begs the question of whose stable and viable BiH we are talking about, i.e. how genuine is the "local ownership", and can it outweigh the construction of peace on the peacebuilders' terms. For instance, for the most part (see, e.g., Council 2004e, July 12), the goal of establishing a safe and secure environment is qualified with the external agenda: i.e. Althea will "contribute to safe and secure environment in line with its mandate, OHR's MIP's core tasks, SAP".

Another recurring statement that characterises the pre-deployment stage is the assertion that "the EU operation will be part of a coherent EU approach" (EU Council Secretariat 2004, November 29; Council 2004c, June 15). The problematique of coherence and effectiveness of the EU's CFSP is investigated in great detail in Juncos Garcia (2007); for this reason, and because the focus of this book is different, this issue will not be dealt with here. However, as became apparent in the case of Artemis, at times the suggestion that CSDP will be part of the wider EU approach (coherent or not) was a strategy to avoid direct responsibility. Consider, for example, the EU's comprehensive approach towards Bosnia, where most of the energy is put into describing the coordination (= coherence) links, rather than talking about the substance of the operation (Council 2004c, June 15).

A recurrent motif is the neat division into the West (core) and the rest (periphery),[24] with all the universally agreed norms, values, etc., located in the core, and the things that need transformation belonging in the periphery. Solana suggests that in BiH, all the EU tools will be deployed "in pursuit of a single objective – the stabilisation and transformation of a post-conflict society into one which some day will be ready for EU membership" (2004c, February 25).

There is a strong case made for seeing EUFOR Althea as a test case for the CSDP. Consider, for example, Solana's prediction: "EUFOR will demonstrate that Europe is capable of taking sensible, coordinated and robust steps to obtain a security environment that benefits its own citizens and those of its neighbours" (2004i, July 15). In other instances, EUFOR Althea is labelled as "the most ambitious mission deployed to date by the EU, with over 7000 men" (Solana 2004j, July 27). Yet, it seems that ambition is more measured in numbers (read: troop size) than in anything else. The latter tendency is prevalent in academic writing as well; for example, Merlingen holds that "Althea was billed by Brussels as a 'make it or break it' operation. Clearly, Althea has made it. Hiccups notwithstanding, it has demonstrated that the EU *can successfully run a sizeable peacekeeping operation*" (2012, 132; emphasis mine).

One of the themes that surface only occasionally concerns local ownership. Thus, regarding this notion, the silence surrounding it is the key to its value to the EU. In many instances, the importance of it is noted, but its substance remains fuzzy. In some instances, in contrast, this notion has a very particular meaning, for example, "local ownership remains the guiding principle. My goal is to ensure a controlled handover of EUFOR's functions to the relevant BiH authorities" (Witthauer 2004, November 29). Clearly, local ownership here is seen in a very limited sense, where the role of the local level is assigned and monitored rather than treated on an equal footing.

Another thread running through the discourses is connected to responsibility. In most cases, the EU does not see that it should shoulder any responsibility for the peacebuilding process; rather it is the local level that should take the lion's share of responsibility. The example below is emblematic of this attitude:

> We can promise effective international support through close co-operation between the EU and NATO. But in the end the challenges of the new era can only be met by the people and political leaders of Bosnia and Herzegovina. They have already come a long way. The next phase begins today — the road ahead is to Europe. The speed of the journey depends on the people of Bosnia and Herzegovina. We remain committed to help. (Solana and de Hoop Scheffer 2004)

Alarmingly, there is little understanding of the gamut of effects that the IC has on the local level. In that, the IC is quick to take the credit but not the blame, even if that is shared. The mainstream accounts of the IC actors do not recognise the need for evaluating their own missions, other for the reason of maximising efficiency and effectiveness during the next one. Thinking about the adverse effects these might have is somehow beyond the mindset of the IC. Critics of peace and conflict studies have connected this to the failure of going beyond the predominant way the IC does business, i.e. the problem-solving framework.

Multiple Others

As with the previous case study, Artemis, the different others the EU converses with are loosely divided into two notional groups, multiple and significant others, based on the discursive material (cf. Neumann and Sending 2007, 679; Bliesemann de Guevara and Kühn 2009).

It seems to be the case that *to a certain degree* and *in a particular sense* the EU takes note of the civil society as playing an indispensable part in peacebuilding. For instance, Ambassador Richard Ryan—speaking on behalf of the EU at the UN—acknowledges that "because it is ordinary citizens themselves who are the main targets of peace-building activities, input provided *on their behalf by civil society actors* is key to its success" (2004, June 22; emphasis mine). In fact, Kaldor et al. (among others) maintain that a genuine participatory approach in the frames of the CSDP is missing (2004). In the context of operation Althea, the rhetorical commitment is made, but this concerns only BiH authorities: "the EU should maintain close consultations with the BiH authorities in particular with the Minister of Defence, regarding the conduct of the EU military operation" (Council 2004e, July 12). Thus, it is crucial to investigate further what stands behind the local as imagined by the EU. At this point, one can spot two tendencies: first, the ambassador a few lines above appears as an advocate of the local, yet his imagination ends with civil society actors who should speak in place of the "ordinary citizens"; second, the engagement with the local is limited to "BiH authorities".

To complement what has been said above, it should be noted that when it comes to the civilian side of the EU's external activities, the civil society is grasped in a more inclusive way. For instance, at the European Council in June 2004, when the "Action Plan for Civilian Aspects of ESDP" was adopted, the civil society was mentioned at some length:

> exchange of information with representatives from non-governmental organisations and civil society should take place on a regular basis. To this end incoming presidencies are invited to facilitate meetings with them during their respective presidencies. NGO and civil society views in relation to the general orientations of EU civilian crisis management are welcome. NGO experience, expertise and early warning capacity are valued by the EU. (2004, June 17–18, 10)[25]

In contrast, when considering the military arm of the EU, any engagement with the "local" amounts to "local authorities" (Council 2004e, July 12). Or, even more narrowly, as stated in the general concept for EUFOR Althea, "EUFOR should develop and maintain a close relationship and dialogue with the Minister of Defence of BiH, and his senior staff" (Council 2004a, April 28).[26] Although the level of engagement might be deeper when it comes to "the civilian face of the EU" compared to the military arm, what remains virtually the same is the substance of this engagement. The dialogue or engagement with the locals, referred to as local ownership, symbolises little more than a maturity test for BiH (authorities) where there is a clear and authoritative judge—the EU (or by extension the IC). For instance, the EU argues in the general concept that "the international community remains committed to helping BiH move closer to European and Euro-Atlantic structures, including through gradual transfer to local ownership" (Council 2004a, April 28, 27). Civil society or the locals remain very limited concepts in the EU's vocabulary: they are mentioned occasionally, but in a very particular sense, i.e. corresponding to the overarching trends of how other IOs interact with the local level. The example below illustrates how the power relations are imagined between the international and local layers of agency by the Political Security Committee (Council 2004f, July 23; UNSC 2004)[27]:

> The continued willingness of the international community and major donors to assume the political, military and economic burden of implementation and reconstruction efforts will be determined by the compliance and active participation by all the authorities in Bosnia and Herzegovina in implementing the Peace Agreement and rebuilding a civil society, in particular in full cooperation with the International Tribunal for the Former Yugoslavia (ICTY), in strengthening joint institutions which foster the building of a fully functioning self-sustaining state, able to integrate itself into the European structures and in facilitating returns of refugees and displaced persons.

This way of representing peacebuilding conveys how different actors are imagined; thus, the IC is assigned the role of an architect of the peace, whereas the local is prescribed to comply with this grand architecture. A further illustration of the power dynamics is well presented in the Office of High Representative's MIP[28]:

> It should be noted that the speed of our progress towards transition – towards a reconfigured IC that has relinquished its executive power – will be determined not by rigid timelines, but by *an ongoing assessment of the situation on the ground*. Is the dynamic of obstructionism in Bosnia and Herzegovina being replaced by a dynamic of reform? Is peace enduring? Is the BiH State viable? Is the country on course for European integration? *Only when we are satisfied that sufficient progress has been made in this respect will we be able to declare our mission implemented*. It follows from this that the faster *our colleagues in the BiH* authorities implement reform, the sooner the OHR can complete its work. (emphases mine)

Intriguingly, the other instance when BiH as an actor is given more space for action is—paradoxically—when the EU lifts the responsibility from its own shoulders, stating: "BiH finally has a clear path to Europe. Whether it gets there of course depends on the BiH institutions themselves. Whether they are prepared to genuinely work together in the interests of the citizens of BiH to deliver the peace and prosperity that Europe offers" (Solana 2004f, May 29; see also Council 2004f, July 23). In addition to shifting the responsibility of implementing the externally manufactured reform package onto the shoulders of BiH authorities, there is another nuance in this statement: that is, Solana prudently frames the opposition between the political elite and the general population in the EU's advantage by implicitly taking the side of the people. Furthermore, in the same interview, Solana further capitalises on this point by saying:

> it is a regrettable fact that eight years after the Peace Agreement was signed, the citizens of Bosnia and Herzegovina continue to be held hostage by political forces, especially in the Republika Srpska (RS), that have failed to meet a key obligation of the Peace Agreement – to uphold BiH's obligations with regard to the International Criminal Court for the former Yugoslavia (ICTY). (Solana 2004f, May 29)

Yet, the main actors that the CSDP missions are supposed to partner with (refer to Council 2004e, July 12) are the local authorities.

There is a tendency by the EU to evoke public legitimacy by, for example, speaking for whole populations: "we have a structure, a force level and a political-military framework that is optimal. This is as it should be, because *we know that the people of BiH* expect much of this mission. *The people of Europe expect* much of this mission too" (Solana 2004i, July 15; emphasis mine). Speaking on behalf of the civil society rather than genuinely engaging with it is a leitmotif of the EU's engagement. The EU's proclivity to speak on someone's behalf further underscores the point made by Spivak that the subaltern do speak but they are not heard (1988).

Relatedly, passivity in different degrees seems to be the underlying assumption in the way the EU and the IC, more generally, relate to BiH. A passive role is habitually assigned to "the people of Bosnia": "We expect from the leaders a dedicated commitment to strengthen your institutions, your democracy, your economy in a responsible manner. The people of Bosnia deserve no less" (Solana 2004m, December 2). Connected to this, Prodi reasons "we need to project stability beyond our borders. That means promoting political and economic reforms that can enable our neighbours to share in our peace and prosperity" (2004, April 1). Although examples abound, there is a clear conflict between the idea of supporting the Balkans in their road to peace that is home-grown versus monitoring the externally imposed reform agenda. For instance, Patten, in referring to the progress in the Western Balkans, maintains: "I have seen substantial improvements in the Region. Greater stability. Functioning democracies. And progress, albeit slow but uneven, towards the implementation of the reform agenda which we have promoted" (2004a, April 28). A similar idea is communicated by Solana when he suggests that "today, the Western Balkans is being steadily brought into the European mainstream" (2004k, September 10). The adopted Comprehensive Policy for BiH (Council 2004d, June 15) further underlines the unequal role of the EU vis-à-vis BiH. The mentioned policy document disregards BiH input when iterating the contributors to the comprehensive EU approach in BiH (although, in the case of the general concept, the BiH authorities were consulted in the preparation stage, see Council 2004a, April 28, 2). Solana presents the division of labour between the EU and the local level (mainly the elite) at the meeting of the EU defence ministers as follows: "we maintain fruitful consultations with the BiH authorities. A visit was conducted at the end of last month to keep those authorities up-to-date with our work, in particular the General Concept, in BiH" (2004d, May 17). Perhaps the gravest issue in this context is that the order in which the EU functions is not questioned. Thus, it is taken for granted, on the one hand, that the peacebuilding agenda is neutral and universal; on the other, that the implementation of the said agenda is a technical matter. In many instances, when the IC "consults" the local actors, it does so already within this external, imposed meaning structure.

To sum up the relation between the EU and the local, I have decided to quote an interview between Solana and a local journalist for the journal *Nezavisne Novine* (2004e, May 28; emphasis mine):

Q: It is announced that mandate for SFOR will be replaced with EUFOR. Can you be more specific and tell us *what is it that citizens of BiH can expect from EUFOR and its presence in Bosnia?*

A: The EU has expressed ... its willingness to lead a military mission in BiH following SFOR. The aim of this EU mission would be twofold: to continue the implementation of the Paris/Dayton Peace Agreement; and to support the Stabilisation and Association Process (SAP). NATO is expected to decide, at its Istanbul Summit, to terminate the SFOR operation by the end of 2004. Thereafter, the EU would lead a military operation making use of the agreed framework on co-operation between the EU and NATO. The process towards this new mission will be led in close co-operation with the EU's partners and with their support. Consultations are ongoing with the authorities in Bosnia and Herzegovina, with High Representative/EU Special Representative Lord Ashdown, with NATO and with other international players including the United States.

This exchange succinctly captures the prevalent tactic of the EU, i.e. to skirt around the "citizens of BiH". Indeed, neither the audience nor the journalist ever learn what the EUFOR offers to the locals.

Significant Others

In contrast to "multiple others", when it comes to the pronounced significant others, partnership "implies mutual respect, fair burden-sharing, common analysis and definition of measures" (Solana 2004k, September 10). This is how the EU-US relations are presented, and their main objective seems to be the argument for a multilateral order where the EU's voice could also be heard. Solana reasons: "if we act together, the US will take heed and listen" (ibid.). In this sense, the multilateral order is advocated by the EU in three different ways: to begin with, it is promoted to carve out a(n equal) role for itself on the international arena; subsequently, it is to contain possible unilateralists; and, last but not least—and connected closely to the first—multilateral order, inclusive of key partners, is defined and offered as the single right *modus operandi* for the enterprise of peace-building.

In creating a place for the EU in the governance of international affairs, Solana propounds that "though the US is today's dominant military actor, it cannot tackle today's complex and multi-dimensional problems on its own" (2004c, February 25). In a similar manner, the member states are tied to the Union. Solana is vocal in convincing the member states of the importance of common action: "It is our task for us to get our act together" (2004k, September 10), for "threats are never more dangerous than when we are divided" (2004c, February 25). Interestingly, responsibility is used to underline both who the significant partners are and why it is imperative for the EU to become a global actor:

> Responsibility refers to the European willingness to provide security in proportion to our position in the world. .... . Due to our size and interests, our history and values, we are also ready to share the burden of global threats with other major players on the international scene. (Solana 2004a, February 17; cf. Solana 2004j, July 27)

Being a player of particular calibre—size, interests, history and values (as suggested above)—means that you have the prerogative to define what responsibility means in international affairs. Therefore, it appears commonsensical for these actors to divide the roles in international affairs among themselves, e.g. "NATO continues to bear the main responsibility for our security", as Prodi maintains, "but we need to ensure we can take action militarily where our American partners are not concerned" (2004, April 1).

Concerning the second point, the EU champions multilateralism to make it harder for the USA to act as a free agent. Solana stresses:

> Stronger security partnerships – and a more effective multilateral system – are essential for our security. Europe's partnership with the United States is irreplaceable. It has underpinned our progressive integration and our security. It benefits not only Europe and the US, but also the international community as a whole. (2004c, February 25)

Furthermore, the EU portrays the EU-US relationship in existential terms when pondering the fruits of their cooperation: "there is no doubt in my mind that, when we act together, America and the Union are the greatest force for international peace and stability. The USA needs the EU. The EU is the only global partner available to the USA and vice versa. This means that we need each other" (Solana 2004k, September 10).

Somewhat paradoxically or perhaps unavoidably, by arguing that the EU is/should be part of the imagined multilateral order, the EU simultaneously (re-)defines it, in order to make room for itself as a global actor:

> The United Nations is at the centre of this system, but can only play its role *if we* [the EU] *have imagination and collective will to strengthen it*, equip it to fulfil its responsibilities and to act effectively. And if we have the courage and determination to act when its rules are broken. (Solana 2004c, February 25)

> Ultimately, I believe that *the best way Europe can contribute to building a stronger UN is by building a strong and capable Europe*; a Europe firmly committed to effective multilateralism. These are not alternatives. They are complementary. (Solana 2004c, February 25; emphasis mine)

Essentially, defining what peace(building) is all about rests with these significant others. This is pointed out by Prodi, who asserts that "we cannot confine our efforts to our member countries. We need to project stability beyond our borders. That means promoting political and economic reforms that can enable our neighbours to share in our peace and prosperity" (2004, April 1; cf. Patten 2004, April 28). This latter idea is also elaborated upon in the ESS (2003), attesting to a rationale well captured in Muppidi's work, whereby "non-Western states are defined, framed, and judged within a framework of categories that takes the Western experience as the universal norm" (2004, 16). Attendant to this problem is the following mindset, where the self is simultaneously particular and universal (read: the EU and the IC), whereas the other (read: the shifting outside of the self) is sweepingly particular (see ibid., 66).

The above two sections—considering how the EU has portrayed different actors in its discourses—explored the degrees of dialogue between the EU and its others. Contrasting these two portrayals bespeaks the overall logic underpinning these dialogues, namely the utterly unequal positions of the EU's dialogue partners. On the one hand, the discussion with the multiple others revolves around their eventual becoming part of the "acceptable standards" on the international arena. The parameters of dialogue vis-à-vis the significant others, on the other hand, hinge on the distribution of roles to uphold the standard framework the multiple others should become part of. As this discussion demonstrates, the key difference between multiple and significant others is that the latter define the circumstances in which the former operate.

Telling EUFOR Althea

Key Goals of Althea

> Most Bosnians know that 80 per cent of the soldiers who will form EUFOR were also part of SFOR. Although there will be a change of badge and flag, there will be no change of policy, tactics or strategy. Delivery on the ground will be exactly the same. (Ashdown 2004b, December 22)

> In a BBC interview in 2003, the then high representative, Lord Ashdown, stated that, "if you want to fight crime … prostitution, drugs, cigarette smuggling - now an issue for today - arms smuggling, on the streets of Manchester, London, Berlin and Paris, you start here in Sarajevo. This is the front line". (quoted in Bancroft 2008)

This section is divided into three parts covering: (i) the cardinal objectives of EUFOR Althea; (ii) the ideas about the end state ("a slice of peace"?)—i.e. how peace is imagined; and lastly (iii), who Althea/peace is for.

The overall aim of Althea, according to the "sanitised version" of the concept for the operation (Council 2004g, September 29), was:

to provide *deterrence* and continued *compliance* as specified in Annexes 1-A and 2 of the General Framework Agreement for Peace (GFAP) in BiH and to *contribute to a safe and secure environment in BiH, in line with* its mandate, required to achieve core tasks of the High Representative (HR's) Mission Implementation Plan (MIP) and the Stabilisation and Association Process (SAP). (ibid., 2–3; emphases mine; Council 2004e, July 12)

It is crucial to note that contributing to a safe and secure environment in BiH is a leitmotif of operation Althea, and principally connected to the idea that BiH should be safe and secure are two concerns. Firstly, avoiding another outbreak of war and violence, which would constitute a rather dangerous security threat for Europe/the EU, and secondly, a safe and secure environment is necessary *for the implementation of the outside reforms* (see, e.g., Council 2004a, April 28, 6–7; 2004b, June 14). The security implied in this leitmotif—as Annexes 1-A and 2 of GFAP confirm—is traditional security (vs. human security; see Kaldor et al. 2004), which means that EUFOR is concerned with negative peace (see Galtung 1969).[29] Thus, Althea's vision of a safe and secure environment in BiH is mainly concerned with keeping BiH safe and secure for materialising certain outside agendas. This chimes with the assertion of the President-in-Office of the Council: "with ALTHEA, we are contributing to the security and stability of Bosnia and Herzegovina, which is important to the reforms in that country" (EP debate 2004, November 16). One can argue that these outside reforms or frameworks cater to the safe and secure environment, yet, as discussed above, in many ways these outside frameworks lack inside backing. To claim that would also imply that the reform agenda and the outside frameworks are able to reflect the realities in BiH better than direct engagement with the locals. But perhaps BiH is not the primary concern on the EU's mind when it comes to the operation. Consider, for example, Commissioner Patten's argument: "the launching of the ALTHEA mission is an important event: important because it will be the first significant military operation undertaken under the European Security and Defence Policy" (see EP debate 2004, November 16; cf. Anderson 2008).

In addition to providing a safe and secure environment, which falls under the key military tasks (KMTs), the operation also included supporting tasks, which will be briefly discussed here.[30] Primarily, this meant that the EUFOR would—as Solana puts it—*"have specific EU tasks.* Its job would be to assist this country's integration into Europe and in particular ... to help the BiH authorities fight the common scourge of organised crime" (2004f, May 29; emphasis mine). Furthermore, as Solana avers,

> one of the main political-military objectives of the EU-led force would be to provide support to the Mission Implementation Plan of the Office of the International Community High Representative (OHR) and, in this way, help support BiH's progress towards European standards. (ibid.)

Different themes are in play here: firstly, as the introductory quote by Ashdown suggests together with Solana's rhetoric in his interviews to Bosnian newspapers (2004f, May 28–29; 2004h, July 14), the crucial message to get across to the BiH audience was reassurance that EUFOR Althea would be identical to the NATO's SFOR. Herein particular emphasis was put on the fact that the number of troops would stay the same. Simultaneously, however, it appears that stressing the particularity of the EUFOR was also pertinent. The latter theme neatly fits the overall EU identity script that argues that the EU is especially well equipped vis-à-vis other actors to tackle crises because it combines civilian and military instruments (see, e.g., Solana 2004c, February 25). Thirdly, the deeply ingrained belief that the EU/Europe and its ways of political organisation—i.e. the European standards—equal progress sums up the idea common to the IC (as defined by the EU) that their way of life is unquestionably both superior and progressive (the need for the West's soul-searching on this matter is well argued for in Chabal's work [2012]).[31]

Perhaps most importantly, the issue of the fight against organised crime (OC) is not elaborated further, and thus, it remains unclear what the EU intends to do in this sphere. The question that arises is whether the EU considers this to be a common-sense matter, and thus self-evident and shared by IC/"all"? Hence, it is useful to consider how the EU has conceptualised OC in the context of the CSDP. As regards different logics of approaching (organised) crime, Berenskoetter's work (2008; cf. Juncos 2009) is useful as it discusses two lenses—utilitarian and critical—that offer different narratives on (organised) crime.[32] Consequently, his work challenges a universal, shared conceptualisation of (organised) crime. Berenskoetter, noting that there is no singular answer to what crime is, tries to pin down the elements of crime. He argues, borrowing from Garland (2002 cited in Berenskoetter 2008), that "one speaks of crime as an act (or practice) deviating from (or 'violating') an established norm". On the basis of this, "a definition of crime is always made", it is suggested "against the backdrop of a definition of order and ... a victim" (2008, 177). Bearing these building blocks in mind, a utilitarian perspective (associated with a problem-solving mindset), as opposed to the critical perspective, provides a fixed definition and adopts the present order uncritically, without addressing the power relations that had led to its establishment. Owing to the approach taken in this work, which is evocative of the critical perspective outlined in Berenskoetter (2008), a number of characteristics can be outlined with regard to the EU's take on organised crime. The ESS argues that the chief target (victim) of organised crime is Europe, whereas failed or weak states are the chief culprits (2003, 4). As a response to organised crime, "the EU pursues an agenda of building order under the umbrella of multilateralism" (Berenskoetter 2008, 184). The ESS champions the active "spreading of good governance" (2003, 10), highlighting that "it is in the European interest that countries on our borders are well-governed" (ibid., 7). The EU's understanding of organised crime follows the utilitarian logic and owing to that, as Berenskoetter points out, the main issue of concern is the coordination dynamics between different EU bodies on the ground (2008, 189). The final characteristic refers to the EU's ossified threat perception from BiH that does not per se resonate with the Bosnians' sentiment.[33] Owing to this reasoning, Berenskoetter points out that crime-fighting becomes order-building (see ESS 2003, 10), namely,

> the frequent emphasis on implementing 'EU style' law and order and 'establishing sustainable policing arrangements under local ownership according to best European and international practice' (Commission 2004d, para. 5) makes quite explicit the EU's aim of exporting its own vision of policing and judicial systems abroad. (2008, 185)

It is worthwhile to consider the logic of order in a more general sense and observe the power dynamics at play:

> A number of countries *have placed themselves* outside the bounds of international society. Some have sought isolation; others persistently violate international norms. It is desirable that such countries should rejoin the international community, and the EU should be ready to provide assistance. Those who are unwilling to do so should understand that there is a price to be paid, including in their relationship with the European Union. (ESS 2003, 10; emphasis mine)

Thus, the EU's objectives in fighting organised crime are overwhelmingly concerned with exporting good governance to BiH. The way OC is framed in the context of CSDP clearly demonstrates power/knowledge dynamics at play. Contrary to Europol reports (2004–2006), arguing that "indigenous OC groups from the European Union (EU), particularly those with extensive international networks, continue to represent the main threat to the EU" (Europol 2005, 5), OC is labelled as an external threat coming from outside the EU (e.g. ESS 2003, 4–5).[34] Furthermore, not only did the EU name OC the main threat for the EU, it was also identified as a "megathreat" for BiH itself (see Merlingen and Ostrauskaite 2005, 310), notwithstanding a somewhat different hierarchy of concerns of the Bosnians (ibid., 311; Juncos 2009, 56–57; Berenskoetter 2008, 192) and despite, as Juncos (2009, 57) maintains, not having a "proper assessment of the impact of organised crime until 2006". In the light of this, it seems that the EU saw OC operating under a single logic; as Juncos suggests (2009, 57), the EU securitised OC and that lead to viewing it as a hard security issue rather than an issue rooted in socio-economic problems. The way EU framed OC raises the question whether OC was designed to fit EUFOR, or should EUFOR have been designed to tackle OC?

Another key motif with regard to the purpose of EUFOR is the argumentation that "the European Union looks forward to continuing working closely with the Alliance in planning and executing this new ESDP mission, on the basis of Berlin Plus. This is a practical example of our strategic partnership in crisis management with NATO" (Solana 2004g, June 28; cf. Ashdown 2004b, December 22). Contrastingly, the ICG, commenting on the EU-NATO collaboration motives and the reason for EU deployment in BiH, argued that "the motives … have less to do with *the real security situation in that country* than with EU eagerness to bolster its credibility as a security actor and U.S. desire to declare at least one of its long-term military deployments successfully over" (2004, June 29; emphasis mine). Furthermore, it is continuously emphasised that the EU's engagement in the Balkans concerns the task of putting "Bosnia irreversibly on the track towards EU membership" (Solana 2004g, June 28; Council 2004h, October 11). It is not the case that the EU is not altruistic enough, but rather that it forces its own logic of how the world operates onto Bosnia as if it was the only right way. Furthermore, the EU paradoxically claims that BiH is irreversibly on the path towards the EU, while in the same breath propounding that despite this, BiH has a genuine choice about its future.

With regard to the overall EU political objectives in BiH, Althea should support the achievement of the various objectives as outlined below (see, e.g., Solana 2004g, June 28; Council 2004a, April 28):

(i) Long-Term Objective: A stable, viable, peaceful and multi-ethnic BiH, cooperating peacefully with its neighbours and irreversibly on track towards EU Membership.

(ii) Medium-Term Objective: Supporting BiH's progress towards EU integration by its own efforts, by contributing to a safe and secure environment with the objective of the signing of a Stabilisation and Association Agreement (SAP).

(iii) Short-Term objectives: To ensure a seamless transition from SFOR (NATO) to EUFOR (EU) in order to help maintain a secure environment for the implementation of the GFAP; the strengthening of local capacity building through support of the BiH authorities in implementing the 16 conditions in the feasibility study as part of the SAP.

All these objectives seem to be connected more to what the EU sees fit—in that a stable, viable and multi-ethnic Bosnia is not defined by the Bosnians but by the EU and/or other outside frameworks already in place—versus Bosnia's own objectives, needs and wishes.[35] In order to further illustrate Bosnia's restricted choices, one can consider the following statement: "at the very end, all these efforts are not about the future of NATO or the EU. *These efforts are about the future of this country. And this future is undoubtedly in Europe, in the European institutions*" (Solana 2004i, July 15; 2004l, September 17; emphasis mine). This more prominent agenda of helping Bosnia into the EU (and also NATO) dominates the operation's objectives: for example, Solana states at an informal meeting of EU defence ministers that "the EU-led mission in BiH will be credible and robust, and it will be directed towards the long-term integration of BiH in the European and Euro-Atlantic structures" (2004b, February 23; 2004l, September 17).

Probably, the biggest paradox of the EU's CSDP missions is that they operate under the assumption that it is possible to draw a clear dividing line between the civilian and military missions/activities, notwithstanding the constant rhetoric of a comprehensive approach. The military operations do not really concern the local as they deal with issues that are somehow commonsensically taken to be divorced from the everyday level. Hence, the label "military" indicates doing something *for*/on *behalf of* the locals rather than doing it *with* them, allowing only minimal space for the locals to voice their understandings. This becomes obvious from the way EUFOR Althea has been designed, which seems to reinforce the IC actors (including its own status on the international arena) more than focus on the security needs of BiH and support those. In the concept for the operation, the safe and secure environment is qualified as follows (Council 2004a, April 28):

> Contribute to a safe and secure environment, support the OHR's MIP and prevent efforts to reverse peace implementation, so that all EU and other International Community (IC) actors may carry out their responsibilities whilst ensuring own force protection (including counter terrorism) and freedom of movement.

Thus, as far as the joint action and the general concept of the operation are concerned, operation Althea promises security in the sense of no violence and stability, so that the IC, including the EU, can proceed with their reforms. Engagement with the local is limited—read: inclusive of the BiH authorities—and does not reflect an equal partnership (cf. the multiple and significant others sections above). Emphasis has been put on the idea that "the agenda of Dayton implementation is gradually being replaced by that of European integration. There are now new opportunities to seize, and new challenges to face" (Solana 2004g, June 28). At times, the EU advertised its approach as something new and unique and thus different from Dayton; however, the paradox lies in the fact that all of its policies are rooted in the status quo framework that was put in place pre-EU engagement. Thus, the argument of replacing the old agenda with an entirely new one seems to be naïve in the extreme, given that Bosnia was already a victim to a locked-in-syndrome where the overwhelming outside agendas have greatly depleted the space for BiH's own agendas.

How Does EUFOR Althea Imagine Peace?

What was the imagined end state of operation Althea? Firstly, the decision to end the operation is based on the EU's own assessment. As far as the local is concerned, it is said that the EU assessment will take into account the views of the BiH authorities (Council 2004a, April 28). As the concept for Althea suggests, the main criterion of success is that "progress towards lasting stability in the country is self-sustaining" (ibid.). The key then is to ensure that there is no resumption of violence, let alone war. Yet, the activities proposed under this rubric are not self-sustaining, as the ultimate concept of security employed by the EU in the context of Althea does not target human security but only military (no violence, no war) security. In this way, it is rather erroneous to use the term self-sustaining if in fact there are no activities proposed that would foster this state of affairs to come about.

Secondly, while the security situation in BiH undoubtedly benefits from the deterrent effect, this does not amount to a self-sustaining approach on its own—especially when the EU connects the deterrent value of the EUFOR to implementing what is foremost an external, and perhaps even more importantly, a top-down and exclusionary endeavour. As an example of this, the exit strategy of EUFOR Althea states: "the military exit strategy is to be based on progress in building efficient state level structures, in particular in the area of security and defence. This objective is primarily the responsibility of the BiH government assisted by EU civilian actors" (Council 2004a, April 28).

In connection to the end state, it is crucial to investigate the meanings of peace that EUFOR Althea communicates. As regards the EU, *in toto*, peace, at least in the Balkan context, is represented as follows: "peace is a fragile plant that calls for constant care and nurturing. There will be no lasting solution in the Balkans *if we do not offer the countries* in the region realistic prospects of joining the European Union" (Prodi 2004, April 1; emphasis mine). Similarly, Solana reaffirms—in line with a liberal-colonial imaginary (Muppidi 2004, 65)—that peace is somehow an article foreign to BiH, and furthermore, the EU is not there to assist but to put BiH "irreversibly" on the road to peace (read: EU membership):

> Bosnia-Herzegovina will be the first case where the EU deploys economic, trade, humanitarian, military and civilian instruments on the ground in pursuit of a single objective – the stabilisation and transformation of a post-conflict society into one which some day will be ready for EU membership. (Solana 2004c, February 25)

Overall, peace is equated with the future goal of EU membership, and the EUFOR Althea's role is essentially to ensure that the civilian activities of the EU proceed without any interruptions. Thus, in reality, EUFOR Althea offers a non-negotiable/inflexible path towards peace, in which everything that is proposed is somehow governed by the already fixed external frameworks (e.g. Dayton, SAP, MIP; cf. the multiple others section).

Who Is Althea for?

To an extent, this issue has already been touched upon above. Interestingly, the EU's information strategy with regard to Althea envisions a slightly more dialogical engagement with the local than the actual operation mandate itself. In that, as stated by the information strategy below, it would seem that the EU operation is in "close co-ordination with NGOs":

> The EUFOR will build on the progress made by NATO (SFOR) and the BiH authorities, taking over the security and stabilisation tasks and in close co-ordination with the efforts of the other EU actors, IOs and NGOs. (Council 2004a, April 28)

However, the mandate of EUFOR Althea, as well as the same concept document that also incorporates a note on the aforesaid information strategy, does not indicate or elaborate on how to work closely with the NGOs. In fact, the EUFOR Althea's engagement with the local starts and ends with the BiH authorities (see, e.g., Council 2004e, July 12). Yet, the link with the BiH authorities is not one heedful of a true partnership, but one that is reminiscent of an unequal relationship where the BiH authorities are designated either a passive role (they are consulted by the EU) and/or they are unfairly made responsible for the upshot of the actions of EUFOR Althea (but also on a more general level, for the overall EU activities in BiH).

The EU, according to the information strategy, "*is deeply engaged in BiH*, through the SAP and the fulfilment of the GFAP in order to maintain a safe and secure environment in BiH" (Council 2004a, April 28; emphasis mine). This statement acquires more substance once the richness of the context (see the sections above) is considered. With the context in mind, one is left with the impression that for the EU, "deep engagement" refers to a *deep intervention in BiH* rather than a *deep engagement with BiH* (that would be meaningful for the locals as well).

The semantics of deep engagement raises a number of questions: (i) is BiH the primary partner/beneficiary of Althea, given that its agency is basically nullified; (ii) if Althea is not primarily for BiH, then for whom is it? Following Muppidi (2004, 70; see also Mac Ginty and Richmond 2013,

769), this research—as has been argued from the start—sees as the *sine qua non* of peace operations a dialogic engagement, which suggests that "a reasonably democratic order – at global or local levels – would support a politics that promotes the participation of those who are the objects of that policy". In this sense, the EU with its operation does not treat BiH as a(n equal) partner, but rather as a patient that needs to be cured in order to become a worthy partner at an uncertain future moment.

The long-term objective of the EU in BiH thus casts the EU-BiH relationship in a certain light. The EU's preoccupation with building the oft-invoked "stable, viable, peaceful and multi-ethnic BiH, cooperating peacefully with its neighbours and irreversibly on track towards EU membership" (e.g. Council 2004a, April 28) carries a number of built-in tensions. Firstly, the imagined BiH does not correspond to the deeds chosen to get it there. In other words, short- and medium-term activities are largely alienated from the local level, with the BiH actors envisaged in rather passive terms when, for instance, it is suggested that in the medium term there should be a "gradual transfer of ownership to BiH authorities" (Council 2004g, September 29). Secondly, the tension between assisting/helping versus offering a ready-made peace package is rather evident, e.g. "all EU actors/instruments, including EUFOR, would contribute to implementing *EU policies towards BiH*: GFAP implementation and European integration through the Stabilisation and Association Process (SAP)" (Council 2004a, April 28; emphasis mine). And finally, is it possible to achieve a viable BiH, if in some stages of the EU engagement (if not in all) the BiH agency is disregarded?

ACTING EUFOR ALTHEA

Owing to the lengthy timeframe of the EU's operation in BiH (2004–present), the analysis of the acting phase of Althea will be divided into two periods, as it is not possible to cover the whole mission.[36] First, the immediate implementation of EUFOR Althea will be investigated (2004–2006). In December 2006, the EU took a preliminary decision to transform Althea, and starting from 27 February 2007, Althea operated under a slightly different mandate.[37] The crucial change here was that the uniqueness requirement that Solana had demanded of Leakey was scaled down. Thus, zooming in on the immediate implementation stage allows for studying the first period of materialising the telling of EUFOR Althea and more broadly realising the telling of the CSDP (= acting them out).

The second period under view, covering roughly 2010–2013, attempts to provide insight on how and where the EUFOR has "progressed".

Acting EUFOR Althea: 2004–2006

EUFOR Althea's Purpose

Solana: Could there be a worse scenario than a self-absorbed Europe, disengaged from *the world we wish to make fairer and safer?* ... Yes, *Europe today is the main vector of peace and democracy right across the world.* (2005c, April 18; emphasis mine)

Solana: Immediately after Dayton, there were clear imperatives: to build the peace and get the country up and running. This was an enormous task. (2005i, November 25)

Patrick Chabal: at bottom the West's sense of its own superiority is rooted in the belief that there is but one way of developing that can secure at one and the same time economic progress, material benefits and a socio-political arrangement that makes possible the most efficient use of the (material and moral) resources we need in order to progress in this fashion. That belief rests on the assumption of a *unilinear* form of development, which effectively translates into Westernisation: modernity is *ipso facto* Western.[38] (2012, 149)

The dual objective of this section is to, firstly, investigate in more detail the three themes of telling EUFOR Althea (as set out above, see the section *Telling EUFOR Althea*) and, secondly, to consider not only the divergences/convergences between the two processes of telling and acting— and beyond, but also to problematise the whole telling–acting process as a medium through which actors operate in the world. The question that entails is, what can one gain from viewing the telling and acting in a processual way, as is done here?

To begin with, I examine the so-called civilian face and the particularity demanded of the EUFOR mission. It is worth noting that, according to the very first force commander of EUFOR Althea, David Leakey,[39] Solana was relentless on EUFOR being "'new and distinct' and" that it "should 'make a difference'" when it succeeded NATO's SFOR (2006, 59–60).[40] According to Leakey, this new and distinct character translated into the operation's "novel 'key military task' to support the High Representative's Mission Implementation Plan and in its 'key supporting task' to support the fight against organised crime" (2006, 59). On balance, to Leakey, it appeared that the "new" was particularly needed to boost the EU's self-image, and to enlarge the EU's foreign political capital. In other words, the positive upshot of the "new" is framed by Leakey as follows: "through combining its military and civil operations, [the EU] achieved a collective and politically significant impact in BiH during 2005, *especially through promotion of the EU 'brand' in the public perception*" (ibid., 67–68; emphasis mine). This way of putting it coheres with Anderson's thesis on the importance of the CSDP to the EU's identity-building project (2008). At this juncture, an interesting tendency emerges: the EU simultaneously seeks to reassure the audience (in Bosnia and beyond) that the EUFOR will be identical to NATO's SFOR, and to accentuate the uniqueness of EUFOR (and thus the difference from its NATO predecessor).

According to Leakey's understanding, the "new and distinct" tasks of "supporting the fight against organised crime" and "supporting the MIP were two sides of the same coin" (2006, 62). The link that Leakey made between the two is based upon his understanding that, as far as MIP was concerned, the main problem it faced was obstructionism—not clearly defined apart from saying that this phenomenon prevents the progress of BiH and the possibility of its entering the EU/NATO. "This obstructionism", he further expands, "manifested itself and was reflected in the organised crime and in the vested interests and corruption of many of the political leaders which pervaded the political and administrative establishments – at all levels" (ibid.). This way of framing the issue suggests that ultimately, the main "enemies" of BiH are to a large extent its elite/authorities (read: the main partners of the EU and, in fact, most of the IC). But perhaps even more quizzically, Leakey's claim indicates that the obstructionism and organised crime the EU is most concerned with relate to those of its elements that hinder the EU reforms. The fact that this problematic affects not only the EU and the IC—or the reform package in its entirety—is something that is not really elaborated upon. As a result, this communicates a tendency of the EU to be occupied with its own agenda and its own definitions of problems to the detriment of how this may affect the people on the ground. This is further illustrated by Solana, when he reports in Brussels on the achievements of EUFOR: "EUFOR has efficiently supported the actions taken by Lord Ashdown and created a safe and secure environment for the BiH authorities to continue their reforms" (2005b, March 18).

Despite the link envisaged between obstructionism and organised crime (see Leakey's reasoning above), the EUFOR does not really explain how it intends to target organised crime; rather the delineation of EUFOR's role in this area is obsessed with clarifying its non-executive mandate vis-à-vis local authorities. Therefore, as Leakey maintains, "EUFOR would help discover a crime or illegality (e.g. fuel smuggling or illegal timber cutting), but would 'freeze the scene' and hand it over to the BiH authorities to deal with the legal and law enforcement technicalities" (2006, 63–64). Solana further muddies the waters when he states that: "EUFOR has *assisted* in a number of operations in the fight against organised crime – an issue, which is today probably posing the most dangerous threat for the country (Council Dec. 2005). And, wherever possible, EUFOR leaves the responsibility to the BiH authorities".[41] These assertions demonstrate how the meaning of support is stretched in that the local authorities are not in the driver's seat. This way of imagining the EU's role towards the local authorities corroborates Merlingen and Ostrauskaite's argument that EUFOR "operated on the assumption that the police was rotten and untrustworthy" (Merlingen and Ostrauskaite 2006, 75). In fact, contrary to the EU's own discourse that frames EUFOR as having a supporting role, a number of sources suggest that initially (mainly in the first year of its operation), "EUFOR organised and executed its own law enforcement operations without lead participation from the EU Police Mission (EUPM) or BiH counterparts" (Friesendorf and Penksa 2008, 677–678; see also Merlingen and Ostrauskaite 2006, 75–76; Juncos 2006). It is crucial to follow in detail the argumentation of the EUFOR's force commander with regard to the need for EUFOR to take on a supporting role in fighting organised crime, in order to inspect more thoroughly EUFOR's role and its relationship with its lauded partners. "This means", as Leakey reasons,

> that EUFOR would not substitute itself for the local authorities. EUFOR would only support, for three reasons: political (the common objective of all the EU actors in BiH is to develop local capacities), legal (EUFOR does not operate under local law) and practical (soldiers cannot generally be transformed into law enforcement agents). (2006, 62)

Perplexingly, the articulation that "the common objective of all the EU actors in BiH is to develop local capacities" does not necessarily match the patronising explanation of EUFOR's concrete *modus operandi*, which again questions the agency of the local authorities and does not tally well with the announced "supporting role", as outlined above (cf. Council 2005, December). Inconsistency also besets Leakey's explanation of one of the objectives of EUFOR—to support the fight against organised crime. Since the following excerpt of discourse demonstrates a number of themes (responsibility, sustainability, EUFOR's relationship vis-à-vis the local authorities, the nature of the EUFOR's attitude), it is worth quoting at length:

> The idea was to create the conditions so that, although EUFOR might be in the lead at the outset, the BiH authorities would gradually take over, lead and initiate operations which they had not previously undertaken. The local law enforcement agencies had respect for EUFOR and were eager to cooperate with it and learn from the way it planned, conducted and reviewed operations. Over the year 2005, the BiH authorities did indeed gradually take over, leading and initiating operations. (2006, 64)

Of course, it is not uncommon to find inconsistency in an actor's discourse, but it is noteworthy to encounter such level of ambiguity in such a short time span. The issue to highlight here is the way the EU understands local ownership, and consequently, how this understanding shapes its policies in general. For the most part, local ownership applies only after the parameters of "how to do peace" are set—note that how they become set is not really problematised—meaning that the locals can gradually *take over* (see the passage above) from, e.g. the EU, but not really author/own peace. In this sense, the concept of local ownership in the EU's vocabulary has a specific meaning, which gives rise to a persistent paradox in the telling and acting of this concept. The concept of local ownership is always pre-filled with the EU-authored content; accordingly, the locals are supposed to own the frameworks they are handed when they gradually become ready to do so.

When it comes to the military tasks, "EUFOR's primary *raison d'etre*", as intimated by Leakey, "was to provide a security reassurance" (2006, 60; also see Council 2005, December 19). This military objective—often referred to as providing a safe and secure environment in Bosnia—is not elaborated upon apart from connecting this aim to activities of stabilisation and deterrence—i.e. no violence. As for the concrete tasks that fall under this objective, Leakey offers an assortment of these:

> EUFOR continued many of SFOR's military operations such as confidence patrolling in remote or unsettled areas; 'harvesting' weapons from the community; supervising the BiH Armed Forces' and the Defence Industry's com-

pliance with the Dayton Agreement; and assisting the BiH police security operations in the community. (2006, 61)

Leakey summarises this core mission—i.e. providing continued deterrence and reassurance—as follows: "EUFOR guarantees the peace by deterring anyone who might try to upset it" (Council 2005, December). In this sense, as the telling phase already communicated, what the "safe and secure environment" entails for the most part is the stability for implementing IC's reform package. However, there are instances, albeit very few, where it is suggested that "the armed forces main task is to provide deterrence and to provide a stable environment for the population" (Council 2005, December).

Although the former proposition—i.e. EUFOR equals security for reforms—is given much more prominence in the EU's discourses, it is worth pondering (see Overhaus 2009, 21) whether it is possible to gauge the impact that the EUFOR has had on the stability and security in BiH. Of all the different questions that arise in that regard, here I only consider one, because I see it as a starting point for all the rest. In order to start measuring the impact on security and stability, first one has to go back to the EU's understanding of security/stability (to an extent these matters are dealt with above). In doing so, it becomes clear that the EU's security/stability assessments go against a number of external assessments of the security situation on the ground. For instance, Kostić reports (2007, 315–316) that the majority of BiH population, when asked, "[do you] feel safe in your place of residence", reply that "they feel totally safe".[42] Although this may seem to indicate EUFOR's success at providing security, one needs to consider that in 2005, "an overwhelming majority of Serbs, Croats and Bosniaks live in areas where their ethnonational group enjoys absolute majority" (Kostić 2007, 291). Thus, the hard security that the EUFOR offers does not really match the situation on the ground, where, as Kostić maintains, the main issue of concern has to do with societal security (see 2007, 28–31)—a term which pertains to threats to group identity (ibid., 28). By analysing the salience of ethnonational identity at elite and population levels, Kostić avers that "all three communities remain highly mobilised around their ethnonational identities" (ibid., 343). It is critical to note that threats posed by this are not primarily related to physical violence, but rather to structural violence (see ibid., 335), in the sense that:

> Despite ten years of international peacebuilding, the crux of wartime incom-
> patibilities has remained unresolved. While the violence has been stopped
> and political discussion has been resumed, members of the three nations
> continue to perceive themselves as being under threat when in a minority
> position, and seem to define their preferences for how the state and society
> should be organised from the perspectives of their own communal concerns.
> (ibid., 298)

In this context, the argument of providing a safe and secure environment
in BiH becomes threadbare if it is not further explained how the EUFOR
proposes to deal with this societal security dilemma that Kostić describes.

The EUFOR, by treating the local as a relatively homogeneous entity
(except for the occasional differentiation between the bad guys [those who
undermine the reform process] and good guys [those who nod to the
reform process]), further aggravates the societal security dilemma, since
it ignores the "communal grievances" (see ibid., 344) and different positions of the ethnonational groups on how to organise the state and society.
Thus, the EUFOR's approach appears to be disconnected from the BiH
context, and furthermore, it seems to be part of activities of the IC that
work forcefully against the local context.

EUFOR Althea Acting Out the Peace: The End State for BiH?

On a general note, it is clear that the "peace" the EU envisages for BiH originates in the EU/Europe/the West. Solana maintains: "Europeans want
their values - human rights, solidarity, justice and peace – promoted around
the world" (2006a, January 27). This, of course, does not mean that European values (including ideas about peace) cannot be very similar, or indeed
identical to the ones in BiH, but to assume a priori that this is the case and to
act by leaving little room for engagement or open dialogue conveys insen-
sitivity to the context. Additionally, this tendency for speaking on behalf
of the whole of Europe continues without a legitimate mandate. Solana
persistently argues that he is certain of what the people of the EU/Europe
like and support: "I am convinced that our citizens want this. The polls
show it consistently. And it is logical too" (ibid.). Furthermore, it is not
only the wishes of Europeans that Solana purports to know, but also the
wishes of the multiple others: "it is not self-indulgent to say that from the
Middle East to Africa, from the Balkans to South East Asia and elsewhere,

the call goes out: can Europe help?" (ibid.). To illustrate this attitude even further, it is worth quoting Solana's reasoning at some length:

> In short, when I travel around Europe, I hear a demand for Europe to play a greater international role. The same is true when I travel around the world. It may be fitting to paraphrase Nike's slogan: let's just do it. The good news is that even in the sensitive area of foreign and security policy, we have come a long way in a short period of time. Like a baby, in foreign policy too, we began talking before we started writing. And we started writing before we started acting. But now we do all three. (ibid.)

It is interesting, though not surprising, that Solana's discourse accommodates diverging ideas. In addition to the more prominent theme discussed above, there are at times hints of a more participatory mood, e.g. in the following assertion:

> In the beginning outsiders have leverage, commitment and resources. But that wears off. If peace is to endure, it should rest on the parties themselves, at the level of both elites and ordinary people. It should be their peace, not ours. Too often when we negotiate an end to a conflict we do not do enough to negotiate the peace. (2006b, June 27)

Although at first sight this may look like a call for a more participatory engagement, this thought operates on a rhetorical level compared to the discourses presented above, in particular, to the conceptualisation of local ownership.

In the context of Artemis, it was possible to show how the telling and acting processes were mobilised by the EU in the aftermath of the operation in order to bolster the CSDP identity/policy. With EUFOR, this is not possible as the mission is still ongoing; nonetheless, it is possible to follow the ideas communicated about the concluded operations. For instance, at this particular instance, Solana presses for a tale of an overall success:

> and where we have acted we have succeeded. We have helped governments take forward *their peace processes* and we have helped to make those processes more sustainable by strengthening their institutions. Most of all, although much remains to be done, of course, in all of these places, we have improved the lives of people and given them hope. (2007, January 29; emphasis mine)

This statement aptly conveys the EU's approach and illustrates the misguided belief of the ownership of the peace process, given that it is impossible to suggest that BiH authorities or the public take forward "their peace process", when even a cursory glance back at the contextual dynamics shows how packed the BiH peace process was with external programmes and agendas. Furthermore, it is repeatedly made clear that EUFOR, as Leakey suggests, "guarantees the peace by deterring anyone who might try to upset it" (Council 2005, December).

Similarly to academic works that have to date been more invested in talking about coordination/effectiveness issues and the like, the EU itself, when drawing conclusions or reflecting on its actions, usually resorts to something akin to what Solana does here:

> If there is a "lesson learned" from interventions in crisis areas such as Bosnia, Kosovo, Afghanistan, Iraq, Sudan/Darfur, the Congo and many others, it is the need to enhance our effectiveness through better co-ordination of civil and military crisis management instruments. (2005f, October 17)

This way of reflecting is a mainstay in the EU's discourses, i.e. the content of the mission is not questioned or problematised. The aspect under scrutiny is mainly the coordination/cooperation dynamics between the EU and various IC actors, or inside the EU (i.e. between different instruments). This echoes Chabal's idea (2012; see esp. Chapter 3 in this book) that the common trait to the West's mindset is the fact that it sees itself as apolitical and non-ideological.

EUFOR Althea: As if BiH Was not There[43]

> EUFOR has been and continues to be a major success for the European Security and Defence Policy (ESDP). (Solana 2005e, October 13)

Similarly to the phase of telling Althea, the main beneficiary of the EUFOR operation in the acting stage is the EU itself. In the words of Solana, EUFOR's relevance and the main recipient of its "success" are summed up as follows:

> EUFOR matters for the simple reason that this is by far our largest military operation. I am pleased how successfully you have demonstrated that the European Union is fully able to carry out such a large-scale operation,

under the Berlin+ arrangements. (2005j, December 6; see also Solana 2005e, October 13)

As the sections above have already given ample clues to the topic under consideration, here I will accentuate the main strain of ideas concerning the addressee of EUFOR's peace.

To begin with, EUFOR Althea serves foremost the interest of the EU in securing for itself a place in the club of global actors. According to Solana, there is a certain understanding of what makes a global actor:

> Indeed we are a global actor. With 25 member states, with over 450 million inhabitants, a quarter of the world's GNP, and around 40% of the world merchandise exports; and with the comprehensive array of instruments – economic, legal, diplomatic, military – at our disposal, that claim is not an aspiration but a statement of fact. (2005a, January 24)

Thus, EUFOR Althea serves as a demonstration of the EU's military muscle that is deemed necessary for occupying the position of a global actor in the international arena. Althea is used as evidence to support the following stance: "we also have significant operational experience" (Solana 2005d, September 26; also Solana 2005g, November 9; 2005h, November 21; 2006a, January 27; 2006c, September 8). Furthermore, "ESDP has made CFSP more credible" (Solana 2007, January 29), and the quantified approach to success continues (see Artemis analysis, Ch. 4): "conducting no fewer than seven operations simultaneously and on four continents has been a key component of ESDP's success" (Council 2006a, June 7). Already at the end of 2005, this argument is made: "but look where we are today. We are united around a single, comprehensive strategy for the region. The Western Balkans are now one of the success stories in EU foreign policy. And it is recognised as such around the world" (Solana 2005e, October 13).

Additionally, the operation (and the EU's activities more broadly) has been articulated as a test case for the EU's foreign policy. Consider, for example, the oft-quoted motif: "the importance of continued EU engagement cannot be overstated. More than any other region in the world, [the Balkans] … are a European responsibility. Simply put, we cannot afford to fail" (Solana 2005d, September 26). With reference to the previous argument, it is further claimed:

maintaining the European membership perspective is the only way we will have real leverage over local leaders so that they take the tough decisions that are needed. It is the only way to achieve the stabilisation and integration of this region, in which we have such an enormous political and moral stake. (ibid.)

The crux of the matter is whether Althea benefits BiH, and to what extent? As far as the official discourse is concerned, Althea "continues to ensure a safe and secure environment" (Solana 2007, January 29; Council 2006b, June 12). However, as demonstrated above, this statement without the contextual nuance is highly ambiguous. Hence, to a certain degree, the EU lives up to its commitment in the telling phase, where it described the BiH context as being in need of military security, by offering traditional security in the acting stage. The problem lies in the fact that the EU's operation defines the problem and then designs the answer accordingly, when it should "listen to" what the problem is and then offer "real" support to resolve it—and not just control disguised as support.

ACTING EUFOR ALTHEA: 2010–2013

The days when EU foreign policy could be dismissed as all talk and no action are long over. (Ashton 2010b, February 6)

By January 2010, together with the reduction of EUFOR troops, the mandate of the operation changed to "include non-executive capacity-building and training tasks as part of the EU's contribution to security sector reform in the country" (Juncos 2013, 150).[44] Furthermore, as of 10 October 2011 (see Council 2011b, October 10), the operation's main focus shifted to "capacity-building and training while also retaining the means to contribute to the Bosnia and Herzegovina authorities' deterrence capacity". At present, the operation's mandate has been extended until 6 November 2019 (UNSC 2018).

The idea of the following section is to focus on the same three elements—the *key tasks*, the *beneficiaries of Althea* and the *end state*—and, by doing so, understand the substance of the operation EUFOR Althea and how it is represented. This exercise will provide insight into what the CSDP is about and demonstrate the value of scrutinising Althea via media of the telling–acting model.

Key Tasks: Simulacra of the Safe and Secure Environment

> At the heart of everything we do lies a simple truth: to protect our interests and promote our values we must be engaged abroad. No one can hope to be an island of stability and prosperity in a sea of insecurity and injustice. Ours is a world in flux. To engage with it effectively, *we need to frame it first*. (Ashton 2010c, March 10; emphasis mine)

> The European perspective remains the overarching framework – both as our objective and as the main incentive for reform. As I stressed everywhere: progress on the path to the EU depends on the commitment to reform at home. (ibid.)

The overarching framework that governs EUFOR Althea is, as the Council puts it, "to support a political process aimed at enabling BiH, *on the basis of the necessary reforms*, to continue to move forward in the EU integration process" (2010a, January 25; emphasis mine). One of the core objectives of the EU's foreign policy, according to Ashton, is "to ensure greater stability and security in our neighbourhood, *by promoting political and economic reforms*. This is important in itself for reasons which are self-evident. But our wider international credibility also depends on getting the neighbourhood right" (2010c, March 10). In order to grasp what this reform agenda means for BiH, at least two aspects need to be considered: who are these "we" that frame security issues, and where does BiH fit in?

Starting from 2010, Althea's mandate changed. Next to the goal of maintaining the safe and secure environment, the operation took on capacity-building and training tasks. The latter rubric comprises the following three groups of activities: (i) exercises, capacity-building and trainings, (ii) local community involvement and (iii) liaison and observation teams' activities.[45] These tasks, together with the continuing deterrent effect, aim at maintaining a safe and secure environment in BiH—or, as COM EUFOR, Major General Bernhard Bair, suggested, the importance of Althea lies in the fact that it is "the guarantor of a safe and secure environment" in BiH.[46]

Materialising EUFOR's New Tasks: Exercises, Capacity-Building and Trainings

The first group of activities includes a number of different endeavours, such as seminars (on, e.g. medical evacuation and search and rescue), exercises (e.g. EUFOR's own rehearsals (refer to Exercise Quick Response), joint trainings (EUFOR together with AF BiH) and courses (e.g. on IT, or emergency rescue from a minefield). Through these activities, the EU defines the relationship between EUFOR and the armed forces of BiH (hereafter AF BiH). Thus, the EUFOR is described as the knowledgable teacher and the AF BiH as the unknowledgeable pupil, or, in other words, "the EUFOR is heading", according the commander of EUFOR, General Heidecker, "in the correct way towards developing the AF BiH trained to international standards and capable of participating in Euro-Atlantic structures and a self-sustainable training system for the AF BiH".[47] One constant in EUFOR's discourse—and by extension the EU and IC's—is the reference to international/UN/NATO standards as the taken-for-granted benchmark against which the state of AF BiH is measured. In this way, the international standards (or European standards) are presented as the only correct way of operating, i.e. the superior know-how to which the EUFOR (and the IC) offers privileged access. This has an effect of constructing an allegedly homogeneous international sphere that operates by these standards, and the "outside" that needs to be educated (enlightened?) along their lines. The standards framework has become a banal structure that the different IC actors subscribe to and promote in BiH (and in the Balkans in general) as a panacea to the problems of Bosnia. Furthermore, the humdrum repetition of the European prospects for the Balkans (see, e.g., Ashton 2010a, January 11; 2010b, February 6; 2010c, March 10; Council 2010a, January 25) hijacks the future of BiH from ordinary Bosnians, in that the (non-)debate over BiH's future hinges on the motif "there is no alternative to Europe" (Van Rompuy 2010, October 20; Bancroft 2010; Jansen 2014). There is a deafening consensus that the praised standards— functioning more as empty signifiers than carriers of real substance—work at "home", and perhaps more importantly, that these standards are shared by everyone, i.e. the troop-contributing countries, who presumedly promote these, know and practice them, notwithstanding the arbitrariness of these standards (see, e.g., ESI 2007).[48] This also raises the question of power, that is, who is the final "judge" in determining that different parties adhere to these standards (leaving aside for the moment the questions of whether this structure should be the starting point in the first place, and whether there is one and correct readily applicable framework altogether) (cf. Caplan 2005)? As has been argued already, the IC has undermined these standards, since imposing their own agendas on BiH leaves very little space for the locals to construct their own alternatives. If democracy is seen as one of these standards, then importing an externally manufactured social contract into BiH would, for the IC, qualify as failing to practice what they preach.[49] "The European Union and the Member-States", notes Ashton, "have an impressive array of instruments, resources, relationships and expertise *to help build* a better, more stable world" (2010e, July 7; emphasis mine). The emphasis should be on "help/assistance", but in many cases it is not, in that, help/support/assistance is seen to apply only at a later date, once the country in question has become more like us, or more like an actor that "we" define as "right". In a way, it appears that the EU does promote a truer and inclusive "help package":

> the EU does not believe that democracy can be exported or imposed, but democratic development and consolidation in third countries can be supported. There is no one single model of democracy. Democracy must come from within and be shaped by each society, based on universal principles, but taking into account the unique historic, geographic and cultural context of that society. (Ashton 2010f, September 15)

Yet, this commendable sentiment exists mainly on the declaratory level, co-existing as it does with contradictory messages in both telling and acting phases (refer to arguments provided above). For instance, "in the Balkans as much as elsewhere", asserts Ashton, "we know that a lasting peace depends *not so much* on foreign intervention but on the efforts and commitment of *local political leaders* themselves" (2010d, May 4; emphasis mine). But then again, the emphasis should be placed on understanding who the EU takes as legitimate local actors. In her second quote, Ashton clarifies this predicament: it is the political elite who are branded legitimate.

To illustrate in more detail what this first group of activities (exercises, capacity-building and trainings) signifies, one activity will be examined further. In 2013, EUFOR conducted a rehearsal of its own deployments to "demonstrate the ability of EUFOR to successfully activate, quickly deploy and integrate two of the four companies held at readiness within its Intermediate Reserves Forces".[50] According to EUFOR, this will demonstrate:

(i) The effective and efficient operation of Intermediate Reserve Forces validating EUFOR's ability to use over the horizon surge forces when and where necessary.

(ii) EUFOR on-going capacity to perform the key military tasks necessary to preserve a safe and secure environment in BiH.[51]

Commenting on EU's rehearsal operations, General Shirreff affirms "the European Union's on-going commitment to the support of a safe and secure environment in BiH".[52] Furthermore, according to EUFOR, this type of exercises, generally speaking, is designed to "demonstrate the commitment of the EU, partners and other international organisations to support the Safe and Secure environment in BiH and to validate EUFOR's ability to surge its troop contingents".[53] This conveys that, to a large extent, the safe and secure environment that the EUFOR promises is situated in the future; in effect, the EUFOR is preparing itself for a counterfactual future event. In parallel, the EUFOR argues that its sole presence works as a deterrent to instability. Accordingly, maintaining a safe and secure environment in BiH acquires a very specific meaning. Namely, the presence of EUFOR, contrary to what the EUFOR communicates, seems to rather be an exercise of fearmongering, since it tirelessly evokes a need to maintain a safe and secure environment (albeit in a strictly military sense). In this, the public (read: ordinary Bosnians [?]) is treated as a passive agent. Consider, for example, the following representation of the state of affairs in BiH by EUFOR: "the public should be reassured that EUFOR retains the capability to support peace and security in BiH". As a consequence, it reserves for itself the privilege to frame and judge the security situation in the country. "When in September 2012 the number of troops deployed in EUFOR Operation Althea was reduced it was done", as EUFOR propounds, "in recognition of the significant improvement in security in this country and the increasing role played by BiH authorities".[54] At this juncture, it is worth invoking the arguments of the Commander of EUFOR (COM EUFOR), Robert Brieger, that throughout the EUFOR's operation there has not been a single incident that required a military response, and that the problems in BiH are beyond military, e.g. organised crime and economic disaster. He goes on to qualify that BiH is secure and stable from a military point of view.[55]

In the course of the mentioned exercise cycle, the AF BiH is to benefit as follows:

> Learning the skills required in international peace support operations, like using English as the working language, drafting and executing Standard Operational Procedures, adhering to Rules of Engagement and other typical international procedures, will help the AF BiH to improve their ability to design and execute own exercise scenarios.[56]

In other words, the EUFOR's rehearsal operation demonstrates its own military muscle, its ability to react to an imagined counterfactual in conjunction with moulding the AF BiH to fit the international standards. "The whole capacity-building industry", Mac Ginty stresses, "is premised on the notion that the people of war-torn societies lack capacity and must be taught and enabled by outsiders. There seems to be little understanding of the profound lack of capacity held by outsiders" (2014, 5). To add to Mac Ginty's observation, consider how Bono questions the discourse of the linear logic of achieving progress: namely, she points to the cracks in the standards of the EU/Europe itself, suggesting that these have been a work-in-progress rather than set once-and-for-all (2006, 154).

In order to draw conclusions on the first group of activities, it is crucial to return to their goal(s). The goals can be situated on a scale from general to specific, where the first relates to the overarching aims of the new tasks of EUFOR since 2010 and the second addresses the specific objectives of the exercises/trainings/capacity-building agenda. First, the overall goal of these "new capacity building and training tasks" is to "contribute to strengthening local ownership and capacity" (Council 2010b, April 26). Furthermore, the overarching frame—redolent of a liberal colonial imaginary (Muppidi 2004, 65)—is described as follows: "EUFOR is supporting the normalisation process and the Rule of Law in Bosnia and Herzegovina in close co-ordination with the International Community and International Organisations". More specifically, the goal is "to ensure AF BiH continues to develop as a modern armed force at the level required for euro-atlantic integration and that its military personnel have the capacity and skill to deploy and positively contribute to international missions overseas", "to assist AF BiH in achieving a robust and self-sustainable training structure".[57] It is crucial to bear in mind that local ownership here has a very specific flavour, in that it refers to a very restricted understanding that the local will be ready/able/qualified once we, the EUFOR, have trained them accordingly. This characteristic is succinctly elaborated upon by the EUFOR itself: "this support [by EUFOR Capacity Building and Training Division] greatly contributes to the development of the AF BiH capability to organise and eventually run their own training system".[58] Or alternatively, the responsibilities currently under EUFOR and/or IC jurisdiction can be "transitioned to BiH ownership" but after the local actors (e.g. AF BiH) have been subjected to exercises/trainings/capacity-building by the "knowledgeable(s)". Bearing this in mind, the EUFOR in 2013 remarks that "soldiers from AF BiH are approaching the level of professionalism required for successful Euro-Atlantic integration".[59]

Materialising EUFOR's New Tasks: Local Community Involvement
All the tasks belonging under the label "local community involvement", are, according to Robert Brieger (COM EUFOR), subsidiary tasks, in that they are not a priority, however, by undertaking these sorts of activities the EUFOR "builds up trust" in BiH. Moreover, because EUFOR, as Brieger elucidates, is part of the international community, it is necessary to be integrated and show the willingness to help within our capacity.[60] These subsidiary tasks include, for instance, holding gender conferences, putting out wildfires, organising school competitions and races. Below a selection of these activities will be discussed in more detail.

The 2011 School competition, organised by EUFOR, had two themes: "Europe without Borders" and "Children of the European Union". In the frames of this art competition "the children were asked to produce a drawing or painting, design a poster, draw a comic strip or, with a group of friends, produce a photo essay", and the prizes for winners included trips abroad, computers and cameras (donated by the IC). In addition to the goals introduced by Brieger, Gen Bair (who was EUFOR commander just before Brieger) said: "this competition provides the youth of Bosnia and Herzegovina an opportunity to express their hopes for their nation to join the European Union".[61] This is a clear instance of the well-known tactic of "winning hearts and minds" rather than true engagement, especially in view of the way EUFOR speaks on behalf of the youth of BiH instead of truly listening to them. In a similar vein, the EUFOR Youth campaign was launched with the following message: "the campaign focuses on the young people of BiH and that the institutions in Bosnia and Herzegovina need to start functioning effectively. Only when this happens can BiH move towards the European Union and get things moving in the right direction to provide a better future for the youth". This campaign is rife with ideological and populist fervour. "The purpose of this campaign", as General Bair states, "is to raise awareness across the country and remind everyone that BiH is standing still and by doing this, we are letting down the youth of BiH. We must make the youth of BiH the winners of both today and tomorrow!"[62] To sum up, the EUFOR notes that it "organises a number of initiatives in support of the youth of the country in order to bring children from across BiH together to show them that they are all the same and that they need to work as one to bring a prosperous future to BiH".

The second activity that is included under this rubric is organising gender conferences. Interestingly, one of these taking place in 2012 was entitled "BiH NGOs, EUFOR and Gender". Its aim, as EUFOR put it, was "to contribute to a better understanding of the valuable work being carried [*sic*] by the various Non-Governmental Organisations (NGOs) in BiH and their important link to the local population". This particular event was only attended by the elite (e.g. ambassadors, representatives of the IOs, BiH authorities). In 2013, there was another gender conference with an aim "to strengthen the gender perspective within the security sector in Bosnia and Herzegovina".[63] In particular, the conference's "topics included ways of implementing UNSCR 1325 on women, peace and security. The conference was attended by high-level EUFOR and AF BiH officials, representatives of non-governmental and international organisations and provided lectures on gender aspects regarding the security sector reforms and best practices". This, in theory, sounds like a positive endeavour. However, the approach taken, i.e. "to provide a floor for the Gender Focal points in the Security Sector of BiH to increase their awareness and gain a conceptual understanding of gender issues in the security sector", is somewhat futile when one contextualises the EUFOR's own knowledge and practices in implementing UNSCR 1325 and/or gender mainstreaming. Richer understanding of this issue vis-à-vis the EUFOR is offered by Batt and Valenius' study in 2006. The authors point to a relevant contextual dynamic within which CSDP operations are deployed in BiH. Namely, Dayton Peace negotiations and the ensuing peace agreement, as well as the mandates of the military and civilian peace operations, did not contain a gender perspective (Batt and Valenius 2006, 5). One of their findings was that although "the top-level officers in both missions [read: EUFOR and EU Police Mission in BiH] demonstrated a positive disposition towards women in the missions ... they had very little knowledge of what gender mainstreaming actually is and what purposes it serves" (2006, 7). Furthermore, investigating the attitudes of staff deployed to BiH suggests that even if generally, senior military officers tended to be supportive of women's participation in peace operations (see ibid., 8), they did have a number of fixed assumptions which meant that although in theory, women's contribution was seen positive, in practice this did not work. Thus, when investigating the views of the members of the Liaison and Observation Team (LOT) in Foca—who were all male—the researchers registered that all of them agreed that "the presence of women colleagues would unnecessarily complicate life in the LOT house", and moreover, "women soldiers would not be appropriate for the LOT's task of liaison with local authorities" (ibid., 8). Although this study was conducted in 2006, and thus may not represent the state of affairs today, it demonstrates EUFOR's engagement patterns at that time and raises some important questions for CSDP military operations in general. In 2006, the researchers remarked: "it seems ESDP missions have not attempted (or if they have, they have not succeeded) to reach the female population in BiH. There is frustration and disillusionment within women's organisations with the EU" (ibid., 12). Also, the women's groups interviewed pointed out that "the EU (and other international organisations) only work with government officials and politicians, not with grassroots organisations" (ibid.). This manner of engagement seems to have not changed much and is not seen as a problem, since in most cases, as Brieger suggests, LOTs obtain their information through patrols and contact official decision-makers in the vicinity.[64] The superficiality of this endeavour is further reinforced by the fact that women and gender seem to surface only in the context of a few gender conferences and are not truly part of the daily activities or mandate of the EUFOR. This, as a result, demonstrates some very troubling lackings in the general portrait of the EUFOR operation that clings to traditional security and thus engages with the locals in an openly superficial manner.

As a result, what these activities demonstrate is, first and foremost, that their aim of building up trust serves certain interests (the EU's and local authorities') and not others (the wider civil society). It also exhibits the at times problematic tendency of outside actors to engage in winning hearts and minds rather than being open to truer forms of engagement. This superficial mode of engagement becomes clear based on the offered examples, which exhibit the limited understanding of who the locals are and what engagement means.

*Materialising EUFOR's New Tasks: Liaison and Observation Teams'
Activities*
LOTs' core purpose is to provide situational awareness, and/or as Brieger argues, LOTs are the "ears and eyes" of the EUFOR operation. The problem with the EUFOR's approach regarding LOTs is that their information gathering techniques—creation of knowledge about BiH—is seen as a straightforward exercise and not one that is saturated with power relations.

According to Brieger, as mentioned above, LOTs' main contact point is with the local authorities. The way the EUFOR represents the local community succinctly demonstrates its understanding of the local. In EUFOR's own words:

> It was readily apparent that the Swiss soldiers had integrated well within the local community which was confirmed when the Ambassador and COM EUFOR later met with City Mayor Ljubo Bešlić, President of the City Council Murat Ćorić and Chief Advisor to the City Radmila Komadina. The Mayor spoke about the importance of the LOT house in the city.[65]

The token relationship between EUFOR and the locals is well illustrated by its activities. For instance, the EUFOR argues that LOT house in Livno built a partnership with the Women's Association of Livno. The partnership amounts to the following: "EUFOR has been able to support the project by advising on the lay-out and the printing of books dealing with these subjects [gender law, the fight against domestic violence, violence amongst children]". It is further suggested by EUFOR:

> This initiative highlights how those manning the LOT houses across Bosnia and Herzegovina are working to develop relations with their neighbours and the local authorities with the aim of helping the local population live together in a stable and multi-ethnic environment.[66]

With this understanding of local dynamics, in which the local population is represented as a passive agent, the EUFOR's engagement with the locals (apart from authorities?) amounts to mere tokenism as the examples above indicate. The engagement of LOT houses with the locals is mostly on their own terms (see, e.g., Commission's Progress Report 2010). Consider, for example, the purportedly "excellent cooperation" between Tuzla LOT house and the local grammar school Os Mejdan: "the principal of OS MEJDAN, Ms Nizama Hamzic, has always agreed to requests from LOT Tuzla to carry out Mine Risk Education training in her school", and "she also appreciates the short presentations concerning the business activities of the LOT which are thoroughly enjoyed by both pupils and teachers".[67] These stories of EUFOR's activities are clearly meant for a much wider public, or perhaps only for the "outside", because they seem to be more concerned with acquiring legitimacy for EUFOR and boosting its image than engaging with the locals. However, it seems that this superficial engagement with the locals has a clear purpose, i.e. to muster support for the operation. According to Brieger, EUFOR is very popular among the locals. This information, as Brieger suggests, comes from LOTs and personal observations.[68]

Beneficiaries of Althea

Though not explicitly underlined, the question of *who EUFOR Althea is for* was embedded in the previous sections. In this section, the attempt is made to tease out the key beneficiaries of Althea more overtly.

The main argument here is that Althea's purpose is to build a credible CSDP and, by extension, a more credible foreign policy for the EU rather than to contribute to peace in BiH. From report to report, the EU's untiring aim is to make "the EU a more capable global actor" (see, e.g., Council 2012, July 13). This seems to reverberate with mainly quantitative capabilities versus substantive capability—i.e. it is evident from the above sections that being/becoming a global actor means demonstrating the ability to act, but not the ability to act meaningfully. It appears that CSDP operations allow the EU to state its credibility for the peacebuilding enterprise more convincingly: "With engagements in the Balkans, in Asia, in Africa and off the coast of Somalia, the EU acts as a provider of security" (ibid.). It is worth noting that cooperation with the locals is not seen as an aim in itself, but rather as a means to something. For instance, the EU frames the importance of civil society/NGOs as follows: "the Council recalled the importance of co-operation with NGOs and civil society as a means to improve the impact of the CSDP missions and operations and encouraged its continuation both in Brussels and in the field, including through regular contacts" (Council 2010b, April 26).

In addition to building a credible image, the EU argues that EUFOR and its non-executive capacity-building tasks help "to improve the quality and know-how of AF BiH units" (Council 2011a, March 14). This assertion carries with it the idea—elaborated above—that there are unified, shared international standards and that EUFOR's approach is just technical. It simply introduces these standards to AF BiH, who apparently do not abide by them. In relation to this, the EUFOR seems to be suggesting that once an actor accepts the international standards, it automatically becomes better or acts in a normatively better way. But perhaps even more importantly, the EUFOR does not question the relationship between means and ends, the core assumption being that it is possible to postpone local ownership until the local conditions are judged "normal"—i.e. in line with international standards—and still build sustainable peace. However, whether this really is the case is something highly debatable, as there is inconclusive evidence that these promoted international standards are better.[69] Also, the development of AF BiH is not the final goal, but rather, as EUFOR itself suggests, EUFOR's non-executive mandate "is geared to ensure AF BiH continues to develop as a modern armed force at the level required for euro-atlantic integration and that its military personnel have the capacity and skill to deploy and positively contribute to international missions overseas".[70] The Euro-Atlantic integration of BiH appears to be one of the key goals and a self-evident route to progress, e.g. refer to the EUFOR statement that "EUFOR is supporting the normalisation process and the rule of law in Bosnia and Herzegovina in close co-ordination with the International Community and International Organisations", and "soldiers from AF BiH are approaching the level of professionalism required for successful Euro-Atlantic integration".[71] In this way, to turn to Rorty, the EUFOR (the EU) seems to be basing its activities on a foundationalist narrative, taking a "jigsaw puzzle view of things", meaning that the EU has achieved progress and now it offers this to BiH. Contrary to this approach, Rorty is of the belief that "there is no such thing as the nature of the state or the nature of society to be understood – there is only an historical sequence of relatively successful and relatively unsuccessful attempts to achieve some combination of order and justice" (2007).

In addition to the AF BiH, the "public" also benefits from EUFOR's activities. Principally, this argument is premised on three suppositions: (i) if war/violence breaks out then, in theory, EUFOR would support peace and security in BiH; (ii) military security and the deterrent function of EUFOR are a *sine qua non* in order to maintain a safe and secure environment in BiH; and (iii) the public itself needs the EU—and by extension the IC—on their path, as EUFOR suggests, *towards* normalisation (cf. Paris 2004; Mac Ginty 2014). The first supposition is built on a counterfactual scenario, i.e. should war break out, then EUFOR would react. The articulation of this counterfactual is problematic, since it points to a status-quo mentality, casting the BiH context in a particular light. The EUFOR's militarised security framework articulates uncertainty on the part of the people of BiH, arguing that: "the public [people of BiH?] *should be reassured* that EUFOR retains the capability to support peace and security in BiH" (emphasis mine).[72] Also, it is suggested that these regular exercises that EUFOR conducts prove "EUFOR's ability to use over the horizon surge forces when and where necessary". Simultaneously, the EUFOR presents the decrease in force numbers as a result of a "significant improvement in security" in BiH "and the increasing role played by BiH authorities".[73] Relatedly, the second assumption suggests, as EUFOR puts forth, that EUFOR's performance of its military tasks is imperative to maintain a safe and secure environment in BiH.[74] Here, the key lies in understanding what exactly the phrase "to maintain a safe and secure environment entails"; as discussed above, this referred to a very limited conceptualisation of security, i.e. military security representing negative peace. The third point implies that EUFOR subscribes to the liberal mode of thinking, which communicates, as Mac Ginty (2014, 2) puts it, "a firm belief in the reformability of people and institutions".

The gist lies in the way the roles are imagined, with the EUFOR as the reformer and the BiH as the reformed. Thus, the concept of local ownership acquires a specific (though not unique) meaning in the context of EUFOR's operation. In a nutshell, it refers to a process of reforms, where a clear asymmetry of power exists, i.e. the EUFOR authors and the AF BiH downloads, and this process is "transformed" when the AF BiH has proven to develop in the right direction, and as a result, the imagined local partners move towards local ownership. Another twist in the plot concerns the EUFOR's cherry-picking of local actors (by an large, local authorities), and this is legitimate because the EU(FOR) has defined security in a way that allows for this manoeuvre. In this context, it is not surprising to read that "the Council welcomed progress with the implementation of the Operation's new capacity building and training tasks, which would contribute to strengthening local ownership and capacity" (Council 2010b, April 26).

End State for BiH and/or CSDP?

> In a way, the Balkans is the birthplace of EU foreign policy. More than anywhere else, it is where we cannot afford to fail. (Ashton 2010c, March 10)

According to Anderson, "foreign and security policy is a powerful tool long used by states to unite and focus the will of the people. As one of the premier symbols of the state, the military stands for power and independence [...] the ESDP is a tool for creating pride among the people and support for the European Union" (2008, 62). In a similar way, many conflict theatres have become the test cases for the EU's CSDP, and thus, the aim of naming EUFOR Althea successful, so that CSDP could be called a success, reverberates in the EU's discourses.

The overall goal and framework within which the Althea operates is the Dayton agenda, expressed as follows: "EUFOR is supporting the normalisation process and the Rule of Law in Bosnia and Herzegovina in close co-ordination with the International Community and International Organisations".[75] In this way, it is possible to argue that Althea offers a slice of "peace" together with a number of other IC actors. Within this framework, Althea promises: (i) to maintain a safe and secure environment in BiH and (ii) to strengthen BiH Armed Forces. Since the different dynamics involved in reaching these goals are discussed in detail above, accordingly here the aim is to capture the chief activities connected to realising these objectives. The broader end state that is imagined by EUFOR is that BiH stays on the course to joining the EU, as General Bair pronounces: "for me the real prize will be for all of the citizens of BiH to join the family of European Union nations and EUFOR will continue to work tirelessly to provide a safe and secure environment so that this can happen" (2010, May 5).[76] The EUFOR, although at first (until roughly 2007) aiming to be different from NATO, during the years 2010–2013 displayed a very limited conception of security which, admittedly, was not in line with the BiH context, whose problems, as COM EUFOR Brieger suggested, were beyond military.[77] As an illustration, consider the following statement by the Chief of Staff of EUFOR, Brigadier General Gerd Bischof: "It is the International Community's distinguished ambition *to prevent the return of violence to this area. Just by serving as a soldier in Camp Butmir we give the people the justified feeling of security*" (2010, August 23; emphasis mine).[78] Yet, side by side with Brieger's assertion, it is argued that EUFOR's "ongoing capacity to perform the key military tasks [is] necessary to preserve a safe and secure environment in BiH". The main question that arises from this is whether providing military security can relate to the everyday security (and the lives) of people in BiH. From the activities that EUFOR engages in (see sections above), it becomes apparent that the main activity to contribute to the safe and secure environment is its deterrent role. However, it is questionable whether this will serve as a means to contribute to sustainable peace (cf. Björkdahl et al. 2009, 4). Brieger argues that since the deployment of EUFOR, no single incident has required a military response and adds that from a military point of view the security situation in BiH is secure and stable.[79] Thus, to sum up, it is worth observing that one of the key activities of EUFOR—deterrence—and its outcome—the safe and secure environment—have brought about a situation of "no war". This contribution to the "no war" situation aggravates the key problems in BiH, as outlined by

Dennis Gratz, who argues that a key issue now is the cementing of status quo which creates apathy and disillusionment among the people of Bosnia (see also Bajrovic et al. 2005). He believes that this is so because the official policy is out of sync with people's needs.[80] The traditional security agenda of EUFOR, because it lacks a broader understanding of security, fails to address the security needs of the people.[81]

The second activity, providing capacity-building and training support to AF BiH, contributes to "strengthening local ownership and capacity" (Council 2010a, January 25). The imagined end result of this process is an AF BiH that is "strengthened" so as to "contribute to international missions overseas".[82] It seems that the aim of strengthening AF BiH is to recruit manpower for peace support operations, as EUFOR maintains: "AF BiH should be able to provide capability oriented and trained personnel in line with international standards, able to participate in Peace Support Operations (PSO)".[83]

All in all, the analysis above has illustrated that the substance of reforms (democracy, security, rule of law, etc.) are seen as an unproblematic function of the correct infrastructure (e.g. robust state institutions, etc.). The operation's efforts are directed at the infrastructure, and the substance is assumed to follow suit. Comparing the telling and acting stages, it becomes evident that there is no discursive contradiction present over this issue in the EU's own eyes. It is problematic that this division is created in the first place, and that neither the form not the substance is at all problematised.

Conclusion: EUFOR Althea as Capital on the International Stage

Self-government to be self-government has merely to reflect the will of the people who are to govern themselves. If they are not prepared for it, they will make a hash of it. I can conceive the possibility of a people fitting themselves for right government through a series of wrong experiments, but I cannot conceive a people governing themselves rightly through a government imposed from without, even as the fabled jackdaw could not walk like a peacock with feathers borrowed from his elegant companion. A diseased person has a prospect of getting well by personal effort. He cannot borrow health from others. (Gandhi 1939, November 25, quoted in Brown 2008)

The EUFOR is only a small part of the overall peacebuilding enterprise that operates within Bosnia. However, it is a part of the overall framework which contributes to an unsustainable governance structure that creates the illusion of self-government (see the excerpt above). Below the main themes that surfaced during the analysis of EUFOR Althea will be highlighted.

The EU in measuring the success of its CSDP missions more often than not resorts to quantifiable data and internal criteria. In the end, numbers and the capacity of the EU to act matter more than the outcome of its operations on the ground. As Ashton triumphantly suggests: "it is striking how far we have come in the last ten years. More than 70,000 men and women have been deployed in this period in more than 20 missions. We do crisis management *the European way*. With a *comprehensive approach*. In support of international law and agreements. And in close cooperation *with key partners*" (2010c, March 10; emphases mine).

The analysis of the EU's military operation in BiH was focused in the discursive context framing the operation. A key finding on this front is that the way BiH has been imagined by the EU has moulded its responses to the BiH context. Also, more generally speaking, investigating the contextual dynamics draws attention to the overwhelming leverage and scope of external frameworks (e.g. Dayton, SAP, etc.). Thus, structurally, it is clear that certain norms and ideas are more prominent on the EU's agenda than others.

The key themes' section both concretises and subverts some of the dominant ideas communicated by the EU in the context of becoming and being a peacebuilder. To reiterate, three topics are worthy of highlighting. Firstly, the mantra "deeds count more than words" seems to have become the very essence of the EU's foreign political outlook and with a rather specific message behind it. The focal point is in staging "action", whereas the process and outcome of "the acting" are consigned to the background. In fact, it appears that the latter two aspects are a non-issue, especially since the acting in itself is seen so positively, particularly in self-referential terms—that is, making the EU into a certain kind of actor, an actor with a *capital*. Secondly, the EU's simultaneous plea for uniqueness and difference from the others in the business of peacebuilding, and for sameness with the IC, signals another worthwhile tactic for assembling capital on the international arena. Thirdly, cues to how the Western peacebuilders are at the helm of envisioning peace(building) are abundant. By delving deep into the telling and acting of EUFOR, the analysis demonstrated how concepts such as local ownership and responsibility are used by the EU, and how the EU relates to its others.

The telling–acting frame employed in the analysis of Althea will be considered in more detail in the final discussion, where evidence from the three case studies will be collated into a more conclusive account. Broadly speaking, the advantage of the frame of *telling and acting* is that it does not solely promise an analysis based on whether these two aspects add up to one another, but rather provides a spectrum of different relationships, e.g. rhetorical, performative, ambiguous, etc., where consistency between the phases is just one possible criterion. What is more revealing is the way how both phases are complicit in imagining, representing and producing meaning.

With reference to telling EUFOR Althea, the major foci included envisaging security in a very traditional sense, imbued with the idea of stability. The security agenda was connected to the outside "needs" rather than internal dynamics. In terms of the EU aiming concurrently at both sameness and difference, an effort is made to link Althea to NATO's SFOR, while at the same time stressing the EU's uniqueness by promoting its supporting tasks—helping BiH to the EU and tackling organised crime. The accents given to these agendas are tightly tied up with two prominent objectives: testing CSDP and the Berlin Plus arrangement with NATO.

The acting phase of Althea comprises a number of emphases, with perhaps the most prominent being the aspiration to connect the meanings of new and distinct to Althea and thus reinforce the overall discourse of the EU as a unique actor. In this way, more emphasis is placed on how this might benefit the overall CSDP discourse than how this might benefit BiH. It seems that the underlying belief is that what is good for the EU is *ipso facto* good for BiH. Further, this chapter explored the EU's understanding of local ownership, concluding that the EU's ideas of assistance and support translate into superintendence, and thus local agency is policed and welcomed only if it corresponds to the externally imposed frames. Given that the main agenda on the security front is ensuring the stability for implementing the IC reform package, the security-related concerns of the population are not addressed as these are not even given any consideration. The local (as far as it is engaged with at all) is always approached on the EU's own terms.

NOTES

1. The idea of the different meanings of spaces is put forth in Kappler's work (2012a; see also Autesserre 2014).
2. Taking cue from postcolonial thought, Todorova explores how the Balkans were imagined as a dichotomous category—as the Europe's *other*—via the phenomenon of *balkanism*, which according to her, "expresses the idea that explanatory approaches to phenomena in the Balkans often rest upon a discourse or a stable system of stereotypes that place the Balkans in a cognitive straightjacket" (2009, 193; cf. Bakić-Hayden 1995; Hughes and Pupavac 2005).
3. For detailed overviews of the EU's activities in BiH both before and after the war consult, for example, the works of Kappler (2012a), Juncos (2005), and Chandler (2005).
4. Sustainability encompasses the premises introduced in Chapter 3 of this book, but see also Lederach (1997).
5. His term lasted from May 2002 to January 2006 (http://www.ohr.int/?page_id=1153).
6. Knaus and Martin note that at the time of Ashdown's term the office of the OHR had grown extremely intrusive. Before 1997, when the "Bonn powers" were put in place, "the OHR had no power to impose anything. Its brief was to act as the Accords' guarantor and to 'facilitate' the signatories' own efforts to implement the peace settlement" (2003, 63). Then, as of 1997, the OHR's mandate was widened to include "vast new powers in the crucial areas of institutional reform, substantial legislation, and the personnel of public office" (ibid., 64). See also Bieber (2006, 83–85) and Kostić (2007, 81–93).
7. See the discussion of leadership without responsibility in Chandler (2010, 76).
8. The report was presented to Javier Solana in Barcelona on 15 September 2004.
9. Juncos argues that the drives behind the EU's Bosnia policy are articulated in detail in the *Comprehensive Policy for BiH* (see Council 2004b, June 14).
10. See, for instance, Epstein (2014), but also the other articles in "Interrogating the Use of Norms in International Relations: Postcolonial Perspectives" (*Forum* 2014).
11. This issue is further elaborated in Chapter 3 of this book.
12. To name a few, the works of Chandler (esp. 2000), Kappler (2012a), the special issue on BiH and peacebuilding (*Special Issue* 2005), Mujkić (2008), Belloni (2007), and Hunt (2011).
13. Hunt, having had a close contact with the policy realm, conveys that "the Foreign Service culture does not value or reward local expertise" (2011, 217).

14. See Caplan (2005) and Ivanić (2005) on the accountability deficit of the IC in Bosnia; see also Jansen (2006); ICG (2001b, November 29).
15. For further details about NATO's effort from IFOR to SFOR consult the ICG (1997, December 15).
16. It is a general practice of the IC to gauge success quantitatively (a tactic well-recorded in the analysis of the EU's Artemis operation in Ch. 4. Moreover, the emphasis put on enhancing the freedom of movement via the betterment of the infrastructure actually skews (unintentionally or not) the manifold problems with returns (of both majority and minority IDPs [internally displaced persons] and refugees) elaborated upon elsewhere (see Heimerl 2005).
17. For instance, Bieber (2006, 3–4) notes that the country "remains deeply divided" and adds, relying on a UNDP report (2003, 27), that "a majority of Serbs and a strong minority of Croats prefer secession from Bosnia, whereas an overwhelming majority of Bosniaks supports the continued existence of Bosnia". See Kostić (2007) for a detailed analysis of the population's and political elite identities around 2005.
18. For more detailed accounts of the way the local is represented by the IC, and the ways in which the local reacts to this, as well as the ways in which the local sees itself without the IC filter, can be found in Kappler's work (see, e.g., Kappler 2012a, b); see also Cubitt (2012, 2013) and Chopra and Hohe (2004).
19. Under the rubric of securitising identity, Belloni (2001, 170, 173) describes the tactics of coercion and consent (following Gramsci's ideas on hegemony) through which, he argues, the "ethnic domination, social fragmentation, and internal group cohesiveness (vis-à-vis opposing ethnic groups) are maintained".
20. Kostić's work demonstrates that both the three national communities and the political elite exhibit remarkable divergences when it comes to the organisation of the state and society (2007, 292, 335).
21. Evans-Kent and Bleiker (2003, 107–116) refer to three vital issues concerning the NGOs in BiH: first, the NGOs in BiH are dependent on donors' agendas, meaning that NGOs struggle to fit the outsiders' project rather than having the outsiders fit theirs; second, there is an unconstructive tension between local and international organisations, especially since the international *modus operandi* aggravates the power asymmetries already in place; third, the authors recognise a certain ad hoc mannerism of NGOs in BiH and add that those that have managed to coordinate their activities have been more successful, yet they also note that there is a fine line between the first and third issue mentioned here.
22. Two comments are apposite here: first, as Juncos notes, no change took place regarding the composition of the forces, in that "essentially the same forces which contributed to SFOR were present in EUFOR (the soldiers

just swapped their badges for the insignia of the European Union Force), but with the major difference that there were no US troops" (2011, 85). Second, and more important, is the fact that "EUFOR was essentially modelled on the previous NATO-led operation SFOR. During the planning phase, the transfer of operational procedures and practices from NATO was of paramount importance. Most of the planning relied on the intelligence and assessments of SFOR on the ground and NATO Headquarters in Mons (Brussels) and EUFOR basically inherited SFOR's OPLAN" (ibid., 91).

23. See also Björkdahl et al. (2009; Kappler and Richmond 2011) who argue that there is not something substantially different in the EU's peacebuilding approach. Note that they concentrate less on the CSDP aspects whereas here it is in the foreground.

24. Tickner has demonstrated how the division of labour in the discipline of IR operates: "the first world/North has come to be viewed as the primary producer of 'finished goods' or scientific theory, while third world/South sites constitute sources of 'data' or, in the best of cases, local expertise, while interpretation – a decisive stage in theory-building – occurs in the North, where knowledge is produced and circulated in order to be consumed worldwide" (2013, 631). Analogously, it could be suggested that the knowledge of the right ways of building peace is confined to the Western space.

25. Yet, at this point this is only a rhetorical commitment and a more comprehensive view of this will be offered in the analysis of EULEX Kosovo.

26. The "general concept" is more commonly known as the Crisis Management Concept (CMC). The CMC is a strategic document identifying the need for a particular CSDP mission, together with the political objectives, aims and possible tasks (for a detailed account of planning and conducting CSDP missions, see Merlingen 2012, Ch. 8).

27. In the context of the CSDP operations, "the Political and Security Committee (PSC) drafts 'Master Messages' to underpin a public information campaign for every operation it undertakes" (Lynch 2005, 26).

28. See   http://www.ohr.int/ohr-info/ohr-mip/default.asp?content_id= 29145 (this link is no longer accessible).

29. Refer also to Richmond's take on human security, which goes well beyond Kaldor's concept. He argues that human security has been defined in different ways (in a continuum from broad to narrow) and in practice its narrow conceptualisation has dominated the IC's use of it (2012–2013, Winter, 210–211).

30. The Key Military Tasks (KMTs) and the Key Supporting Tasks (KSTs) are set out in the Concept of the operation (Council 2004a, April 28).

31. Richmond (2012, 361) discusses the tension in the international community's approach to local ownership, namely, the fact that local agency is

seen as crucial, yet it is, as he argues, "moderated by the allusions to universal norms, principles and standards." This in turn draws attention to the embedded power relations, where those who have not defined these norms must still follow them.

32. Though the author offers a third perspective in view of the noted "lack"—i.e., the resistance aspect of domination—it is here subsumed under the critical project since the author's proposed third perspective shares its commitments (see Berenskoetter 2008, 191–194).

33. See, for example, the report of European Stability Initiative (2007) that casts light on the ambiguity of police reform, the lack of debate that surrounded it, and moreover, the question of (organised) crime in BiH and whether that really was as serious a threat as the EU claimed.

34. Consult the Europol reports here: https://www.europol.europa.eu/latest_publications/31.

35. All the outside peacebuilding efforts, including the EU's, were based on a vision of BiH as a unified and centralised state without entities and cantons. Thus, the whole peacebuilding enterprise operated in a way against the wishes of some parts of BiH's population. As Kostić's work (2007, 293–295) demonstrates, in 2005 Serbs were clearly opposed to a centralised BiH, whereas Bosniaks supported this wholeheartedly, Croats, for their part, preferred the establishment of a three-entity federation in BiH.

36. See Dijkstra (2013, 104) for a brief overview of the timeframe of the operation.

37. Operation Althea has been reconfigured many times, for further details about the latest extension consult: http://unscr.com/en/resolutions/doc/2443.

38. Blaney and Inayatullah refer to a similar "temptation" by the "European core to treat its self-understandings as universal and international society as merely an extension of a European self". This logic of self-other relations is, according to the authors, the key hindrance to conversation (2004, 357–358; see also Prashad 2007).

39. Major General David Leakey was Commander of the European Force (EUFOR) in Bosnia and Herzegovina between December 2004 and December 2005.

40. Allegedly, the "new and distinct" feature of Althea was not something that was shared among the architects of the operation, in that Solana's vision was not supported by the member states (see Juncos 2006). Yet, as Dijkstra observes, because Solana was able to influence Leakey, the first phase of the operation was somewhat more ambitious than the official mandate would suggest (2013, 122–123; cf. Leakey 2006).

41. Refer back to the discussion of how the OC is framed by the EU in the telling part.

42. This sociological survey was conducted in the summer of 2005. In addition to Kostić's work, see other sources that do not see the hard security as the main problem in BiH (e.g. ESI 2007; Bajrovic et al. 2005).

43. The second part of this heading is paraphrased from the title of Slavenka Drakulić's novel *As if I Am Not There* (1999) to convey the absurdity of connecting EUFOR Althea with BiH.

44. The EUFOR Capacity Building and Training Division reached full operational capacity on 1 July 2010 (see http://www.euforbih.org/index.php?option=com_content&view=section&id=20&Itemid=150, under the rubric capacity building and training; note that this information is no longer available on the EUFOR Althea's official web page: http://www.euforbih.org).

45. These categories are taken from the web page of EUFOR Althea: http://www.euforbih.org.

46. Refer to http://www.euforbih.org/index.php?option=com_content&view=section&id=20&Itemid=150 (rubric "Exercises and trainings"; this rubric no longer exists on the EUFOR web page, last accessed August 2014).

47. Op. cit., note 44.

48. EUFOR troop-contributing countries, according to the operation's web page: 17 EU member states and 5 partner nations: Albania, Chile, the Former Yugoslav Republic of Macedonia, Switzerland and Turkey.

49. See, for instance, "Council Conclusions on Democracy Support in the EU's External Relations" (Council 2009, November 17).

50. Op. cit., note 44.

51. Ibid.

52. Ibid.

53. Ibid.

54. Ibid.

55. Personal interview at Camp Butmir, Sarajevo, 23 August 2012.

56. EUFOR web page (see rubric "Capacity building and training"). Op. cit., note 44.

57. Ibid.

58. Ibid.

59. Ibid.

60. Op. cit., note 55.

61. See http://www.euforbih.org/index.php?option=com_content&view=section&id=20&Itemid=150 (rubric "Local Community Involvement"; this rubric no longer exists on the EUFOR web page, last accessed August 2014).

62. Ibid.

63. Ibid.

64. Op. cit., note 55.

65. See http://www.euforbih.org/index.php?option=com_content&view=section&id=20&Itemid=150 (rubric "Liaison and observation teams"; this rubric no longer exists on the EUFOR web page, last accessed August 2014).
66. Ibid.
67. Ibid.
68. Op. cit., note 55.
69. It seems, as suggested above, that rather than referring to a clear-cut substance, the label "international standards" in the EU's discourse seems to be used to legitimise its actions. To further investigate the content of these standards as they are applied on the ground, one would need to conduct an ethnographic study (this would mean wider access to the operation on the ground).
70. Op. cit., note 46.
71. Ibid.
72. Ibid.
73. Ibid.
74. Ibid.
75. Ibid.
76. This information was accessed in August 2012 under the rubric "EUFOR news" at the EUFOR home page http://www.euforbih.org/index.php?option=com_content&view=section&layout=blog&id=20&Itemid=176; this information is not available any longer, last accessed August 2014.
77. Op. cit., note 55.
78. Op. cit., note 76.
79. Op. cit., note 55.
80. Personal interview with the head of the political party *Naša stranka*, Sarajevo, 20 August 2012.
81. See for instance Bojicic-Dzelilovic and Kostovicova (2011) and Kaldor and Beebe (2010).
82. Op. cit., 46.
83. Op. cit., note 44.

References

Anderson, Stephanie B. 2008. *Crafting EU Security Policy: In Pursuit of a European Identity*. Boulder: Lynne Rienner.

Ashdown, Paddy. 2002. "Inaugural Speech by Paddy Ashdown, the New High Representative for BiH." BiH State Parliament, May 27. http://www.ohr.int/ohr-dept/presso/presssp/default.asp?content_id=8417.

Ashdown, Paddy. 2004a. "Report to the European Parliament by the OHR and EU Special Representative for BiH, January–June 2004." November 3. http://www.ohr.int/other-doc/hr-reports/default.asp?content_id=33446.

Ashdown, Paddy. 2004b. "Interview: Paddy Ashdown, the High Representative in BiH and Special Representative of the EU." December 22. http://www.ohr. int/ohr-dept/presso/pressi/default.asp?content_id=33834.

Ashton, Catherine. 2010a. "European Parliament Hearing—Opening Remarks." Brussels. In *EU Security and Defence: Core Documents 2010*, vol. XI, compiled by Catherine Glière, January 11. Paris: EUISS. http://www.iss.europa. eu/uploads/media/CoreDocs-2010_EN.pdf.

Ashton, Catherine. 2010b. "Catherine Ashton—Munich Security Conference." Munich. In *EU Security and Defence: Core Documents 2010*, vol. XI, compiled by Catherine Glière, February 6. Paris: EUISS. http://www.iss.europa. eu/uploads/media/CoreDocs-2010_EN.pdf.

Ashton, Catherine. 2010c. "Address by Catherine Ashton at the Joint Debate on Foreign and Security Policy—European Parliament Plenary." Strasbourg. In *EU Security and Defence: Core Documents 2010*, vol. XI, compiled by Catherine Glière, March 10. Paris: EUISS. http://www.iss.europa.eu/uploads/media/ CoreDocs-2010_EN.pdf.

Ashton, Catherine. 2010d. "Statement by High Representative Catherine Ashton at the UN Security Council." New York. In *EU Security and Defence: Core Documents 2010*, vol. XI, compiled by Catherine Glière, May 4. Paris: EUISS. http://www.iss.europa.eu/uploads/media/CoreDocs-2010_EN.pdf.

Ashton, Catherine. 2010e. "Speech by HR Catherine Ashton to the European Parliament on the Creation of the EEAS." Strasbourg. In *EU Security and Defence: Core Documents 2010*, vol. XI, compiled by Catherine Glière, July 7. Paris: EUISS. http://www.iss.europa.eu/uploads/media/CoreDocs-2010_EN.pdf.

Ashton, Catherine. 2010f. "Declaration by HR Catherine Ashton on the Occasion of the International Day of Democracy." Brussels. In *EU Security and Defence: Core Documents 2010*, vol. XI, compiled by Catherine Glière, September 15. Paris: EUISS. http://www.iss.europa.eu/uploads/media/CoreDocs-2010_EN.pdf.

Autesserre, Séverine. 2014. *Peaceland: Conflict Resolution and the Everyday Politics of International Intervention*. New York, NY: Cambridge University Press.

Bajrovic, Reuf, et al. 2005. "National Human Development Report: Better Local Governance in Bosnia and Herzegovina." http://www.ba.undp.org/content/ dam/bosnia_and_herzegovina/docs/Research&Publications/NHDR/BiH_ NHDR_2005_Better_Local_Governance_En.pdf.

Bakić-Hayden, Milica. 1995. "Nesting Orientalisms: The Case of Former Yugoslavia." *Slavic Review* 54 (4): 917–931. https://doi.org/10.2307/ 2501399.

Bancroft, Ian. 2008. "Spot the Difference: Representations of Post-conflict Bosnia and Herzegovina which Reiterate 'Otherness' Undermine Progress and the Prospect of EU Membership." *The Guardian*, June 22. http://www. theguardian.com/commentisfree/2008/jun/22/balkans.eu.

Bancroft, Ian. 2010. "'European Standards' Hinder Balkans." *The Guardian*, April 22. http://www.theguardian.com/commentisfree/2010/apr/22/european-standards-hinder-balkans.

Batt, Judy, and Johanna Valenius. 2006. *Gender Mainstreaming: Implementing UNSCR 1325 in ESDP Missions*. Paris: EUISS. https://www.iss.europa.eu/content/gender-mainstreaming-implementing-unscr-1325-esdp-missions.

Belloni, Roberto. 2001. "Civil Society and Peacebuilding in Bosnia and Herzegovina." *Journal of Peace Research* 38 (2): 163–180. https://doi.org/10.1177/0022343301038002003.

Belloni, Roberto. 2007. *State Building and International Intervention in Bosnia*. London: Routledge.

Berenskoetter, Felix. 2008. "Under Construction: ESDP and the 'Fight Against Organised Crime.'" *Journal of Intervention and Statebuilding* 2 (2): 175–200. https://doi.org/10.1080/17502970801988073.

Bieber, Florian. 2006. *Post-war Bosnia: Ethnicity, Inequality and Public Sector Governance*. Basingstoke: Palgrave Macmillan.

Bjelić, Dušan I. 2002. "Introduction: Blowing Up the 'Bridge'." In *Balkan as Metaphor: Between Globalization and Fragmentation*, edited by Dušan I. Bjelić and Obrad Savić, 1–22. Cambridge, MA: MIT Press.

Björkdahl, Annika, Stefanie Kappler, and Oliver Richmond. 2009. "The EU Peacebuilding Framework: Potentials and Pitfalls in the Western Balkans and the Middle East." *JAD-PbP*. Working Paper No. 3, 1–55. http://www4.lu.se/upload/LUPDF/Samhallsvetenskap/Just_and_Durable_Peace/WorkingPaper3.pdf.

Black, Ian. 2003. "Ashdown Backs Creation of EU Bosnia Force." *The Guardian*, October 8. http://www.theguardian.com/world/2003/oct/08/eu.warcrimes.

Blaney, David L., and Naeem Inayatullah. 2004. *International Relations and the Problem of Difference*. New York: Routledge.

Bliesemann de Guevara, Berit, and Florian P. Kühn. 2009. "The 'International Community'—Rhetoric or Reality? Tracing a Seemingly Well-Known Apparition." *Sicherheit und Frieden/Security and Peace* 27 (2): 73–79. http://www.sicherheit-und-frieden.nomos.de/fileadmin/suf/doc/Aufsatz_SuF_09_02.pdf.

Bojicic-Dzelilovic, Vesna, and Denisa Kostovicova. 2011. "Transnational Networks and State-building in the Balkans." openDemocracy, January 17. http://www.opendemocracy.net/vesna-bojicic-dzelilovic-denisa-kostovicova/transnationalnetworks-and-state-building-in-balkans.

Bono, Giovanna. 2006. "The Perils of Conceiving of EU Foreign Policy as a 'Civilising Force'." *Internationale Politik und Gesellschaft* 1: 150–163. http://library.fes.de/pdf-files/id/ipg/03647.pdf.

Bridoux, Jeff, and Milja Kurki. 2014. *Democracy Promotion: A Critical Introduction*. Abingdon: Routledge.

Brown, Judith M., ed. 2008. *Mahatma Gandhi: The Essential Writings*. Oxford: Oxford University Press.

Brummer, Klaus. 2007. "Superficial, Not Substantial: The Ambiguity of Public Support for Europe's Security and Defence Policy." *European Security* 16 (2): 183–201. https://doi.org/10.1080/09662830701529794.

Calic, Marie-Janine. 2005. "The EU Military Operation in Bosnia and Herzegovina." *CFSP Forum* 3 (2): 12–14. http://www.lse.ac.uk/internationalRelations/centresandunits/EFPU/EFPUpdfs/CFSPForum3-2.pdf.

Caplan, Richard. 2005. "Who Guards the Guardians? International Accountability in Bosnia." *International Peacekeeping* 12 (3): 463–476. https://doi.org/10.1080/13533310500074549.

Chabal, Patrick. 2012. *The End of Conceit: Western Rationality After Postcolonialism*. London: Zed Books.

Chandler, David. 2000. *Bosnia: Faking Democracy After Dayton*. 2nd ed. London: Pluto Press.

Chandler, David. 2003. "The European Union and Governance in the Balkans: A Unequal Partnership." *European Balkan Observer* 1 (2): 5–9. http://www.davidchandler.org/wp-content/uploads/2014/10/EBO.pdf.

Chandler, David. 2005. "From Dayton to Europe." *International Peacekeeping* 12 (3): 336–349. https://doi.org/10.1080/13533310500074077.

Chandler, David. 2006. "Back to the Future? The Limits of Neo-Wilsonian Ideals of Exporting Democracy." *Review of International Studies* 32 (3): 475–494. http://www.jstor.org/stable/40072199.

Chandler, David. 2010. "The EU's Promotion of Democracy in the Balkans." In *EU Foreign Policy in a Globalised World: Normative Power and Social Preferences*, edited by Zaki Laïdi, 68–82. Abingdon: Routledge.

Chopra, Jarat, and Tanja Hohe. 2004. "Participatory Intervention." *Global Governance* 10 (3): 289–305. http://www.jstor.org/stable/27800530.

Council of the European Union. 2004a. "General Concept for an ESDP Mission in Bosnia and Herzegovina, Including a Military Component." 8928/04. Brussels, April 28. http://data.consilium.europa.eu/doc/document/ST-8928-2004-REV-1/en/pdf.

Council of the European Union. 2004b. "Council Decision of 14 June 2004 on the Principles, Priorities and Conditions Contained in the European Partnership with Bosnia and Herzegovina." 2004/515EC. *Official Journal of the European Union*, L221, 22, June 10–16.

Council of the European Union. 2004c. "ESDP Presidency Report." 10547/04. Brussels, June 15. http://register.consilium.europa.eu/doc/srv?l=EN&f=ST%2010547%202004%20INIT.

Council of the European Union. 2004d. "European Security Strategy: Bosnia and Herzegovina/Comprehensive Policy." 10099/04. Brussels, June 15. http://data.consilium.europa.eu/doc/document/ST-10099-2004-INIT/en/pdf.

Council of the European Union. 2004e. "Council Joint Action 2004/569/CFSP of 12 July 2004 on the European Union Military Operation in Bosnia and Herzegovina." *Official Journal of the European Union*, L252, July 12.

Council of the European Union. 2004f. "ESDP Mission, Including a Military Component, in Bosnia and Herzegovina (BiH)—Updated Master Messages." 11569/1/04 REV 1, July 23. http://register.consilium.europa.eu/doc/srv? l=EN&t=PDF&gc=true&sc=false&f=ST%2011569%202004%20REV%201& r=http%3A%2F%2Fregister.consilium.europa.eu%2Fpd%2Fen%2F04%2Fst11% 2Fst11569-re01.en04.pdf.

Council of the European Union. 2004g. "Concept for the European Union (EU) Military Operation in Bosnia and Herzegovina (BiH)—Operation ALTHEA." 12576/04, September 29. http://register.consilium.europa.eu/ doc/srv?l=EN&f=ST%2012576%202004%20INIT.

Council of the European Union. 2004h. "2608th Council Meeting: General Affairs and External Relations." 12767/04. Luxembourg, October 11. https://www.consilium.europa.eu/uedocs/cms_data/docs/pressdata/en/ gena/82210.pdf.

Council of the European Union. 2005. "ESDP Newsletter: European Security and Defence Policy." Issue 1, December. http://www.iss.europa.eu/publications/ detail/article/esdp-newsletter-2/.

Council of the European Union. 2006a. "Annual Report from the Council to the European Parliament on the Main Aspects and Basic Choices of CFSP, Including the Financial Implications for the General Budget of the European Communities (2005)." 9069/06. Brussels, June 7. http://data.consilium.europa.eu/doc/ document/ST-9069-2006-INIT/en/pdf.

Council of the European Union. 2006b. "Presidency Report on ESDP." 10418/06. Brussels, June 12. http://register.consilium.europa.eu/doc/srv?l= EN&f=ST%2010418%202006%20INIT.

Council of the European Union. 2009. "Council Conclusions on Democracy Support in the EU's External Relations (2974th External Relations Council Meeting)." Brussels, November 17. http://www.consilium.europa.eu/ uedocs/cms_data/docs/pressdata/en/gena/111250.pdf.

Council of the European Union. 2010a. "2992nd Council Meeting: Foreign Affairs." 5686/10. Brussels, January 25. http://www.consilium.europa.eu/ uedocs/cms_data/docs/pressdata/en/foraff/112569.pdf.

Council of the European Union. 2010b. "3009th Foreign Affairs Council Meeting, CSDP." 8979/10. Luxembourg, April 26. http://europa.eu/rapid/press- release_PRES-10-90_en.htm?locale=en.

Council of the European Union. 2011a. "Operation Althea—Quarterly Report to the United Nations." 7716/11. Brussels, March 14. http://register.consilium. europa.eu/doc/srv?l=EN&f=ST%207716%202011%20INIT.

Council of the European Union. 2011b. "3117th Council Meeting: Foreign Affairs." 15309/11. Luxembourg, October 10. http://europa.eu/rapid/press-release_PRES-11-357_en.htm.

Council of the European Union. 2012. "Report by the High Representative on CSDP." 12616/12, July 13. http://data.consilium.europa.eu/doc/document/ST-12616-2012-INIT/en/pdf.

Cubitt, Christine. 2012. "Responsible Reconstruction After War: Meeting Local Needs for Building Peace." *Review of International Studies* 39 (1) (April): 91–112. https://doi.org/10.1017/s0260210512000046.

Cubitt, Christine. 2013. "Constructing Civil Society: An Intervention for Building Peace?" *Peacebuilding* 1 (1): 91–108. http://dx.doi.org/10.1080/21647259.2013.756274.

Daalder, Ivo H. 1997. "Bosnia After SFOR: Options for Continued US Engagement." *Survival: Global Politics and Strategy* 39 (4): 5–18. https://doi.org/10.1080/00396339708442938.

Dijkstra, Hylke. 2013. *Policy-Making in EU Security and Defense: An Institutional Perspective*. Basingstoke: Palgrave Macmillan.

Drakulić, Slavenka. 1999. *As If I Am Not There: A Novel About the Balkans*. Translated by Marko Ivić. London: Abacus.

Dunn, Kevin C. 2003. *Imagining the Congo: International Relations of Identity*. New York: Palgrave Macmillan.

Epstein, Charlotte. 2014. "The Postcolonial Perspective: An Intro." *International Theory* 6 (2): 294–311. https://doi.org/10.1017/s1752971914000219.

EU Council Secretariat. 2004. "EU Military Operation in Bosnia and Herzegovina: Factsheet," November 29. http://eu-un.europa.eu/articles/en/article_4089_en.htm.

European Commission. 2002. "Bosnia and Herzegovina Country Strategy Paper 2002–2006." http://ec.europa.eu/enlargement/pdf/financial_assistance/cards/publications/bosnia_country_strategy_en.pdf.

European Commission. 2003. "Report from the Commission to the Council on the Preparedness of BiH to Negotiate SAA with the European Union." Brussels, November 18. http://eur-lex.europa.eu/legal-content/EN/TXT/?uri=CELEX%3A52003DC0692.

European Commission. 2004. "Commission Staff Working Paper: Bosnia and Herzegovina Stabilisation and Association Report 2004." Brussels. http://ec.europa.eu/enlargement/pdf/bosnia_and_herzegovina/cr_bih_en.pdf.

European Council. 2004. "Action Plan for Civilian Aspects of ESDP," June 17–18. https://www.consilium.europa.eu/uedocs/cmsUpload/Action%20Plan%20for%20Civilian%20Aspects%20of%20ESDP.pdf.

European Parliament. 2004. "Althea Mission in Bosnia and Herzegovina." Strasbourg, November 16. http://www.europarl.europa.eu/sides/getDoc.

do?pubRef=-//EP//TEXT+CRE+20041116+ITEM-008+DOC+XML+V0/
/EN&language=EN.
European Security Strategy (ESS). 2003. "A Secure Europe in a Better World—The European Security Strategy." Brussels, December 12.
European Stability Initiative (ESI). 2007. "The Worst in Class: How the International Protectorate Hurts the European Future of Bosnia and Herzegovina." http://www.esiweb.org/index.php?lang=en&id=156&document_ID=98.
Europol. 2005. "EU Organised Crime Report." The Hague. https://www.europol.europa.eu/content/publication/european-union-organised-crime-report-2005-1499.
Evans-Kent, Bronwyn, and Roland Bleiker. 2003. "Peace Beyond the State? NGOs in Bosnia and Herzegovina." *International Peacekeeping* 10 (1): 103–119. https://doi.org/10.1080/714002396.
Fagan, Adam. 2005. "Civil Society in Bosnia Ten Years After Dayton." *International Peacekeeping* 12 (3): 406–419. https://doi.org/10.1080/13533310500074515.
"Forum: Interrogating the Use of Norms in International Relations: Postcolonial Perspectives." 2014. *International Theory* 6 (2). https://doi.org/10.1017/S175297191400013X.
Friesendorf, Cornelius, and Susan E. Penksa. 2008. "Militarised Law Enforcement in Peace Operations: EUFOR in Bosnia and Herzegovina." *International Peacekeeping* 15 (5): 677–694. https://doi.org/10.1080/13533310802396277.
Galtung, Johan. 1969. "Violence, Peace and Peace Research." *Journal of Peace Research* 6 (3): 167–191. https://doi.org/10.1177/002234336900600301.
Goldsworthy, Vesna. 2002. "Invention and In(ter)vention: The Rhetoric of Balkanisation." In *Balkan as Metaphor: Between Globalisation and Fragmentation*, edited by Dušan I. Bjelić and Obrad Savić, 25–38. Cambridge: MIT Press.
Hansen, Lene. 2006. *Security as a Practice: Discourse Analysis and the Bosnian War.* London: Routledge.
Heimerl, Daniela. 2005. "The Return of Refugees and Internally Displaced Persons: From Coercion to Sustainability?" *International Peacekeeping* 12 (3): 377–390. https://doi.org/10.1080/13533310500074200.
Hellmüller, Sara. 2014. "A Story of Mutual Adaptation? The Interaction Between Local and International Peacebuilding Actors in Ituri." *Peacebuilding* 2 (2): 188–201. https://doi.org/10.1080/21647259.2014.910914.
Hobson, John M. 2012. *The Eurocentric Conception of World Politics: Western International Theory, 1760–2010.* Cambridge: Cambridge University Press.
Hughes, Caroline, and Vanessa Pupavac. 2005. "Framing Post-conflict Societies: International Pathologisation of Cambodia and the Post-Yugoslav States." *Third World Quarterly* 26 (6): 873–889. http://www.jstor.org/stable/4017815.
Hunt, Swanee. 2011. *Worlds Apart: Bosnian Lessons for Global Security.* Durham: Duke University Press.

ICG (International Crisis Group). 1997. "A Peace, or Just a Cease-Fire? The Military Equation in Post-Dayton Bosnia and Herzegovina." Report No. 28. Sarajevo, December 15. http://www.crisisgroup.org/~/media/Files/europe/balkans/bosnia-herzegovina/Bosnia%2011.pdf.

ICG. 2001a. "No Early Exit: NATO's Continuing Challenge in Bosnia." Report No. 110. Sarajevo and Brussels, May 22. http://www.crisisgroup.org/~/media/Files/europe/Bosnia%2040.pdf.

ICG. 2001b. "Bosnia: Reshaping the International Machinery." Report No. 121. Sarajevo and Brussels, November 29. http://www.crisisgroup.org/~/media/Files/europe/Bosnia%2043.pdf.

ICG. 2004. "EUFOR: Changing Bosnia's Security Arrangements." Europe Briefing No. 31. Sarajevo and Brussels, June 29. http://www.crisisgroup.org/en/regions/europe/balkans/bosnia-herzegovina/b0031-eufor-changing-bosnias-security-arrangements.aspx.

Ignatieff, Michael. 2003. *Empire Lite: Nation-Building in Bosnia, Kosovo and Afghanistan.* London: Penguin. Kindle edition.

Ivanić, Mladen. 2005. "The International Community and Bosnia-Herzegovina." *Cambridge Review of International Affairs* 18 (2): 275–282. https://doi.org/10.1080/09557570500164777.

Jansen, Stef. 2006. "The Privatisation of Home and Hope: Return, Reforms and the Foreign Intervention in Bosnia-Herzegovina." *Dialectical Anthropology* 30: 177–199. https://doi.org/10.1007/s10624-007-9005-x.

Jansen, Stef. 2013. "If Reconciliation Is the Answer, Are We Asking the Right Questions?" *Studies in Social Justice* 7 (2): 229–243. http://brock.scholarsportal.info/journals/SSJ/article/view/1045/1015.

Jansen, Stef. 2014. "Bosnia and Herzegovina: Putting Social Justice on the Agenda." *openDemocracy*, February 18. http://www.opendemocracy.net/can-europe-make-it/stef-jansen/bosnia-and-herzegovina-putting-social-justice-on-agenda.

Juncos, Ana E. 2005. "The EU's Post-conflict Intervention in Bosnia and Herzegovina: (Re)Integrating the Balkans and/or (Re)Inventing the EU?" *Southeast European Politics* 6 (2): 88–108. http://www.seep.ceu.hu/archives/issue62/juncos.pdf.

Juncos, Ana E. 2006. "Bosnia and Herzegovina: A Testing Ground for the ESDP." *CFSP Forum* 4 (3): 5–8. http://www.lse.ac.uk/internationalRelations/centresandunits/EFPU/EFPUpdfs/CFSPForum4-3.pdf.

Juncos, Ana E. 2009. "Of Cops and Robbers: EU Policy on the Problem of Organised Crime in BiH." In *Neighbourhood Challenge: The EU and Its Neighbours*, edited by Bezen Balamir-Coşkun and Birgül Demirtaş-Coşkun, 47–68. Boca Raton: Universal Publishers.

Juncos, Ana E. 2011. "The Other Side of EU Crisis Management: A Sociological Institutionalist Analysis." In *EU Conflict Prevention and Crisis Management:*

Roles, Institutions, and Policies, edited by Eva Gross, and Ana E. Juncos, 84–100. Abingdon: Routledge.

Juncos, Ana E. 2013. *EU Foreign and Security Policy in Bosnia: The Politics of Coherence and Effectiveness.* Manchester: Manchester University Press.

Juncos Garcia, Ana E. 2007. "Coherence and Effectiveness of the EU's Common Foreign and Security Policy in Bosnia and Herzegovina (1991–2006)." PhD diss., Loughborough University.

Kaldor, Mary. 1999. *New and Old Wars: Organised Violence in a Global Era.* Cambridge: Polity Press.

Kaldor, Mary. 2010. "Putting People First: The Growing Influence of 'Human Security'." Interview. *Yale Journal of International Affairs* 5 (2). http://yalejournal.org/2010/07/20/putting-people-first-the-growing-influence-of-'human-security'/.

Kaldor, Mary, and Shannon Beebe. 2010. *The Ultimate Weapon Is No Weapon: Human Security and the New Rules of War and Peace.* Philadelphia, PA: PublicAffairs.

Kaldor, Mary, et al. 2004. "A Human Security Doctrine for Europe: The Barcelona Report of the Study Group on Europe's Security Capabilities." Barcelona. http://www.lse.ac.uk/internationalDevelopment/research/CSHS/humanSecurity/barcelonaReport.pdf.

Kappler, Stefanie. 2012a. "'Mysterious in Content': The European Union Peacebuilding Framework and Local Spaces of Agency in Bosnia-Herzegovina." PhD diss., University of St Andrews. http://hdl.handle.net/10023/2536.

Kappler, Stefanie. 2012b. "Liberal Peacebuilding's Representation of 'the Local': The Case of Bosnia and Herzegovina." In *Hybrid Forms of Peace: From Everyday Agency to Post-liberalism*, edited by Oliver P. Richmond and Audra Mitchell, 260–276. Basingstoke: Palgrave Macmillan.

Kappler, Stefanie, and Oliver P. Richmond. 2011. "Peacebuilding and Culture in Bosnia and Herzegovina: Resistance or Emancipation?" *Security Dialogue* 42 (3): 261–278. https://doi.org/10.1177/0967010611405377.

Knaus, Gerald, and Felix Martin. 2003. "Lessons from Bosnia and Herzegovina: Travails of the European Raj." *Journal of Democracy* 14 (3): 60–74. http://www.journalofdemocracy.org/sites/default/files/KnausandMartin.pdf.

Knaus, Gerald, and Marcus Cox. 2004. "Bosnia and Herzegovina: Europeanisation by Decree?" In *The Western Balkans: Moving On*, Chaillot Paper No. 70, edited by Judy Batt, 55–68. Paris: EUISS. http://www.iss.europa.eu/uploads/media/cp070.pdf.

Kostić, Roland. 2007. *Ambivalent Peace: External Peacebuilding, Threatened Identity and Reconciliation in Bosnia and Herzegovina.* Report No. 78. Uppsala: Department of Peace and Conflict Research.

Krastev, Ivan. 2002. "The Balkans: Democracy without Choices." *Journal of Democracy* 13 (3): 39–53. https://doi.org/10.1353/jod.2002.0046.

Krotz, Ulrich, and Joachim Schild. 2013. *Shaping Europe: France, Germany, and Embedded Bilateralism from the Elysée Treaty to Twenty-First Century Politics.* Oxford: Oxford University Press.

Leakey, David. 2006. "ESDP and Civil/Military Cooperation: Bosnia and Herzegovina, 2005." In *Securing Europe? Implementing the European Security Strategy,* Zürcher Beiträge zur Sicherheitspolitik No. 77, edited by A. Deighton and Victor Mauer, 59–68. Zurich: Center for Security Studies.

Lederach, John Paul. 1997. *Building Peace: Sustainable Reconciliation in Divided Societies.* Washington: United States Institute of Peace.

Lynch, Dov. 2005. "Communicating Europe to the World: What Public Diplomacy for the EU?" EPC Working Paper No. 21. http://www.isn.ethz.ch/Digital-Library/Publications/Detail/?ots591=0c54e3b3-1e9c-be1e-2c24-a6a8c7060233&lng=en&id=16968.

Mac Ginty, Roger. 2014. "Why Do We Think in the Ways That We Do?" *International Peacekeeping* 21 (1): 107–112. https://doi.org/10.1080/13533312.2014.893154.

Mac Ginty, Roger, and Oliver P. Richmond. 2013. "The Local Turn in Peace Building: A Critical Agenda for Peace." *Third World Quarterly* 34 (5): 763–783. https://doi.org/10.1080/01436597.2013.800750.

Merlingen, Michael. 2012. *EU Security Policy: What It Is, How It Works, Why It Matters.* Boulder: Lynne Rienner.

Merlingen, Michael, and Rasa Ostrauskaite. 2005. "Power/Knowledge in International Peacebuilding: The Case of the EU Police Mission in Bosnia." *Alternatives* 30: 297–323. https://doi.org/10.1177/030437540503000303.

Merlingen, Michael, and Rasa Ostrauskaite. 2006. *European Union Peacebuilding and Policing: Governance and the European Security and Defence Policy.* Abingdon: Routledge.

Mujkić, Asim. 2008. *We, the Citizens of Ethnopolis.* Sarajevo: Centar za ljudska prava Univerziteta.

Muppidi, Himadeep. 2004. *The Politics of the Global.* Minneapolis: University of Minnesota Press.

Neumann, Iver B., and Ole Jacob Sending. 2007. "'The International' as Governmentality." *Millennium—Journal of International Studies* 35 (3): 677–701. https://doi.org/10.1177/03058298070350030201.

Overhaus, Marco. 2009. "Operation Althea and the EU Police Mission in Bosnia and Herzegovina: Implementing the Comprehensive Approach." In *The EU as a Strategic Actor in the Realm of Security and Defence? A Systematic Assessment of ESDP Missions and Operations* (SWP Research Paper), edited by Muriel Asseburg and Ronja Kempin, 16–29. Berlin. http://www.swp-berlin.org/fileadmin/contents/products/research_papers/2009_RP14_ass_kmp_ks.pdf.

Paris, Roland. 2004. *At War's End.* New York: Cambridge University Press.

Patten, Chris. 2004. "The Western Balkans—The Road to Europe (Speech)." Berlin, April 28. http://eu-un.europa.eu/articles/en/article_3450_en.htm.

Prashad, Vijay. 2007. *The Darker Nations: A People's History of the Third World.* New York: New Press.

Prodi, Romano. 2004. "Europe and Peace." Speech at the University of Ulster, April 1. http://europa.eu/rapid/press-release_SPEECH-04-170_en.htm.

Richmond, Oliver P. 2009. "The Romanticisation of the Local: Welfare, Culture and Peacebuilding." *The International Spectator: Italian Journal of International Affairs* 44 (1): 149–169. https://doi.org/10.1080/03932720802693044.

Richmond, Oliver P. 2010. *Palgrave Advances in Peacebuilding: Critical Developments and Approaches.* Basingstoke: Palgrave Macmillan.

Richmond, Oliver P. 2012. "Beyond Local Ownership in the Architecture of International Peacebuilding." *Ethnopolitics: Formerly Global Review of Ethnopolitics* 11 (4): 354–375. https://doi.org/10.1080/17449057.2012.697650.

Richmond, Oliver P. 2012–2013. "Human Security and Its Subjects." *International Journal* 68 (1) (Winter): 205–225. https://doi.org/10.1177/002070201306800113.

Richmond, Oliver P. 2013. "The Paradox of Peace and Power: Contamination or Enablement?" *Pax in Nuce*, November 28. http://paxinnuce.com/2013/11/28/the-paradox-of-peace-and-power-contamination-or-enablement/.

Richmond, Oliver P., and Audra Mitchell. 2012. "Introduction—Towards a Post-liberal Peace: Exploring Hybridity via Everyday Forms of Resistance, Agency and Autonomy." In *Hybrid Forms of Peace: From Everyday Agency to Post-liberalism*, edited by Oliver P. Richmond and Audra Mitchell, 1–38. Basingstoke: Palgrave Macmillan.

Rorty, Richard. 2007. "Democracy and Philosophy." *Eurozine*, November 6. http://www.eurozine.com/articles/2007-06-11-rorty-en.html#footNote1.

Rupnik, Jacques. 2011. "The Balkans as a European Question." In *The Western Balkans and the EU: 'The Hour of Europe'*, edited by Jacques Rupnik, 17–27. Paris: EUISS. http://www.iss.europa.eu/uploads/media/cp126-The_Western_Balkans_and_the_EU.pdf.

Ryan, Richard. 2004. "Statement by Ambassador Richard Ryan, Permanent Representative of Ireland to the United Nations, on Behalf of the European Union, to the Security Council, the Role of Civil Society in Post-conflict Peace-Building." New York, June 22. http://www.eu-un.europa.eu/articles/en/article_3605_en.htm.

Schnabel, Julian (director). 2007. *Le Scaphandre et Le Papillon* (movie). France: Pathé.

Solana, Javier. 1996. "The Intervention Force in Bosnia: Much Done, More to Do." *The New York Times*, August 9. http://www.nytimes.com/1996/08/09/opinion/09iht-edjav.t.html.

Solana, Javier. 2004a. "Croatia and the European Perspective." Zagreb, February 17. http://www.eu-un.europa.eu/articles/en/article_3217_en.htm.

Solana, Javier. 2004b. "Summary of the Report by Javier Solana on a Possible EU Deployment in BiH Presented to the EU Council of Foreign Ministers," February 23. http://www.ohr.int/en/ohr_archive/summary-of-the-report-by-javier-solana-eu-high-representative-for-cfsp-on-a-possible-eu-deployment-in-bih-presented-to-the-eu-council-of-foreign-ministers/.

Solana, Javier. 2004c. "The European Strategy—The Next Steps?" Helsinki, February 25. http://www.eu-un.europa.eu/articles/en/article_3230_en.htm.

Solana, Javier. 2004d. "Meeting of EU Defence Ministers: Summary of the Remarks Made by Javier Solana." In *EU Security and Defence—Core Documents 2004*, vol. V, Chaillot Paper No. 75, 71–80, May 17. Paris: EUISS. http://www.iss.europa.eu/uploads/media/cp075e.pdf.

Solana, Javier. 2004e. "Interview with Javier Solana." *Nezavisne Novine*. Banja Luka, May 28. http://www.consilium.europa.eu/uedocs/cms_data/docs/pressdata/en/sghr_int/80699.pdf.

Solana, Javier. 2004f. "Interview with Javier Solana." *Oslobodjenje*. Bosnia and Herzegovina, May 29. http://www.consilium.europa.eu/uedocs/cms_data/docs/pressdata/en/sghr_int/80698.pdf.

Solana, Javier. 2004g. "Summary of Remarks at the Istanbul NATO Summit." Istanbul, June 28. http://www.eu-un.europa.eu/articles/en/article_3619_en.htm.

Solana, Javier. 2004h. "Interview with Javier Solana by Nidzara Ahmetasevic." *Slobodna Bosna*. Bosnia and Herzegovina, July 14. http://www.consilium.europa.eu/uedocs/cms_data/docs/pressdata/en/sghr_int/81463.pdf.

Solana, Javier. 2004i. "Summary of Remarks during His Visit to Sarajevo, Bosnia and Herzegovina," July 15. http://www.eu-un.europa.eu/articles/en/article_3670_en.htm.

Solana, Javier. 2004j. "EUHR Solana's Remarks at the Conference of Ambassadors in La Farnesina." Rome, July 27. http://www.eu-un.europa.eu/articles/en/article_3711_en.htm.

Solana, Javier. 2004k. "Conférence Annuelle de l'Institut d'Etudes de Sécurité de l'Union Européenne. Discours du Haut Représentant de l'Union Européenne pour la Politique Étrangère et de Sécurité Commune." Paris, September 9–10. http://www.eu-un.europa.eu/articles/en/article_3791_en.htm.

Solana, Javier. 2004l. "Summary of the Remarks at the Informal Meeting of EU Defence Ministers in Noordwijk," September 17. http://www.eu-un.europa.eu/articles/en/article_3816_en.htm.

Solana, Javier. 2004m. "Launch of the EU 'ALTHEA' operation in Bosnia and Herzegovina," December 2. http://www.eu-un.europa.eu/articles/en/article_4116_en.htm.

Solana, Javier. 2005a. "Shaping an Effective EU Foreign Policy (Speech)." Brussels, January 24. http://eu-un.europa.eu/articles/fr/article_4251_fr.htm.

Solana, Javier. 2005b. "Résumé des Interventions de Javier Solana à la Réunion Informelle des Ministres de la Défense de L'Union Européenne." Luxembourg, March 18. http://eu-un.europa.eu/articles/en/article_4482_en.htm.

Solana, Javier. 2005c. "Speech by Javier Solana at the Institut d'Etudes Politiques." Paris, April 18. http://www.consilium.europa.eu/uedocs/cms_data/docs/pressdata/en/discours/84584.pdf.

Solana, Javier. 2005d. "Speech by Javier Solana at the Annual Conference of the Institute for Security Studies of the European Union." Paris, September 26. http://www.iss.europa.eu/uploads/media/speech05-10.pdf.

Solana, Javier. 2005e. "Summary of Remarks by Javier Solana at the Informal Meeting of EU Defence Ministers." Lyneham. In *EU Security and Defence: Core Documents 2005*, vol. VI, October 13. Paris: EUISS. http://www.iss.europa.eu/uploads/media/cp087e.pdf.

Solana, Javier. 2005f. "Address by EUHR Solana on Civil-Military Co-ordination." London, October 17. http://eu-un.europa.eu/articles/en/article_5143_en.htm.

Solana, Javier. 2005g. "Europe's International Role (Speech)." Bratislava, November 9. http://eu-un.europa.eu/articles/fr/article_5281_fr.htm.

Solana, Javier. 2005h. "Summary of Remarks by Javier Solana at the Ministers of Defence Meeting." Brussels, November 21. http://www.consilium.europa.eu/uedocs/cms_data/docs/pressdata/en/discours/87059.pdf.

Solana, Javier. 2005i. "Speech by Javier Solana at the Policy Dialogue 'Dayton at Ten: Drawing Lessons from the Past'." Brussels, November 25. http://www.consilium.europa.eu/uedocs/cms_data/docs/pressdata/en/discours/87125.pdf.

Solana, Javier. 2005j. "Remarks of Javier Solana at the EUFOR Change of Command Ceremony." Sarajevo, December 6. http://www.consilium.europa.eu/ueDocs/cms_Data/docs/pressdata/EN/discours/92023.pdf.

Solana, Javier. 2006a. "Speech at the Sound of Europe Conference." Salzburg, January 27. http://www.consilium.europa.eu/uedocs/cms_data/docs/pressdata/en/discours/88179.pdf.

Solana, Javier. 2006b. "Mediating Today's Conflicts for Tomorrow's Peace" (Speech). Oslo Forum, June 27. http://www.consilium.europa.eu/uedocs/cms_data/docs/pressdata/en/esdp/90605.pdf.

Solana, Javier. 2006c. "Europe's Answers to the Global Challenges" (Speech). University of Copenhagen, September 8. http://www.consilium.europa.eu/uedocs/cms_data/docs/pressdata/en/discours/90938.pdf.

Solana, Javier. 2007. "From Cologne to Berlin and Beyond—Operations, Institutions and Capabilities—Address by EUHR Solana." Berlin, January 29. http://eu-un.europa.eu/articles/es/article_6720_es.htm.

Solana, Javier, and Jaap de Hoop Scheffer. 2004. "Guiding Bosnia along the Road to Brussels." *The New York Times*, July 15.

Special Issue. 2005. *International Peacekeeping* 12 (3). http://www.tandfonline.com/toc/finp20/12/3.

Spivak, Gayatri Chakravorty. 1988. "Can the Subaltern Speak?" In *Marxism and the Interpretation of Culture*, edited by Cary Nelson and Lawrence Grossberg, 271–313. Basingstoke: Macmillan.

Tickner, Arlene B. 2013. "Core, Periphery and (Neo)Imperialist International Relations." *European Journal of International Relations* 19 (3): 627–646. https://doi.org/10.1177/1354066113494323.

Todorova, Maria. 2009. *Imagining the Balkans*. Updated edition. Oxford: Oxford University Press.

UNDP. 2003. "Bosnia and Herzegovina: Human Development Report/Millennium Development Goals 2003." Bosnia and Herzegovina. http://hdr.undp.org/sites/default/files/bosnia_and_herzegovina_2003_en.pdf.

UN Security Council. 2004. *Resolution 1575*. New York: United Nations. http://www.consilium.europa.eu/uedocs/cmsUpload/N0461922.pdf.

UN Security Council. 2018. *Resolution 2443*. New York: United Nations. https://www.un.org/press/en/2018/sc13567.doc.htm.

Van Rompuy, Herman. 2010. "Remarks by Herman van Rompuy, President of the European Council, Following His Visit to Bosnia and Herzegovina," October 20. http://eu-un.europa.eu/articles/en/article_10236_en.htm.

Wagner, Wolfgang. 2005. *The Democratic Legitimacy of European Security and Defense Policy*, Occasional Paper No. 57, 1–35. Paris: EUISS. http://www.iss.europa.eu/uploads/media/occ57.pdf.

Wagner, Wolfgang. 2006. "The Democratic Control of Military Power Europe." *Journal of European Public Policy* 13 (2): 200–216. https://doi.org/10.1080/13501760500451626.

Witthauer, Hans Jochen. 2004. "COM EUFOR Meeting with BiH Minister of Security," November 29. http://www.euforbih.org/index.php?option=com_content&view=article&id=200:com-eufor-meeting-with-bih-minister-of-security&catid=105:press-statements.

CHAPTER 6

EULEX in Kosovo: EULEKSPERIMENT

The logic of outside actors, such as UNMIK, "[exercising] significant productive and coercive power over the Kosovars, in the name of promoting
the norms of democracy, human rights and the rule of law," is an apt summary of the logic that has pervaded Kosovo (Gheciu 2005, 122). Indeed,
the international community (IC) seems to be rather complacent when
wielding terms like democracy and human rights. They take these terms
to be the essential characteristics that they possess and use them in such a
binary way that there can be no criticism towards how they employ these
terms (Musliu and Orbie 2014). Although there are a number of aspects to
how these values are promoted, I will focus on a couple of more prominent
trends that appear throughout the peacebuilding efforts. The promotion
of these norms usually installs an asymmetrical power structure where the
norm promoters unequivocally are the symbols of these norms and the
host societies on the receiving end are represented as lacking these; thus,
the standing of the host societies is significantly undercut already from
the start.[1] This prompts another rather problematic dynamic, since as the
peacebuilding enterprise claims these norms as integral to its identity, it
quashes from the beginning any criticism towards itself. Farther, it understands and represents these norms in a particular way—very often taking
the liberal tradition as superior—and thus leaves little room for alternatives
(Bridoux and Kurki 2014; Pugh 2005; YIHR 2010). The way this overall

© The Author(s) 2020
B. Poopuu, *The European Union's Brand of Peacebuilding*,
Rethinking Peace and Conflict Studies,
https://doi.org/10.1007/978-3-030-19890-9_6

frame functions in the context of the EU's rule of law mission in Kosovo (EULEX) will be unfolded in the analysis below. The aim is not to discredit the EU-foregrounded norms per se, but rather to draw attention to the structural imbalance of wielding them, i.e., who decides and defines the content of the terms and thus also gets to decide who lacks the stated qualities. Another facet to keep in mind is that wielding these norms does not mean that the external actors are omnipotent (Sending 2011). Rather, it creates structural dynamics that do not, of themselves, have definitive effects (Franks and Richmond 2008; Mac Ginty 2011), but which merit investigation in the particular contexts.

Within this chapter, the telling and acting of EULEX will be considered in an attempt to capture in detail the support the EU provides with its CSDP missions. Excavating EULEX in this manner allows for a critical examination of the above-mentioned norms and how the EULEX makes use of them. Read closely together with the previous two case studies, this move should provide a more solid basis from which to openly discuss the value of CSDP operations. The structure of this chapter follows the already familiar logic: its aim is to present the contextual setting in which EULEX came to operate, in order to highlight how EULEX both borrows from the wider peacebuilding enterprise and is also at the same time trapped by it. The contextual part is divided into three overlapping layers: (i) the EU/European context; (ii) the wider peacebuilding context; and (iii) the local context. The latter provides some insight into the different themes and emphases on the ground before EULEX was launched, yet in many ways these are restricted and thus offer a glimpse into the matter rather than a full-blown analysis. This will be followed by an analysis of EULEX through the medium of telling and acting—consonant with the theoretical premises introduced in the conceptual Ch. 2 and 3—that allows for nuancing the response the EULEX gave to Kosovo.

THE EU/EUROPEAN CONTEXT

The creation of a stable, secure and multi-ethnic society in Kosovo is at the heart of the EU's political conditionality. *Many more steps need to be taken before Kosovo succeeds in creating a society* which fully respects people of all ethnic backgrounds.

The Commission *will continue helping* Kosovo to make progress *towards its European aspirations*, provided the political leaders of Kosovo demonstrate a clear commitment to the respect of democratic principles, human rights, protection of minorities, rule of law, market economic reform and values on which the European Union is based. Ultimately, *Kosovo's future is in the hands of its people. They should spare no effort to ensure the implementation of the Standards*, which are essential prerequisites for making their goal of European integration a reality. (Commission 2005, April 20; emphasis mine)

This section maps the key themes that characterise the EU's involvement in Kosovo since 1999.[2] It does not aim to produce a linear chronological overview of the different EU policies. Instead, the focus is set on the overall normative and ideational frame that allows for examining the main tenets of the EU's policy towards Kosovo and, by extension, the Balkans.[3] Hopefully, this approach paints a clearer picture of the dynamics of the EU's engagement with Kosovo and of the contextual and structural specifics EULEX came to operate in.[4]

The Kosovo's European perspective, European perspective of Western Balkan countries, European course of these countries and their progress towards the EU all figure as recurrent motifs in the EU's discourse (Commission 2005, April 20, 2006, January 27, 2008, March 5). The problem with this discourse is that it fixes and decides Kosovo's future/progress solely from the EU's vantage point, thus dismissing Kosovo's perspective on its own future. For instance, consider how the Commission sets the priorities/agenda for Kosovo: "the European perspective must become an integral part of all policies in Kosovo" (Commission 2005, April 20). Furthermore, as the epigraph to this section illustrates, the agency and decision-making of Kosovo is presented as an oxymoron: on the one hand, the EU policies (Stabilisation and Association Process [SAP]; European Partnership) set the priorities and standards for Kosovo together with other external frameworks (e.g. Stability Pact [later Regional Cooperation Council]; UNMIK; KFOR, etc.); on the other hand, the EU still argues that "Kosovo's future is in the hands of its people" (see the above quote). As a result, Chandler's analysis is apt as it points out how the words partnership and ownership in reality carry only a nominal weight from Kosovo's position (2007). Keukeleire, Kalaja and Çollaku note that the Commission's activities on the ground are driven by two predominant "paradigms", the "institution-building paradigm" and the "enlargement paradigm", but as these are pursued without a consideration of the contextual dynamics (i.e. the authors point to the divergence between the EU-set priorities and the priorities of Kosovars themselves), these avenues for EU policy are myopic and ultimately do not serve Kosovo's interests (2011, 200). Furthermore, the authors point out yet another underlying paradigm directing EULEX—the "stability paradigm"—which, because of its narrow focus (that usually translates into a negative peace agenda), in effect undermines the other two paradigms (ibid.).

A number of general objectives towards Kosovo can be grouped under the theme of "stabilising the region" (see esp. Commission 2008, March 5). Under this theme, an array of aims and objectives are presented ad nauseam (e.g. to build a lasting peace and democracy, to facilitate Kosovo's progress towards a democratic, multi-ethnic society) despite the fact that these aims do not always complement one another, mirror the situation on the ground, or represent neutral agendas with transparent power relations. To the contrary, they form a group of objectives that are in tension with one another, and perhaps more importantly, they demonstrate well the relationship the EU *imagines* for itself and Kosovo. One of the issues that come to light is the belief that expertise comes from outside (Bridoux and Kurki 2014). It is suggested that "the European/Accession Partnerships agreed in December 2005 for the Western Balkan countries define the priorities on which the countries should concentrate", and "EU's objective is to promote stability, security and prosperity in the Western Balkans through the region's progressive integration into the European mainstream" (Commission 2008, March 5). Hence, the agenda of what needs to be done in the Balkans, i.e., the content of the above-mentioned aims (e.g. lasting peace), is disproportionately produced outside of Kosovo (cf. the analysis in Ch. 5). Furthermore, from numerous policy documents it becomes clear that the EU's counterparts in the European Partnership Policy are portrayed as immature and not civilised enough to fill the contents of the aims the EU has put forth. By contrast, there is an understanding that the EU/Europe (and by extension the IC) has achieved the qualities that it promotes in Kosovo and the Western Balkans and is thus particularly well placed to export these to the outside (Hobson 2012; Prashad 2007). In this way, peace acquires a specific externally articulated attire. This is particularly evident when it comes to the EU's treatment of civil society, but in effect captures the whole of Kosovo. In fact, one of the underlying problems is the very imagining of Kosovo as an actor. In that, the EU is complicit of a rather simplistic treatment, where for the most part Kosovo's society is seen as an undifferentiated whole (e.g. statements that suggest that EU's actions are for the entire population of Kosovo, providing for the needs of its citizens; or Kosovo's population is seen only in binary terms; that is,

Kosovo Albanians as a homogeneous group are set against equally homogeneous Kosovo Serbs). Simultaneously, Kosovo's population is depicted as passive and consequently muted (in everything that SAP and European Partnership are done for them, rather than together with them). Perhaps most alarmingly, the way in which the EU relates to the civil society signals that it needs to be created and developed before it can autonomously act. In the EU's own words:

> The European Union is actively supporting the United Nations Mission in Kosovo and NATO (KFOR) and is working closely with the Provisional Institutions of Self-Government (PISG) *to facilitate Kosovo's progress towards the creation of a democratic and multi-ethnic society* in which all communities can live in peace and prosperity. (Commission 2005, April 20)

It seems that the EU's policy framework for Kosovo (and in truth for the whole region) is premised on the idea that the recipe for peace lies in the EU's membership offer, and that Kosovo will achieve peace if it becomes part of the "mainstream of European political and economic life" (Commission 2006, January 27; cf. O'Brennan 2013). This idea of converting the "underdeveloped" Kosovo into an arguably "developed" country (read: one that has reached the terminus of development and is thus qualified to govern others) is nothing new in the IC's approach to post-conflict societies. Duffield's characterisation of this logic is fitting: "development has always functioned as a moral trusteeship. It is a relation of external tutelage and educational direction aimed at making what is incomplete – and as such, potentially dangerous to itself and others – whole and functional" (2011). This is not to deny that the EU can contribute towards peace in Kosovo, but rather to emphasise that the overall approach the EU has adopted is rather harmful as it negates and/or leaves no room for Kosovo's agency. Thus, if there is an enormous power asymmetry built into the "Peace-land" (Autesserre 2014; Bridoux and Kurki 2014) that has descended upon Kosovo, it does not help that the EU's overall approach is overly paternalistic. In this sense, the argument that "the EU perspective remains essential for the stability, reconciliation and the future of the Western Balkans" (Council 2008d, July 17) is charged with colonial mentality, revealing the positioning of the actors involved and the assumptions about who, owing to their position, has the right to define peace for the other. A closely related theme is the one that postpones Kosovo's ownership in the context of building peace, implying that Kosovo needs to be first remade in the image of the West, and only then can it slowly start to claim ownership over the external frameworks. Throughout the EU's policy documents, it is maintained that civil society needs to be created and developed (see the quotes above), and that the EU will help to achieve greater political maturity in the region (Council 2008d, July 17). Another illustration of this comes from the European Parliament (2007, March 29), which

> (i) points out to the Kosovo authorities that the international community expects them to focus their efforts on developing the institutional and administrative capacity required in order ultimately to take over the responsibilities hitherto exercised by UNMIK;

> (ii) to work seriously and constructively towards the establishment of a multi-ethnic, multicultural, multi-faith, tolerant country and society that respects the rights of all ethnic groups.

Although the above quote illustrates the way ownership acquires a very specific meaning in the EU's use, it also points to the fact that the EU's policy is elite-oriented (Keukeleire et al. 2011).

The Wider Peacebuilding Context in Kosovo

> Ahtisaari: While independence for Kosovo is the only realistic option, Kosovo's capacity to tackle the challenges of minority protection, democratic development, economic recovery and social reconciliation on its own is still limited. Kosovo's political and legal institutions must be further developed, with international assistance and under international supervision. This is especially important to improve the protection of Kosovo's most vulnerable populations and their participation in public life. (Ki-moon 2007, March 26)

It has become axiomatic to point out how stifled Kosovo is by outside frameworks. It is critical to evince that despite the overwhelming power wielded by the IC in moulding Kosovo by setting its agenda of reforms, it is Kosovo that, in the end, is solely responsible for the implementation of this agenda. For instance, as Ahtisaari maintains, "notwithstanding this strong international involvement, Kosovo's authorities are ultimately responsible and accountable for the implementation of the Settlement proposal" (Ki-moon 2007, March 26). This way of framing the relationship between the IC and Kosovo is emblematic of the multiple external peacebuilding efforts in Kosovo. In other words, the IC tries to define Kosovo's future without taking responsibility for it. The strategies to evade accountability are rooted in the overall structural setting within which everything unfolds (see esp. Prashad 2007). Owing to the structural asymmetry in place, the parameters of reforms are overwhelmingly in the hands of outside actors, whereas the burden of implementing these reforms is conveniently delegated to those who should benefit from these reforms.[5] Moreover, as Gheciu (2005, 127–128) demonstrates, the prevailing mindset of the internationals was rooted in the idea that people were not ready to engage independently in democratic political processes. This section, while not covering the wider peacebuilding efforts in their entirety, focuses on UNMIK's take on rule of law—which is significant as it was the forerunner to EULEX.[6]

In addition to other responsibilities, UNMIK was spearheading the re-establishment of the Kosovo judiciary and security services up to the time of Kosovo's unilateral declaration of independence in February 2008 (Peterson 2010, S23). Below, I examine a number of traits in UNMIK's approach to the rule of law (hereafter RoL). One of the primary issues with the RoL discourse is, as Peterson points out, the fact that it tries to convey the RoL in a manner that nullifies power relations. Thus, RoL programming is presented as something beyond both politics and scrutiny by evoking neutrality and objectivity of law (ibid., S23–S24). To illustrate this, consider the issue of choosing which law would govern the territory of Kosovo. As Peterson shows (ibid., S24), the choice was made for "Albanian" law so as to appease (Albanian) jurists. This choice is deeply political, seeing as the main conflict issue was the question of who controls Kosovo (Hehir 2010a, 190–191). Simultaneously, this is a sign of favouring stability—again, not a neutral choice. Effectively, this emphasis is the main article of liberal peacebuilding, reflecting a particular sensibility (Peterson 2010, S23). Consequently, it is clear that this choice had political repercussions:

> While an obvious moral and political victory for the Albanian population, this decision has had ramifications for relationships with both the Serbian minority and the state of Serbia, which, due to decisions such as these, came to view UNMIK as favouring the Albanian cause. Stemming in part from this move, the Serbian minority in Kosovo has been reluctant to utilise or cooperate with newly formed legal institutions, often turning to parallel Serbian state courts that continue to operate within Kosovo's borders. (ibid., S25)

On a wider note, it is clear that this choice was not executed keeping in mind the contextual dynamics, that is, the highly polarised attitudes of Kosovo Albanians vs. Kosovo Serbs (Hehir 2010a, Ch. 10). Rather than supporting reconciliation, this action in the name of the RoL worsened the relationship between the two communities (Blagojevic 2007; Peterson 2010, S25). With regard to security institutions, the same logic repeats itself. According to Peterson (2010, S26), "the KLA [Kosovo Liberation Army] negotiated a deal whereby 50 per cent of applications for the new police force would be reserved for ex-KLA members despite the KLA representing roughly two per cent of the population". Consequently, UNMIK has extensively participated in moulding Kosovo in a certain way—consolidating the power of some and further aggravating the already acute divisions—and in the course of its RoL programming, it has upheld stability (i.e. negative peace) at the expense of justice and reconciliation. Furthermore, the UNMIK's approach was redolent of institution-building with an apparent lack of feel for the context (as demonstrated above)—thus trust-building was sidelined. Peterson also points to the offhand view taken towards ensuring accountability (2010, S28). Not only was accountability seen as a peripheral question when it came to Kosovo institutions, it was also a half-hearted matter when it came to UNMIK itself (see esp. Visoka 2012). Arguably, UNMIK had failed to live by the values it was promoting in Kosovo.

The above demonstrates how the paradigm of stability and institution-building dominated UNMIK's approach with little concern for transforming relationships. Importantly, the values that are so ardently promoted do not always fit together. For instance, Security Council Resolution 1244 (1999) argues that the situation in the Balkans constitutes a threat to international peace and security, and thus, stability becomes the guiding principle. At the same time, the IC wants to ensure the conditions for a peaceful and normal life to Kosovars, which refers to agendas, such as reconciliation and social justice, which can be at variance with the first goal, namely stability. Additionally, the various values are promoted in a unidirectional way, leaving questionable the promoters' own adherence to them (Gheciu 2005).

The Local Setting in Kosovo

In Kosovo our aim is not nation building but institution building: we are fostering institutions and attitudes that will be able to build themselves. This doesn't mean cloning EU societies. In Kosovo, we're aiming at achieving fundamental standards that apply to all stable and functioning societies. (Steiner 2003)[7]

Michael Steiner's term as the SRSG is deeply problematic since he seriously subverted the agency of the Kosovars, in particular the Kosovo Provisional Institutions of Self-Government (PISG).[8] From his actions, it becomes apparent that his main focus was on getting good publicity for the UNMIK and increasing its credibility, even if this meant undermining the standing of its counterparts (ICG 2003, September 3, 2–4; Gheciu 2005, 137). In the end, he managed to antagonise the government and engender distrust towards both UNMIK and the institutions it was supposed to "help" establish. Furthermore, illustrating the overall logic of how international/European standards are wielded by the IC, Steiner is of the view that a peacebuilding mission "must change the host society's bad habits – even if they are 'traditional'" (2003).[9] Some aspects of local contextual dynamics will be presented below with an eye to the IC's pattern of engagement with them.

Generally, the IC seemed unwilling—or unable—to grasp the context in which it was operating. This can be demonstrated by the fact that it did not even try to take note of the pre-existing local capacities, but came with a relatively partisan attitude, emblematic of the one donned by Steiner. Albeit far from perfect, as both Clark (2000) and Mertus (2001) comment, the local civil resistance movement and human rights culture (the respective terms of the mentioned authors) represented solid local experience on which UNMIK could build. As Mertus suggests, the Kosovar parallel society of the 1990s was underpinned by human rights norms. The human rights discourse that pervaded the society was closely tied to the political strategy of non-violence. Although the human rights culture was strong, it was incomplete (Mertus 2001, 25). Incompleteness was manifested in the rather oppositional terms in which human rights were treated. Thus, while equality between human beings was underlined, "the central value of human rights: respect for the Other", as Mertus notes, was in the background (ibid., 23). In view of this, the window of opportunity to genuinely help and support the human rights culture in Kosovo, in particular by making it more inclusive, was there, but the IC chose not to react in a timely or, indeed, constructive manner. This pattern of application of human rights is captured by Mertus (2001, 26):

For years, NATO allies turned a blind eye to systemic human rights abuses in Kosovo, issuing only an occasional empty threat to the Milosevic regime. The US and other NATO countries decided to take up the human rights flag only after the emergence of the Albanian paramilitary organisation, the Kosovo Liberation Army (KLA). Only at that point did it appear as if the conflagration in Kosovo could result in a massive population displacement that would spill across country borders, disrupting trade and social relations among NATO countries.

This self-serving attitude towards human rights eroded the trust of the people of Kosovo towards the IC, but perhaps even more damagingly, it made the population cynical about the notion of universal human rights (ibid.). This development boosted two varied dynamics between the IC and Kosovar political actors. On the one hand, the Kosovar political actors pointed out "an inconsistency between the norms that the international administration claimed to embody, and practices of exclusion of Kosovo's citizens from decision-making processes affecting their lives" (see Gheciu 2005, 134); on the other, the norms of democracy and human rights began to be used as a "platform for mutual blaming" (ibid., 142). The post-agreement stage (after the adoption of the 1244 Resolution [1999]), as Mertus observes, did not fare much better in sustaining a human rights culture in Kosovo (2001, 29). Because a deeper knowledge of the human rights culture of Kosovo was missing from the IC's approach, it has come to represent a farrago of missteps. Context sensitivity was not the only lacuna: another serious problem presented itself in the overarching colonialist mindset of the IC that sabotaged the relationship between the IC and its local counterparts.[10] Mertus has recorded in detail this IC mindset in action—as have others (e.g. Gheciu 2005; Lemay-Hébert 2011). For instance, Mertus brings out an instance where international gender experts deemed their approach superior to that of the local gender experts (2001, 31). Here, the aim is not to point towards a straightforward influence of the international architecture vis-à-vis the local—as this rarely is the case (see esp. Mac Ginty 2011)—but to stress the overall tendencies of the international efforts, which have, on the whole, been top-down and largely ignorant of local knowledge. It is critical to bear in mind that the way the locals have responded to the top-down efforts of international actors varies (see, e.g., Franks and Richmond 2008).

In many ways, the legacy of the described approach set the tone for years to come. Coupled with the primary aim of building institutions, this strategy of detachment from the local context manifests that instead of tapping into the local potential and empowering it, the IC has, in some instances, reinforced ethnic intolerance. The IC has not been keen on building trust or encouraging a transformation of relationships, which, in view of the rather divisive conception of human rights culture in Kosovo, appeared necessary (see Blagojevic 2007). Instead, the IC has disregarded trust-building altogether and offered a new template for Kosovo's populace to live by, i.e., the discourse of multi-ethnicity (Hehir 2010b). The latter in itself would not have been a problem if it was borne out of a genuine engagement with Kosovo Albanians and Serbs, as opposed to the imposition of policies that allegedly (ethnic quotas, decentralisation; see Hehir 2010b) advanced multi-ethnicity (see also Higate and Henry 2013, 70).

CAPTURING EULEX KOSOVO

What we *do* abroad is shaped by *who we are*. (Solana 2008f, October 7)

This section captures the telling phase of EU's rule of law mission in Kosovo. It forms the first part of the following analysis, which is divided into two parts: (i) telling and (ii) acting identity, which capture discourses surrounding the commencement and the implementation of the mission in Kosovo.

Key Themes of EULEX Kosovo

Brussels states that the central concept of EULEX is local ownership (Council Winter 2009c, 9; de Kermabon in Council 2008c, July). However, the problem arises when one enquires what stands behind the oft-used label "local ownership". No neat understanding of the concept exists within the EU: it differs depending on the context and who communicates it. It becomes apparent that most conceptual documents[11] tend to be negligibly more detailed—though not often consistent—when it comes to defining who the local is, or what is meant by local ownership in the first place. Whereas if we look beyond the conceptual documents—to, e.g., mission mandates, comments and communications regarding a specific mission, and beyond—the concept of local ownership, more often than not, becomes a mere slogan (read: local ownership is important).[12] To illustrate this, I provide some indications about how the EU relates to the term "local", and offer a more nuanced discussion in the section *Multiple others* (see below). The EU has identified local ownership as one of its guiding principles in the context of the CSDP support to Security Sector Reform (SSR):

> SSR will be conducted under local ownership. This local ownership is defined as the appropriation by the local authorities of the commonly agreed objectives and principles. This includes the commitment of the local authorities to actions on the ground, including their active support of the implementation of the SSR mission's mandate; implementation and sustainability of SSR are their responsibility. The clear affirmation by the EU of its values, principles and objectives as well as consultation with local authorities at all stages should make local ownership possible. (Council 2005, October 13)

The EU seems to *define* the local rather than to *support* it (cf. Mac Ginty and Richmond 2013), as evident in the following key themes that run through the conceptual documents:

    i. in any given mission rapid build-up of the local capacity and subsequent handover to local ownership is essential (Council 2003, May 26);

    ii. to ensure local ownership as soon as possible (ibid.);

    iii. close cooperation with local authorities (ibid.);

    iv. facilitate development of CSOs; local NGOs require training and need to strengthen their capacities in order to play an effective role in the process of European integration (Rehn 2008, April 17);

    v. in cases where the competence of personnel in the field of rule of law may justifiably be questioned on the basis of the said personnel's educational background, it should be carefully assessed what approach to be employed, i.e., whether they should be substituted or whether assistance in the shape of strengthening (monitoring/mentoring) should be initiated (Council 2003, May 26);

    vi. experts from academic and non-governmental organisations could be called upon to carry out activities related to the implementation of the mandate of a crisis management mission (ibid.);

    vii. exchange of information with representatives from non-governmental organisations and civil society should take place on a regular basis (Council 2004, June 15).

In sharp contrast to the above, the critical camp of peace and conflict studies argues that local ownership "refers to the extent to which *domestic actors control both the design and implementation of political processes*; in post-conflict contexts, the term conveys the commonsense wisdom that any peace process not embraced by those who have to live with it is likely to fail" (Donais 2009, 3; emphasis mine; see also Hellmüller 2014). The term local in the context of the EULEX mission, for the most part, refers only to one segment of society, i.e., to the "competent Kosovo institutions" (Council 2008a, February 4). In general, these institutions are not portrayed as equal partners, but rather as passive recipients; they are not part of creating or thinking about peace, but rather seen as mere implementers of a predetermined "correct" approach. For instance, Solana establishes a clear division of roles when he says: "or take the Western Balkans. The scale of the EU commitment *to putting that region* on a path of sustainable peace, reconciliation and growth is unprecedented" (2008f, October 7; emphasis added). In similar terms, the locals with whom the EU engages have a very well-delineated task "to convert the EULEX vision into a reality".[13] A slightly more inclusive stance towards the locals is taken in the "Report on the Implementation of the European Security Strategy" (2008, December 11), where it is maintained that "civil society and NGOs have a vital role to play as actors and partners", yet this remains all that is said, with no further elaboration provided.[14] This way of dealing with substantive issues is very characteristic of the EU. Rayroux (2013) has coined a useful term to define this kind of political evasion, calling it "constructive ambiguity". Interestingly, constructive ambiguity allows the EU to speak with one voice, while at the same time keeping the divergent national preferences intact (see ibid.). And, in this case, it allows the EU to bend "local ownership" into a direction it finds suitable.

A topic that receives much more coverage than the one described above concerns the UN as *the* authority on post-conflict peacebuilding. The rigour with which this topic is pursued demonstrates a particular order that the EU sees fit to govern the "enterprise of global peacebuilding". However, reinforcing a certain (normative) order by constantly and relatively uncritically referring to the ultimate goodness of the UN's established order has implications (cf. Jabri 2013). For example, in the "EU-US summit declaration" (2008, June 10), a certain "we" (read: the EU and the US) is established and entrusted with a particular mission: "we seek a world based on international law, democracy, the rule of law and human rights, and strengthened by broad and sustainable market-based economic growth". The statement signals that should this world not live up to their vision, then the US and the EU would be particularly well placed to make the necessary correctives. It becomes clear from the way the enterprise of peacebuilding is presented that the EU, together with the broader IC, considers themselves its architects. For instance, it is maintained that

> the scale of the EU commitment to putting that region [the Western Balkans] on a path of sustainable peace, reconciliation and growth is unprecedented. From Bosnia Herzegovina to Kosovo, from Serbia to FYROM Europe is seen as an indispensable anchor of stability and development. (Solana 2008f, October 7)

Assuming authorship of the enterprise of peacebuilding seems to come naturally: "one area where Europe can and must take more initiatives is in developing new rules and institutions for a more complex and unstable world" (Solana 2008g, October 30). Yet, at this point of time, there is also a recognition of "a more complex and less 'Western' world" (ibid.), and thus an argument is put forward by Solana to proactively involve "others": "too often *we* discuss these issues in terms of integrating *the new powers* into the *global system we devised*. But we better prepare for the new powers having their own ideas on how the system must be run and reformed" (ibid.; emphasis mine). Beyond the statement that "we need all *relevant players* 'present at the creation' of the new system", Solana—addressing the member states—contends that the member states step up and materialise a credible EU foreign policy and thus be involved in shaping the world— or exist in a world "shaped by and for others" (ibid.; emphasis mine). However, even though the main characteristics that the EU brings out in the "global enterprise of peacebuilding" may well be captured by the term "liberal peace" (cf. Richmond 2006), this does not indicate a state of equilibrium between the different actors engaged in it. For example, Solana promotes, though not explicitly, the view that although the EU and US can be seen as partners, the EU/Europe is still qualitatively different from the US: "one of the things Europe can do is get beyond totalising theories like the war on terror and get into the differences between China and Russia ..." (2008g, October 30).

The next topic touches upon the main characteristics of the EU's approach to peacebuilding. Solana argues that "values are at the core of our external actions and an expression of our collective identity", adding "this is why the European approach to international relations is characterised by the primacy of international law; the search for consensual solutions; and a commitment to making multilateral institutions effective" (2008f, October 7). Characteristically, this approach is legitimised by a reference to a historical analogy. Namely, Solana—having a certain mnemonic power position—avers that "not only is this approach *right*. It is also very *effective*, as the history of Europe over the last fifty years demonstrates" (2008f, October 7; emphasis added). Interestingly, Solana is trying, simultaneously, to underline the existence of a consensus on how the international community does peacebuilding, and to stress the uniqueness of the EU's approach: "Europe's niche and added value is the very fact that it has a feel for complexity" (Solana 2008g, October 30). This connects well with the overall idea of devising bespoke solutions (ibid.). The crux of the matter, however, is in the question of who authors these bespoke solutions. The EU merely suggests the need for them, but does not see a problem in who designs these solutions. In fact, the way the multilateralist order is presented—"global and complex issues require global answers" (Solana 2008f, October 7); "too often we discuss these issues in terms of integrating the new powers into the global system we devised" (Solana 2008g, October 30)—demonstrates succinctly the division of roles between those who are allowed to imagine the global and those who are muted.

Closely connected to the above is an idea that still seems to haunt the EU—its credibility as a global actor. As Solana reasons, "if Europe wants to be heard, it has to offer more than just advice" (2008g, October 30). This echoes the urgency that was the key driving force behind the EU's actions in 2003.[15] Perhaps this logic already points to the knotty problem in peacebuilding, namely the question of *for whom* it is, and *how* it *can be* done. The EU's position seems to be underpinned by the problem-solving approach, which means that it rarely questions the way it does things, or why it engages in certain activities. For instance, engaging in peacebuilding is justified by, in the first instance, ensuring Europe's security and meeting the expectations of its citizens. However, the latter statement is not directly connected to peacebuilding per se, but rather to the importance of having the capabilities to "be ready to shape events" (Implementation Report 2008, December 11). Hence, peacebuilding is more often seen as a tool to ensure that the EU remains relevant in world politics than anything else (see, e.g., Solana 2008b, February 28). Equally controversial seems to be the way the EU usually approaches conflicts and how it imagines its role (Solana 2008c, June 4). Predominantly, the EU approaches the above themes by talking (and very extensively) about the quantifiable aspects (e.g. improving capabilities, coordination-cooperation dynamics), while the more substantive issues are dealt with in the margins or not at all (cf. Mac Ginty 2012). In case the more substantive issues are addressed, they are usually seen as common-sense categories that do not require debate.[16]

Another recurrent theme is Solana's call that "we must match our rhetoric with concrete action" (Solana 2008a, February 10). The explanation why this is relevant is given, for example, here:

> having people on the ground is changing the way outsiders see us. Slowly, people outside Europe are beginning to see that Europeans are not only people who talk or give money. But who are also willing to take risks and have people on the ground. Besides, deploying people is also changing our own mental maps. We no longer see ourselves as something like the World Bank. We are becoming a political actor with interests to defend and values to promote. (Solana 2008b, February 28)

The final discourse relates to the importance of the "significant others" for the EU.[17] It is stated that "the EU has made substantial progress over the last five years. We are recognised as an important contributor to a better world" (Implementation Report 2008, December 11). Manifestly, this reveals that for the EU, the important aspect of success is being recognised by other authorities in the business of building peace—versus building peace that resonates with the locals.

Multiple Others

Although it does take note of the importance of "the local", the EU tries to co-opt the locals into following its plans versus listening to their demands, allowing space for them to act autonomously, or making use of their resources. This position is reiterated in a number of EU documents; for instance, it is suggested that the aim of enhancing the cooperation with NGOs/CSOs is "to contribute to increasing operational efficiency" (Council 2009a, March 17). Yet, as noted above, the "local" is not a straightforward label: it acquires a different content depending on who authors it (cf. Richmond 2012). This section explores the identity of the EU's multiple others in the context of EULEX and the nature of their relationship, but also, on a more general level, how the EU relates to "the local(s)". As with the other two case studies, this exercise is based on analysing the discursive material.

The key multiple others that are identified in the context of EULEX Kosovo are the Kosovo institutions (Council 2008a, February 4, see also the accompanying Factsheet). The relationship between EULEX and Kosovo institutions is defined in the mandate as one of assistance in their progress towards the following objectives: "sustainability, accountability, multi-ethnicity, freedom from political interference, and compliance with internationally recognised standards and European best practices".[18] Crucially, the EU claims that the above objectives constitute a "shared vision" of Kosovo institutions—"a vision that EULEX would help to achieve"— and furthermore: "what is envisaged by the Mission Statement is a process of reform: i.e., moving Kosovo's police, justice and customs from their 'current state' to a more 'desirable state' of the 6 principal mission aims" (ibid.; Solana and Rehn 2007, March 29). However, concurrently with the claim of a "shared vision", EULEX states: "through a strategy based on the principle of 'local ownership' all the interested parties have worked hard to convert the EULEX vision (based on the six aims in the Mission Statement) into a reality".[19]

Similarly to the BiH case, partnership is one of the key words the EU uses to describe the relationship between itself and Kosovo.[20] This partnership is not something that envisions an equal say in the matter, but rather, from the very start, Kosovo is inserted into numerous outside frameworks (e.g. UNSC Resolution 1244 and Ahtisaari plan) and steered towards externally defined goals that are seen necessary for Kosovo to become "normal" (e.g. meeting European standards/internationally recognised standards/European best practices and European perspective; "the Balkans are changing for the better" [Implementation Report 2008, December 11]), which makes it difficult for Kosovo to voice its own ideas. Furthermore, Kosovo is in most cases designated the role of an apprentice who both learns and implements the outside reforms (see EULEX *Joint* 2008, October 22; Council 2008a, February 4). In addition to the fact that what the partnership amounts to is defined by the EU, it is of an exclusionary nature, i.e., most commonly referring only to the official authorities (i.e. Kosovo institutions).

In general, when Kosovo is referred to *in toto* (and for the most part it is)—as in "all members of society" (see Factsheet in Council 2008a, February 4); "the people of Kosovo" (Solana 2009b, July 14)—its agency is minimised, in the sense that it is treated as a passive and homogeneous agent in need of guidance. In this capacity, it is also lumped together with other countries perceived to be in a similar structural position with regard to the

EU. For example, the EU sees itself as the one shaping events (together with the identified significant others—see the section just below), and Kosovo, together with other countries (of which some are listed in the Implementation Report (2008, December 11) under the section "Building Stability in Europe and Beyond"), is seen as those in need of guidance. Accordingly, Kosovo and beyond are on the receiving end of policies fashioned by a group of actors that the EU sees as the shapers of events, or alternatively as those building stability (cf. Duffield 2007). This dynamic—a form of biopolitics (see ibid.)—can be characterised as an instance of unquestioned power relations, where the premise informing both the ESS (2003) and the Implementation Report (2008, December 11)[21] is that all that is labelled "progressive"—stability and prosperity—originates from the multilateral order that the EU names and defines together with other IC actors. Besides, a common characteristic of the IC approach to conflict theatres is the "empty-shell perspective" (Lemay-Hébert 2011, 195–197; Hughes and Pupavac 2005). This perspective treats the conflict-torn territories as both *tabulae rasae* and dysfunctional, thus constructing the IC's intervention as both functional and legitimately grounded. Follow, for instance, the way the head of mission (HoM) imagines the relation between EULEX and Kosovo:

> *if we want to help create a peaceful and democratic society*, which is needed for the stability of the region, everybody, all the communities must be able to rely on a strong rule of law situation. (Council 2008c, July; emphasis mine)

The qualitative gap between multiple and significant others is discernible from, inter alia, the Implementation Report (2008, December 11), which draws a clear indication of roles: that is, there are the builders of stability—the so-called actors of multilateralism (see EU-US Summit Declaration 2008, June 10)—and then there are those who are subject to this stability building. The major difference lies in the access to labelling on the global scale, and the consequences of that. This is to say, the EU together with its significant others can and does define the subject positions of the actors designated to the group of multiple others, with the consequence of creating common-sense regimes that then govern and inform the policies of the significant others towards these multiple others (Bourdieu 1989; Frueh 2004).

Perhaps most importantly, as the understanding of local ownership is limited and also rather ambiguous within the EU, it is evident that the entire

EULEX mission suffers from this evasive engagement. Although the EU has a living document on enhancing cooperation with NGOs and CSOs, the relationship between the EU (here the focus is on the CSDP) and the "local(s)" abounds with problems.[22] Firstly, although rhetorically the need to cooperate with NGOs/CSOs is recognised, it is usually seen as either a component that contributes to the success of the CSDP mission (see, e.g., Council 2006, December 8)—begging the question of who the mission is for—or the mission mandates, as a rule, do not identify NGOs/CSOs (or anything beyond these categories, for that matter) as partners. Secondly, it is not explained why, in the context of CSDP, the only other actors the EU has chosen as local partners beyond the elite is NGOs/CSOs (the difference between these two categories also remains murky). Owing to this, the group of actors with whom the EU engages on the ground is limited, which in turn hints at the EU's understanding of how to build peace. It is noteworthy that it was not before 2008 that the EU conducted an overview of its engagement with locals (Council 2009a, March 17). This assessment, in addition to being one-sided—in that it does not include the voice of any of the local actors[23]—reveals a number of worrisome trends (ibid.). In relation to the CSDP, it was noted that "the ESDP missions [*sic*] approach is a targeted one, identifying NGOs with specific activities related to the missions' tasks (e.g. human rights, gender issues)". In respect of the substance of cooperation, the report argued that "the most common activity mentioned was information exchange". The overview indicated that "while contacts with NGOs were wide-ranging and frequent, they were most often ad hoc". It also refers to the fact that some partners are seen as more valuable than others (see above the distinction the EU evokes between multiple vs. significant others), namely,

> while the ESS places considerable emphasis on the need for the EU to act with other partners in crisis management (in particular the UN, and key regional organisations such as OSCE, NATO, ASEAN, etc.) in the framework of effective multilateralism, it makes no specific mention of cooperation with NGOs/CSOs. (ibid.)

On a more positive note, "the importance of EU relations with NGOs/CSOs", it is suggested, "should be addressed in development of EU policy and doctrinal papers". In sum, what this review signals is that there is no clear strategy on how the EU can and should engage with the local. These observations become especially mind-boggling in relation to the fact that initially, the key principle of the EULEX mission was local ownership.[24]

Significant Others

Europe ... has to face up to new threats to its security and to its values of democracy and liberty. These new threats are more diverse, less visible and less predictable. *The EU has to provide credible responses to these threats,* whatever their source, whatever their form, through prevention, deterrence and response, *in close coordination with its principal partners in the world and with the relevant international organisations,* in particular the United Nations, which has global responsibility for peace and security. (Council 2008e, December 3; emphasis mine)

We will work together [read: the EU and the UN] to ensure that the multilateral system takes action to protect the freedoms of individuals, and will hold all regimes that fail to protect the human rights of their people accountable. (EU-US Summit Declaration 2008, June 10)

As noted above, there is a qualitative difference—that the EU has acknowledged as well (see Council 2009a, March 17)—in how the EU relates to and represents its "others". In this section, the EU's relationship with its closest partners will be under scrutiny.[25] Broadly speaking, it is possible to say that the main dividing line between significant and multiple others, according to the EU, lies in the actor's ability to define the multilateral order. In other words, the significant others are those actors that have impacted themselves on the international arena and continue to make a certain global order commonsensical by repeatedly uttering claims to global leadership and/or to the global scope of their role (see Muppidi 2004, esp. 28, 60–61).

The first aspect that I will touch upon is the concept of effective multilateralism, and how it establishes a particular globality that—taking cue from Muppidi—makes certain particularities seem universal (2004, 65–67). In this respect, the EU identifies two key significant others: the US and the UN, who, as far as the EU is concerned, are the major architects of *a particular* multilateral order (Implementation Report 2008, December 11). To illustrate this, consider:

The strategic partnership between the EU and the U.S. is firmly anchored in our common values and increasingly *serves as a platform from which we can act in partnership to meet the most serious global challenges and to advance our shared values, freedom and prosperity around the globe*. (EU-US Summit Declaration 2008, June 10; emphasis mine; see also Solana 2008b, February 28)

The dynamic of how different partners of the EU are represented is underpinned by the unquestioned legitimacy of a certain global order. This mindset is manifested in the following statement: "in this decisive year for the Western Balkans, *we underline the importance of the European and transatlantic perspective* as an essential element in promoting stability and economic progress *for the whole region*" (EU-US Summit Declaration 2008, June 10).

These significant others have a lot of resources—in contrast to the multiple others—to frame the global. Consider, for instance, the ESS (2003) and the Implementation Report (2008, December 11) as well as the various statements that on a daily basis enforce a particular state of affairs that accords these significant others the role of the architects of the international order. For example, "with shifting threats, we [Europe/the EU, by extension other significant others] see shifts in the way to deal with them. There are more actors, and more flexible constellations. In this new international security architecture, Russia is a key partner" (Solana 2008a, February 10, 2008f, October 7).

Ostensibly, this section can only capture some of the traits of how the EU relates to its significant others and how this relationship is qualitatively different from the one the EU has with its multiple others. To take cue from Simone de Beauvoir, there appears to be a specific oppression by hierarchy that permeates the EU's representations of its others (1956). Although it is clear that not all significant others have the same standing (e.g. the difference between the EU's discourse towards the BRICS vs. the UN, US; see, e.g., Solana's reasoning [2008g, October 30]), it is also patent that a "significant other" is more of a partner than any of the "multiple others" are. This attitude is evident across the EU. For instance, it is maintained that "the European Union will continue to cooperate with the UN, KFOR, OSCE and other international actors in order to preserve stability in the region [the Western Balkans]" (Council 2008b, February 18).

Thus, there is a paradox written into the EU's representation of "its others". While the EU argues for local ownership (even if in its shallow version), it is simultaneously, markedly subscribed to the agendas of its significant others (Solana 2008g, October 30). In structural terms, this creates a situation where a power and knowledge imbalance is thriving on an international arena that operates on the basis of a particular common sense that masquerades as the universal way of good life.

Telling EULEX Kosovo: Ambiguity as a Strategy

Key Goals of EULEX

The stakes for the EU in terms of regional security and stability, internal development and international credibility are so high that the EU cannot afford to let its CSDP flagship fail. (Keukeleire and Thiers 2010, 354; emphasis mine)

Yves de Kermabon: Our mission will benefit all communities. (Council 2008c, July)

This section will be guided by three questions: What were the key goals of EULEX Kosovo; what was the mission's end state—i.e., how was peace imagined—and finally, who was EULEX Kosovo for?

To begin with, the main objectives of EULEX Kosovo will be probed. As the introductory quote to this section suggests, the pressure for the EU to succeed is critical, and this is recognised not only by the academics, but also by various EU officials and member states (see, e.g., Solana 2005, November 9). More often than not, however, this success is seen as more vital for strengthening the EU's foreign political image than for the benefit of Kosovo. Moving from general to more specific, it is argued by the Council of the EU that the overall aim of EULEX Kosovo is "to support the Kosovo authorities at all levels to meet European standards" (Council 2008c, July). In more detail, the joint action (Council 2008a, February 4)—which provides the legal basis for the mission—offers a list of goals that EULEX aims to reach:

EULEX Kosovo shall assist the Kosovo institutions, judicial authorities and law enforcement agencies in their progress towards sustainability and accountability and in further developing and strengthening an independent multi-ethnic justice system and multi-ethnic police and customs service, ensuring that these institutions are free from political interference and *adhering to internationally recognised standards and European best practices.* (ibid.; emphasis mine)

Keukeleire and Thiers point out that the proposed cure (i.e. the standards and best practices) for Kosovo's many issues "is, in practice, causing many troubles to the Kosovars and is sometimes even becoming part of the problem" (2010, 361). To elaborate further, "there is no international consensus whatsoever", they posit,

> on what the best standards and practices are. Kosovar politicians and civil servants were confronted with international actors (the US, UN, EU and individual EU member states) competing with each other in promoting and imposing *their own interpretation* of best international standards or European best practices – often leading to a cacophony of advice to be borne by the Kosovar counterparts. (ibid.; emphasis mine)

Additionally, it is crucial to note that these standards and best practices seem such a commonplace that they are not elaborated upon.[26] In turn, this positioning of Kosovo (or the entire Western Balkans region) institutes a clear boundary between the EU and Kosovo, where the former functions as an example that the latter, in order to reach the purported normalcy of these standards, needs to follow and imitate. Indeed, the EU has a lot to offer, yet ignoring local standards or best practices hints that there is a superiority/inferiority hierarchy at play—the other is seen, approached and evaluated according to one's own background (see Inayatullah and Blaney 2004, 11; also Chabal 2012; Escobar 1995, 111)—where the overarching objective is to Europeanise/internationalise Kosovo and the Balkans. In this respect, Inayatullah and Blaney's observation of the self and other's contact zone—which is "constituted in and by their relations to each other"—is apposite to this situation (2004, 9): "Instead of recognising the possibility of the overlap of self and other, boundaries are rigidly drawn, carefully policed, and mapped onto the difference between good and evil" (ibid., 10). At this instance, one can notice the ease with which the EU presents the superiority/inferiority of the EU's Self vs. the Kosovo Other as a common-sense state of affairs. Thus, implicit in the mandate's objectives is a very particular portrayal of both EULEX (and by extension the EU) and Kosovo, which is further entrenched in the methodology, or the way EULEX will realise its mandate.

This methodology is explained by the first head of mission (HoM) of the EULEX Kosovo, Yves de Kermabon (Council 2008c, July), as follows (this is quoted at some length to demonstrate the contradictions that abound in this methodology):

The mandate of the mission is to *monitor, mentor and advise the local authorities* in the broader field of rule of law, while *retaining certain executive powers to be used in a corrective way*. The EULEX experts will cover all aspects in police, justice and customs and our professionals will be co-located with their Kosovo counterparts. The *key concept is local ownership and accountability: the Kosovo authorities will be in the driver's seat*. But, let me be very clear on one thing: *If I need to use executive powers, be sure that I will*. Should the Kosovo authorities fail to meet their responsibilities in the areas of organised crime, war crimes, inter-ethnic crimes, terrorism, corruption, financial crime or property issues, I will not hesitate to take the necessary action. Though I hope I can avoid the use of these powers as much as possible. (emphasis mine; also Council 2008a, February 4)

This methodology, as Keukeleire and Thiers suggest, reveals that the EU's "assistance" to the Kosovo institutions takes many forms, "including methods that imply a more active and even intrusive role of the EU: it includes not only 'advising,' *but also* 'mentoring,' 'monitoring' and even assuming 'executive responsibilities'" (2010, 361–362; emphasis mine). The HoM's statement above also exhibits the tension present in the methodology and the aims/goals/values promoted; that is, the concept of local ownership becomes rather thin once the chosen methodology is considered.[27]

Although not explicitly, the EU divides the tasks of the mission into executive and non-executive, without being aware of the problematic dichotomy this move entails (Council 2008a, February 4). See, for instance, the HoM's explanation of the nature of the mission: "it is intended principally as a monitoring, mentoring, and advisory (MMA) mission, whilst retaining a number of limited executive powers" (EULEX Report 2009). Implicitly, therefore, this indicates that there are less intrusive/non-intrusive methods vs. the more intrusive ones. The advantage of putting it this way lies in the ability to say that EULEX Kosovo is not in the lead but rather assists and supports (albeit the question *whom?* is buried deep in the ground), and hence is different from UNMIK.[28] Evidently, the salient question is whether the mentoring, monitoring and advising (MMA) activities can be seen as wholly non-executive, or whether they carry executive tasks in disguise. The MMA is guided by the following logic: first, EULEX maps the "current state" (i.e. the existing problems, stressing that the Kosovo institutions do not start from a "zero state" because they have already been subjected to the UNMIK mission, see EULEX Report [2009]). Second, enter the concept of local ownership, and now the Kosovo institutions become responsible for implementing the tasks necessary to reach the objectives of the mission.

Though the adjective "competent" is inserted before the Kosovo institutions in the mandate (Council 2008a, February 4), the MMA does not really take this into account. Keukeleire and Thiers (2010, 361) succinctly sum up the essence of these tasks, which is worth quoting at some length:

> Whereas *"advising"* refers to the provision of expert information and professional counseling to the Kosovo authorities, *"mentoring"* indicates that … the EULEX staff actively assist the Kosovo staff in the development of new skills and knowledge by coaching or showing how a task can be carried out, convey their own experience and skills and encourage the Kosovo staff to take action and discuss the consequences of decisions and actions. *"Monitoring"* means that the EULEX staff observe and assess how the Kosovo rule of law institutions and staff are performing in relation to the aims of the EULEX mission, which is done through a comprehensive system of measuring performance. Or in less diplomatic terms: *EULEX also has the task to control the Kosovo institutions and to evaluate the progress they make.* (emphasis mine)

In this sense, the MMA actions are not entirely distinct from the executive responsibilities, in that they encapsulate the logic of *global governmentality* that—as Vrasti suggests—"manifests its force not through the actual number of people or states it controls, but by acting as a standard of reference against which all forms of life (individual, communal, political) can be assessed according to modern conceptions of civilisation and order" (2011, 16). The MMA side of the EULEX mission will be further probed in the "acting EULEX" section, whereas the paragraph below will demonstrate the link between the MMA and the rule of law. Due to the indivisible relationship between them, the MMA cannot but be seen as an inherently political endeavour.

The main object of monitoring, mentoring and advising is to instruct, the *local authorities* in the *broader field of rule of law* (Council 2008c, July). Having already problematised European/international standards and best practices as the proposed cure to Kosovo's rule of law situation and the methods chosen to implement them, what remains is the question of how the EU and EULEX understand and conceptualise the RoL.[29] A short, but telling answer to this problematique is given by the EULEX mission's staff themselves (see EULEX Report 2009, 7): "the desired end state *envisages rule of law institutions* that are able to operate "without international intervention and substitution" (emphasis mine). The EULEX approach to

RoL demonstrates a clear focus on institution-building and thus is more concerned with the procedural side of the rule of law than the substantive side.[30] The latter, as Mani explains (1999, 17), puts emphasis on the fact that the "rule of law is more than just rule *by* law, and encompasses structural, procedural as well as substantive components"; that is, laws are about justice. Being clearly focused on the betterment of the RoL institutions of Kosovo—either by strengthening and/or substituting for them (Council 2003, May 26)—EULEX's concept of RoL is interpreted in a minimalist way and thus renders Kosovo's people both vulnerable and passive. Consider the statement by the HoM: "if we want to help create a peaceful and democratic society, which is needed for the stability of the region, everybody, all the communities must be able to rely on a strong rule of law situation" (Council 2008c, July). The people are not just detracted from contributing to the RoL—they are also seen unfit to do that, as they are not yet peaceful and democratic enough. In addition to disregarding Kosovo's people, EULEX in effect also mistrusts the Kosovo institutions (refer back to the discussion of local ownership). Also, the EU's conceptual document for missions in the field of RoL in crisis management (Council 2003, May 26) is suspicious about local resources. It seems to advance two different logics: first, locals in themselves are not seen as a valuable asset, necessitating a "rapid build-up of the local capacity and subsequent handover to local ownership"; or alternatively, it is suggested that the local legal system needs to live up to the international standards (ibid.). Second, when local efforts are taken into account, it is under the supervision and direction of the EU; that is, the success of a RoL mission—scripted by the EU—lies in the local authorities' readiness "to be fully involved from the beginning in the achievement of the objectives" (again, scripted by the EU and, more generally, by the enterprise of peacebuilding that, structurally speaking, has the upper hand in devising any mission objectives).

How Does EULEX Imagine Peace?

In investigating how the end state has been conceptualised by the EU/EULEX, the trajectory of the following analysis will start from the general and move to the more particular. The underlying rationale of EULEX in Kosovo—and in fact for the whole enterprise of peacebuilding, according to Solana—is to maintain stability (EU-US Summit Declaration 2008, June 10; Solana 2008e, July 18; Council 2008b). To illustrate this, Solana suggests: "I want to underline that stability in Kosovo as well as of the whole Balkan region is essential and remains a high priority for the EU" (2008d, June 21). The quest for stability becomes the reason why other objectives are pursued; for instance, it is suggested that "it is critical for international efforts to deepen rule of law in Kosovo in order to contribute to greater stability in the region" (EULEX *Joint* 2008, October 22). One of the most ardent opposition forces to the international presence in Kosovo is the Vetëvendosje![31] whose leader, Albin Kurti, has pointed out that "the international presence in Kosova is international domination based upon the paradigm of stability" (2011, 89; see also YIHR 2010, 29–36). He adds to this:

> This paradigm of stability has conceptually militarised security. The number of international police and military troops became the measure of security in Kosova, not the well-being of citizens and their future prospects. Security in Kosova is a non-economic security (the promise of a market economy simply brought us a market without an economy). The international rule imposed a discourse stripped of words like 'defence' and even 'protection,' where only security remains, as army turned into police, and rule of law recalled by rulers of law, de-linked from the ideas of justice and rights. (ibid., 91)

Other signposts signalling stability and what it means in the context of EULEX are its emphasis on the fact that it is a technical mission and that it operates within the supposedly status-neutral frame of the UN. These two characteristics that are repeatedly underlined by the mission highlight that it operates within the boundaries of the status quo. By extension, this demonstrates a lack of contextual understanding, since what is promoted is not in the interest of Kosovars (see, e.g., Papadimitriou and Petrov 2012, 759–760). Unquestionably, the non-recognition of Kosovo's self-proclaimed independence means that the EU is skirting around this issue, and thus before this issue is tabled, it is hard to see how EULEX contributes to anything other than negative peace.[32] Since the status issue is in limbo, Ioannides and Collantes-Celador (2011, 436) ask an apposite question: "for what and for who [*sic*] is EULEX creating security institutions?" In this connection, they also note that "the EU does not have real leverage on Kosovo's political leaders, since it does not recognise the very institutions whose development it is supporting" (ibid.; also Papadimitriou and Petrov 2012). Thus, the overarching aim of stability that EULEX pursues does not really correspond to the *ideas of positive peace*. The overall logic of EULEX seems to fit exactly the aim of the objective of negative peace, which is to avoid potential future conflict (see Mani 1999, 21).

It is critical to underline that the approach that EULEX has taken is premised on the argument it is a technical mission (Gashi 2008b, December 10). This is a strategic move to naturalise the EU's mission, communicating that what the EU is doing is commonsensical, a mere technical fix (see Mac Ginty 2012). In fact, by naming its mission technical, the EU banishes the dimension of the political—i.e., relations of power—from its mission (e.g. Mouffe 2009, 2013, 21–22). This argument serves a number of purposes. First, it is habitually made to escape having to attend to the contextual dynamics. For example, EULEX repeatedly sidesteps dealing with the problem of parallel structures in North Kosovo (Visoka and Bolton 2011, 205; KIPRED 2009), constantly referring to Kosovo institutions as if they applied unproblematically to the whole of Kosovo. Furthermore, and perhaps more perniciously, the emphasis is on the reform of institutions, but not on the reform of the structural issues that considerably affect the RoL. Second, by attaching the label "technical" to its approach, the EU/EULEX seems to believe that improving RoL is an *a*political, neutral, matter-of-fact activity, without alternatives, and merely to do with improving institutions. Paradoxically, as Peterson's study suggests, although RoL programming claims to be neutral and apolitical, it is nonetheless highly politicised, since the end goal is a very specific "state", namely liberal peace (2010, esp. S18). In more specific terms, Peterson adds, the politicisation of RoL is mirrored by clinging to stability at all costs, even at the cost of the rule of law itself.

The fact that positive peace is removed from EULEX's agenda is also visible in the logic of its approach. It is maintained that "the initial mandate is for two years but the mission is foreseen to be terminated when the Kosovo authorities have gained enough experience to guarantee that all members of society benefit from the rule of law" (Solana 2008i, December 5). This dynamic of engagement suggests that EULEX believes that peace can and will trickle down from the correctly—EU/internationally certified—built institutions. This approach is not specific to EULEX per se, but is also characteristic of the overall "enhanced EU engagement in Kosovo": "The European Union is about to enhance its presence in Kosovo. It will do this by a threefold effort with the same overall objective: to support the Kosovo authorities at all levels to meet European standards" (Council 2008c, July). These emphases demonstrate that EULEX's focus is on *building institutions not peace* and, as discussed above, that its approach to the rule of law is narrow. It is evident that, to a large extent, this agenda is achieved without true cooperation with the Kosovo authorities—not to mention the people of Kosovo. Moreover, EULEX is more concerned with *building for* than *building with* the local counterparts.

Although the division between general and particular is not a straightforward one, it can be argued that perhaps the more particular end state can be connected to the six principal aims that have guided EULEX's actions (see above; Council 2008a, February 4). As discussed in the context of EULEX's relationship to civil society, this way of relating to Kosovo mirrors a specific understanding of conflict societies, in that they are seen as empty-shells in need of filling with approved content (EU(ropean)/international). This also shows that the EU artificially draws a line between European/international standards and Kosovo standards. This logic becomes more problematic when it is assumed that by reforming Kosovo institutions, EULEX is, by extension, creating a peaceful/democratic/multi-ethnic society, as if the people of Kosovo did not have these traits and as if they were not able to build peace themselves. Thus, the more particular end state that the EU is imagining is at odds with reality, since EULEX deals with Kosovo as if its society had been expunged by the conflict and needs to be re-created.

Who Is EULEX for?

Essentially, this question can be answered—at least tentatively—by turning to the chief foci of EULEX. One of the overarching aims of EULEX was stability, and this was articulated by a number of different actors within the EU and beyond in order to maintain the status quo and avoid a relapse into conflict, future violence.[33] The idea of stability intrinsically links Kosovo to outside frameworks, e.g., European or transatlantic perspectives. Thus, the external actors manage change, which amounts to different reform packages that are geared towards creating a stable, democratic and multi-ethnic society (EU-US Summit Declaration 2008, June 10). Yet, the key problem with this is that the external authorial voice has already decided on the path towards this objective, which means that structurally speaking, Kosovo is in an inimical position. The inequality built into imposing a decision of *what path* to follow and *how* refers to the fact that the outside "solution" structure is much heftier, and it is presented and articulated in a way that makes it hard to propose an alternative. Further, contextual sensitivity seems to be thin, in that the emphasis is on filling the society with (pre-approved) substance rather than appreciating and acknowledging its resources (refer back to the empty-shell argument above). The label "stability" is used in a dichotomous way: Kosovo is presented as unstable, and the EU's approach (or the outside influence more generally) is portrayed as stabilising. Yet, it has become evident that the multiple outside frameworks have caused and continue to cause instability (see esp. Peterson 2010). In this context, consider the effects of the UN's rule and the riots of 2004 that happened to a large extent due to the UN's policy line of "standards before status" (see Lemay-Hébert 2013, 95–97). Also, it is worth highlighting that the EU's shifting stance on what EULEX would be about, together with the internal divisions within the EU on the status issue, created not only confusion but resistance. As Papadimitriou and Petrov (2012, 759; see also Gashi 2008a, December 4) remark, the EU was greeted with a series of graffiti that appeared across the streets of Pristina in late 2008: "No EUMIK, no EULEX", or "EULEXperiment".[34]

Finally, the imagined end state of EULEX Kosovo is closely tied to the EU's understanding of both globalisation and the global system (these phenomena are viewed as separate). One of the assumed categories in the EU's approach to post-conflict Kosovo is the belief in the entirely internal logic of this conflict. That is to say, the wider background—especially the global system—against which the Kosovo conflict unfolded is not problematised (see Fierke 2007, 155; Bellamy 2002). This line of thought introduces an a priori power relation into the role allocation, whereby the IC is seen as a legitimate actor—i.e., they offer repair—to respond to conflicts and also define their parameters; whereas the conflict zones—labelled as in need of repair—do not hold any sway in this. Subsequently, it seems common sense to suggest, as the EU does, that "global problems require global solutions" (Solana 2008h, November 5) and that the EU is particularly well positioned to "[extend] the internal success of the European project. From peace on our continent to promoting peace in the world" (Solana 2008b, February 28). Together with the discourses on shaping events and effective multilateralism (both themes were discussed above), stability and the creation of a stable, democratic and multi-ethnic society acquires a specific meaning, in that there are global actors—or, alternatively, shapers of events—who assume that their understandings of the global problems are universal and their solutions function as a nostrum (see esp. Kurki 2013). Consider, in this context, the slogan "shape and share" that should inform the EU's politics (Solana 2008g, October 30).[35] Paradoxically, in the EU's discourse, globalisation is likened to a process without an author (see, e.g.,

Solana 2008g, October 30; Implementation Report 2008, December 11; ESS 2003), whereas the global system is authored by a select few (incl. the EU) to tackle the "dark side of globalisation".[36] This move is needed so that it could be argued that the shapers of the global system—distinct from the ones shaping globalisation—try to manage the global problems produced by globalisation's "invisible hand" (see Artemis case study where this is touched upon [Ch. 4], and Jahn's [2012] discussion on democracy promotion). Notice how—albeit implicitly—certain values are linked to both globalisation and the global system (not to be seen necessarily as stable categories).[37]

Acting EULEX Kosovo: 2008–2011

This section will be divided into two periods in order to mark the change in focus between the immediate implementation phase (roughly end of 2008 to 2011) and the period following the "re-think" (2012–2013). This division is based on EULEX's announcement in March 2012 that a modified EULEX will start work as of 14 June 2012.[38]

EULEX's Purpose

The handling of *our periphery* [the Balkans] is essential for our credibility in international politics.

The key question is: can we stabilise our own neighbourhood?

My answer is: we cannot afford not to (Solana 2009a, July 11, 2009c, July 28; emphasis mine).

If we don't "export" stability, we risk "importing" instability (Ferrero-Waldner 2009, September 29).

The Council noted the important and specific role played by the mission [EULEX Kosovo] in strengthening the stability of the region *in line with its European perspective.* (Council 2010a, April 26; emphasis mine)

The aim here is to investigate, similarly to the telling section, the three themes—objectives, the end state, and addressee(s) of peace—that provide insights into EULEX Kosovo *in action.*

It should be noted that the full operational capability of the EULEX mission was reached on 2009b, April 6, although deployment started in

December 2008. Marking full deployment, Solana reiterated the focus of the mission, "to make the rule of law institutions work better and faster for the benefit of all the people in Kosovo" (Council 2009b, April 6; see also the attached Factsheet). As de Kermabon demonstrates, faster and better translates into the following: "the long-term plan is to bring these institutions to a European level" (Karadaku 2010, April 12). In addition to providing support to Kosovo authorities, the "key priorities of the mission are to address immediate concerns regarding protection of minority communities, corruption and the fight against organised crime" (ibid.). Below these elements will be fleshed out and discussed with a view to further nuancing the EU's rule of law mission in Kosovo.

The umbrella objective of EULEX is to reform the RoL in Kosovo. In order to understand what this means, I will investigate the conceptualisation of *rule of law in use*—a Wittgensteinian enquiry in spirit (1967)—with due attention given to the conceptual debates about the rule of law. The concept of rule of law, Kleinfeld Belton remarks, is usually defined in two competing ways: on the one hand, there are "those [today, mainly legal scholars] who define the rule of law by its ends – and thus argue about which ends deserve inclusion"; on the other hand, others—notably, "the practitioner, political, and journalistic communities"—have largely overlooked this debate and focus on institutional reform (2005, 5–7). Approaching the rule of law by its ends[39] demonstrates that there is no single recipe to the rule of law—despite the certainty with which practitioners (incl. EULEX) approach it—but that all ends need to be considered in context; that is, the substantive element is as important, if not more, as the procedural one. Overall, as a number of authors note (e.g. Kleinfeld 2012; Hurwitz and Huang 2008; Carothers 2006), the IC's *modus operandi* vis-à-vis the rule of law is presently institutions-based—thus fitting under the first-generation approach as defined by Kleinfeld (2012). This, according to Kleinfeld (2012, Ch. 1; cf. Mani 2008; Rajagopal 2008), means that laws and institutions are at the forefront of rule-of-law reform to the detriment of "treating rule-of-law reform as a cultural or political problem". She further adds that by directing one's attention to the institutions, there is a danger of merely scratching the surface as "many rule-of-law problems are located primarily not in ... legal bodies, but in the broader relationships *between the state and society*" (ibid.; emphasis mine).[40]

In contrast to the first-generation approach, the second-generation RoL reform "encourages broad thinking about the cultural and political roots of rule-of-law failures. It implicitly pushes reformers to look at the actual needs of societies, rather than apply cookie-cutter programmes. It leans against technocratic thinking" (Kleinfeld 2012, Ch. 1). Furthermore, it is suggested that

> at its root, the rule of law is defined by the checks and balances among structures of power within a country and the cultural norms and habits that define how public servants – from police to court clerks to politicians – treat citizens, how they are treated by those they serve, and how citizens act toward one another and society as a whole. Power and culture, not laws and institutions, form the roots of a rule-of-law state. (ibid., 358)

Most importantly, the latter approach stands for a contextually sensitive and participatory practice, which suggests two conclusions. The relationship between state and society should be prioritised, and thus, it does not seem reasonable to rally for an approach that is disproportionately institution-based, especially if the rule of law has to be meaningful for the people. There is no clear linear causation between establishing the "right" institutions and guaranteeing the rule of law; instead, Kleinfeld suggests a different causation: "when the power structures and cultural norms are supportive, a country's laws and institutions will follow" (ibid.). Relatedly, rule of law institutions in and of themselves do not change the state of the rule of law if people do not participate and respect these institutions (ibid., Ch. 1; cf. Peterson 2010).

These conclusions allow for springing from the general to the more specific, in that, as Kleinfeld suggests, "it makes sense to look at rule-of-law reform as working to change four major parts of society", namely laws, institutions, power structures and social and cultural norms (ibid., Ch. 1). The first two of these four areas should be seen—as the second-generation approach would have it—only as the means to changing the last two (see esp. ibid., Ch. 4). To buttress this claim, the author refers to previous practice on RoL reform that has mainly been about top-down perfecting of institutions (Kleinfeld 2012, Ch. 4). For instance, Linn Hammergren's work (see ibid., Ch. 4) demonstrated that it is possible to achieve institutional success without much effect on the rule of law. Furthermore, it is stressed that there is no single right way to reform institutions: it is not a matter of following a mathematical equation (ibid.; see also Ch. 6 where she makes a case of employing different tactics together; Carothers 2006, esp. Ch. 2). Thus, the unquestionable *modus operandi* of institutional reform favoured by the IC is challenged in Kleinfeld's work and elsewhere (see, e.g., Golub 2006), especially in view of the underlying perception of the Western practice as superior, or having reached either a model status of universal standards that are homogeneous in character (see Kleinfeld Belton 2005, 19). In contrast, Kleinfeld brings out a number of methods and debates their overall worth—again pointing out that there is no one sure-fire way of promoting RoL. Troublingly, when considering the actual practice in this field (see esp. Kleinfeld 2012, Ch. 5), she concludes that a top-down mindset has become predominant to the detriment of bottom-up approaches:

> When I interviewed European Commission staff in Albania, Romania, and Indonesia, all expressed reservations and distrust for bottom-up reform, concern about its effectiveness as well as its legitimacy, and uncertainty over their own abilities to choose partners wisely. (ibid.)

This attests to the trend she finds prevalent in RoL programmes, where "real, meaningful participation of locals is often a missing element" (ibid., Ch. 7).

Addressee(s) of Peace

In terms of the outlined approaches to the rule of law, the EULEX mission definitely displays affinity with the first-generation approach. Both its mandate and the *modus operandi* on the ground suggest that the rule of law reform was mainly targeting institutions. Thus, unquestioningly, the whole operation revolves around "moving Kosovo's police, justice and customs from their 'current state' to a more 'desirable state' of the six principal mission aims".[41] Indeed, according to Kleinfeld (2012), the crux of rule of law lies in the relationship between state and society, yet EULEX's main "partners" are the Kosovo authorities (see, e.g., EULEX Report 2009). Furthermore, the mission's understanding of the rule of law is limited, since the overall aim is to reform institutions as an end in itself. The acting stage from the "start" defined the rule of law through perfecting institutions (see, e.g., EULEX Report 2009). This means that certain assumptions about the rule of law are made to the effect that the rule of law can be guaranteed if a state has functioning rule of law institutions—which is somewhat reminiscent of Roland Paris's approach (2004).

Furthermore, it is assumed that the rule of law will trickle down to the populace who are envisaged as a passive, if at times troublesome, entity.

The passivity of the populace of Kosovo is expressed in a number of ways, for instance, "one of the mission's aims is to help create an environment where people can experience for themselves the advantages of stability, predictability and security; in other words 'the rule of law'" (Council Winter 2009c). The perception of the populace (or certain parts of it) as being troublesome is communicated less openly. Partly, this relates to the Kosovo authorities and is couched in the following terms (cf. with the other two case studies [Chs. 4 and 5]):

> *The rate of development* is dictated largely by the resources and capabilities of the police officers, customs staff, prosecutor, judges and court administrators; they own and control the change process, whilst EULEX assists with MMA. (de Kermabon in EULEX Report 2010, 5; emphasis mine; see also Gashi 2008b, December 10)

> 'We can work with the institutions to improve the situation,' said Reeve [Deputy Head of EULEX], 'but the work will not to be done by EULEX. The work will be done by the Kosovo institutions. *All we will do is point out the areas that need improvement*'[42];

It bears emphasising that with this move, EULEX conveniently makes the Kosovo authorities solely responsible for the rule of law reforms initiated in the context of the mission. Conversely, the populace is portrayed in a passive manner and/or its agency is erased. The strongest argument in this regard is silence or dismissal on the part of EULEX. While EULEX has paid lip service to the importance of local ownership, in reality it is clear that there has been no real engagement with the locals, not to mention the very limited understanding of local ownership that EULEX tells and acts (refer to the discussions above, but see also Sabovic 2010, 116–117; EULEX Reports 2009–2011). When the head of EULEX, Yves de Kermabon, is confronted with the issue of local resistance to EULEX, he simply replies that protests are a good sign and adds that in France there are also very often protests. Furthermore, he states that the EULEX mission is "in the interest of the Kosovo, and of the population" (Gashi 2008b, December 10). Note how the EU has a propensity to speak on behalf of the people of Kosovo rather than making an effort to engage with them.

It is crucial here to illustrate the huge disconnect between EULEX and its programmes, on the one hand, and the local agendas in their multiplicity, on the other. If the presumed logic of EULEX's rule of law is that fixing the institutions means that Kosovo has a functioning rule of law system, then the local reality is not amenable to this plan. From February to May 2010, a group of researchers conducted an in-depth study in order to understand the human security situation in Kosovo (Kostovicova et al. 2012). Their approach was genuinely participatory, as they left room for Kosovars to voice what they *did* to address insecurity in their daily lives.[43] What their research uncovered, inter alia, was that there are three key terms—self-reliance, informality and community cohesion—that characterise, security-wise, people's everyday experiences (ibid., 576). Kosovo's citizens, as the study suggests, are self-reliant and to a large extent do not have faith in state institutions, thus the public realm that the internationals are building and reforming is something that the locals have withdrawn from in their everyday lives (ibid., 576–581). Informality, referring to "practices of non-compliance, avoidance, evasion or disregard of the formal rules regulating polity, economy and society" (ibid., 578), is a double-edged sword since, on the one hand, "recourse to informality" undermines the "provision of public facilities" and "hence has impaired the security of people and communities of Kosovo"; on the other, "it has been a strategy and a means to resolve the problems and demands of everyday life" (ibid.). This, of course, does not per se indicate that well-functioning institutions that *do indeed serve the public needs* are not vital, but rather that perhaps there should be a different approach, if, as it turns out, the *public sphere* as it stands now is a major source of insecurity.

Turning to specific activities envisaged in the context of EULEX, it is worthwhile to consult EULEX's Catalogue of Programmatic MMA Actions (2011, August).[44] These actions are "*designed* to implement change and reform processes *within* the Rule of Law Institutions in Kosovo" (ibid.; emphasis mine). It is crucial to bear in mind the instances when the rhetoric of EULEX is grander than its actual achievements. If in the beginning of the mission EULEX confirmed that it was implementing its mandate throughout Kosovo, then in the first EULEX Report its staff admitted—in a footnote—that "MMA activities in the north of Kosovo have been patchy due to political circumstances beyond the scope of this report" (2009, 11).[45] Furthermore, what EULEX activities suggest is that the bulk of its actions belongs to the category of devising strategy and MMA. Another group of activities can be designated as equipment and infrastructure development. In order to give a more elaborate portrayal of how the EU represents its RoL activities on the ground, I will now critically inspect some of these activities.

The major thread running through these EULEX-proposed reform activities is the argument that they adhere to internationally recognised standards and European best practices. This in itself is not problematic, yet similarly to the findings of EU Police Mission in Bosnia (see Merlingen and Ostrauskaite 2005), EULEX in Kosovo wields the claim to international standards and European best practices as *the truth claim* when it comes to building peace. This *par excellence* exhibits the power/knowledge dynamic (Barkawi and Laffey 2006, 346–347) that is told and acted via the CSDP. Although the EU standards are a stable label in EULEX's discourse representing its activities on the ground, it is noteworthy that "EULEX personnel is not always aware of what those EU standards are, particularly as EULEX staff includes a small contingent of non-EU secondees" (Derks and Price 2010, 20).

The following analysis of a number of activities on the ground is based on EULEX's consecutive reports, where the first one (from 2009) functions as the rationale for the following ones. It is crucial to note that the 2009 report defines both the problems of rule of law in Kosovo and the proposed "cure" to solve these problems. Therefore, despite all the efforts to cloak the mission as merely technical, it is nonetheless inherently political (Higate and Henry 2013).

EULEX: *Bettering Kosovo's Rule of Law Institutions*

Development, Duffield (2007, Ch. 1) holds, "is a regime of biopolitics" that splits humanity "into developed and underdeveloped species-life". In a similar vein, the EU's mission in Kosovo is emblematic of biopower (see also Merlingen and Ostrauskaite 2005), in that the mission allocates specific roles of provider and beneficiary. These roles function on the basis of a distinction between the universal (ad nauseam references to European/international standards and best practices) and the specific (Kosovo's "current state;" see EULEX Report 2009) and the common-sense relationship postulated between the two, whereby the "particular" moves towards the "universal" with, of course, the help (read: monitoring, mentoring, advising, etc.) from the latter. Boaventura de Sousa Santos (2015), adding to Duffield's critique, queries the binary representation of development vs. underdevelopment by questioning the rationale of formulaic precepts of development and asking "why everyone needs to be developed in the same way?" In his work, he demonstrates how the type of knowledge we command influences how we understand the world, and how certain knowledge has a privileged position. He argues that in order to vie for a more just world, one needs to "broaden the conversation of humankind" (ibid.).

The police component is EULEX's largest component, notwithstanding EULEX's acknowledgement that "compared with Kosovo Police, the criminal justice system and judiciary as a whole are considerably weaker …" (EULEX Report 2009, 14; ICG 2010, May 19). Below, I will discuss a number of aspects of EULEX's approach towards Kosovo's RoL institutions.

It is not explained how bettering the RoL institutions will contribute to improving the state of rule of law in Kosovo. Instead, it seems that EULEX works under the assumption that bettering RoL institutions through a top-down approach will automatically affect the wider agenda of rule of law (read: beyond rule of law institutions).[46] Apposite in this context is Kleinfeld's observation of the first-generation approach to rule of law reform, of which EULEX seems to be an illustration:

> one of the key differences between first- and second-generation rule-of-law reform is that first-generation reform focused on altering laws and institutions to make them look more like those in 'rule-of-law countries.' Too often, these laws and institutions became ends in themselves, altered toward no clear goal other than modernity. (2012, Ch. 4)

Rather than seeing "better" RoL institutions as a means to the rule of law reform, in EULEX they are largely seen as ends in themselves (see Kleinfeld Belton 2005). Furthermore, EULEX defines what constitutes "better" RoL institutions in lieu of the locals whom the institutions should serve.

Throughout the EULEX Reports (2009–2011), the mission's agenda is confined to building Kosovo's RoL institutions. The major problem lies in the way this is done, in that EULEX improves RoL institutions *for* the Kosovo people without their input. Because EULEX's idea of "local ownership" is extremely superficial, in EULEX's practice this boils down to assigning the role of local implementers and/or contributors to the actions designed by EULEX (EULEX Report 2010, 6; George 2009, December 16). For example, EULEX suggests with reference to the Kosovo Judicial Council (KJC) that it will "ensure that the KJC Disciplinary Committee becomes operational" (EULEX Report 2009, 94). This activity is premised on EULEX's assessment that "core accountability mechanisms are currently not operational" (93). Progress with this activity was summarised as follows: "most of the Office of Disciplinary Council (ODC) vacancies filled", and the ODC was transferred from the ministry of justice to KJC (EULEX Report 2011, 34). Whether this progress metric guarantees accountability within KJC is left completely untouched. What it demonstrates is the superficial and technocratic outputs that do not necessarily reflect betterment in the rule of law. In fact, it can be argued that the overall "measurement of success" is based on an inward-looking logic, which indicates that EULEX measures not outcomes, but outputs.

It is crucial to bear in mind that in the first EULEX Report (2009), EULEX first frames the rule of law problems and then proposes solutions do it. EULEX is more interested in lowering conventional crime rather than transnational organised crime (TOC) and corruption[47]—albeit the latter is seen as a challenge for the Kosovo Police (hereafter KP). In this way, the key emphasis on KP revolves around tackling (conventional) crime effectively. This is despite the following acknowledgement:

> As indicated, Kosovo's recorded crime levels in that year [2006] stood at just under 3000 per 100 000 population, *considerably lower than the average across a sample group of eleven EU member states.* However, within the context of the former-Yugoslavia the level of recorded crime in Kosovo appears to be comparatively high. It is noteworthy that the incidence of crime in Kosovo is almost three times the level found in the contiguous territory of the Former Yugoslav Republic of Macedonia (FYROM), a country with a similar population and urban/rural mix. Indeed, that Kosovo has 30% more recorded crime than the Croatia ... is a probable cause for concern. (EULEX Report 2009; emphasis mine)

In contrast, the report of the United Nations Office on Drugs and Crime (UNODC) published in 2008 suggests both that conventional crime in the Balkans is generally lower compared to Western European States (UNODC 2008, 5, 9–10, 35–43; see also UNODC 2011), and that traditional TOC has decreased considerably (UNODC 2008, 12–16, 55–85, 97; see also Bliesemann de Guevara 2013). This, as Bliesemann de Guevara (2013) points out, should not signal that TOC is absent from the Balkans, but rather that the stereotypical image of the Balkans as drenched in TOC needs to be interrogated, as opposed to accepting it at face value (cf. Arsovska and Kostakos 2010).[48] Furthermore, the UNODC report (2008, 17–20, 85–107) communicates that far more problematic than TOC are economic crime and corruption, such as tax evasion, smuggling of legal goods and misappropriation of public funds (see Bliesemann de Guevara

2013, 211–212; ICG 2010, May 19). In the light of the above, it seems questionable that one of EULEX's major focal point vis-à-vis the KP is tackling crime effectively (see EULEX Report 2009), especially if it is not spelled out what the crime problem in Kosovo appertains to. It is also quite telling that the accounts of crime—i.e. EULEX's account of crime versus UNODC's account—differ.

The mission's activities are premised on the idea that EULEX holds the key to expert knowledge (see Merlingen and Ostrauskaite 2005). It is suggested that "EULEX should provide expert advice", and there is a constant reference to the need of RoL institutions to aspire and evolve towards European best practices (see EULEX Report 2009, 47, 71; Kleinfeld Belton 2005, 19). It is crucial to note how KP becomes hemmed in by EULEX's visions that seem to be rooted in the dominant idea of policing that gained ground in the end of the twentieth century (see Sheptycki 2003, 45). In this way, for instance, intelligence-led policing (ILP) is presented as an indisputable way forward for KP (e.g. EULEX Reports 2009, 37; 2010, 18; 2011, 17). As Sheptycki notes, this overlooks the fact that policing is underpinned by particular understandings and norms of policing (2003; see also Edwards and Gill 2003, 265). Also, policing is part and parcel of the overall enterprise of peacebuilding, where certain types of knowledge are more privileged than others. In this way, ILP is not just a more "advanced" way of policing: it is related to the knowledge paradigms promoted by the liberal peace. According to Sheptycki, ILP "rests on a technological revolution aimed directly at controlling crime and criminals" (ibid., 45), "especially 'serious and organised crime'" (ibid., 47). In fact, the ILP approach is more concerned with controlling crime rather than analysing its underlying conditions. Moreover, as the shift towards ILP coincided with the emergence of the TOC discourse, the top-down setting of priorities regarding what ILP should focus on became even more noticeable (ibid.).

The activities conceived by EULEX are predominantly technocratic in character, inward-looking, ahistorical, and implemented without reference to the major structural issues, or the wider scheme of things. EULEX operates largely in isolation from both the other actors and the wider context of rule of law. In view of the fact that the EULEX both defines the problem(s) that it then goes on to solve, it is no surprise that the grand strategy for KP is to improve it towards a mystical "desired end" that remains rather opaque, apart from offering as a panacea the aspiration towards European standards. This is a tactic that is rehearsed throughout EULEX's policy towards Kosovo, functioning as a shield from criticism and as a legitimacy clause that seems to suggest that the EULEX has carte blanche in Kosovo because of these standards that the EU has ostensibly achieved, but Kosovo lacks. This is arbitrary power at its best, and its overarching discourse has framed the context so asymmetrically that it seems almost irrational even to think about whether the EU(LEX) itself always lives up to the standards it sets for others (Capussela 2011); or whether the only way to "progress" is in tune with these standards (Drakulic 2007).

In this light, reforming KP seems in no significant way connected to the wider scheme of things, and to reveal this, one only needs to ask, how will the micromanagement of KP by EULEX help the general state of rule of law in Kosovo? One of the key emphases in EULEX is put on tackling crime effectively, which in itself would not be a problem. However, it does become problematic in view of EULEX's lack of interest in why crime is there, and the automatic assumption that in order to reduce crime, one needs to "better" the institutions that deal with it. It is in this context that the following measures advocated by the EULEX should be seen (see EULEX Report 2009, 21–34; see also EULEX 2011, August): to help/micromanage the "relevant KP senior staff in the design and implementation of an effective strategy to reduce the overall volume of crime" (EULEX Report 2009, 25); "to mentor and advise the relevant KP senior staff in the design and implementation of an effective policy of recording, collecting and collating crimes under categories that are of concern to the public and private industry, and match the categories used by EU member states" (ibid.); and so forth. It is striking that this is done without any reference to Kosovo's society or the wider contextual implications of crime.

Owing to the narrow approach that EULEX has taken towards RoL, there are a number of noteworthy erasures, including overlooking local security concerns (Bennett and Saferworld 2011), disregarding contextual dynamics and apathetic attitude towards the North of Kosovo. As became evident from the above discussion, the EU's priority with regard to KP is to mould it in the image of itself, rather than to consider how KP could be responsive to local security needs. Gordon emphasises the importance of genuine local involvement, as

> without ensuring substantive and inclusive local ownership of SSR programmes, security and justice sector institutions will not be accountable or responsive to the needs of the people and will, therefore, lack public trust and confidence. This would leave the state vulnerable to renewed outbreaks

of conflict. It will be suggested that public trust and confidence in state security and justice sector institutions, and, ultimately, the state itself, can be promoted in many ways, including through incorporating community safety structures into the framework of SSR programmes. (2014, 127; Donnelly et al. 2013)

EULEX does not in any way foster a bottom-up approach to security, precluding a genuine engagement with the local in its many forms, e.g., the Municipal Community Safety Councils (MCSC) (KCSS 2010). This dismissal of the locals has had its negative impact, which is evident, for instance, in people's lack of trust in security and justice providers, or state institutions more generally (Bennett and Saferworld 2011, ii; KCSS et al., October 2010, 7).

Another major absence, or, rather, misconstrual of the context, is the idea that defective institutions are the reason for Kosovo's poor rule of law situation. This is not stated explicitly, but it becomes apparent once EULEX activities towards Kosovo RoL institutions are examined. As far as the North of Kosovo goes, EULEX has been unable to deal with this issue (Visoka and Bolton 2011, 205–206), and this not only because of the structural obstacles (i.e. its status-neutral position) but also because of its overall approach—with stability at the heart—to Kosovar context and rule of law. EULEX's limited understanding of crime (as discussed above) and the overall preoccupation with stability, coupled with a penchant for top-down logic of engagement,[49] may be seen as responsible for the failure to deal with high-level corruption (KCSS et al., October 2010, 8) and the issue of political interference in judiciary, which is highlighted in EULEX's own report of 2009 (87; EULEX Report 2010, 25). Yet, political interference (IKS 2010, 9) is not targeted in any way, and it is just something that is mentioned in passing throughout the reports. In reality, as a number of sources claim, political interference in the judiciary is not just an issue of local authorities' abuse of the rule of law (YIHR 2010), but also of outside actors who sometimes sacrifice the rule of law for the sake of stability (see Braak 2012, 60–61).[50] Furthermore, although EULEX has taken note of the problem of political interference, its policy of putting institutions first not only fails to consider this issue, but also ignores the possibility that its actions might instead reinforce the power base of the already powerful (see YIHR 2010).

In sum, EULEX is occupied with perfecting the Kosovo rule of law institutions with the underlying assumption that "better" police/justice/customs institutions translate into a "better" rule of law. This vision is limited and strips the local of their constructive agency, in that not a single evaluation touches upon how the perfecting of the said institutions has impacted the rule of law in a wider sense. What remains outside the purview of EULEX is the simple question: How has the wider society benefitted from the reform of these institutions?

ACTING EULEX KOSOVO: 2012–2013

The year 2012 does not represent a rupture in EULEX's approach, but rather a cosmetic exercise in improving the image of EULEX in the Kosovar's eyes (Council 2012, June 5). The need to reflect on its mission was not brought about by self-reflection, but rather by the fact that it had grown unpopular among the Kosovars (e.g. Saferworld reports, UNDP reports).[51] Also, the European Court of Auditors released a critical report on EU's activities in the field of rule of law (2012). This section will continue the format followed across the case studies, discussing key activities together with the end state scenario(s) and the authorship of peace.

EULEX 2.0: More of the Same?

De Marnhac to Lajčák: 'we all have the same goal of bringing Kosovo closer to EU standards.' (EULEX 2012a, February 2)

De Marnhac: '... Kosovo is on the right track, so long as its institutions and society continue to aspire to the principles and values which the EU promotes.' (EULEX 2012d, March 27)

Official from the EU Office in Kosovo: 'we [the EU] are not here for the sake of being nice or being good. ... We are here, of course, for the good of Kosovo. But, at least, I mean, that's the aim, but [*sic*] in the understanding that the good of Kosovo also coincides or is compatible with the EU interest in addressing the rule of law. Eh? So, the mission is the expression of the Common Security Policy.'[52]

Given that the biggest change in EULEX's mission mandate in 2012 had to do with the downsizing, amid the mounting dissatisfaction with EULEX, the EU Civilian Operations Commander's Hansjoerg Haber's statement that "EULEX has done a great job" seems off the mark (EULEX 2012b, March 7; EULEX Report 2012, 6). Below, I examine a number of developments in EULEX from 2012 onwards to see what else (if anything) has changed in the mission's approach.

It seems that 2012 saw a boost in the "engagement" with the locals. For example, EULEX organised a series of outreach activities, the gist of which was, in its own words,

> to contribute to the process of strengthening awareness of rule of law and encouraging young people to take an active interest in EULEX's work and achievements as well as wider issues of justice, police and customs. (2012c, March 19)

On the whole, this can be considered as a positive move, particularly in view of the report that many people do not feel adequately informed about EULEX (Bennett and Saferworld 2011, 18). However, this is not where the Kosovars would like the engagement to end, in that they would like to see more interaction between EULEX and the people (ibid.). Perhaps a more questionable engagement of EULEX was its campaign with the slogan "EULEX is doing nothing". The aim of this campaign was to point out two things: the wish to challenge the view that nothing is being done in the fight against corruption by EULEX, and the need to stress that EULEX "can only do so much", and that the major burden is on local authorities (EULEX 2012e, June 12; Aliu 2012). The EULEX Report details the relationship between EULEX and local NGOs (2012, 38–41), revealing that the contacts with NGOs are established on EULEX's terms—based on how it is convenient for the mission to relate to the locals. This is reflected in the offered avenues for cooperation, including information sharing with local NGOs; the organisation of workshops by EULEX with the aim to introduce findings from EULEX annual progress reports (ibid., 40–41); or the overly technocratic endeavours to reap local legitimacy, such as the contact point established with the Youth Dialogue Programme to convey the information about the programmatic approach (the EULEX's *modus operandi* in Kosovo) and a rather limited attention paid towards MCSCs (ibid., 41).

Despite EULEX's effort to paint a picture of a partnership between local NGOs and itself, this has not materialised in any genuine sense. Paradoxically, the EULEX Programme Manager admits that at this point, the NGO perspective is lost.[53] But rather than admitting that this is a matter of concern, the Programme Manager further adds that public opinion as such does not matter, since justice is not about popularity—it is about facts (ibid.). A number of NGOs point out that EULEX is not in any way accountable to the people of Kosovo and that EULEX is more concerned about its own activities, rather than creating a space for its alleged local partners to voice their opinion.[54]

The logic of the other key strategies of EULEX remained, on the whole, unchanged (Kursani 2013). In this way, the overarching premise guiding EULEX in Kosovo is that because of institutional weaknesses, the rule of law is compromised. This is evident in the fact that institution-building is isolated from structural problems and, in fact, from any context. This belief and its planned execution are captured in the imagined end results of the MMA activities (now named strengthening activities). All of the objectives listed in the EULEX report are premised on the assumption that if we get the institutions right, then the rule of law is guaranteed (2012, 45), featuring benchmarks from "progress on issues related to fair, transparent and sustainable staff recruitment, management, and policy making in the RoL area" to "an enhanced Kosovo Police performance on organised crime, war crimes and corruption and capacity/willingness to take additional tasks". This does not signal a farsighted and sustainable approach, or an outcome for that matter, as EULEX tries to fix Kosovo institutions in isolation from the contextual dynamics. This is noticeable in the fact that the people of Kosovo are not considered—or in any way empowered— to be part of "fixing" the institutions: rather, their agency is eroded, and their input dismissed. On the other side of the contextual dismissal are the Kosovo authorities, although here the dismissal carries an entirely different meaning. Here, the power dynamics are ignored, and there is a misplaced hope that fixing Kosovo's RoL institutions without factoring in the role of government authorities—especially the widely reported issue of political interference (Kursani 2013)—will succeed.

Furthermore, despite the rhetorical promise of EULEX that the Kosovo RoL institutions are its partners, they are, similarly to the local NGOs, passivised, their single role being to absorb the teachings of EULEX. In this way, while EULEX is supposed to support the Kosovo RoL institutions' move towards accountability, this same European standard does not apply to itself. When querying EULEX about its lessons learned and its accountability mechanism, the answer was: "we are not here to evaluate our own work, we are here to evaluate the work of Kosovo institutions".[55] Furthermore, "in the eyes of many civil and other professional beneficiaries in the public sector in Kosovo, EULEX staff has not provided any significant expertise to them" (Kursani 2013, 13–14). It is interesting to observe that for EULEX, its strengthening approach (spreading the European best practices) is a priori legitimate: 70% of EULEX's work is to do with MMA (strengthening the RoL institutions), which arguably translates into recommendations without the aspect of enforcing them.[56] The fact that EULEX tries to position itself strategically as both a technical mission, in order to relieve itself of responsibility and underline its neutral and apolitical stance, and a mission that is supposed to stand for the rule of law (one of the core values of the EU), creates certain controversy. In a conversation with the EULEX Programme Manager, this issue was explained as follows:

> There might be a misunderstanding also due to our [*sic*], that's my personal opinion, the nature of the mission. I don't think rule of law is a technical issue, rule of law is much more than that ... It's definitely a social issue. So the idea that rule of law can be technically brought into a nation is wrong. If we ever provided space for that assumption to enter the heads of the local population then we were wrong. Because it doesn't work this way. It takes years and decades to come to a level of rule of law as the one [pause] we have in mind. ... If we are to talk about technicalities then, I think, this mission brilliantly did this job. Because if we are talking about the judicial infrastructure which needed to be in place then it is there. We started in 2009 and now in 2012 you have a functioning Kosovo Judicial Council, functioning Kosovo Prosecutorial Council, a Supreme Court, Constitutional Court. Do they function? [long pause] That's a different question. But, if we're talking about the technical building up of capacities then I don't think anybody can prove us wrong.[57]

This way of putting it definitely challenges other telling- and acting-stage discourses that tried to represent EULEX as both a technical mission and as a rule of law mission at the same time. The rule of law aspect of EULEX is often emphasised, for instance, in Van Rompuy's remark: "rule of law is one of the defining values of the EU, and one of our most important priorities in Kosovo" (2010, July 6). Or, to recap, here is the HoM's, de Kermabon's view: "The aim is to significantly improve the rule-of-law situation to the benefit of all the communities in Kosovo" (Council Winter 2009c). Conversely, in order to leave the impression that EULEX's impact can only be seen in progressive terms without any consideration of power relations; that is, it is entirely apolitical and neutral, the label "technical" is used repetitively, as if a mere reference to that label would depoliticise the mission (see, e.g., Council Summer 2010b). However, as the analysis has thus far demonstrated, EULEX's conceptualisation of rule of law is very thin, meaning that the EULEX's telling and acting of rule of law can be likened to technical fixes. In this way, the illusion of the rule of law that EULEX tries to create by offering the technical aspects of the rule of law (read: EULEX's version of rule of law) has been interrogated throughout this analysis.

The executive branch of EULEX's approach is rooted in a parochial strategy of dealing with the symptoms of crime rather than addressing the root causes and supporting local capabilities (in their multiplicity and beyond detached institution-building) in devising more ingenious solutions, rather than the band-aid solutions enforced now. The underlying reasons for an exclusively law enforcement-oriented response from EULEX rest on a binary understanding of crime, signalling a rather simplified reading of licit and illicit activities.[58] According to Banfield (2014, 4, 17), the lack of a deeper reaction to crime originates from a restricted understanding of its character (cf. IKS 2010; Pugh 2006). Overwhelmingly, the response has been limited to law enforcement, as opposed to, for instance, socio-economic development (Banfield 2014, 30; Pugh 2013b). Unsurprisingly, EULEX's key activities focus on "investigating, prosecuting and adjudicating sensitive cases related to organised crime, corruption, war crimes, and property and privatization issues" (EULEX Report 2012, 45). One of the reasons for the executive mandate is the fact that "Kosovo's judiciary is inefficient and permeable to political interference, corruption and intimidation" (see Capussela 2015, 6). This might be the case; however, Kosovo's judiciary is an intrinsic part of the wider context in which it operates. A more sustainable approach—which, according to EULEX's mandate, should be its aim, albeit because of the compartmentalised attitude towards the rule of law, the pledge to sustainability remains short-lived—would go beyond the symptoms and aid with tackling of the root causes of crime. The predominant response of the EULEX to the problems identified within its executive mandate reflects the adopted policy of stability with the overarching aim of maintaining the status quo. It also, and perhaps even more importantly, demonstrates the power coded into the largely undisputed manner in which the definition of Kosovo's ills is authored by EULEX (taking into account the legacy which it inherited). Lastly, it is crucial to note to the fact, as pointed out by Capussela (2015, 74–81), that until 2013, EULEX's executive role was characterised by a policy of passivity. Taking stock of the cases EULEX took upon itself, a pattern emerges that demonstrates that EULEX was upholding elite interests, and thus cases probing into high-level crime were marginalised (ibid.).[59]

Who Is EULEX Accountable to?

Being accountable should be a *sine qua non* of peace operations, as accountability ensures that the principles and standards the IC demands of conflict-affected societies also apply to itself (see Visoka 2013, 2–3; HRW 2008, March 10). In the light of the poor accountability mechanisms in UNMIK and KFOR, the urgency of addressing this issue in Kosovo becomes apparent.[60] The question of accountability—similarly to the overall pattern of EULEX in Kosovo—follows a top-down logic.[61] "External legitimacy", referring to the habit of acquiring consent from the IC and a reiteration of good intentions in building peace to the wider audience (Visoka 2012, 189), is a mainstay of IO practice that has also found application in EULEX. Palm aptly points out the difference between effectiveness, which refers to the IO's loyalty to the mandate, and accountability, which translates into acknowledgement and responsibility for actions and ensuring space for multiple local stakeholders (2009, 8–9). EULEX puts more emphasis on being effective, whereas accountability is not always seen as a problem, at least not on a deeper level. In fact, it is suggested that EULEX prevailingly sees accountability in terms of itself and Brussels.[62] However, as Visoka argues (2013, 3), when compared to the current practice of both the UN and EU, EULEX demonstrates a much more advanced approach.

The mission's accountability falls into three baskets: operational, internal and external accountabilities.[63] Operational accountability refers to the practice of producing reports to measure statistically Kosovo's authorities' performance against the EULEX-set benchmarks; in addition, it also comments on the mission's own progression, even if this is limited to mandate loyalty. The second pillar of operational accountability is the Human Rights and Gender Office, which ensures that EULEX adheres to international standards of human rights and gender mainstreaming. According to Kosovo Women's Network report (2011, 25–26) that investigated the implementation of UNSCR 1325 in Kosovo, to a large extent the topic of gender was a peripheral issue for EULEX and, as one former EU official recalls, although EULEX paid lip service to the importance of UNSCR 1325, in practice the EULEX attitude was that "women are not our business" (ibid., 25). Internal accountability "consists of legal and disciplinary accountability, which are regulated by a code of conduct and other internal disciplinary instruments to liaison with judiciary mechanisms of the participating states in EULEX mission" (Visoka 2013, 3). EULEX's commitment to external accountability is envisaged as follows: (i) political accountability to Brussels; (ii) political accountability to Kosovo authorities, primarily consisting in regular contacts through the Joint Rule of Law Board; (iii) social accountability to the people of Kosovo, i.e., providing transparent and timely information on the mission's activities to Kosovo's civil society, journalists and people; (iv) financial accountability to the Commission; and (v) external human rights accountability—the establishment of the Human Rights Review Panel (HRRP).[64]

Despite this detailed presentation of its accountability mechanism, there are a number of weaknesses, especially when it comes to accountability to the local population. Accountability to the locals remains skin-deep, and the failings of EULEX in this are well documented in the works of Visoka (2013) and Palm (2009). Despite the efforts to differentiate EULEX from UNMIK, EULEX's HRRP suffers similar problems to the consecutive accountability mechanisms set up by UNMIK (see Visoka 2012). The bodies of both institutions did not live up to the demand of HRW to put into place effective independent accountability mechanisms (2008, March 10). Visoka (2013) demonstrates how the accountability of EULEX is compromised by the limited mandate of the HRRP (it can issue non-binding recommendations to the HoM of EULEX) and its restricted autonomy (authored by Brussels, financial and political dependence on EULEX). Furthermore, the accountability to the people of Kosovo and Kosovo authorities is nominal, in that both are involved on the EULEX's terms (consider the preceding analysis of the acting stage of EULEX). The key line of inclusion of the local is through inviting civil society organisations (CSOs) to meetings where EULEX programme reports are introduced (see Palm 2009, 13–14). Consider an excerpt from Palm's findings, which captures the mood of one-sided cooperation well:

> Interviews with Mission staff members indicate that EULEX would like to see CSOs taking a more proactive role and that [there] is a certain degree of frustration that CSOs do not always respond adequately to the Mission's initiatives. Interviews with CSOs, on the other hand, suggest that their limited engagement in EULEX-led initiatives may be due to the perception that 'cooperation' is, to some extent, limited to information rather than genuine dialogue in which they are able to share their expertise and experience. (ibid., 13)

EULEX = Frankenstein?

What is the imagined end state of EULEX? Despite the reconfiguration of 2012, it is evident that EULEX wants to complete its original mandate despite what this might mean for Kosovo. EULEX's lack of feel for the context is demonstrated by the very fact that in rethinking its mandate, it did not address the mounting criticism and distrust of the locals towards itself and the RoL institutions it tries to "better" (see, e.g., Muja 2012). According to Florian Qehaja, the EULEX's attitude towards Kosovo NGOs has not been satisfactory, and in the last two years, it has deteriorated because of EULEX's reluctance to accept criticism.[65] EULEX carries the patina of local ownership while true respect for the local input is missing. What is equally troubling, especially in terms of respecting the accountability structures set up, is that the HRRP was not involved or consulted during the reconfiguration process (Visoka 2013, 13). This is not to dismiss the reform of RoL institutions but rather to suggest that this cannot be done in detachment from the local context. Consider also the fact, as pointed out by Kursani (2013, 11), that the civilian mission has not been lead by a person versed in the rule of law; rather, the mission's first two heads— Generals Yves de Kermabon and Xavier Bout de Marnhac—have been former KFOR commanders. Indeed, the emphasis needs to be placed on the EULEX-scripted end state, since as far as the above-mentioned activities convey, EULEX operates as if it was mending the RoL institutions in a laboratory and because of that, local ownership is skin-deep.

EULEX Kosovo—for whom is it? "State institutions", Boege et al. (2009, 31) note, "work because they are embedded in social and cultural norms and practices". EULEX has tunnel vision in supporting Kosovo's rule of law institutions, namely, it has tried to micromanage these by subtracting the civil society and in effect trying to fill the role that the civil society is supposed to play. As the EU's contact with the people of Kosovo has been minimal—apart from the patronising rhetoric of what EULEX will do/be for the people of Kosovo every now and then—it does not come as a surprise that their legitimacy in the eyes of the locals has dropped considerably. In many ways, the locals are seen more as a problem than a solution when it comes to the rule of law. For instance, when a EULEX Programme Manager relates to the corruption issue in Kosovo during an interview, he understands and portrays the matter in a way that suggests that at the root of this problem is the mindset of the people of Kosovo.[66] In this way, throughout the international intervention in Kosovo the problems that need fixing are reduced to the Kosovar (and/or the Balkan) context as if it had been a hermetic society untouched by its multiple others (refer back to the agenda-setting power of the outside actors in the beginning of this chapter). The illustration offered above should be treated cautiously, as it does not represent the mission's views in their entirety, although elements of this view have been voiced by other mission staff as well (Hargreaves 2014), and apropos other issues as well, for example, concerning the treatment of crime. This reinforces the claim that the crux of interrogating the purpose of EULEX lies in the way it has told and acted the rule of law. And this has revealed the domination of external agendas and frames of understanding, a great emphasis put on stability, and the superficial accent placed on accountability, which leaves one with a rather similar conclusion to the other two case studies. In other words, and no less paradoxically, EULEX is designed for the credibility of the CSDP, in order for EU to have a say in international affairs.

Conclusion: Silo Mentality Tout Court

It seems rather self-evident to state, as do Bridoux and Kurki (2014, 88), that "democracy is not an apolitical, non-ideological or neutral concept". Yet, the above analysis demonstrated that despite promoting European norms and best practices, of which democracy is part and parcel, EULEX tries present its mission as a technical rule-of-law mission: it denies any alternative meanings of good life, while presenting its own mission as universally valid. To compound this further, the way in which EULEX does this is in many ways far from democratic. Thus, throughout both telling and acting its mission, a certain rather inconsistent positioning reveals. For the most part, expert knowledge (European/international standards towards which Kosovo should aspire) is confined to the West; yet the advantage conferred by this privileged knowledge evaporates in the context of declaring EULEX "a technical mission". This rather self-righteously puts forward the argument that what EULEX's mission is putting in place is so natural and commonsensical that there is no need to ponder its substance matter (see also Kurki 2013), and what is at stake is rather becoming more effective in what it does—as what it does is undoubtedly right. Below, some of the accents of this chapter will be reiterated.

To begin with, the contextual frame that sets the parameters of the manoeuvring room for EULEX's entry into Kosovo highlighted a number of themes. Overall, the IC provides a hollow promise of local ownership where a certain path to progress is chosen for Kosovo, while the responsibility for implementing this vision is conveniently placed on Kosovo's shoulders. Also, very often the central aim of keeping stability—which usually just translates into "no violence/conflict" mantra—overrides issues of social justice and other values that the IC is keen to promote but not to follow through. Taking note of the local setting, it becomes apparent that not only did the IC demonstrate a lack of engagement with the local actors, but it also evinced a patchy understanding of the local context.

The telling and acting lenses on EULEX have served as an indication that the chief emphasis does not need to be on telling versus acting, in the sense of pointing out possible inconsistencies between them, but rather on both phases of identity narration as they are equally filled with rhetorical and performative matter, as well as inconsistencies. Strikingly, in the case of the EU's CSDP genre, the very fact of deploying on the ground is already considered a success. The value of the telling and acting lenses lies in the nuance that they provide, where the telling phase might offer more in an answer to the *what*-question, whereas the acting stage might proffer more in an answer to the *how*-question. The major problem with EULEX is that from the very beginning, it harnesses the concept of local ownership to its mission, while at the same time indulging in a very restricted understanding of it. Basically, the locals' input and agency is postponed until they are deemed fit—that is, until the completion of the EULEX's mission of making Kosovo's society peaceful and democratic. Meanwhile, in the narrow reading, local ownership is reduced to EULEX's relationship with Kosovo authorities, understood as a very specific role allocation of beneficiary vs. recipient. Another bundle of tensions arises from the conceptual discordance between the three-pronged aim of assuring stability, supporting the rule of law, and advocating for European standards, all of which also fit poorly with the technical premise of EULEX's mission. The difficulties with how the EU(LEX) tells and acts these objectives are well recorded in the main body of this work, so they will not be repeated again.

Notes

1. Pugh astutely points to a common assumption among peacebuilders: they generally find fault with the society in question rather than the overall structure in which this society functions (2005, 24).
2. For a chronology of EU's policies in Kosovo consult: http://eeas.europa.eu/delegations/kosovo/eu_kosovo/political_relations/index_en.htm.

3. See Kurki (2013, Ch. 8) for a detailed interrogation of the conceptual underpinnings of the EU's democracy support.
4. Note that a number of themes with regard to the Balkans were mentioned in the Althea analysis, see Ch. 5.
5. This dynamic is well presented in Dauphinee's work (2003).
6. For general overviews of the peacebuilding efforts in Kosovo, consult, e.g., Hehir (2010a/Hehir 2010b), Visoka and Bolton (2011), Higate and Henry (2013), Gheciu (2005), ICG reports (e.g., 2003, September 3).
7. He was the UNMIK's Special Representative of the Secretary-General for the period 14 February 2002–8 July 2003 (http://www.unmikonline.org/Pages/SRSGs.aspx).
8. The stage for this sort of unlimited power abuse was set by one of the first SRSG's, Bernard Kouchner (Mertus 2001, 28; also Lemay-Hébert 2011).
9. In this context, Hughes and Pupavac's remarks prove insightful (2005), see also Lemay-Hébert (2011).
10. Gheciu notes the prevailing view in 1999–2000 within KFOR and UNMIK decision-making circles, namely that "the people of the province were far from ready to engage in democratic political processes" (2005, 127).
11. By conceptual documents I mean, e.g., "Recommendations for Enhancing Co-operation with NGOs and CSOs in the Framework of EU Civilian Crisis Management and Conflict Prevention" (Council 2006, December 8; Council 2009a, March 17); "Action Plan for Civilian Aspects of ESDP" (European Council 2004, June 17–18); documents on the rule of law (Council 2002, November 19; Council 2003, May 26; Council 2010c, December 20); and security sector reform (Council 2005, October 13). Most of these documents are living documents, meaning they are continuously updated and revised.
12. Mac Ginty and Richmond (2013) discuss what the "local turn" means in *different contexts* and how the IOs have difficulties approaching the local without undermining it because of their mindset, which is rooted in universalism.
13. See the EULEX Kosovo official web page, where the EULEX MMA Tracking Mechanism is discussed (www.eulex-kosovo.eu/en/tracking/). Note that this site is no longer operational, last time accessed June 2015. The MMA logic is also summed up in the first EULEX Report (2009).
14. Indeed, the conceptual labour is done on a general level and if specifics are mentioned then the concept suffers from inconsistencies. In that, the meaning of local remains unclear—though usually referring to just NGOs and/or local authorities. Similarly, the importance of the emphasis on the local context becomes superficial if one considers the fact that as a rule the mandates of the CSDP missions lack any serious commitment towards local actors (beyond local authorities and beyond the role of implementer) (refer to the conceptual documents mentioned in Note 11).

15. Note the Joint UK-France Declaration (2008, March 27) that created an air of urgency for the CSDP to achieve success on the civilian front in 2008.
16. This becomes especially clear from the conceptual documents of the EU (see Note 11).
17. In most cases, the difference between the multiple and the significant others is the configuration of dialogue; that is, in the case of the former there is a much clearer tendency "to speak in place of the other", whereas in the latter case, speaking together with/to the other prevails (Mbembe 2008). Thus, the boundaries between these groups are artificial, what defines them is the quality of being more one than the other. Also, these imagined groups are subject to empirical analysis and cannot be defined a priori.
18. Op. cit., Note 13.
19. Ibid.
20. Note that in the Report on the Implementation of the ESS (2008, December 11), it is suggested that post-conflict stabilisation and reconstruction "is most successful when done in partnership with the international community and local stakeholders".
21. Repeatedly identified as the key strategic and conceptual—notwithstanding the vagueness in terms—documents that arguably direct the EU's actions.
22. See the following Council documents (2006, December 8; 2009a, March 17), but also the Presidency Conclusions (Council 2008d, July 17).
23. This overview was conducted as follows: "The DGE IX Director ... sent a letter to all civilian Heads of Missions (HoMs) and EU Special Representatives (EUSRs) with a series of questions in annex in order to assess the cooperation between these key EU actors on the ground and NGOs/CSOs deployed in the same areas, specifically on the range, frequency and substance of their contacts/relations" (Council 2009a, March 17).
24. See http://www.eulex-kosovo.eu/en/news/000217.php.
25. Note that the aim here is not to offer comprehensive coverage of all of the EU's strategic partners, but rather to critically examine and contextualise the ones that at this specific instance appear in the EU's discourse.
26. This observation demonstrates perhaps most clearly the need for a creative combination of discourse and practice approaches. At this juncture, a deeper on-site engagement would have proven beneficial to enquire further into the ways in which these standards are understood by the EU staff.
27. Op. cit., Note 13.
28. UNMIK's blazing unpopularity—its failure "to secure popular legitimacy among Kosovars from all communities" (Lemay-Hébert 2011, 193)—is recorded by numerous sources and in relation to diverse issues, and recognised to a degree, by the UN itself (see UNSC 2008), as well as EULEX, whose officials, according to Sabovic (2010, 115–116), often distance themselves from UNMIK. Within the EU, UNMIK's legacy is treated inconsistently, with assessment ranging from outright condemnations (see

Zuccarini's [the Deputy Head of EU Planning Team in Kosovo] damning position on UNMIK in Lutolli and Maloku [2008, February 6]) to euphemistic comments: "The UN has made commendable work in Kosovo since 1999 but *due to changed circumstances* the international presence now has to be adjusted" (Solana 2008d, June 21; emphasis mine).

29. For a comprehensive discussion on the topic of rule of law, see, e.g., Hurwitz and Huang's edited book (2008), Kleinfeld (2012), Kleinfeld Belton (2005).

30. Note also that the conceptual documents (see Note 11) that centre on the rule of law accentuate institution- and capacity-building as the building blocks of rule of law.

31. For more information about its mandate and activities, see http://www.vetevendosje.org/en/ (also see Lemay-Hébert [2013, 93–94]). For a detailed analysis of the legitimacy gap between the internationals and the locals, consult, e.g., Lemay-Hébert (2013).

32. Although, in principle, the mission is status-neutral, in practice, as Ioannides and Collantes-Celador report, the mission, in order to function, acts "status positive" (2011, 433). The key here is that to act "status positively", EULEX cannot but take part in politics. Thus, the "technical mission" banner is rather misleading.

33. Note that this particular agenda—of preserving stability—is a mainstay in the EU's discourses (see Council 2008a, February 4; Council 2008b, February 18; see Annex A in GAERC 2003, June 16). Yet the concrete content and meaning of this agenda remains ambiguous. Most often, the commitment towards stability communicates a move towards the EU/Europe (see, e.g., Annex A in GAERC 2003, June 16).

34. The resistance was also manifest in a protest organised by several Kosovo Albanian NGOs in early December "to say 'No' to EULEX's deployment" (Gashi 2008a, December 4); Kosovo Serbs from their side signed a petition against EULEX (Gashi 2008b, December 10).

35. This spirit is evident in the two strategic documents, the ESS (2003) and the Implementation Report (2008, December 11), which exude the key principles of the EU's foreign and security policy.

36. See in this context Solana's thoughts on how the IC has to tackle the dark side of globalisation, which is portrayed as authorless (2007, October 1).

37. See De Sousa Santos (2007) on the production of globalisation and its link to human rights discourse.

38. The EULEX's current mandate extends to 14 June 2020. See http://www.eulex-kosovo.eu/?page=2,60.

39. Crucially, although Kleinfeld Belton brings out the usual suspects considered as the ends of rule of law reform, such as "making the state abide by law, ensuring equality before the law, supplying law and order, providing efficient and impartial justice, and upholding human rights" (2005, 7), she

puts a premium on the fact that these ends are spatio-temporally sensitive, manifold and separable, and that tension can exist between them (ibid.; Kleinfeld 2012).

40. Refer to Kleinfeld (2012, Ch. 1) for an illustrative list of typical activities carried out in the frames of the first-generation approach (see also Golub 2006).

41. Op. cit., Note 13.

42. See http://www.eulex-kosovo.eu/en/news/000172.php.

43. Cf. Higate and Henry's take on *everyday security* (2013, 17).

44. In addition to the EULEX-compiled catalogue of activities, it is useful to consider EULEX Reports (2009–2012) and other material detailing EULEX activities on the official web page http://www.eulex-kosovo.eu.

45. Some submit that the EU is taking a "light" approach in the North in view of the sensitivity among some EU member states to the status issue (Derks and Price 2010, 10).

46. This is a habitual assumption within statebuilding literature, which usually leads, as Berdal and Zaum note, to "conceptualising and treating societies subject to statebuilding interventions as passive and static" (2013, 7).

47. Problematically, although TOC as a concept is already knotty, what makes it even more so is EULEX's praxis of not defining or explaining what it means by it (cf. UNODC report's [2008] praxis).

48. While the Balkans is too easily stereotyped as the hub of TOC, it is also a common practice to see organised crime in binary terms; that is, organised crime happens outside of the EU/Europe and thus the EU/Europe needs to secure its borders against this threat (see Scherrer 2010; Edwards and Gill 2003).

49. It is conspicuous that despite flirtations with the term local ownership, the overall approach of EULEX towards Kosovo's justice system can be characterised by rule from above. As EULEX itself maintains, "at the strategic level, the Joint Rule of Law Coordination Board (JRCB) is coordinating all matters pertaining to Kosovo's Rule of Law sector" (EULEX Report 2011, 6; see Derks and Price 2010, 23–24 for details). Furthermore, as Derks and Price (2010, vi) suggest, "EULEX's initial interest [in civil society] was superficial and has fallen short of actual participation or input into programmes".

50. Allegedly, the selective application of rule of law has not just taken place in the case of EULEX, as its former Chief Prosecutor, van Vreeswijk, claims (see Braak 2012, 60–61), but also in the case of UNMIK, as suggested by its former head (August 2004–July 2006), Jessen-Petersen (see Qosaj-Mustafa 2010, 5).

51. To an extent, this was recognised by the mission itself, see EULEX Report (2012, 44).

52. Personal interview at the EU Office in Kosovo, Pristina, 2012, November 29.
53. Personal interview, Pristina, 2012, November 30.
54. Personal interview (via Skype) with Seb Bytyci from IPOL, 2012, November 23.
55. Personal interview with EULEX spokesperson Irina Gudeljevic, Pristina, 2012, November 26.
56. Op. cit., Note 51.
57. Op. cit., Note 53.
58. It is also crucial to note that structurally speaking, the mainstream law-enforcement approach does not problematise the capitalist system (structures of inequality that persist today, Piketty 2014) in which TOC functions. On account of this, the IC habitually compartmentalises the problem and deals increasingly with one element of it, i.e., the "fragile" states.
59. In this light, it is worthwhile to consider the discussions above, detailing the IC's practice of juggling with stability and rule of law. Florian Duli (personal interview, the Kosovar Stability Initiative [IKS], Pristina, 2012, November 30) points to a similar trend in the EU's practice, in that it takes on only politically palatable cases. She also, in this context, brings out stability as the key frame the EU deploys in Kosovo, which accounts for its strategy to maintain the same players as they are the most obedient.
60. See the HRW reports, e.g., 2007, June 14, 2008, March 10, but also Higate and Henry (2013), Gheciu (2005, 126), Braak (2012, Ch. 5).
61. The issues of accountability are more comprehensively dealt with by, e.g., Visoka (2012, 2013) and Palm (2009).
62. Personal interview with the executive director of KCSS, Pristina, 2012, November 27.
63. http://www.eulex-kosovo.eu/?page=2,23.
64. http://www.hrrp.eu/about.php.
65. Personal interview with the executive director of KCSS, Pristina, 2012, November 27.
66. Op. cit., Note 53. The incident is based on the following *encounter* between the mentioned Programme Manager and unspecified high school students of Kosovo. Namely, during one of EULEX's outreach campaigns, the Manager asked the students the following question: What would they do if their father, who works in a ministry, would tell them that tomorrow they can start working at the ministry with him without applying, a job interview, etc.? The Manager reports that all of them would accept this offer. And when he further enquired whether they would consider this an instance of corruption, they answered "no". Which led the Manager to conclude that this is "a social issue" that a technical mission (read: EULEX) cannot fix.

References

Aliu, Fatmir. 2012. "EU Kosovo Mission Fights Back Against Critics." *Balkan Insight*, June 14. http://www.balkaninsight.com/en/article/eulex-fights-back-to-critics.

Arsovska, Jana, and Panos A. Kostakos. 2010. "The Social Perception of Organised Crime in the Balkans: A World of Diverging Views?" In *Defining and Defying Organised Crime: Discourse, Perceptions and Reality*, edited by Felia Allum et al., 113–129. London: Routledge.

Autesserre, Séverine. 2014. *Peaceland: Conflict Resolution and the Everyday Politics of International Intervention*. New York, NY: CUP.

Banfield, Jessie. 2014. *Crime and Conflict: The New Challenge for Peacebuilding*. London: International Alert. http://www.international-alert.org/resources/publications/crime-and-conflict.

Barkawi, Tarak, and Mark Laffey. 2006. "The Postcolonial Moment in Security Studies." *Review of International Studies* 32: 329–352. https://doi.org/10.1017/s0260210506007054.

Bellamy, Alex J. 2002. *Kosovo and International Society*. Basingstoke: Palgrave Macmillan.

Bennett, Christine, and Saferworld. 2011. *Public Perceptions of Safety and Security in Kosovo: Time to Act*. London: Saferworld. http://www.saferworld.org.uk/resources/view-resource/553-public-perceptions-of-safety-and-security-in-kosovo.

Berdal, Mats, and Dominik Zaum. 2013. "Power After Peace." In *Political Economy of Statebuilding: Power After Peace* (Kindle edition), edited by Mats Berdal and Dominik Zaum, Ch. 1. Abingdon: Routledge.

Blagojevic, Bojana. 2007. "Peacebuilding in Ethnically Divided Societies." *Peace Review: A Journal of Social Justice* 19 (4): 555–562. https://doi.org/10.1080/10402650701681186.

Bliesemann de Guevara, Berit. 2013. "A 'Black Hole' in Europe? The Social and Discursive Reality of Crime in Bosnia-Herzegovina and the International Community's Tacit Complicity." In *Transnational Organised Crime: Analyses of a Global Challenge to Democracy*, edited by Heinrich-Böll-Stiftung and Regine Schönenberg, 211–231. Bielefeld: Transcript Verlag.

Boege, Volker, Anne Brown, Kevin Clements, and Anna Nolan. 2009. *On Hybrid Political Orders and Emerging States: What Is Failing—States in the Global South or Research and Politics in the West?* Berlin: Berghof Research Center for Constructive Conflict Management. http://www.berghof-foundation.org/fileadmin/redaktion/Publications/Handbook/Dialogue_Chapters/dialogue8_boegeetal_lead.pdf.

Bourdieu, Pierre. 1989. "Social Space and Symbolic Power." *Sociological Theory* 7 (1): 14–25.

Braak, Bruno Jim. 2012. "The Locals Are Lost: Using Local Perceptions to Evaluate the Effectiveness and Legitimacy of International Peace Missions (UNMIK, KFOR, OSCE, ICO and EULEX) in Kosovo." Master's thesis, University of St Andrews.

Bridoux, Jeff, and Milja Kurki. 2014. *Democracy Promotion: A Critical Introduction*. Abingdon: Routledge.

Capussela, Andrea. 2011. "EULEX in Kosovo: A Shining Symbol of Incompetence." *The Guardian*, April 9. http://www.theguardian.com/commentisfree/2011/apr/09/eulex-kosovo-eu-mission.

Capussela, Andrea. 2015. "EULEX's Performance of Its Executive Judicial Functions." In *State-Building in Kosovo: Democracy, Corruption and the EU in the Balkans*, edited by Andrea Lorenzo Capussela. London: I.B. Tauris. http://eulexannex.wix.com/draft.

Carothers, Thomas, ed. 2006. *Promoting the Rule of Law Abroad: In Search of Knowledge*. Washington, DC: Carnegie Endowment for International Peace. Kindle edition.

Chabal, Patrick. 2012. *The End of Conceit: Western Rationality After Postcolonialism*. London: Zed Books.

Chandler, David. 2007. "EU Statebuilding: Securing the Liberal Peace Through EU Enlargement." *Global Society* 21 (4): 593–607. https://doi.org/10.1080/13600820701562850.

Clark, Howard. 2000. *Civil Resistance in Kosovo*. London: Pluto Press.

Council of the European Union. 2002. "Comprehensive EU Concept for Missions in the Field of Rule of Law in Crisis Management, Including Annexes." 14513/02. Brussels, November 19.

Council of the European Union. 2003. "Comprehensive EU Concept for Missions in the Field of Rule of Law in Crisis Management, Including Annexes." 9792/03. Brussels, May 26.

Council of the European Union. 2004. "ESDP Presidency Report." 10547/04. Brussels, June 15. http://register.consilium.europa.eu/doc/srv?l=EN&f=ST%2010547%202004%20INIT.

Council of the European Union. 2005. "EU Concept for ESDP Support to Security Sector Reform (SSR)." 12566/4/05 REV 4. Brussels, October 13.

Council of the European Union. 2006. "Recommendations for Enhancing Co-operation with Non-Governmental Organisations (NGOs) and Civil Society Organisations (CSOs) in the Framework of EU Civilian Crisis Management and Conflict Prevention." 15574/1/06 REV 1. Brussels, December 8.

Council of the European Union. 2008a. Council Joint Action 2008/124/CFSP of 4 February 2008 on the European Union Rule of Law Mission in Kosovo. Official Journal of the European Union, L 42/92. February 16.

Council of the European Union. 2008b. "Press Release: 2851st Council Meeting General Affairs and External Relations." 6496/08. Brussels, February 18.

http://www.consilium.europa.eu/uedocs/cms_data/docs/pressdata/en/gena/98818.pdf.

Council of the European Union. 2008c. "Kosovo—Preparations for Enhanced Engagement." ESDP Newsletter Issue 6: 17–20. July.

Council of the European Union. 2008d. "Brussels European Council 19–20 June 2008: Presidency Conclusions." 11018/1/08. Brussels, July 17.

Council of the European Union. 2008e. "Statement on Tighter International Security." 16751/08. Brussels, December 3.

Council of the European Union. 2009a. "Draft Review of Recommendations for Enhancing Co-operation with Non-Governmental Organisations (NGOs) and Civil Society Organisations (CSOs) in the Framework of EU Civilian Crisis Management and Conflict Prevention." 10114/1/08 REV 1. Brussels, March 17.

Council of the European Union. 2009b. "Javier Solana, EU High Representative for the CFSP, Welcomes EULEX Full Operational Capability." Brussels, April 6. http://consilium.europa.eu/uedocs/cms_Data/docs/pressdata/en/esdp/107145.pdf.

Council of the European Union. 2009c. ESDP Newsletter, No. 7. Brussels, Winter. http://www.iss.europa.eu/uploads/media/ESDP_Newsletter_007.pdf.

Council of the European Union. 2010a. "3009th Foreign Affairs Council Meeting, CSDP." 8979/10. Luxembourg, April 26. http://europa.eu/rapid/press-release_PRES-10-90_en.htm?locale=en.

Council of the European Union. 2010b. CSDP Newsletter, Issue 10. Brussels, Summer. http://eeas.europa.eu/csdp/publications-and-documents/csdp_newsletter/index_en.htm.

Council of the European Union. 2010c. "Draft EU Concept for CSDP Justice Missions (Within the Rule of Law Framework)." 18173/10. Brussels, December 20.

Council of the European Union. 2012. "Council Decision 2012/291/CFSP of 5 June 2012 Amending and Extending Joint Action 2008/124/CFSP on the European Union Rule of Law Mission in Kosovo." *Official Journal of the European Union* L 146/46, June 6.

Dauphinee, Elizabeth A. 2003. "Rambouillet: A Critical (Re)Assessment." In *Understanding the War in Kosovo*, edited by Florian Bieber and Židas Daskalovski, 99–119. London: Frank Cass Publishers.

De Beauvoir, Simone. 1956. *The Second Sex*. Translated and edited by H. M. Parshley. London: Jonathan Cape.

Derks, Maria, and Megan Price. 2010. *The EU and Rule of Law Reform in Kosovo*. The Hague: Netherlands Institute for International Relations 'Clingendael'.

De Sousa Santos, Boaventura. 2007. "Human Rights as an Emancipatory Script." In *Another Knowledge Is Possible: Beyond Northern Epistemologies*, edited by Boaventura de Sousa Santos, 3–40. London: Verso.

De Sousa Santos, Boaventura. 2015. "Visions and Propositions for a More Just World." Lecture Given at the Université Catholique du Louvain, April 20, Belgium. http://alice.ces.uc.pt/en/index.php/homepage-videos/visions-and-propositions-for-a-more-just-world-video-lecture-louvain-belgium/.

Donais, Timothy. 2009. "Empowerment or Imposition? Dilemmas of Local Ownership in Post-conflict Peacebuilding Processes." *Peace & Change* 34 (1): 3–26. https://doi.org/10.1111/j.1468-0130.2009.00531.x.

Donnelly, Thomas, Ferdinand Nikolla, Anil Poudel, and Bibash Chakraborty. 2013. *Community-Based Approaches to Safety and Security: Lessons from Kosovo, Nepal and Bangladesh.* London: Saferworld. http://www.saferworld.org.uk/resources/view-resource/741-community-based-approaches-to-safety-and-security.

Drakulić, Slavenka. 2007. "Bathroom Tales: How We Mistook Normality for Paradise." *Eurozine*, April 10. http://www.eurozine.com/articles/2007-10-04-drakulic-en.html.

Duffield, Mark. 2007. *Development, Security and Unending War: Governing the World of Peoples.* Cambridge: Polity Press. Kindle edition.

Duffield, Mark. 2011. "Mark Duffield on Human (In)Security, Liberal Interventionism and Fortified Aid Compounds." *Theory Talks*, July 21. http://www.theory-talks.org/2011/07/theory-talk-41.html.

Edwards, Adam, and Peter Gill. 2003. "After Transnational Organised Crime? The Politics of Public Safety." In *Transnational Organised Crime: Perspectives on Global Security*, edited by Adam Edwards and Peter Gill, 264–281. London: Routledge.

Escobar, Arturo. 1995. *Encountering Development: The Making and Unmaking of the Third World.* Princeton: Princeton Univ. Press.

European Council. 2004. *Action Plan for Civilian Aspects of ESDP.* June 17–18. https://www.consilium.europa.eu/uedocs/cmsUpload/Action%20Plan%20for%20Civilian%20Aspects%20of%20ESDP.pdf.

European Court of Auditors. 2012. *European Union Assistance to Kosovo Related to the Rule of Law.* Luxembourg: ECA. http://www.eca.europa.eu/Lists/ECADocuments/SR12_18/SR12_18_EN.PDF.

EULEX. 2011. "Catalogue of Programmatic Monitoring, Mentoring and Advising (MMA) Actions," August. http://www.eulex-kosovo.eu/docs/tracking/2011-08-ACTION-FICHES-PUBLIC-new.pdf.

EULEX. 2012a. "Press Release: Lajčák Expresses Support for EULEX," February 2. http://www.eulex-kosovo.eu/en/pressreleases/0227.php.

EULEX. 2012b. "A Stronger, Leaner, More Efficient EULEX—EU Civilian Operations Commander," March 7. http://www.eulex-kosovo.eu/en/news/000344.php.

EULEX. 2012c. "Press Release: EULEX Organises Series of Lectures in Schools Throughout Kosovo," March 19. http://www.eulex-kosovo.eu/en/pressreleases/0246.php.

EULEX. 2012d. "Press Release: Head of Mission Communiqué," March 27. http://www.eulex-kosovo.eu/en/pressreleases/0253.php.

EULEX. 2012e. "Press Release: EULEX Is Doing Nothing," June 12. http://www.eulex-kosovo.eu/en/pressreleases/0298.php.

EULEX Joint. 2008. "EULEX Kosovo—Joint Press Statement." In *EU Security and Defence Core Documents 2008*, vol. IX, compiled by Catherine Glière. Paris: EUISS. http://www.iss.europa.eu/uploads/media/cp117.pdf.

EULEX Report. 2009. *EULEX Programme Report 2009*. Pristina: EULEX Programme Office. http://www.eulex-kosovo.eu/?page=2,1.

EULEX Report. 2010. *EULEX Programme Report 2010: Building Sustainable Change Together*. Pristina: EULEX Programme Office. http://www.eulex-kosovo.eu/?page=2,1.

EULEX Report. 2011. *EULEX Programme Report 2011: Bolstering the Rule of Law in Kosovo: A Stock Take*. Pristina: EULEX Programme Office. http://www.eulexkosovo.eu/?page=2,1.

EULEX Report. 2012. *EULEX Programme Report: Rule of Law Beyond the Headlines*. Pristina: EULEX Programme Office. http://www.eulex-kosovo.eu/?page=2,1.

European Commission. 2005. "Communication from the Commission: A European Future for Kosovo." (COM(2005) 156 Final). Brussels, April 20. http://eurlex.europa.eu/legal-content/EN/TXT/?uri=CELEX:52005DC0156.

European Commission. 2006. "Communication from the Commission: The Western Balkans on the Road to the EU: Consolidating Stability and Raising Prosperity." (COM(2006) 27 Final). Brussels, January 27. http://eur-lex.europa.eu/LexUriServ/LexUriServ.do?uri=COM:2006:0027:FIN:EN:PDF.

European Commission. 2008. "Communication from the Commission to the European Parliament and the Council: Western Balkans: Enhancing the European Perspective" (COM(2008) 127 Final). Brussels, March 5. http://eur-lex.europa.eu/legalcontent/EN/TXT/?uri=celex:52008DC0127.

European Parliament. 2007. "European Parliament Resolution of 29 March 2007 on the Future of Kosovo and the Role of the EU (P6_TA(2007)0097)." Brussels, March 29. http://www.europarl.europa.eu/sides/getDoc.do?type=TA&reference=P6-TA-2007-0097&language=EN&ring=A6-2007-0067#ref_1_1.

European Security Strategy (ESS). 2003. "A Secure Europe in a Better World—The European Security Strategy." Brussels, December 12. http://www.consilium.europa.eu/uedocs/cmsUpload/78367.pdf.

EU-US Summit Declaration (Brdo). 2008. In *EU Security and Defence: Core Documents 2008*. Vol. IX. Compiled by Catherine Glière. Paris: EUISS. June 10. http://www.iss.europa.eu/uploads/media/cp117.pdf.

Ferrero-Waldner, Benita. 2009. "Speech by Benita Ferrero-Waldner, European Commissioner for External Relations and ENP, to European Parliament's Foreign Affairs Committee (AFET)." Brussels, September 29. http://europa.eu/rapid/press-release_SPEECH-09-424_en.htm?locale=FR.

Fierke, Karin. 2007. *Critical Approaches to International Security*. Cambridge: Polity Press.

Franks, Jason, and Oliver P. Richmond. 2008. "Coopting Liberal Peace-Building: Untying the Gordian Knot in Kosovo." *Cooperation and Conflict* 43 (1): 81–103. https://doi.org/10.1177/0010836707086738.

Frueh, Jamie. 2004. "Studying Continuity and Change in South African Political Identity." In *Identity and Global Politics: Empirical and Theoretical Elaborations*, edited by Patricia M. Goff and Kevin C. Dunn, 63–78. New York: Palgrave Macmillan.

GAERC. 2003. "2518th Council Meeting." 10369/03. Luxembourg, June 16. http://data.consilium.europa.eu/doc/document/ST-10369-2003-INIT/en/pdf.

Gashi, Krenar. 2008a. "Foggy Dawn for New EU Mission in Kosovo." *Balkan Insight*, December 4. http://www.balkaninsight.com/en/article/foggy-dawn-for-new-eu-missionin-kosovo.

Gashi, Krenar. 2008b. "We Can't Perform Miracles Overnight." *Balkan Insight*, December 10. http://www.balkaninsight.com/en/article/we-can-t-perform-miracles-overnight.

George, Alexandra. 2009. "EULEX Enlists the Support of Civil Society," December 16. http://www.eulex-kosovo.eu/en/news/000191.php.

Gheciu, Alexandra. 2005. "International Norms, Power and the Politics of International Administration: The Kosovo Case." *Geopolitics* 10 (1): 121–146. https://doi.org/10.1080/14650040590907695.

Golub, Stephen. 2006. "A House Without a Foundation." In *Promoting the Rule of Law Abroad: In Search of Knowledge* (Kindle edition), edited by Thomas Carothers, Ch. 5. Washington, DC: Carnegie Endowment for International Peace.

Gordon, Eleanor. 2014. "Security Sector Reform, Statebuilding and Local Ownership: Securing the State or Its People?" *Journal of Intervention and Statebuilding* 8 (2–3): 126–148. https://doi.org/10.1080/17502977.2014.930219.

Hargreaves, James. 2014. "The EULEX Legacy in the Kosovo Courts." *Osservatorio Balcani e Caucaso* (OBC). November 4. http://www.balcanicaucaso.org/eng/Regions-and-countries/Kosovo/The-EULEX-Legacy-in-the-Kosovo-Courts-156872.

Hehir, Aidan, ed. 2010a. *Kosovo, Intervention and Statebuilding: The International Community and the Transition to Independence*. Abingdon: Routledge.

Hehir, Aidan. 2010b. "The Efficacy of the International Administration's Policy of Coerced Co-operation in Kosovo." EISA Conference Paper, Sweden.

Hellmüller, Sara. 2014. "A Story of Mutual Adaptation? The Interaction Between Local and International Peacebuilding Actors in Ituri." *Peacebuilding* 2 (2): 188–201. https://doi.org/10.1080/21647259.2014.910914.

Higate, Paul, and Marsha Henry. 2013. *Insecure Spaces: Peacekeeping, Power and Performance in Haiti, Kosovo and Liberia.* London: Zed Books. Kindle edition.

Hobson, John M. 2012. *The Eurocentric Conception of World Politics: Western International Theory, 1760–2010.* Cambridge: Cambridge University Press.

HRW. 2007. "Better Late Than Never: Enhancing the Accountability of International Institutions in Kosovo," June 14. http://www.hrw.org/sites/default/files/reports/kosovo0607web.pdf.

HRW. 2008. "Kosovo: EU Should Ensure International Mission Is Accountable," March 10. http://www.hrw.org/news/2008/03/09/kosovo-eu-should-ensure-international-mission-accountable.

Hughes, Caroline, and Vanessa Pupavac. 2005. "Framing Post-conflict Societies: International Pathologisation of Cambodia and the Post-Yugoslav States." *Third World Quarterly* 26 (6): 873–889. http://www.jstor.org/stable/4017815.

Hurwitz, Agnès, and Reyko Huang, eds. 2008. *Civil War and the Rule of Law: Security, Development, Human Rights.* Boulder: Lynne Rienner Publishers.

ICG. 2003. "Two to Tango: An Agenda for the New Kosovo SRSG." Europe Report No. 148. Pristina/Brussels: ICG. September 3. http://www.crisisgroup.org/en/regions/europe/balkans/kosovo/148-two-to-tango-an-agenda-for-the-new-kosovo-srsg.aspx.

ICG. 2010. "The Rule of Law in Independent Kosovo." Europe Report No. 204. Pristina/Brussels, May 19. http://www.crisisgroup.org/en/regions/europe/balkans/kosovo/204-the-rule-of-law-in-independent-kosovo.aspx.

IKS (Kosovar Stability Initiative). 2010. "Untying the Knot: The Political Economy of Corruption and Accountability in Kosovo." Policy Paper. Pristina: IKS. June 29. http://www.iksweb.org/repository/docs/enuntying_the_knot_491401.pdf.

Ioannides, Isabelle, and Gemma Collantes-Celador. 2011. "The Internal-External Security Nexus and EU Police/Rule of Law Missions in the Western Balkans." *Conflict, Security & Development* 11 (4): 415–445. https://doi.org/10.1080/14678802.2011.614127.

Inayatullah, Naeem, and David L. Blaney. 2004. *International Relations and the Problem of Difference.* New York: Routledge.

Jabri, Vivienne. 2013. "Peacebuilding, the Local and the International: A Colonial or a Postcolonial Rationality?" *Peacebuilding* 1 (1): 3–16. https://doi.org/10.1080/21647259.2013.756253.

Jahn, Beate. 2012. "Rethinking Democracy Promotion." *Review of International Studies* 38 (4): 685–705. https://doi.org/10.1017/s0260210511000763.

Joint UK-France Declaration. 2008. In *EU Security and Defence: Core Documents 2008*. Vol. IX. Compiled by Catherine Glière. Paris: EUISS. March 27. http://www.iss.europa.eu/uploads/media/cp117.pdf.

Karadaku, Linda. 2010. "De Kermabon: Status Quo Unsustainable in Northern Kosovo." Cesran International. April 12. http://cesran.org/de-kermabon-status-quounsustainable-in-northern-kosovo.html.

KCSS (Kosovar Center for Security Studies). 2010. "Assessment of the Democratic Oversight and Governance Mechanisms of Municipal Community Safety Councils." Pristina: KCSS. http://www.qkss.org/en-us/Policy-Papers/Assessment-of-the-Democratic-Oversightand-Governance-Mechanisms-of-Municipal-Community-Safety-Councils-88.

KCSS, et al. 2010. "Progress Report: Made in Kosovo." Pristina. October. http://www.institutigap.org/documents/32617_KosovarProgressReport.pdf.

Keukeleire, Stephan, Arben Kalaja, and Artan Çollaku. 2011. "The European Union's Policy on Kosovo." In *European Foreign Policy Legal and Political Perspectives*, edited by Panos Koutrakos, 172–202. Cheltenham: Edward Elgar Publishing.

Keukeleire, Stephan, and Robin Thiers. 2010. "EULEX Kosovo: Walking a Thin Line, Aiming for the Rule of Law." In *The European Union and Peacebuilding*, edited by Steven Blockmans et al., 353–374. The Hague: T.M.C. Asser Press.

Ki-moon, Ban. 2007. "Letter Dated 26 March 2007 from the Secretary-General Addressed to the President of the Security Council (S/2007/168)," March 26. http://www.unosek.org/docref/report-english.pdf.

KIPRED (Kosovo Institute for Policy Research and Development). 2009. "Kosovo at a Crossroad: Decentralisation and the Creation of New Municipalities." Policy Brief No. 14. Pristina: KIPRED.

Kleinfeld Belton, Rachel. 2005. "Competing Definitions of the Rule of Law: Implications for Practitioners." Carnegie Papers No. 55. Washington: Carnegie Endowment for International Peace.

Kleinfeld, Rachel. 2012. *Advancing the Rule of Law Abroad: Next Generation Reform*. Washington: Carnegie Endowment for International Peace. Kindle edition.

Kostovicova, Denisa, Mary Martin, and Vesna Bojicic-Dzelilovic. 2012. "The Missing Link in Human Security Research: Dialogue and Insecurity in Kosovo." *Security Dialogue* 43 (6): 569–585. https://doi.org/10.1177/0967010612463489.

Kurki, Milja. 2013. *Democratic Futures: Revisioning Democracy Promotion*. Abingdon: Routledge. Kindle edition.

Kursani, Shpend. 2013. "A Comprehensive Analysis of EULEX: What Next?" Policy Paper. Pristina: KIPRED.

Kurti, Albin. 2011. "JISB Interview: Kosova in Dependence: From Stability of Crisis to the Crisis of Stability." *Journal of Intervention and Statebuilding* 5 (1): 89–97. https://doi.org/10.1080/17502977.2011.541787.

KWN (Kosovo Women's Network). 2011. "1325 Facts and Fables: A Collection of Stories About the Implementation of UNSC Resolution 1325 on Women, Peace, and Security in Kosovo." Pristina: KWN. http://www.womensnetwork.org/documents/20130120165559661.pdf.

Lemay-Hébert, Nicolas. 2011. "The 'Empty-Shell' Approach: The Setup Process of International Administrations in Timor-Leste and Kosovo, Its Consequences and Lessons." *International Studies Perspectives* 12 (2): 190–211. https://doi.org/10.1111/j.1528-3585.2011.00427.x.

Lemay-Hébert, Nicolas 2013. "Everyday Legitimacy and International Administration: Global Governance and Local Legitimacy in Kosovo." *Journal of Intervention and Statebuilding* 7 (1): 87–104. https://doi.org/10.1080/17502977.2012.655622.

Lutolli, Labinot, and Krenare Maloku. 2008. "EULEX Will Not Be like UNMIK." *Balkan Insight*, February 6. http://www.balkaninsight.com/en/article/eulex-will-not-be-like-unmik.

Mac Ginty, Roger. 2011. *International Peacebuilding and Local Resistance: Hybrid Forms of Peace*. Basingstoke: Palgrave Macmillan.

Mac Ginty, Roger. 2012. "Routine Peace: Technocracy and Peacebuilding." *Cooperation and Conflict* 47 (3): 287–308. https://doi.org/10.1177/0010836712444825.

Mac Ginty, Roger, and Oliver P. Richmond. 2013. "The Local Turn in Peace Building: A Critical Agenda for Peace." *Third World Quarterly* 34 (5): 763–783. https://doi.org/10.1080/01436597.2013.800750.

Mani, Rama. 1999. "Contextualising Police Reform: Security, the Rule of Law and Post-conflict Peacebuilding." *International Peacekeeping* 6 (4): 9–26. https://doi.org/10.1080/13533319908413796.

Mani, Rama. 2008. "Exploring the Rule of Law in Theory and Practice." In *Civil War and the Rule of Law: Security, Development, Human Rights*, edited by Agnès Hurwitz and Reyko Huang, 21–45. London: Lynne Rienner Publishers.

Mbembe, Achille. 2008. "What Is Postcolonial Thinking?" *Eurozine*, January 9. http://www.eurozine.com/articles/2008-01-09-mbembe-en.html.

Merlingen, Michael, and Rasa Ostrauskaite. 2005. "Power/Knowledge in International Peacebuilding: The Case of the EU Police Mission in Bosnia." *Alternatives* 30: 297–323. https://doi.org/10.1177/030437540503000303.

Mertus, Julie. 2001. "The Impact of Intervention on Local Human Rights Culture: A Kosovo Case Study." *Global Review of Ethnopolitics* 1 (2): 21–36. https://doi.org/10.1080/14718800108405095.

Mouffe, Chantal. 2009. *The Democratic Paradox*. London: Verso.

Mouffe, Chantal. 2013. *Agonistics: Thinking the World Politically*. London: Verso.

Muja, Armend. 2012. *Kosovo Security Barometer.* Pristina: KCSS. http://www.qkss.org/en/Reports/Kosovo-Security-Barometer-124.

Muppidi, Himadeep. 2004. *The Politics of the Global.* Minneapolis: University of Minnesota Press.

Musliu, Vjosa, and Jan Orbie. 2014. "The International Missions in Kosovo: What Is in a Name?" *European Foreign Affairs Review* 19 (3): 411–428.

O'Brennan, John. 2013. "The European Commission, Enlargement Policy and Civil Society in the Western Balkans." In *Civil Society and Transitions in the Western Balkans,* edited by Vesna Bojicic-Dzelilovic, James Ker-Lindsay, and Denisa Kostovicova, 29–46. Basingstoke: Palgrave Macmillan.

Palm, Malin. 2009. *Accountability and Effectiveness of CSDP Missions: The Role of Civil Society.* Brussels: EPLO. http://www.eplo.org/institutions-and-policies.html.

Papadimitriou, Dimitris, and Petar Petrov. 2012. "Whose Rule, Whose Law? Contested Statehood, External Leverage and the European Union's Rule of Law Mission in Kosovo." *Journal of Common Market Studies* 50 (5): 746–763. https://doi.org/10.1111/j.1468-5965.2012.02257.x.

Paris, Roland. 2004. *At War's End.* New York: Cambridge University Press.

Piketty, Thomas. 2014. *Capital in the Twenty-First Century.* Translated by Arthur Goldhammer. Cambridge: The Belknap Press of Harvard University Press.

Peterson, Jenny H. 2010. "'Rule of Law' Initiatives and the Liberal Peace: The Impact of Politicised Reform in Post-conflict States." *Disasters* 34 (1): S15–S39. https://doi.org/10.1111/j.1467-7717.2009.01097.x.

Prashad, Vijay. 2007. *The Darker Nations: A People's History of the Third World.* New York: The New Press.

Pugh, Michael. 2005. "The Political Economy of Peacebuilding: A Critical Theory Perspective." *International Journal of Peace Studies* 10 (2): 23–42. http://www.jstor.org/stable/41852928.

Pugh, Michael. 2006. "Crime and Capitalism in Kosovo's Transformation." In *Kosovo Between War and Peace: Nationalism, Peacebuilding and International Trusteeship,* edited by Tonny Brems Knudsen and Carsten Bagge Laustsen, 116–134. Abingdon: Routledge.

Pugh, Michael. 2013. "Statebuilding and Corruption: A Political Economy Perspective." In *Political Economy of Statebuilding: Power After Peace* (Kindle edition), edited by Mats Berdal and Dominik Zaum, Ch. 6. Abingdon: Routledge.

Qosaj-Mustafa, Ariana. 2010. *Strengthening Rule of Law in Kosovo: The Fight Against Corruption and Organised Crime.* Pristina: KIPRED. http://www.kipred.org/repository/docs/Strengthening_Rule_of_Law_in_Kosovo-_The_Fight_Against_Corruption_and_Organised_Crime_602831.pdf.

Rajagopal, Balakrishnan. 2008. "Invoking the Rule of Law: International Discourses." In *Civil War and the Rule of Law: Security, Development, Human*

Rights, edited by Agnès Hurwitz and Reyko Huang, 47–67. London: Lynne Rienner Publishers.

Rayroux, Antoine. 2013. "Speaking EU Defence at Home: Contentious Discourses and Constructive Ambiguity." *Cooperation and Conflict*. https://doi.org/10.1177/0010836713495001.

Rehn, Olli. 2008. "Civil Society at the Heart of the EU's Enlargement Agenda." Brussels, April 17. http://europa.eu/rapid/press-release_SPEECH-08-201_en.htm?locale=en.

Report on the Implementation of the European Security Strategy (Implementation Report). 2008. "Providing Security in a Changing World." S407/08. Brussels, December 11. https://www.consilium.europa.eu/ueDocs/cms_Data/docs/pressdata/EN/reports/104630.pdf.

Richmond, Oliver P. 2006. "The Problem of Peace: Understanding the 'Liberal Peace.'" *Conflict, Security & Development* 6 (3): 291–314. https://doi.org/10.1080/14678800600933480.

Richmond, Oliver P. 2012. "Beyond Local Ownership in the Architecture of International Peacebuilding." *Ethnopolitics: Formerly Global Review of Ethnopolitics* 11 (4): 354–375. https://doi.org/10.1080/17449057.2012.697650.

Sabovic, Senad. 2010. "Intervention and Independence in Kosovo: The EULEX Rule of Law Mission." In *The European Union and Human Security: External Interventions and Missions*, edited by Mary Martin and Mary Kaldor, 112–127. Abingdon: Routledge.

Scherrer, Amandine. 2010. "International Policy Discourses on Transnational Organised Crime: The Role of an International Expertise." In *Defining and Defying Organised Crime: Discourse, Perceptions and Reality*, edited by Felia Allum et al., 55–68. London: Routledge.

Sending, Ole Jacob. 2011. "The Effects of Peacebuilding: Sovereignty, Patronage and Power." In *A Liberal Peace? The Problems and Practices of Peacebuilding* (Kindle edition), edited by Susanna Campbell, David Chandler, and Meera Sabaratnam, 55–69. London: Zed Books.

Sheptycki, James. 2003. "Global Law Enforcement as a Protection Racket: Some Sceptical Notes on Transnational Organised Crime as an Object of Global Governance." In *Transnational Organised Crime: Perspectives on Global Security*, edited by Adam Edwards and Peter Gill, 42–58. London: Routledge.

Solana, Javier. 2005. "Europe's International Role (Speech)." Bratislava, November 9. http://eu-un.europa.eu/articles/fr/article_5281_fr.htm.

Solana, Javier. 2007. "Countering Globalisation's Dark Side." *Europe's World*. October 1. http://europesworld.org/2007/10/01/countering-globalisations-dark-side/#.VAjJU1ZguoI.

Solana, Javier. 2008a. "Summary of the Address: 'Where Is Russia Going? A New Attempt for an All-European Security Order.'" Munich, February 10. http://

www.consilium.europa.eu/uedocs/cms_Data/docs/pressdata/en/discours/98707.pdf.

Solana, Javier. 2008b. "Europe in the World: The Next Steps (Cyril Foster Lecture)." S087/08. Oxford, February 28. http://www.consilium.europa.eu/uedocs/cms_data/docs/pressdata/en/discours/99116.pdf.

Solana, Javier. 2008c. "Address to the European Parliament on EU Foreign, Security and Defence Policy by Javier Solana." S194/08. Brussels, June 4. https://www.consilium.europa.eu/ueDocs/cms_Data/docs/pressdata/EN/discours/101004.pdf.

Solana, Javier. 2008d. "On UN Reconfiguration of the Civilian Presence in Kosovo." S223/08. Brussels, June 21. http://www.consilium.europa.eu/ueDocs/cms_Data/docs/pressdata/EN/declarations/101371.pdf.

Solana, Javier. 2008e. "Summary of Intervention of Javier Solana Before the Meeting of International Organisations Active on the Ground in Kosovo (EU, NATO, UN, OSCE)." S257/08. Brussels, July 18. http://www.consilium.europa.eu/uedocs/cms_data/docs/pressdata/en/discours/101889.pdf.

Solana, Javier. 2008f. "Remarks by EU High Representative Javier Solana at the Conference 'National Interests and European Foreign Policy (Berlin)'." In *EU Security and Defence: Core Documents 2008*, vol. IX, compiled by Catherine Glière. Paris: EUISS. October 7. http://www.iss.europa.eu/uploads/media/cp117.pdf.

Solana, Javier. 2008g. "Annual Conference of the Institute for Security Studies of the European Union—Speech by Javier Solana," In *EU Security and Defence: Core Documents 2008*, vol. IX, compiled by Catherine Glière. Paris: EUISS. October 30. http://www.iss.europa.eu/uploads/media/cp117.pdf.

Solana, Javier. 2008h. "Javier Solana addressed Today the Foreign Affairs Committee of the European Parliament and the Chairs of the Foreign Affairs and Defence Committees of the National Parliaments on Recent Developments Concerning the Main Issues on the International Agenda," November 5. http://eu-un.europa.eu/articles/en/article_8274_en.htm.

Solana, Javier. 2008i. "Javier Solana, EU High Representative for the CFSP, Announces the Start of EULEX Kosovo." S400/08. Brussels, December 5. http://www.consilium.europa.eu/uedocs/cms_Data/docs/pressdata/en/declarations/104524.pdf.

Solana, Javier. 2009a. "Europe's Global Role—What Next Steps? (Ditchley Foundation Lecture)." London, July 11. http://eu-un.europa.eu/articles/fr/article_8875_fr.htm.

Solana, Javier. 2009b. "Summary of Remarks to Reporters by EUHR Solana During Kosovo Trip," July 14. http://eu-un.europa.eu/articles/en/article_8884_en.htm.

Solana, Javier. 2009c. "ESDP at 10: What Lessons for the Future?" Brussels, July 28. http://www.consilium.europa.eu/uedocs/cms_data/docs/pressdata/en/discours/109453.pdf.

Solana, Javier, and Olli Rehn. 2007. "Summary Note on the Joint Report by Javier Solana, EU High Representative for the CFSP, and Olli Rehn, EU Commissioner for Enlargement, on the State of Preparations of the Future EU and International Presence in Kosovo." Brussels, March 29. http://europa.eu/rapid/press-release_MEMO-07-121_en.htm.

Steiner, Michael. 2003. "For Example, Kosovo: Seven Principles for Peace Building." Speech Delivered at the London School of Economics and Political Science, January 27. http://eprints.lse.ac.uk/23456/1/DP22_ForExampleKosovo.pdf.

UNODC. 2008. *Crime and Its Impact on the Balkans and Affected Countries.* Vienna: UNODC.

UNODC. 2011. *Corruption in Kosovo: Bribery as Experienced by the Population.* Vienna: UNODC.

UN Security Council. 1999. *Resolution 1244 (1999).* New York: United Nations. June 10. http://www.un.org/Docs/scres/1999/sc99.htm.

UN Security Council. 2008. "Kosovo Situation Calm, but Political Transition Following Declaration of Independence More Complex than Expected." SC/9512. http://www.un.org/press/en/2008/sc9512.doc.htm.

Van Rompuy, Herman. 2010. "President of the European Council, Following His Visit to EULEX Headquarters." PCE 152/10. Pristina, July 6. http://www.consilium.europa.eu/uedocs/cms_data/docs/pressdata/en/ec/115689.pdf.

Visoka, Gëzim. 2012. "The 'Kafkaesque Accountability' of International Governance in Kosovo." *Journal of Intervention and Statebuilding* 6 (2): 189–212. https://doi.org/10.1080/17502977.2012.655603.

Visoka, Gëzim. 2013. "The EULEX Accountability in Kosovo." Policy Study No. 2. Pristina: Kosovo Institute of Peace. https://www.academia.edu/7598243/EULEX_Accountability_in_Kosovo.

Visoka, Gëzim, and Grace Bolton. 2011. "The Complex Nature and Implications of International Engagement after Kosovo's Independence." *Civil Wars* 13 (2): 189–214. https://doi.org/10.1080/13698249.2011.576158.

Vrasti, Wanda. 2011. "Universal But Not Truly 'Global': Governmentality, Economic Liberalism, and the International." *Review of International Studies* (Online Version) 1–21. https://doi.org/10.1017/s0260210511000568.

Wittgenstein, Ludwig. 1967. *Philosophical Investigations.* 3rd ed. Translated by G. E. M. Anscombe. Oxford: Basil Blackwell.

YIHR (Youth Initiative for Human Rights). 2010. *State of Constriction? Governance and Free Expression in Kosovo.* Prishtina: YIHR. http://www.civilrightsdefenders.org/files/State-of-Constriction-YIHR-Kosovo.pdf.

CHAPTER 7

Conclusion

This book interrogated how the EU has told and acted its CSDP identity throughout its three core missions: Artemis in the DRC, EUFOR Althea in BiH and EULEX in Kosovo. The contextually close reading of EU missions—using the fluid categories of *telling and acting*, stressing the *dialogical ways of being*, and taking heed of the concept of *just peace* as a particular guide to building peace—allowed to tap into the specific meanings the EU had of peace, the ways in which it imagined its relationships with its varied "partners", and perhaps most controversially, the way that being/becoming a global actor has been front and centre of the CSDP. The mentioned analytical apparatus has given a solid platform for a relational study of the CSDP. In fact, these concepts have introduced the inescapable in-betweenness of the object of study, making it impossible to glean *just a story* as there is always a multiplicity of inextricably intertwined stories. This notwithstanding, Chimamanda Ngozi Adichie urges us to take the positionality of *a* story seriously (also Butler 2004):

> It is impossible to talk about the single story without talking about power. There is a word, an Igbo word, that I think about whenever I think about the power structures of the world, and it is 'nkali.' It's a noun that loosely translates to 'to be greater than another.' Like our economic and political worlds, stories too are defined by the principle of *nkali*: How they are told, who tells them, when they're told, how many stories are told, are really dependent on power.

© The Author(s) 2020
B. Poopuu, *The European Union's Brand of Peacebuilding*,
Rethinking Peace and Conflict Studies,
https://doi.org/10.1007/978-3-030-19890-9_7

Power is the ability not just to tell the story of another person, but to make it the definitive story of that person. The Palestinian poet Mourid Barghouti writes that if you want to dispossess a people, the simplest way to do it is to tell their story and to start with, 'secondly.' Start the story with the arrows of the Native Americans, and not with the arrival of the British, and you have an entirely different story. Start the story with the failure of the African state, and not with the colonial creation of the African state, and you have an entirely different story. (Adichie 2009)

Embarking on a research quest equipped with the chief tenets of critical theories has, furthermore, made me responsive to the idea that questions of ontology and epistemology are best treated as relational categories, and that they do not concern merely the research object, but also the researcher as a party to that process (see esp. Hamati-Ataya 2010). Making use of the analytical categories of telling and acting has enabled me to study the EU's CSDP in motion and as a process, and the sheer spatio-temporal detail this has provided has been illuminating. This move has also raised some intriguing questions about ontological and epistemological concerns vis-à-vis telling and acting that could be regarded as starting points for further debate. As pointed out above, Adichie brings out an important aspect of storytelling, namely power, which permeates the social realm and, through the creation of different lenses and positions, encourages both different readings and story-telling practices. The critical commitments made in this work have allowed me to get beyond a single story—notwithstanding the gravitation towards a single story in the EU's own discourse—but at the same time recognising that the approach taken here is not exhaustive of other stories and starting points.[1] This, in a nutshell, was the ambition of this book—to interrogate the story of the EU's CSDP identity without losing sight of other stories. In this chapter, I will revisit a number of themes that were touched upon throughout the three case studies, in order to capture some of the chief stories the EU has told about itself and its social surroundings.

Interrogating the telling and acting of the EU has enabled me to flesh out the EU's CSDP identity. Curiously, while the CSDP deals with peace and conflict, the EU has restrained from labelling itself either a conflict manager or a peacebuilder. If this is mentioned at all, then the EU shows a clear preference for the term crisis/conflict management. Compared to this, the EU has been far more obsessed with both *being* and *becoming* a global actor. This reveals the somewhat problematic status of the CSDP. It is apparent that the CSDP is a means to becoming/being a global actor. This argument is underpinned by the way the EU has chosen to speak about the CSDP, which focuses overwhelmingly on building up capabilities rather than the thornier issues of the substance of this policy. In itself, this attitude signals that the CSDP is a taken-for-granted policy (at least as far as the substance goes). This work was interested in the substance of the CSDP and its implications, and in consequence, it has been constantly deconstructing the habitual commonsense of the CSDP. It has adopted the generic label of "peacebuilding" to refer to all the different ways of addressing conflicts without deciding a priori on the identity of the actor (see Fetherston 2000). The critical approach to the EU's CSDP identity has been a refreshing endeavour since critically inclined analyses have been rather rare in the pertinent literature. Hopefully, the present work has demonstrated that these kinds of engagements, which probe the common-sense framing of the CSDP, are indispensable as they stress the idea of dialogue when dealing with peacebuilding.

I have approached the EU's CSDP identity by investigating how it was expressed via media of telling and acting. This analytical move allowed me—in a deeply contextual way—to interrogate the meanings the EU put forth in the context of the CSDP. On that basis, I will now revisit the recurrent themes that surfaced within this book to answer the questions *what goods does the CSDP offer*, and *who the CSDP is for*. This exercise does not necessarily permit generalisation beyond the CSDP, as the Commission has its own profile in peacebuilding (see esp. Björkdahl et al. 2009, 2011; Kappler 2012a, b; Pogodda et al. 2014). Yet, the CSDP read together with the Commission's approach to peacebuilding provides an insightful perspective on the EU's responses to conflict-affected countries.

Contextual investigations have portrayed the vast frames of meaning of which the CSDP operations became part. All of the case studies have shed light on the degree to which the EU's operations have been structurally constrained by the already present contexts (such as Dayton, SAP or the accumulated and distributed knowledge about the conflict in question). For example, in the context of operation Artemis, it was very clear that the primary narratives of the peacebuilding apparatus in place in the DRC were upheld by the EU as well. As a result, the EU subscribed to the two dominant beliefs on how to approach the conflict theatre in question: the idea that the national level remains the main contact point for the outsiders and that the fixing of the state (institutions) should be the main peacebuilding activity. The fact that the EU underwrites these premises—even though in the DRC it had a more traditional crisis management profile, with keeping peace (read: stability) and ensuring traditional security at its core—is constitutive of and shapes the EU's way of responding to conflicts. Promoting the top-down approach to conflict has considerable repercussions for the potential of the EU to offer something new and unique as is sometimes trumpeted. At this juncture, the habitually reiterated idea that the UN is the primary authority in the field of peace and conflict becomes problematic if this is used as an alibi to further entrench the top-down mindset of peacebuilding. Relatedly, the tension between, on the one hand, the unquestioned endorsement of the UN's *modus operandi* in peacebuilding, and, on the other hand, the articulation of a unique role for the EU, unfolds within the case studies. Arguably, the latter part of the argument is not convincing, because it often just amounts to claiming that the EU has an all-encompassing/comprehensive approach to conflicts, yet the proof usually resides in the fact that the EU has both civilian and military capabilities. The silence around substantive matters is deafening. Clearly, sustainable and meaningful peacebuilding, as Keukeleire, Kalaja and Çollaku point out, does not stop with having the capabilities or proclaiming an all-encompassing policy, it also needs to resonate with the locals on their terms (2011, 201–202).

The just peace lens introduced in Chapter 3 is promising since it has equipped me with a critical frame adept at questioning the received wisdom of the EU's CSDP. Equally, the just peace lens demonstrated that peace is always contextual—as it is to do with people's lives. Further, it underlined the value of inclusive discussions over "peace goods". In this sense, the critical and ethical commitment behind it is about more just social arrangements. The conceptual apparatus of just peace pierces through specific peace goods on offer and brings out their particularity as opposed to their purported universality/neutrality. Therefore, for the EU to truly claim that it is aiming for just peace—capturing the value and need of meaningful engagement and social justice—it needs to foster more openness and inclusivity when it comes to understanding conflicts and about its role and the partnerships built thereafter.

The EU places enormous emphasis on "acting" (sometimes referred to as credibility). It becomes clear that this quality quite simply translates into being able to operate on the international arena and consequently being recognised by the significant others (such as the UN, US). It also, and rather troublingly, works in the evaluation stage as an easy stamp of approval. To illustrate this, on many occasions the mere deployment of the mission served as an indicator of success, despite the particulars of this acting. Furthermore, the acting—in the sense of launching a mission—was seen as a necessary component to buttress the EU's global actor profile.

Throughout the analysis, a number of discourses shed light on the understandings that constitute the CSDP. I believe that these discourses have been fairly well presented within the empirical chapters. Here, I want to go back to a thought that Ashton clearly voices in 2010, but which applies to the spatio-temporal scope of this work from the start. This thought is important because it uncovers the mechanics of describing and creating what is "normal". Ashton argues that in order to engage with the world effectively, "*we* need to frame it first" (Ashton 2010, March 10; emphasis mine). As the case studies manifest, this idea is incorporated within the CSDP logic, becoming visible where a certain kind of knowledge is privileged, and where a crude role allocation is maintained through an explicit framing of the world. For example, all of the empirical chapters uncovered an asymmetrical relationship, where it is evident that the "we" that does the framing is not inclusive of the local voices (except in a perfunctory/symbolic role, made digestible to the EU). Therefore, the structural imbalance goes beyond the resource levels, deep into the meaning-making realm, which exposes a rather grim view of the state of affairs. For instance, the categories of *multiple* and *significant others*, which emerged in the course of the analysis of the case studies, illustrate how the telling and acting of the EU matters in "reality". These categories manifest how diverse groups of actors are understood and hence acted towards. Contrasting these labels, it becomes clear that there is a huge gap between them: there are those who share/bring/shape peace (read: the significant others) and then there are those who first "necessitate" and then "suffer" this peace (read: the multiple others). As a major caveat, it should be noted that the offered apprehension mirrors the EU's take on the matter, but it does not in any way directly imply causality. To wit, the locals are not clay waiting to be moulded by the EU, they are incredibly resourceful and are not unidirectionally affected by the EU's actions (see Kappler 2012a, b; Richmond 2014), albeit they can be considerably constrained by them (i.e. opportunities that turn into constraints/oppressive frames, etc.). Furthermore, there are numerous value judgements that the EU makes when talking about these groups that often end up in mere binarism (esp. the universal vs. particular conundrum). Note, however, that this dichotomy is not a black-and-white matter, it is increasingly the property of those allowed to frame it (see Muppidi 2004).

The issue of standards pervades more prominently the BiH and Kosovo cases. It is via this discourse on European/international standards that the EU reveals its hegemonic inclinations. There are many dynamics to the relationships framed in terms of spreading the boon of the European standards to others, albeit the EU itself prefers to see it as a more or less technical issue. The various facets of this discourse are illustrated throughout the case studies. A key ill of this gesture is the structural imbalance that it instils and reinforces. Despite the fact that the countries under scrutiny have suffered a conflict, it does not necessarily make them bereft of the standards the EU purports to offer and master. Arguably, the task of rebuilding the many constructive relationships that made up the social fabric of those countries and which have broken down in the course of the conflict does not require treating those countries as apprentices learning a new trade. In fact, quite the opposite is desirable of genuine peacebuilding, namely, it should *help with*—not *control*—the peace process. The view that some parts of the world have somehow once and for all figured out democracy/human rights/rule of law, etc., and others, for various reasons, have not mastered these, communicates a deeply colonial view of politics, let alone peacebuilding (see Chabal 2012).

Closely connected to the above issue is the concept of local ownership and the ways in which the EU understands it. The tension here can be summed up—although not in its entirety—by the concurrent *promise of agency* and *simulation of agency*. This oxymoronic premise places the locals in a rather impossible situation, because the EU sets the agenda and then makes the locals responsible for implementing it, and thus forgetting about its own role in the equation.

Telling and acting, i.e. *meaning in use*, echo a spatio-temporal nuance of an actor's identity. They provide a glance—although not complete (if that were even humanely possible)—on how identity is played out. One of the reasons for engaging with both of these moments is that they radiate an actor's identity in a more complete manner. The other reason for taking these moments seriously is the emphasis the EU itself sets on acting. Particularly, the EU prized acting (read: deployment of missions in terms of quantity) not as an end in itself; in fact, quite the opposite: acting was prized as an enabler for being/becoming a global actor. It appears that in the EU's parlance, agency is linked to acting alone, and acting per se suffices for "meaningful" agency in the EU's opinion. This emphasis on acting per se glosses over the substance of acting. For this reason, this study has taken the relationship between telling and acting as a vehicle for understanding how the EU missions relate to, and represent, the object of their mandates and policies. For example, the particular way of framing the rule of law in the context of the EULEX Kosovo operation is an outcome of the process of telling and acting. Telling and acting, as the case studies reaffirm, do not correspond to a linear logic, and this does not just concern the relationship of consistency (which habitually becomes the single most important way of interpreting this relationship), but also the diverse logics they take (of which consistency is but one), sometimes more unidirectional than at other times, but never readily computable. What mattered the most in the context of this analysis is the in-motion quality that they bring into the portrayal of the EU's CSDP and the fact that they operate in relation—in *dialogue*—to one another. Perhaps that is one truth to take from here: it has struck me as a researcher—and a beginner at that—that there are so many sides to these two aspects of telling and acting that at times I have felt overwhelmed by the sheer possibilities they created, and on many occasions I have felt rather inexpert in capturing their dynamism.

In sum, this book has researched the EU's CSDP through the EU's telling and acting of it. The focus on these two sites of identity has made it possible to tap into the goods which the EU purports to offer through its CSDP, and to discover that, for the most part, the overall good that the EU has been preoccupied with has been to bolster its profile on the international stage. Although concomitantly, the EU has experimented with particular understandings of security and rule of law, its Common Security and Defence Policy has not left the terminus called *liberal peace*. This does not inevitably translate into self-interested behaviour *tout court*; rather it communicates a certain amount of vanity and myth of the essential goodness of its ways.

Note

1. It is crucial to be aware of the stories of peace (formation) from the ground up that have, as recent scholarship on peace and conflict studies demonstrates, greatly contributed to creating peace (e.g. Richmond 2014; Firchow 2018).

References

Adichie, Chimamanda Ngozi. 2009. "Chimamanda Ngozi Adichie: The Danger of a Single Story." TEDGlobal Conference. https://www.ted.com/talks/chimamanda_adichie_the_danger_of_a_single_story/transcript?language=en.

Ashton, Catherine. 2010. "Address by Catherine Ashton at the Joint Debate on Foreign and Security Policy—European Parliament Plenary." Strasbourg. In *EU Security and Defence: Core Documents 2010*, vol. XI, compiled by Catherine Glière, March 10. Paris: EUISS.

Björkdahl, Annika, Stefanie Kappler, and Oliver Richmond. 2009. "The EU Peace-building Framework: Potentials and Pitfalls in the Western Balkans and the Middle East." *JAD-PbP* Working Paper No. 3, 1–55. http://www4.lu.se/upload/LUPDF/Samhallsvetenskap/Just_and_Durable_Peace/WorkingPaper3.pdf.

Björkdahl, Annika, Stefanie Kappler, and Oliver Richmond. 2011. "The Emerging EU Peacebuilding Framework: Confirming or Transcending Liberal Peacebuilding?" *Cambridge Review of International Affairs* 24 (3): 449–469. https://doi.org/10.1080/09557571.2011.586331.

Butler, Judith. 2004. *Precarious Life: The Powers of Mourning and Violence.* London: Verso.

Chabal, Patrick. 2012. *The End of Conceit: Western Rationality After Postcolonialism.* London: Zed Books.

Fetherston, A. B. 2000. "Peacekeeping, Conflict Resolution and Peacebuilding: A Reconsideration of Theoretical Frameworks." In *Peacekeeping and Conflict Resolution*, edited by Tom Woodhouse and Oliver Ramsbotham, 190–218. London: Frank Cass.

Firchow, Pamina. 2018. *Reclaiming Everyday Peace: Local Voices in Measurement and Evaluation After War.* Cambridge: CUP.

Hamati-Ataya, Inanna. 2010. "Knowing and Judging in International Relations Theory: Realism and the Reflexive Challenge." *Review of International Studies* 36 (4): 1079–1101. https://doi.org/10.1017/S0260210510000550.

Kappler, Stefanie. 2012a. "'Mysterious in Content': The European Union Peacebuilding Framework and Local Spaces of Agency in Bosnia-Herzegovina." PhD diss., University of St Andrews.

Kappler, Stefanie. 2012b. "Liberal Peacebuilding's Representation of 'the Local': The Case of Bosnia and Herzegovina." In *Hybrid Forms of Peace: From Everyday Agency to Post-Liberalism*, edited by Oliver P. Richmond and Audra Mitchell, 260–276. Basingstoke: Palgrave Macmillan.

Keukeleire, Stephan, Arben Kalaja, and Artan Çollaku. 2011. "The European Union's Policy on Kosovo." In *European Foreign Policy Legal and Political Perspectives*, edited by Panos Koutrakos, 172–202. Cheltenham: Edward Elgar Publishing.

Muppidi, Himadeep. 2004. *The Politics of the Global.* Minneapolis: University of Minnesota Press.

Pogodda, Sandra, Oliver Richmond, Nathalie Tocci, Roger Mac Ginty, and Birte Vogel. 2014. "Assessing the Impact of EU Governmentality in Post-Conflict Countries: Pacification or Reconciliation?" *European Security.* https://doi.org/10.1080/09662839.2013.875533.

Richmond, Oliver P. 2014. *Failed State Building: Intervention and the Dynamics of Peace Formation.* New Haven: Yale University Press.

INDEX

CPSIA information can be obtained
at www.ICGtesting.com
Printed in the USA
LVHW031526050123
736468LV00003B/225